Museums

Museums

A History

John E. Simmons

ROWMAN & LITTLEFIELD
Lanham • Boulder • New York • London

Published by Rowman & Littlefield
An imprint of The Rowman & Littlefield Publishing Group, Inc.
4501 Forbes Boulevard, Suite 200, Lanham, Maryland 20706
www.rowman.com

86-90 Paul Street, London EC2A 4NE, United Kingdom

British Library Cataloguing in Publication Information Available

Library of Congress Cataloging-in-Publication Data

Names: Simmons, John E.
Title: Museums : a history / John E. Simmons.
Description: Lanham, MD : Rowman & Littlefield, [2016] | Includes
  bibliographical references and index.
Identifiers: LCCN 2016008763 (print) | LCCN 2016011079 (ebook) | ISBN
  9781442263628 (hardcover : alk. paper) | ISBN 9781538171516 (pbk. : alk.
  paper) | ISBN 9781442263635 (electronic)
Subjects: LCSH: Museums—History. | Museum techniques—History.
Classification: LCC AM5 .S58 2016 (print) | LCC AM5 (ebook) | DDC 069/.09—
  dc23
LC record available at http://lccn.loc.gov/2016008763

Contents

List of Figures, Tables, and Boxes   vii

Preface   xi

Acknowledgments   xix

1   What Is a Collection? What Is a Museum?   1

2   Hoards and Tombs: Collections in the Ancient World,
    to 700 BCE   11

3   The Temple of the Muses: The Conjunction of Objects and
    Knowledge, Classical Antiquity, 700 BCE–400 CE   29

4   The Power of Objects: Medieval Collections, 400–1400   45

5   Of Cabinets and Kings: Renaissance Collections, 1400–1600   59

6   The Museum Enlightened, 1600–1800   93

7   Emergence of the Modern Museum, 1800–1900   139

8   Museums in a World Gone Awry, 1900–1970   177

9   Learning to Read Objects (Again): The Post-Postmodern Museum   213

References   261

Index   287

Figures, Tables, and Boxes

FIGURES

1.1 Dulwich Picture Gallery, London   8

2.1 Dr. François Bordes (1919–1981) demonstrating flint knapping at the University of Kansas in the early 1970s   13

2.2 Knapped projectile point showing cutting edge made by conchoidal fracturing. Scale is marked in one-centimeter blocks   14

2.3 Petroglyphs in Whoopup Canyon (Weston County, Wyoming), ca. 12,000 BCE   17

2.4 Clay tablet from Nippur, Iraq, ca. 3300 BCE. Photograph courtesy of the Earth and Mineral Sciences Museum and Art Gallery, The Pennsylvania State University   19

4.1 Moat and walls of a crusader fortress in Caesaria, Israel   47

4.2 Buddhist stupas at Wat Phra Mahathat, Nakhon Si Thammarat, Thailand   50

5.1 Snake stone   74

5.2 The Hortus Botanicus in Leiden   79

5.3 The cabinet of curiosities of Calzolari, 1622   83

5.4 The cabinet of curiosities of Imperato, 1599   84

5.5   The cabinet of curiosities of Besler, 1616   85

6.1   Das Kircher-Museum im Collegium Romanum, 1679   101

6.2   The Museum Wormianum, 1655   115

6.3   The cabinet of curiosities of Settala, 1666   117

6.4   The Cospi collection, 1677   118

6.5   The Vincent collection, 1706   119

6.6   Title page of the 1686 reprint of the catalog of rarities
         belonging to the Royal Society and preserved at
         Gresham College   127

6.7   The American Philosophical Society Hall, Philadelphia   136

7.1   The 1894 Conservatory at the Horniman Museum, London   140

7.2   The Field Museum, Chicago   149

7.3   The Natural History Museum, London   158

7.4   Comparison of generalized patterns of evolution of museums   166

7.5   The Castle, headquarters of the Smithsonian Institution,
         Washington, DC   171

9.1   The Newseum, Washington, DC   222

9.2   Visitor center, White Sands National Monument, New Mexico   223

9.3   Former telegraph office in Aracataca, Colombia;
         now a municipal museum   258

TABLES

2.1   Ancient Evidence of Material Culture   16

3.1   The Muses   31

5.1   General Collection Classification Schemes, 1400–1823   67

5.2   Quiccheberg's Categories, 1565   70

5.3   Quiccheberg's Museums, Workshops, and Storerooms, 1565   71

6.1   The Nature of Museum Collections   95

6.2   Organization of the Tradescant Collection, 1656   104

6.3   The Collection of Sir Hans Sloane Based on the 1725 Inventory   114

6.4 Specimens in Cabinets of Natural History 124

6.5 Organization of the Catalog of the Royal Society, 1681 129

7.1 Founding Dates for Some Representative Museums 141

7.2 Visitors to the British Museum, 1807–1840 154

9.1 Museums in the United States 224

BOXES

1.1 Collecting Animals 3

2.1 Flint Knapping 14

2.2 The Development of Writing 20

3.1 A Visit to Alexandria 32

3.2 Plato, Forms, and Cabinets of Curiosities 35

4.1 Relics Sacred and Profane 50

5.1 Ancient Wisdom, Modern Knowledge 62

5.2 Snake Stones 74

5.3 Relics and the Protestant Reformation 75

5.4 The Medici Dynasty 77

5.5 The Cabinet of Carlo Ruzzini, from the Diary of John Evelyn 80

5.6 Aldrovandi, Master Cataloger 81

5.7 Movable Type and Peripatetic Catalogs 89

6.1 Francis Bacon's Travel Tips 100

6.2 A Closer Look at the Tradescant Catalog 107

7.1 Losing One's Marbles 147

7.2 The Darwin Effect 157

7.3 The Past Is Cast 168

8.1 Mr. Frisky, Docents, and Choo-Choos 180

8.2 The Translated Museum 190

8.3 The Long, Strange Saga of the Barnes: What Is (and Is Not) a Museum? 196

9.1   From Binary to Primary: Computers in the Museum   215

9.2   Learning How We Learn   232

9.3   The Case of the Māori   237

9.4   Changing Environmental Standards   252

Preface

Museography does not deal with questions of why, but how.

—Maroević 1998:100

Museums have long fascinated me—not just museums themselves but also the way that they are perceived by the public and how they are portrayed in literature and film. I find it paradoxical that museums are simultaneously ridiculed as old-fashioned institutions while being admired as sources of accurate information (AAM 2015). The neglected, chaotic museum collection covered in a thick layer of dust is a standard trope in newspaper stories, fiction, and movies, even though the vast majority of museum collections are clean and ordered. The museum is frequently employed as a metaphor for boring and old-fashioned, although more people visit museums in the United States than attend professional sporting events (AAM 2015). It is almost as if there are two sorts of museums—those that exist in the public imagination and those that the public loves to visit.

In fiction, museums may be the scene of murder, nefarious activities, or dubious experiments (in Dan Brown's 2009 novel *The Lost Symbol*, a museum storage facility is the scene of both murder and secret research). In film, threatening monsters stalk collection storage (*The Relic*, 1996), darkened dioramas come to life (*Night at the Museum*, 2006), cops and robbers have shoot-outs in the galleries (*Jigsaw*, 1949), and criminals hide from the police (in Alfred Hitchcock's 1929 film *Blackmail*, a tense pursuit through the British Museum ends with the villain crashing through the glass of the reading room dome and falling to his death). Perhaps the best use of a museum setting in film is in *Russian Ark* (2002). The entire film consists of a single continuous ninety-six-minute shot filmed inside the Hermitage Museum in St. Petersburg, during which three hundred years of Russian history are recounted. The Hermitage is seen in the film both as a museum and as the Winter Palace at the time of the Russian monarchy.

However museums are perceived, their evolution has been driven by people trying to understand the world they live in. Throughout history, humans have made sense of the chaos around them by assembling collections, microcosms that mirror the macrocosm, abstractions from the real world (Pearce 1992). Collections have order—the order may be apparent only to the collector, but it is order nevertheless. Collections are made because collectors find affinities among the objects that they can use to arrange and array them. In this sense, the history of museums is really the history of how humans organize and classify the world as they navigate through life using objects (Pearce 1992; Simmons and Muñoz-Saba 2003). As one critic phrases it, "To collect is not to mirror the world, but to remake it" (Poliquin 2012:16). Collecting and keeping objects is a universal human trait. It is an impulse that runs very deep and was expressed by the earliest human ancestors. The difference between a chance accumulation of objects and the making and preserving of a collection can be said to be the difference in being human or not.

In this book I present a critical examination of the history of museums from the point of view of museum collections—how and why objects have been collected, the transition of objects from their original contexts to collections, and what the content and organization of collections can tell us about the human beings who assembled them. I begin in chapter 1 ("What Is a Collection? What Is a Museum?") by discussing how collections and museums are defined and what distinguishes museum collections from other assemblages of objects. Because collections pre-date museums, chapter 2 ("Hoards and Tombs") considers the earliest history of collecting up to about 700 BCE. The story starts with the most ancient of collections—the useful everyday objects and grave goods known from archaeological evidence and oral traditions. In chapter 3 ("The Temple of the Muses"), collections from classical antiquity through 400 CE are evaluated, particularly the ancient institution that is the philosophical foundation of the modern museum.

Chapter 4 ("The Power of Objects") and chapter 5 ("Of Cabinets and Kings") cover the years 400–1600, as the precursor institutions to modern museums emerged and the concept of the power of the object was firmly established. Over the course of these chapters, the emphasis shifts from private collections to concentrate on the development of the first museums. Although the private collector has been an important force in the acquisition of objects throughout history (and although many private collections wind up in museums), my focus is on the development of museum collections, not on the history of collecting—many authors have analyzed collecting with an emphasis on private collecting (e.g., Blom 2002; Muensterberger 1994; Pearce 1994, 1995; Rigby and Rigby 1944). One of the most fascinating aspects of the history of collecting is the interplay and conflict between commercial values, cultural values, and collecting objects, which is discussed in chapter 6 ("The Museum Enlightened, 1600–1800") and chapter 7 ("Emergence of the Modern Museum, 1800–1900"), as the development of the modern museum in Europe is explored in more detail in the period from about 1600 to 1900. How and why the European model of the museum has been successfully exported and redefined in diverse cultures around the world is the subject of chapter 8 ("Museums in a World Gone Awry"), and what is happening now and might happen to museums in the next millennium is addressed in chapter 9, "Learning to Read Objects (Again)."

We lack direct knowledge of why many objects were collected, particularly before the people who made collections began writing about what they did in the 1600s, so for much of this history, it has been necessary to use ancillary sources of information to get an idea of what was going on. Some of the sources I have used are rather far removed from traditional museology but provide valuable insight into museum history. To better understand the overall context for collections, trends and general characteristics of the societies and the literature produced by collecting cultures are used to discern worldviews and, in some instances, the motivations of collectors. I have found that there is a close association between literature and collections—both the written word and the objects in collections are forms of preserving cultural memory, as well as interpreting the world around us. As Marjorie Swann points out, in the mid-fifteenth century the word *collection* referred to gathered historical or literary materials and was only later applied to assemblages of objects (Swann 2001).

The dates and the definitions of the time periods that I use are approximate—the history of museums cannot easily be broken into the neat chronological blocks that we might like, and even if it could, there is the problem that some museums evolve rapidly while others change slowly (I have seen several contemporary museums that are essentially late nineteenth century in the arrangement and presentation of their collections). I have used BCE (Before the Common Era) and CE (of the Common Era) to position the chronology of information within a global, multicultural context.

WHAT SHOULD WE CALL THE COMPONENTS OF COLLECTIONS?

I have generally used the word *object* to refer to a component of a collection, unless the context calls for a more specific term, such as *artifact* or *specimen*. According to the *Oxford English Dictionary*, the word *object* means something thrown or put in the way of something else, as an obstacle or hindrance that interrupts or obstructs. An object is something physical that can be perceived, thus an object is capable of being seen, touched, or otherwise sensed. The root of the word *object* is the Latin *objectum* (meaning "thrown in the way"); its first recorded use in English was in 1398. By contrast, an *artifact* is something made or modified by human beings, which generally excludes the components of natural history collections. The word *artifact* is derived from the Latin words *arte* (skill) and *factum* (to do). One of the first recorded use of the word in English was by Samuel Taylor Coleridge (1772–1834) in an 1821 essay in *Blackwood's Magazine*. Coleridge wrote, "The conception of all these, as realized in one and the same artéfact, may be fairly entitled, the Ideal of an Ink-stand" (Coleridge 1821:256). An argument can be made that, because natural history specimens are collected and prepared by human beings, they qualify as artifacts; however, this argument ignores the significance of a specimen in the context of systematic biology as a representational object (e.g., International Commission on Zoological Nomenclature 1999).

The word *specimen* is commonly used for the components of natural history collections, despite its Aristotelian typological connotations. A specimen is defined as a representative part of a whole or a pattern or a model but more often refers to a part typical of a group or whole or something that belongs in a particular category (hence the name of Walt Whitman's 1882 Civil War memoir *Specimen Days and Collect*). The word *specimen* comes from the Latin word *specere* (to look at). The first recorded use in English was in 1619 in the sentence "Our Resurrection shall be like our Saviour's: His and ours make a mutual Aspect; His the Specimen, and ours the Complement" (Jones 1708:491). In short, a specimen is an individual chosen as a representative of a group.

Two other words that have been used as general terms for any component of a museum collection are *item* and *thing*. An *item* can be a statement, maxim, or admonition or an article or unit included in an enumeration or total or one of the distinct parts of a whole. *Item* is derived from the Latin *ita* (meaning "thus"). *Thing* specifically refers to something inanimate or a meeting or assembly. It can refer to an entity of any kind or a spatial entity. *Thing* is derived from an old Goth word, *theihs* (time). I find both these words vague, unsatisfactory, and too imprecise for use in describing the components of museum collections.

A word that I have previously suggested could be used for the components of museum collections is *element* (Simmons 2006). *Element* means a constituent part of a whole (which is what a component of any collection is); it also has meaning in reference to a member of a set, and collections can be defined as sets of elements (Simmons 2015; Simmons and Muñoz-

Saba 2003). *Element* comes from the Latin word *elementum*, the original meaning of which is uncertain. However, despite my recommendation, the use of *element* for the components of collections has not yet become part of museum jargon.

THEORETICAL PERSPECTIVES

Most of the work that has been done on the history of collecting has focused on individual collectors but rarely has addressed the relationships between private collections and museum collections. Some historians have criticized the hubris of early collectors for believing their collections to be universal in scope and assuming that their objects would last forever, which I believe is a misinterpretation of history. Most collectors seem to have worried extensively about the fate of their beloved objects, constantly seeking better ways to preserve and care for them but being limited by available preservation technology (Simmons 2015), which is still a great concern in museums. As I discuss at various points in this study, most collectors knew that their collections were far from comprehensive (which is what stimulated them to keep collecting) and that their beloved objects were subject to deterioration, no matter how hard they tried to preserve them.

Most of the work that has been published on the history of museums has concentrated on the development of a particular kind of museum (e.g., art museums or history museums) or on museums from a specific geographic region or has assumed that museum history begins in the late Renaissance. Almost all of these histories emphasize the exhibition of objects, which presents museum history from the point of view of an outsider looking in. What museums show to their visitors is certainly important—exhibitions play a significant role in producing meaning and shaping knowledge (Moser 2006)—but exhibitions are based on museum collections, not the other way around. In fact, there would be no museums if there were no collections, so my primary emphasis is on what objects were collected, why were they collected, how were they preserved, and how were they used. Nevertheless, I have drawn extensively from the body of scholarly work that has been done on the history of collecting and the history of museums, which has often proven to be a rich source of knowledge and ideas (and sometimes amusement). I have credited my sources throughout the text, but I take responsibility for any unintentional misinterpretations or misrepresentations of their work.

It is fascinating to look at the descriptions of early collections and read old museum catalogs. I believe that modern museums have lost something to the inexorable forces of reductionism as they have become more specialized institutions. The juxtaposition of diverse objects in the older collections often led to insights and recognitions of relatedness that are hard to find in today's museums. As I discuss in the first chapter, merely exhibiting objects does not make a museum a museum—it is the interactions of objects and people that make a museum. The emphasis on the appearance (or presumed appearance) of early museums is at the root of many oversimplifications of what museums are about, particularly in popular descriptions. Cabinets of curiosities (chapter 5) are often described as hodgepodge assemblages of objects. The arrangement of a collection as depicted in an engraving of a cabinet of curiosities may look disordered to us, but it was not—it was arranged in a way that made sense to its organizer. There is order in the perceived relationships among the objects (whether actual or imaginary). A modern viewer may have trouble understanding what order meant to someone living in the Renaissance, but there was order and logic in the collections nevertheless. Ordering, or classifying objects, is closely related to collecting objects.

I have structured this book around two principal frameworks: (1) the evolution of collections, particularly their chronological history in different parts of the world, and (2) the significance of the objects in collections and how objects are classified as reflections and refractions of human culture. My theoretical perspective is based largely on the museological theories promulgated by Ivo Maroević (1937–2007), his students, and other scholars who have explored his ideas (e.g., Desvallées and Mairesse 2010; Maroević 1998; Stránsky 1970; van Mensch 2000), along with document studies (sensu Wood and Latham 2014). For an overall perspective on world history, I have relied generally on the sixth edition of a delightful tome, *The Penguin History of the World* by J. M. Roberts and Odd Arne Westad (2013), and on a number of specialist works, as cited. As Neil MacGregor points out in *The History of the World in 100 Objects*, museums tell histories through objects in the belief that they will lead to a better understanding of the world (MacGregor 2011).

To help understand objects in collections and human culture, I have looked to world literature, based generally on *The Norton Anthology of World Literature* (Lawell and Mack 2001; Puchner et al. 2012). Literature provides a useful context for the study of the development of collections and museums, and in particular, literature can provide evidence for the musealization of objects (defined in chapter 1) in a culture and the ordering of collections through time. By looking at large-scale trends in storytelling, human expression, philosophy, religion, and literature, much is revealed about the worldview of the creators and their contemporary audiences (Damrosch 2008). It is important to remember that literature began before writing and that writing began before written literature. Writing was used for mundane data recording for centuries before oral traditions were recorded in written form (Fischer 2001). Literature began as oral stories, songs, and poems transmitted from generation to generation to convey history, morals, and ethics, as well as to entertain and to consolidate cultural affinities. Gradually, as oral traditions were recorded, they became fixed and more distant from the cultures from which they came. Much of early world literature consists of epics, representational stories featuring larger-than-life characters (Voth 2007), and these stories may also serve as cultural, historical, or religious documents. The *Epic of Gilgamesh*, the *Iliad*, the *Odyssey*, and *Beowulf* are examples of epics with idealized characters; the stories from the *Tanakh* (Old Testament) and the *Bhagavad Gita* are examples of religious epics (Voth 2007). Humans are storytellers, and literature is our way of telling our stories about who we are, who we think we are, and who we want to be. Likewise, humans are collectors, and the content of collections can tell us much about what humans thought was important at a particular moment of time and what memories they wanted to preserve for the future. The examination of collections within the scope of cultural history and literature (a revealing record of human myth) provides an understanding of the long and complex relationships between humans and objects in a collection context.

Museums share a common, often parallel history with other collecting institutions, most notably libraries, zoological parks, and botanical gardens. Although some references are made to these sister institutions, my main emphasis is on the history of museums rather than institutions that house primarily paper-based documents or living organisms.

Acknowledgments

I owe my interest in museums in large part to my parents, who taught me that museums are wonderful and special places. Our family rarely passed up the chance to visit museums during our camping vacations around the country. Although my siblings were not quite so enamored with museums, I was sufficiently captivated with the idea of collecting and interpreting objects that, when I was twelve years old, I created my own museum in a corner of the basement.

The history of museums is the story of a lot of curious people whose broad knowledge base and intense interest in the world around them enabled them to see connections between objects that others overlooked. Building a broad base of knowledge and nurturing such curiosity is fundamental to a liberal arts education. I was lucky to have been an undergraduate at the University of Kansas at a time when a true liberal arts curriculum was still promoted and to have been educated on a campus with several museums and an excellent library system. Like most students, during my undergraduate years, I did not fully appreciate how very useful courses in history, art, literature, music, philosophy, science, foreign languages, and mathematics would be to me in later life, nor did I understand how much I was learning in the campus environment outside of the classroom. Somehow, I managed to acquire far more knowledge during my undergraduate years than my exceedingly mediocre grades indicated—evidence of the power and influence of informal learning.

As an undergraduate, I had the good fortune to meet three professors who were also curators at the Museum of Natural History and who provided me with experiences that demonstrated how knowledge is produced from the study of museum collections. The curator of archaeology, Alfred E. Johnson, allowed me to enroll in archaeology field school the summer before I officially began my freshman year. Once I arrived on campus, I was hired by curators William E. Duellman and Linda Trueb to work in the Division of Herpetology. These experiences were my first exposure to scientific collecting, museum collections, and collection-based research. I continued to work in the Museum of Natural History throughout my prolonged undergraduate career, primarily in herpetology but also with short stints in public education and exhibits. Duellman and Trueb made it possible for me to participate in extensive fieldwork, including spending a year in the Amazon and another year traveling the length of the Andes (Duellman 2015).

After graduation, I worked first as a zookeeper (at the Fort Worth Zoological Park) and then as a collections manager (at the California Academy of Sciences and later at the Biodiversity Research Center at the University of Kansas). I completed my master's degree in historical administration and museum studies in the 1980s, when museum studies was still relatively undefined as an academic field. Rather than being trained as specialists, we were provided with a well-rounded understanding of museums as complex, evolving institutions in a program that emphasized both theory and practice. My graduate advisor, Philip S. Humphrey, was a firm believer in the value of a liberal arts education and encouraged the critical examination of museums in many contexts and from diverse points of view.

The single most important experience in my development as a museum professional came about because of an opportunity brought to my attention by a coworker, Cathy Dwigans, who encouraged me to apply for the National Institute of Conservation's Collections Care Pilot Training Program for Natural History in 1987 at the Los Angeles County Museum of Natural History. Participation in this program completely changed the way I thought about museums in general, collections care in particular, and my own work in collections. I began teaching museum studies in 1998 and served as director of the Museum Studies Program at the University of Kansas from 2001 to 2007, which further expanded my understanding of museums and their role in society.

I thank my editor at Rowman & Littlefield, Charles Harmon, for giving me the opportunity to coalesce my diverse ideas about the history of museums in this book, which was a wonderful excuse to spend time reading stacks of books and articles I had long wanted to have an excuse to read. I deeply appreciate the editorial skills of Janice Braunstein and Niki Guinan of Rowman & Littlefield, whose diligence has greatly improved the text.

Many friends and colleagues provided encouragement, references, and suggestions that have proven extremely useful while preparing this history, and I am grateful to each of them for their help, particularly John Coppola, William López, Elizabeth Merritt, Sally Shelton, and Julianne Snider. John Talent generously shared with me his in-depth knowledge about one of his personal heroes, Ulisse Aldrovandi. Kiersten Latham provided constant encouragement to write this book; generously provided me with several fundamental references and many ideas; served as a sounding board for my interpretations of history; and most important, introduced me to the work of Ivo Maroević and the concept of document studies. A special thank-you goes to my colleagues in the Maestría en Museología y Gestión del Patrimonio at the Universidad Nacional de Colombia for their insights on museum history in a global context, particularly Edmon Castell and Marta Combariza and most especially William López, with whom I have enjoyed many hours of discussions about museums as we strolled through the streets of Bogotá and visited numerous exhibitions and bookstores. Many of the students I have taught over the years, particularly those at the University of Kansas, the Universidad Nacional de Colombia, and Kent State University, have responded enthusiastically to my presentations of museum history, providing further motivation to complete this study.

This book is dedicated to Julianne Snider, without whom this project would never have been started, much less finished. Julianne provided advice, support, and encouragement throughout its development; brought to my attention several critical sources that I did not know existed; patiently critiqued my ideas and gently told me when I was wrong; critically read and edited several parts of the text; and has made our home an oasis for pursuing our dreams. This book would not exist without her.

1

—⟨ೂ/⟩—

What Is a Collection?
What Is a Museum?

DR. JOHNSON'S EVOLVING DEFINITION

In 1755, Dr. Samuel Johnson (1709–1784), the irascible lexicographer and author of one of the most influential dictionaries of the English language, defined *museum* as a "repository of learned curiosities" (quoted in Murray 1904:36). I like this definition because the phrase *learned curiosities* reflects the interactions between objects and people that produce knowledge in museums.

Based on how museums are represented in popular culture, most people still think of museums primarily as venues in which objects are exhibited. This is misleading, as most museums exhibit only a small percentage of the objects in their collections (Heritage Preservation 2005). In practice, museums value objects for many more reasons than just for their exhibitionary qualities. The most significant feature of a museum is its collection of objects, many or most of which are never put on public view. What distinguishes museums from similar institutions is how museums use and interpret objects in all ways, not just for display.

The original use of the word *museum* (derived from the Greek *mouseion*) was to describe a temple of the muses, particularly the primarily philosophical institution (or place of contemplation and teaching) that existed in the third century BCE in ancient Alexandria (discussed in chapter 3). However, collections have a much longer history than do museums, beginning long before the Alexandrian Temple of the Muses was founded. Archaeological evidence shows that our hominid ancestors began collecting shortly after they became bipedal, which means that collecting is a deeply ingrained human trait related to the way humans use objects to navigate their way through the world. The acquisition and use of objects is so fundamental to human beings that it has been suggested that the "origins of the twin concepts of preservation and interpretation, which form the basis of the museum, lie in the human propensity to inquire and acquire" (Lewis 1985:481). Although humans are not the only animals that pick up and use objects, we are the only animals that make true collections (see box 1.1).

When the word *museum* entered the English language in the early 1600s, it was variously spelled *musaeum* (the Latin spelling), *muséum*, or *museum*. In 1730, some fifteen years prior to Johnson's definition, the *Dictionarium Britannicum; Or a More Compleat Universal Etymological English Dictionary* defined a museum as a "Study or Library; also a College or publick Place for the resort of learned Men" (Bailey 1730:n.p.). Thus, during the 1700s, there were two separate definitions of the word *museum*: one emphasizing the physical structure housing the collection, the other emphasizing the collection housed in the physical structure—but both centered around the idea of the association of objects and learning.

Curiously, the word *museum* did not appear in the 1841 edition of Noah Webster's *An American Dictionary of the English Language*, despite the fact that there had been museums in North America since 1773. In the revised edition published in 1856, *museum* was defined as a "collection of natural, scientific, or literary curiosities, or of works of art" (Buchanan 1901:42), emphasizing the collection but not the physical structure it was housed in.

The *Universal Dictionary of the English Language* by Robert Hunter and Charles Morris, published in 1897, defined *museum* as a "room or building used as a repository for works of art or science; a collection or repository of natural, scientific, or literary curiosities; a collection of objects illustrating the arts, sciences, manufactures, or natural history of the world, or some particular part" (Hunter and Morris 1897:3229), which more completely integrated the concepts of the physical space occupied by the collections and the collections themselves. This basic definition was tweaked over the next few decades in dictionaries published in both England and the United States. By 1913, the Funk and Wagnalls *Standard Dictionary of the English Language* defined *museum* as a "building devoted to the collecting and preserving of works of nature, art, and antiquity, or to the exhibition of rare and instructive articles in the arts, science, or literature; also, the collection itself, as of interesting specimens in natural history, mineralogy, painting, and sculpture" (Funk 1913:1634).

There were other conceptions of what museums were and were not. In 1890, the German art historian and philosopher Julius Langbehn (1851–1907) wrote that a museum was a place "Where every separate object kills

BOX 1.1.
Collecting Animals

Humans are not the only animals that pick up and save objects. Among the best-known nonhuman collectors are wood rats, magpies, and bowerbirds.

Wood rats (popularly called pack rats) are any of nineteen species of the rodent genus *Neotoma* that range from Mexico into the United States (MacDonald 2006). Wood rats build complex nest structures in cracks, crevices, caves, and trees using plant materials and other debris. Wood rats actively collect nesting materials and build onto their nests throughout their lives. As they scamper about looking for stuff to add to their nests, wood rats often appear to be attracted to specific objects, particularly shiny ones—sometimes they will drop the object they are carrying if they come across a new object that catches their attention along the way.

A wood rat nest is referred to as a midden (a term also used in archaeology to refer to a refuse heap). Wood rat middens are used by multiple generations—some nests have been used continuously for 50,000 years or longer. For this reason, wood rat nests are valued by researchers as records of vegetative and climate change. Wood rat middens are held together in part by the rat's urine, which crystallizes into a substance called amberat that helps protect the materials from deterioration.

The Eurasian or common magpie (*Pica pica*) is a corvid (a relative of crows and jays). Magpies have an undeserved reputation for being particularly attracted to shiny objects when, in fact, they do not just pick up things that sparkle but most anything that catches their attention. In some folk traditions, magpies are considered to be thieves, as in the 1817 opera by Gioachino Rossini (1792–1868) named *La Gazza Ladra*, or *The Thieving Magpie*. The folk belief probably comes from the fact that people tend to notice magpies when they pick up shiny objects but not when they pick up other objects or food items.

The twenty species of bowerbirds (family *Ptilonorhynchidae*) are found in the forests of the Austro-Papuan region. Most male bowerbirds pick up brightly colored objects and arrange them on their display grounds (called bowers) as part of an elaborate ritual to attract mates (Welty 1979).

All of these are examples of organisms selecting, picking up, using, and storing objects, which tells us that the use of objects is deeply embedded in the DNA of many animals, so it should not be a surprise that we find the collecting of objects to be practiced by other hominids as well as our own species. Many different kinds of animals use objects—what makes humans different is that we craft the objects for our purposes before they are needed and then keep the objects to use again and again (MacGregor 2011).

every other and all of them together the visitor" (Langbehn 1890:17). The Italian poet and futurist Filippo Tommasco Marinetti (1876–1944) wrote:

> Museums, cemeteries! . . . Identical, surely, in the sinister promiscuity of so many bodies unknown to one another. Museums: public dormitories where one lies forever beside hated or unknown beings. Museums: absurd abattoirs of painters and sculptors ferociously slaughtering each other with color-blows and line-blows, the length of the fought-over walls! That one should make an annual pilgrimage, just as one goes to the graveyard on All Souls' Day—that I grant. That once a year one should leave a floral tribute beneath the *Gioconda*, I grant you that. . . . But I don't admit that our sorrows, our fragile courage, our morbid restlessness should be given a daily conducted tour through the museums. Why poison ourselves? Why rot? (Marinetti 1909:1)

What could be characterized as cynical definitions were issued by both museum supporters and detractors. In 1889, George Brown Goode (1851–1896), the assistant secretary of the Smithsonian Institution, famously quipped, "An efficient educational museum may be described as a collection of instructive labels, each illustrated by a well-selected specimen" (Goode 1889:262). In 1916, at the eleventh annual meeting of the American Association of Museums, Benjamin Ives Gilman (1852–1933), then a member of the organization's board, jokingly characterized a museum as a "place where things out of date were gathered in order to become more so" (Gilman 1916:53). In the 1970s, Joseph Mordaunt Crook (b. 1937) wrote, "The modern museum is a product of Renaissance humanism, eighteenth-century enlightenment and nineteenth-century democracy" (Crook 1972:32).

One thing noticeably missing from all of these definitions of *museum* is any characterization of the visitors or in fact any purpose for the collection beyond study. The concept of museums as institutions open to the general public is fairly new. In 1946, the definition of *museum* adopted by the International Council of Museums (ICOM) in its constitution stated, "The word 'museums' includes all collections open to the public, of artistic, technical, scientific, historical or archaeological material, including zoos and botanical gardens, but excluding libraries, except in so far as they maintain permanent exhibition rooms" (ICOM 2016:n.p.). By 1951, ICOM had modified the definition to include purpose:

> The word museum here denotes any permanent establishment, administered in the general interest, for the purpose of preserving, studying, and enhancing by various means and, in particular, of exhibiting to the public for its delectation and instruction groups of objects and specimens of cultural value: artistic, historical, scientific and technological collections, botanical and zoological gardens and aquariums. Public libraries and public archival

institutions maintaining permanent exhibition rooms shall be considered museums (ICOM 2016:n.p.).

By 1970, the word *museum* was being widely applied, sometimes to institutions that did not have collections (contrary to most of the historic definitions cited here). The Accreditation Committee of the American Association of Museums (AAM, now American Alliance of Museums) stated that a museum is an "organized and permanent non-profit institution, essentially educational or aesthetic in purpose, with professional staff, which owns and utilizes tangible objects, cares for them and exhibits them to the public on some regular schedule" (Alexander and Alexander 2008:2). Curiously enough, the AAM itself has no official definition of *museum* (only its Accreditation Committee does), but the organization does consider zoological parks, botanical gardens, aquariums, planetariums, and nonprofit galleries that exhibit but do not own objects to be museums.

In the United States, the legal definition of *museum* was provided in the founding legislation for the Institute of Museum Services (now the Institute of Museum and Library Services, or IMLS) in 1996: "A public or private nonprofit agency or institution organized on a permanent basis for essentially educational or aesthetic purposes, which, utilizing a professional staff, owns or utilizes tangible objects, cares for them, and exhibits them to the public on a regular basis" (Malaro and DeAngelis 2012:3). The problem with this definition is that it restricts the use of *museum* to those organizations that exhibit objects (even if the organization doesn't own the objects it displays), while excluding institutions that own, use, and care for collections but do not exhibit them to the public. In her 1970 history of museums, pioneer museologist Alma S. Wittlin (1899–1990) wrote that the "International Council of Museums (ICOM) succinctly defined a museum as an establishment in which objects are the main means of communication. If we agree with this definition, an establishment in which objects are not used at all or are not used as main carriers of messages are not museums, whatever their qualities may be otherwise" (Wittlin 1970:203).

As the history of collections and museums is traced, we eventually arrive at institutions that reflect the most widely accepted contemporary definition of *museum*, adopted by ICOM at its twenty-first general conference in Vienna, Austria, in 2007, which first stresses nonprofit status, then permanence, followed by public service, and only then mentions collections: "A museum is a non-profit, permanent institution in the service of society and its development, open to the public, which acquires, conserves, researches, communicates and exhibits the tangible and intangible heritage of humanity and its environment for the purposes of education, study and enjoyment" (ICOM 2016:n.p.).

COLLECTIONS AND THE MUSEALIZATION OF OBJECTS

Pinpointing the origin of collections is problematic, but recognizing what distinguishes a collection from an accumulation of objects is much easier—collections are made on purpose, while accumulations just happen (Simmons 2015; Simmons and Muñoz-Saba 2003). To make a collection, someone must select the objects for a reason, which means that some sort of relationship between the objects—some sort of order—must be recognized. As Susan Pearce points out, the order may not make sense to anyone other than the collector, but all collections have order (Pearce 1994). Historically, establishing and maintaining order in the collection (in storage, on exhibition, and in the catalog) has been a fundamental aspect of museums.

Systems of order have changed greatly over the centuries both as reflections of our understanding of the objects and as the result of the continual musealization of objects. For example, most natural history collections are organized according to internationally accepted hierarchical systems (e.g., class, order, family, genus, species); a history collection might be organized by the kind or function of the object or the date of its creation; and an art collection might be organized by type of media, artist's name, or accession number—but all have order (Latham and Simmons 2014).

Because the story of collecting begins in prehistory with the association of objects and the remains of hominids, a distinction must be made between an object that is used once and discarded and an object that is collected. From a theoretical point of view, what distinguishes a collected object from other objects is that a collected object is musealized when it is removed from its original context to become part of a collection—in other words, when the object is physically and conceptually removed from its original natural or cultural environment and becomes part of a collection, it transcends functional reality to serve as a document in a different context (Desvallées and Mairesse 2010; Maranda 2009; Maroević 1998). Objects can be musealized without becoming part of a museum collection.

Not only is musealization a change in the status of the object, musealized objects also continue to acquire new meanings and contexts throughout their lives as musealia (collection objects). Maroević has defined *musealia* as "real and potential museum objects, that is, objects with the traits of museality" (Maroević 1998:134). *Museality* is defined as the "characteristic feature of an object to become a document of reality by being relocated from its authentic environment into a museum reality" (Maroević 1998:134).

Musealization imbues objects with special and distinctive meanings (a sword that was used as a weapon becomes musealized when it is intentionally buried in a tomb rather than being passed on to another sword wielder). In a museum, the continuous process of the musealization of objects often produces unexpected information due to the formation of new connections and meanings associated with the objects, which is a fundamental aspect of museology and museological theory. In Maroevic's theoretical structure, applied and theoretical museology are united but with four limitations based on musealization—those of (1) the museum objects; (2) the functions of preservation and use of the objects; (3) the institutions in which the functions of preservation and use take place; and (4) societal attitudes (Maroević 1998).

PASSIONATE COLLECTORS AND THE POSSESSIONS OF THE DEAD

Most collectors are passionate about their collections. In 1661, as Cardinal Giulio Raimondo Mazzarino (1602–1661) lay dying, he expressed his regret at having to leave behind his collection of objects, even though he believed he was bound for an eternity in heavenly paradise (Wittlin 1970). Mazzarino collected art and jewels and had a particular fondness for diamonds—some of the diamonds from his collection were ultimately given to Louis XIV and ended up in the Louvre. In Bruce Chatwin's short novel *Utz*, a Czechoslovakian collector of Meissen porcelains (Kaspar Utz) is so closely connected to his objects that he cannot leave them and refuses to defect to the West, even though he has opportunities to do so (Chatwin 1988). After Utz's death, it is discovered that his collection has mysteriously disappeared. The fictional Kaspar Utz is based on a real collector named Rudolph Just (1895–1972), whose collection also disappeared after his death, only to reappear thirty years later on auction at Sotheby's (Riding 2001).

Many of the earliest known collections are grave goods, the objects buried with the dead that are physically or symbolically intended to be used by the deceased in the afterlife or objects that are so deeply associated with the dead that they have greater value in the tomb than they would if left among the living. There are many motivations for placing objects in graves—it is a custom as old as human burials. As is discussed in chapter 2, Neanderthals buried objects with their dead, as have people of almost every subsequent human culture. In some instances, the value of the entombed objects encouraged grave robbing, a desecration that is the exact opposite of what the burial intended. From the pharaohs of Egypt to the Wari royalty in ancient Peru, many cultures have taken elaborate steps to protect tombs from robbers, usually to little avail. All too often, the value of the grave goods makes violations of cultural taboos and the work of breaking into sealed tombs worth the risk and effort. Sometimes it is the cultural value rather than the monetary value of grave goods that causes the objects to be retrieved from the grave. When Elizabeth Siddal (1829–1862), the beautiful young wife of pre-Raphaelite poet and painter Dante Gabriel Rossetti (1828–1882), died from an overdose of laudanum in 1862, he placed in her coffin the only copy of a manuscript containing most of his unpublished poems. However, in 1869, Rossetti changed his mind and had the coffin exhumed and the manuscript retrieved so that he could publish the poems (Simons 2008).

The ultimate expression of not wanting to leave objects behind can be found in the number of museum founders who are buried in the institutions they started, sometimes in the collections. These range from the well-known to the obscure. A neo-Greek style mausoleum (built of yellow brick) in the midst of the Dulwich Picture Gallery (figure 1.1) in London contains the bodies of the museum's first benefactors, the collectors Noel Desenfans (1745–1807), his wife Margaret Morris (1731–1813), and Sir Francis Bourgeois (1756–1811). The ashes of founders Henry Clay Folger and Emily Jordan Folger rest in the Folger Library in Washington, DC (Blom 2002). The mortal remains of Albert M. Brooking (1880–1946), founder of the Hastings Museum (Hastings, Nebraska), are buried in the basement of the museum he created. Once I was shown a small urn containing ashes of the founder of a natural history collection,

Figure 1.1.   Dulwich Picture Gallery, London.

housed in a drawer along with some of his favorite specimens. Thus not just objects can be musealized—so can the collectors of the objects.

ORDO AB CHAO

Why do humans make collections? In the process of collecting, objects are named, organized, and classified to make them useful for understanding the seeming chaos of the world around them—*ordo ab chao* (order from chaos). *Classification* has been defined as the "orderly arrangement of a set of particulars that instantiate some intentionally defined, abstract, generality—a universal, what some would call a natural kind" (Kluge 2005:8). Stephen Jay Gould (1941–2002) wrote, "Taxonomy, or the science of classification, is the most underrated of all disciplines. Dismissed by the uninformed as philately gussied up with jargon, classification is truly the mirror of our thoughts, its changes through time the best guide to the history of human perceptions" (Purcell and Gould 1986:14). There is a curious parallel between the human need to organize and to classify and creation myths—just as it is necessary to give objects names in order to place them in a taxonomy, so in most cultural traditions the establishment of a taxonomic system is a fundamental part of the creation myth, in order to give names to things. For example, in the Judeo-Christian-Islamic creation myth, the first task of the first human is giving names to all the animals. How important this naming of things is in the human environment was aptly illustrated by Gabriel García Márquez (1927–2014) when he imagined the founding of the town of Macondo in *One Hundred Years of Solitude*, writing, "The world was so recent that many things lacked names, and in order to indicate them it was necessary to point" (García Márquez 1970:1).

OBJECTS, PRESERVATION, AND MUSEUMS

The concepts of collecting and preserving are closely related because, for collections to be truly meaningful, they had to survive into the future. The natural durability of some objects determined what has survived from the earliest collections. The preservation of organic materials is particularly difficult, which means that many objects made of leather, plant material, bone, or wood have deteriorated, while objects made of stone or ceramic have survived. Because of this differential preservation, what little knowledge we have of early collections is skewed. For example, clay tablets are more easily preserved than are papyrus scrolls, and papyrus scrolls are longer lasting than are texts written on animal hides.

The oldest method for the long-term preservation of organic materials is dehydration, which is the basis for mummification. Human and animal mummies were made on purpose at least 8,000 years ago in Peru and Chile and at least 5,000 years ago in Egypt. Mummification techniques have varied widely from place to place and over time, but in essence, a mummy is made by removing much of the soft tissue (which is prone to rapid deterioration), extracting the moisture from the remaining tissue (sometimes using dehydrating salts, sometimes allowing environmental dehydration to take place), and then wrapping the body in skins or textiles, often treated with oils and resins for protection from pests (Andrews 1998; Arriaza 1995).

Even objects that are made of durable materials, such as stone or gold, are subject to deterioration. In effect, the preservation of objects in museum collections requires constant vigilance and care. For example, although several catalogs of Renaissance collections have survived, very few of the objects that were in those collections are still extant.

SUMMARY

For purposes of locating the beginnings of collections and museums, Dr. Johnson's definition of *museum* as a collection of learned curiosities will suffice, but as the evolution of these institutions is explored in greater detail, the definition of *museum* also evolves as we work our way forward to the modern museum. Museums did not suddenly appear as institutions similar to those we know today—they developed slowly from private collections to public collections, from treasure troves to objects preserved for the public good. The gradual transformation of collections into museums did not always proceed in a linear fashion but varied from place to place and time to time along many divergent paths, assisted by a few conceptual fits and starts. There is no definable moment in history when the museum appears, although we can identify the major trends and foundational concepts among the prehistoric hoards, palace rarities, church treasuries, and cabinets of curiosities that preceded the emergence of the modern museum in the Age of Enlightenment.

2

——⁓⁓⁓——

Hoards and Tombs

Collections in the Ancient World, to 700 BCE

The study of ancient collections is difficult due to sparse archaeological evidence and few verifiable written records. Although archaeological excavations have unearthed many ancient collections, we know that not all of the objects originally in those collections survived the passage of time due to the nature of the materials they were made of. We are thus left to wonder and speculate about exactly which objects were originally collected and why.

In her study of museum history, Alma S. Wittlin (1899–1990) argued that an account of premuseum collections based on chronology or geography was not as useful as categorizing collections by function because "collections both reflect and affect human ways of life" (Wittlin 1970:4). Wittlin proposed grouping collections into six categories: (1) economic hoard collections, (2) social prestige collections, (3) magic collections, (4) collections made as expressions of group loyalty, (5) collections intended to stimulate curiosity and inquiry, and (6) collections assembled as means of emotional experience. Wittlin provided examples for each category of collection, which gives some perspective on the issue, but the problem with classifying ancient collections by function is that it requires making assumptions that may be based on little or no evidence. I believe that a better way to understand collections before there were museums, particularly ancient collections, is to consider their composition and preservation—knowing which objects were collected and how they were preserved can shed light on the motivation of the collectors and provide clues to possible uses of the objects.

THE EVOLUTION OF MATERIAL CULTURE

Collection objects are part of *material culture,* the physical evidence of cultural practices. *Material culture* is best defined as "that sector of our physical environment that we modify through culturally determined behavior" (Deetz 1977:24). Most any object can become part of material culture if it is utilized by human beings. Unfortunately, much of the evidence of material culture has not been preserved in the archaeological record because the objects have deteriorated. For example, archaeologists are far more likely to find a cache of stone tools than they are to find the leather bag that the tools were carried in or the seeds and feathers that were used to decorate the leather bag. Nevertheless, identifying the origins of material culture in humans can help reveal the earliest known collections.

The earliest indication of material culture in humans is the production of stone tools, which began about 3 million years ago in Africa, where humans evolved. Two million years ago, humans started to disperse from Africa into other parts of the world. By at least 100,000 years ago, there is evidence of symbolic expression, art, and cultural diversity in at least three human species—*Homo erectus, Homo neanderthalensis,* and *Homo sapiens.* One of these three species (*Homo sapiens*) was able to migrate far from Africa to colonize such remote places as Australia (about 60,000 years ago) and the Americas (at least 30,000 years ago). For reasons that are not clear, by around 25,000 years ago, all species of the genus *Homo* except *Homo sapiens* had become extinct (Higham et al. 2014).

Improved analytical methods have recently made it possible for scientists to unravel some of the mysteries of ancient human DNA and to better understand material culture by studying very small bits of pigments, resins, and other materials ancient humans used and left behind. Detailed studies of the flaking of stone tools and microscopic examination of their cutting surfaces have greatly enhanced our understanding of tool manufacture and use. One way that scientists study how stone tools were made and used is by duplicating the tools found at archaeological sites (figure 2.1).

There is an important distinction between *tool use* and *tool making. Tool use* is defined as the use of an object as an extension of a mouth, beak, hand, or claw to achieve an immediate goal, such as food gathering, bodily care, or defense (sensu van Lawick-Goodall 1971). Tool use is practiced by many animals other than humans. For example, some bowerbirds dip fibers from tree bark into paste they make by chewing colored fruits, and during mating season, North American porcupines may masturbate by straddling a stick as they walk on their hind legs (Carrighar 1965). *Tool making* refers to the alteration of an object in order to perform a task, such as flint knapping to make stonecutting implements (see figure 2.2 and box 2.1).

Figure 2.1.   Dr. François Bordes (1919–1981) demonstrating flint knapping at the University of Kansas in the early 1970s.

There are examples of object modifications that may or may not qualify as tool making, such as when a chimpanzee strips the leaves from a twig and uses it to capture termites to eat (van Lawick-Goodall 1971), but in general tool making is defined as the intentional selection, modification, and retention of an object for repeated use in the future.

The oldest tools that can be associated with a known hominid species were found with the 2.5-million-year-old remains of an individual of a human ancestor, *Australopithecus afarensis*, in Hadar, Ethiopia. The tools are stone (which is not surprising because stone endures long after other materials deteriorate). We don't know if these hominids also had tools made of bone, antler, or wood, but it is likely that they did in order to make their stone tools. We do know that these ancient hominids were selecting, modifying, and using tools and carrying the tools around with them. Recently, much older stone tools (dating back 3.3 million years) have been found in Kenya. Which hominid species made these tools is not known, but their quality indicates that the makers "already had considerable abilities in terms of planning depth, manual dexterity and raw material selectivity" (Harmand et al. 2015:310).

The artifacts that comprise material culture sometimes provide evidence of symbolic expression (the use of symbols to convey meaning),

BOX 2.1.
Flint Knapping

The process of shaping a stone into a tool is called *knapping*, or *flaking*. The stones most commonly used are flint, chert, and obsidian because the way they fracture (called conchoidal fracturing) leaves a sharp cutting edge. Figure 2.2 shows a knapped projectile point with sharp cutting edges made by conchoidal fracturing. A few sharp blows from a heavy hammer stone are used to break rough flakes off of a stone core. The rough flakes may be used as crude cutting tools, or they may be finely shaped and sharpened for a specific use. Shaping and sharpening of flakes is accomplished by using a softer object, such as a piece of antler, bone, or very hard wood to break off small slivers of stone along the edges of the piece. The process of fine shaping is called *pressure flaking*.

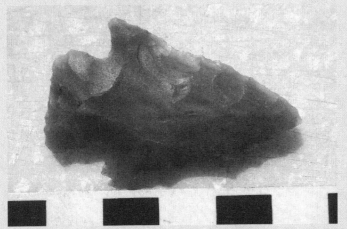

Figure 2.2. Knapped projectile point showing cutting edge made by conchoidal fracturing. Scale is marked in one-centimeter blocks.

Knocking sharp flakes from a stone core can be learned fairly quickly, but the fine work of pressure flaking to produce a sharp cutting blade or a spear point, dart point, or arrowhead requires considerable skill, time, and patience (Whittaker 1994). Probably because of the work invested in making them, finished stone tools were often saved and resharpened multiple times.

Stone tools vary widely in the sophistication of their craftsmanship, depending on their intended use. The small, thin flakes removed while shaping a larger stone are very sharp and make effective cutting implements, but producing a tool that can be repeatedly resharpened or a carefully balanced blade takes immense planning, skill, and practice.

While contemplating the significance of a two-million-year-old shaped stone tool found at Olduvai Gorge in northern Tanzania (now in the collection of the British Museum), Neil MacGregor observed,

> The extra chips on the edge of the chopping tool tell us that right from the beginning, we—unlike other animals—have felt the urge to make things more sophisticated than they need to be. Objects carry powerful messages about their makers, and the chopping tool is the beginning of a relationship between humans and the things they create which is both a love affair and a dependency. . . . [I]n this sense, it is making things that makes us human. (MacGregor 2011:13)

which is an indication that the objects have been musealized (taken from their original functional reality and placed in another context, as discussed in chapter 1). The earliest evidence of symbolic expression comes from objects that were buried in Neanderthal graves. Although we can only speculate as to why particular objects were placed in ancient burials, their inclusion as grave goods is also evidence of their musealization.

NEANDERTHAL COLLECTIONS

The human lineage known as Neanderthals (*Homo neanderthalensis*) evolved around 500,000 to 300,000 years ago. The first Neanderthal skulls found in modern times came from the Engis Caves in Belgium in 1829. Their scientific name, *Homo neanderthalensis*, is derived from the location where the holotype specimen was found in 1856, the Feldhofer Cave in the Neander Valley, about twenty-three kilometers east of Düsseldorf, Germany. For decades, it was assumed that Neanderthals were primitive creatures—the archetypal knuckle-dragging, grunting cavemen who wielded crude clubs. However, recent research has radically changed that image. DNA analysis shows that Neanderthals differed genetically from *Homo sapiens* by just 0.12 percent and that they frequently interbred with *Homo sapiens*, possibly to the point that, rather than dying off (as was long thought), they instead may have been gradually absorbed into *Homo sapiens* (many people of European ancestry alive today have some Neanderthal DNA). Neanderthals lived in organized social groups and used painting, sculpture, body adornment, and music as means of symbolic expression (table 2.1). In addition, there is evidence of technological innovations by Neanderthals, including the ability to control fire and to refine pitch to make an adhesive to secure blades to hafted tools (Wragg Sykes 2015).

Table 2.1. Ancient Evidence of Material Culture

Evidence of Material Culture	Date	Reference
Oldest known representation of a human face, carved on mammoth tusk, France	25,000 years ago	Walker 2015
Oldest indisputable depiction of a human being (called the Venus figurine), Höhle Fels Cave, Germany	35,000 years ago	Walker 2015
Stone with carved patterns, Neanderthal cave occupation site, Gibraltar	39,000 years ago	Walker 2015
Pentatonic flute carved from vulture bone, Höhle Fels Cave, Germany	40,000 years ago	Higham et al. 2012
Zoomorphic figure of a lion-headed human, carved in mammoth ivory, Höhle im Hohlenstein Cave, Germany	40,000 years ago	Walker 2015
Feather ornaments, Neanderthal burials, France and Iraq	50,000 years ago	Radovčić et al. 2015
Manganese and iron oxide pigments used for painting, Neanderthal occupation site, Israel	60,000 years ago	d'Errico et al. 2010
Shell beads, Neanderthal occupation sites, Israel and Algeria	100,000–135,000 years ago	Vanhaereny et al. 2006
Eagle talon jewelry, Neanderthal occupation site, Croatia	130,000 years ago	Radovčić et al. 2015
Ochre pigments, Neanderthal occupation site, South Africa	160,000–250,000 years ago	Marean et al. 2007; Roebroeks et al. 2012

CULTURAL DIVERSIFICATION AND COLLECTING

As humans continued to spread across the globe and make use of resources through technological innovations, their cultures became diverse, rapidly differentiating from each other in terms of dress, architecture, behavior and belief, technology, and thought (Roberts and Westad 2013). In addition to stone tools, early humans left behind other physical evidence, including bone needles, nets, traps, fishing gear, spears, and grave goods. As they traveled across the vast expanses of Eurasia, humans developed techniques for food preservation, conducted ceremonies and rituals, and began living in groups larger than nuclear family units (Roberts and Westad 2013).

Humans have a long history of symbolic expression using graphic symbols (the precursors to writing) and mnemonics (memory tools). Further evidence of symbolic expression is found in the manufacture of

Figure 2.3. Petroglyphs in Whoopup Canyon (Weston County, Wyoming), ca. 12,000 BCE.

shell beads, ivory and bone carvings, and cave and rock paintings (hand stencils, petroglyphs, and petrographs and pictoglyphs), even though in most cases it is not possible to interpret what these symbols meant to their makers (Fischer 2001; Walker 2015). Cave paintings and carvings have been found across Africa, Europe, Asia, Australia, and the Americas, dating from the earliest known human habitations of those areas (figure 2.3). Neil MacGregor cites the example of a sculpture of a swimming reindeer made from a mammoth tusk around 13,000 years ago at the end of the last ice age in Montastruc, France, as evidence that humans were exploring order and patterns as they were making art (MacGregor 2011).

The most ancient humans were hunter-gatherers. Cooperative hunting was required to obtain large animals and maintain food supplies, and it is an indication that experiences were being communicated from person to person as part of an oral tradition (Roberts and Westad 2013). Around 8000 to 9000 BCE, some hunting-gathering humans began cultivating crops and domesticating livestock (Langone, Stutz, and Gianopoulos 2006; MacGregor 2011). The subsequent development of metallurgy enabled significant changes in material culture—by 7000 to 6000 BCE, some human societies were using copper. Humans soon discovered how to make bronze, an alloy of copper and tin that is a much stronger and more useful compound. Other sophisticated technological advances were made in this same period, including the ability to perform trepanation, a surgical procedure in which a hole is cut in the skull of a living person, usually to remove damaged bone (Prioreschi 1991).

By about 6000 BCE, in the region of the Fertile Crescent (an area of ancient Mesopotamia around the Tigris and Euphrates Rivers), several kinds of wild barley and wheat were under cultivation. Meanwhile, the people who had reached the Americas by crossing the Bering Strait had domesticated wild teosinte (maize, or corn), and several species of animals had been domesticated for exploitation by humans in Peru, central Africa, and eastern China (Langone, Stutz, and Gianopoulos 2006).

The first identifiable cities and states developed between 4000 and 2000 BCE in the river valleys of North Africa and Asia, primarily in present-day Iraq, Egypt, Pakistan, and India. Archaeological evidence (primarily from grave goods and the excavation of occupation sites) suggests that there were significant inequalities of wealth and power between the rulers and the ruled (MacGregor 2011), with most of the collecting being practiced by those who possessed greater wealth.

In Mesopotamia, clusters of Neolithic villages and scattered temples were united to form the city of Sumer, the first true urban culture (Roberts and Westad 2013). Sumerians were the first to harden copper (by alloying it with lead, antimony, and tin), and they learned how to make iron around 1200–1000 BCE (Sarton 1970a). Sumerian craftsmen worked with gold, perfecting filigree and granulated gold work, as well as silver, lapis lazuli, and ivory (Sarton 1970a), producing objects with little direct practical use but desirable in collections, as indicated by their frequent selection as grave goods. With its concentration of workers, Sumer was the first place that skilled craftsmen were able to mass-produce a commodity—in this case, fine pottery (the concept of the wheel was developed around 3500 BCE, used first for making pottery and only later for transport of materials). To sustain the group of craftsmen, sufficient agricultural production and trade goods were also needed. With this urbanization, musealized art and artistic expression became more apparent in daily life in the form of public monuments (sensu Roberts and Westad 2013).

ORAL TRADITIONS, WRITING, AND LITERATURE

It is not known precisely when writing began, in part because many early writing materials (such as bark, bamboo strips, wooden tablets, wax tablets, parchment, and papyrus) do not preserve well (Diringer 1953). Writing is a form of symbolic expression that was first used for bookkeeping, inventories, and contracts rather than narratives (Casson 2001; Fischer 2001). However, the development of writing proved very useful as a means for rulers to exert control over their subjects (MacGregor 2011). The earliest

Figure 2.4. Clay tablet from Nippur, Iraq, ca. 3300 BCE. Photograph courtesy of the Earth and Mineral Sciences Museum and Art Gallery, The Pennsylvania State University.

known writings are clay tablets from about 3300 BCE from the city of Uruk, on the lower Euphrates River between Babylon and the Persian Gulf (Diringer 1953). The soft clay was marked with a stylus in a writing system that consisted of numerals and pictograms (figure 2.4). More than three-quarters of the 150,000 or so cuneiform inscriptions that have been found in Mesopotamia are inventories, letters, business records and receipts, and administrative records (Fischer 2001). Pictograms representing particular objects were extremely useful for making records of ordinary things but not for recording abstract thoughts or poetic ideas (see box 2.2).

Oral traditions function as cultural memory, entertainment, a way to memorialize the past, and an affirmation of cultural identity (Voth 2007). Before the development of written languages, the stories, songs, poems, and group histories that make up oral traditions were passed from one generation to another for tens of thousands of years to encourage social interactions and as assurance that knowledge was transferred and preserved. Over time, oral traditions began to be recorded as written literature. Writing down what had once been transmitted orally changed not only the way the information was communicated but also the role of literature in human society by preserving or fixing the stories and histories, making the meanings of rituals and beliefs more explicit (Roberts and Westad 2013).

Although the majority of Sumerian clay tablets are legal and economic documents (Kramer 1944), they are also the source of the oldest known

BOX 2.2.
The Development of Writing

The writing used on clay tablets is largely cuneiform (from the Latin words *cuneus*, meaning wedge, and *forma*, meaning shape). Cuneiform writing was also inscribed on stone, wax, ivory, metal, glass, and other substrates (few of which have survived) but rarely on papyrus (Fischer 2001). It is somewhat ironic that the reason so many clay tables have survived is that the fires that destroyed many other writing materials served to preserve writings on clay by baking it (see figure 2.4). Fires also preserved the earliest examples of the arrangement of documents in collections by destroying the buildings housing the archives while preserving intact the order of the clay tablets (Fischer 2001).

As one scholar of ancient history points out, the "scribe writing on clay had not by any means the same freedom as his Egyptian colleague writing on glossy papyrus. The latter was like a painter or draftsman; the former could only make two or three kinds of signs or wedges" (Sarton 1970a:63–64). As a result, the users of cuneiform script did not develop a tradition of calligraphy, despite the fact that, due to the "inertia of tradition" (Sarton 1970a:64), cuneiform writing continued to be used for centuries.

Clay was abundant and inexpensive, and clay tablets were much easier to make than papyrus sheets. Clay tablets could be simply dried to preserve them or baked for a greater degree of durability. In addition, clay tablets could be protected in clay envelopes (called shrinks) and secured with a seal that had to be broken for the document to be read. It was the use of clay tablets that led the Sumerians to develop the concept of archives and archival organization (Sarton 1970a). On the other hand, the flexibility of papyrus meant that the Egyptians were able to develop the scroll (the forerunner of the modern book), which was a much more efficient system for storing and retrieving information than the use of multiple clay tablets.

Papyrus writing material was made from the plant of the same name, an aquatic sedge (*Cyperus papyrus*). Papyrus was an important plant, not just for writing, but also as a building material, in making boats, and in other uses. The "bulrushes" used to make the basket that held the infant Moses in the biblical Exodus account were actually papyrus (Casson 2001).

In Egypt, papyrus scrolls were stored in wooden boxes or chests, stacked on shelves, or placed on end in clay jars. In temple collections, papyrus scrolls were arranged by subject or by author, often with labels made from small pieces of clay that were attached to the scroll with string to identify the contents (Murray 2009). The labeling and proper storage were critical—the papyrus libraries could be large, and the writing on them could not be read unless the scrolls were unrolled.

As early as 2600 BCE, there were papyrus records containing detailed descriptions of medical ailments and how they should be treated and cured. Perhaps the best known of the Egyptian medical texts is the *Ebers Papyrus*, written about 1550 BCE on a scroll that is more than 65 feet long and contains more than 700 remedies and incantations to cure diseases and injuries (Langone, Stutz, and Gianopoulos 2006).

The next advance in writing came about with the development of a system of graphic symbols to represent the sounds employed in spoken language—the symbols could be combined to form words rather than using different pictograms to represent individual objects. The transition from pictograms to graphic symbols, which has been called the change from *incomplete writing* to *complete writing*, occurred around 3700 BCE. This was a crucial point in the history of writing systems because complete writing enabled the writer to record ideas and concepts rather than just lists and inventories. Complete writing was rapidly adopted, spreading from the Nile up through the Indus Valley (Fischer 2001). According to one expert, "Though there are other possible interpretations, the cumulative weight of evidence urges the consideration that the idea of complete writing may have emerged only once in humankind's history. . . . All other writing systems and scripts are, then, perhaps derivatives of this one original idea . . . that emerged between 6,000 and 5,700 years ago in Mesopotamia" (Fischer 2001:33).

It has been argued that the development of writing systems had a greater impact on the evolution of human culture and society than any other invention, even though writing produced not the birth of great literature but the birth of bureaucracy (MacGregor 2011).

literary texts, consisting of poems, hymns, stories about the gods, and epic tales. The Sumerian epic stories were usually tales of great struggles followed by the triumph of an extraordinary human. For example, in one tale, the king Enmerkar is credited with inventing writing on clay tablets and was said to have reigned for 420 years.

The best known Sumerian narrative is the *Epic of Gilgamesh*, which tells the story of the spiritual quest of a ruler, Gilgamesh of Uruk. Considered to be the first great work of world literature, the story is only known today because it survived on clay tablets that were found in 1853 by an Assyrian archaeologist named Hormuzd Rassam (1826–1910). The tale has deep roots in the Mesopotamian oral tradition and includes the earliest known story of a worldwide flood (apparently based on the flooding of the Tigris and Euphrates Rivers). The story may have passed from the oral tradition into a written form as early as 2700 BCE, but the oldest surviving written version is a seventh century copy on twelve clay tablets from the library of Assurbanipal of Assyria (Voth 2007) from a version dating to about 1200 BCE.

The *Epic of Gilgamesh* has been described as a "mixture of pure adventure, of morality, and of tragedy" (Sandars 1972:7) but has also been interpreted as a parable describing the change from pastoral life to urban life, or from innocence to knowledge (Voth 2007). The text makes reference to several musealized objects, such as the special weapons that were made to slay the monster Humbaba and the cedar door that was built for Nippur. Gilgamesh was the name of a historic person who lived sometime between 2800 and 2500 BCE. In the story, however, he is depicted as a demigod with superhuman strength who lived for 126 years, a brutal and rapacious king. Gilgamesh has a fight with Enkidu, who was sent by the gods to destroy him, but afterward, the two become friends and journey together to the Cedar Mountain, where they kill a monstrous chimeric giant named Humbaba in order to steal sacred trees to build a gate for Uruk. In the process, Gilgamesh rejects the advances of the goddess Ishtar and, as a result, angers the gods, who send the Bull of Heaven to punish him. Gilgamesh and Enkidu manage to slay the beast, but as retribution, the gods cause Enkidu to die of a strange illness. Gilgamesh, saddened by the loss of his friend, sets out on a perilous journey to uncover the secret of eternal life. Although he discovers much during his many adventures, Gilgamesh also learns that all humans must die. Gilgamesh returns home when he realizes that the only thing that will live on after him is what he has built—in effect, the only things that are immortal (besides the gods) are the objects he has musealized by collecting, an expression of the increasing awareness of the importance of preservation of material culture for the perpetuation of societal ideals and meanings.

The first Egyptian hieroglyphs were developed before 3000 BCE and were used until 394 CE. Despite the fact that hieroglyphs were used for nearly 4,000 years, it was fourteen and a half centuries after the last hieroglyphs were written before they were deciphered by modern scholars (Roberts and Westad 2013). In contrast to Mesopotamia, writing in Egypt almost from its inception was used not only for administrative matters but also to record events intended for posterity on public monuments and walls. In part, the Egyptians could make records of public events because of the success of their agricultural production, which generated enough food to enable many public works to be constructed (Roberts and Westad 2013). Another significant aspect of Egyptian culture was the pervasiveness of religion as a framework for managing society and particularly Egyptian religion's apparent obsession with death, expressed in elaborate mummy-making and associated rituals, including the massive collections of musealized grave goods that were preserved in funeral chambers (Roberts and Westad 2013). As a result of the influence of religion in Egyptian society, the majority of ancient Egyptian literature consists of prayers, rituals, medical texts, and legal documents (Sarton 1970a). Egyptian society placed a high value on social cohesion, which was expressed in the selection of funerary objects that would be needed by the owner in the afterlife. The objects that were musealized as grave goods by the Egyptians stand in stark contrast to funerary collections from Mesopotamia, which emphasized individual heroic achievement rather than cohesive preparation for the afterlife.

LATER ANCIENT COLLECTIONS: 3000–2000 BCE

There are a number of scattered accounts of objects in later collections that give us an indication of how common collecting had become. An Akkadian ruler, Naram-Sin (2678–2641 BCE), owned a stone drinking cup that was inscribed with his name. After his death, the cup passed from owner to owner for three hundred years before turning up in the collection of a royal priestess of the moon god Nanna in the Sumerian city of Ur, who added her own name to it and kept it in the collection held in the temple. The temple burned in 1885 BCE, but the cup was found in its remains in 1400 BC (Rigby and Rigby 1944).

By the third millennium BCE, the Sumerian archives in Ebla (in modern-day Syria, about fifty kilometers south of Aleppo) held extensive collections of clay tablets that were used to teach writing to student scribes. Excavations of Ebla in 1974–1975 unearthed a room measuring three and a half by four meters that was filled with tablets containing various administrative documents, preserved in place as the result of a fire that occurred between 2300 and 2250 BCE. The tablets, which had been housed on wooden shelves, remained in their original order when the shelves burned away. From this discovery, we know that the tablets were stored upright, separated by small fragments of baked clay (Casson 2001). In a collection of tablets excavated at Nippur (Nibru), another Sumerian city, several catalog tablets were found, dating to around 2000 BCE (Kramer 1944). These catalog tablets list the titles of other tablets in the collection, which is important because they represent a significant step toward systematizing the contents of a collection. Later, identifying notes were routinely added to clay tablets (Casson 2001).

COLLECTING AND COLLECTIONS: 2000–700 BCE

During the period from 2000 to 700 BCE, although most people in the Middle East lived in scattered communities, they created many sophisticated objects using a variety of materials, including bronze and gold—objects assumed to have been designed to make an impression or to demonstrate power and that were intended to survive long into the future (MacGregor 2011). A diverse array of materials was in circulation thanks to extensive trade routes. For example, beads found at a second-millennium site in Mycenae were manufactured in Britain from Baltic amber (Roberts and Westad 2013). Archaeologists have been able to trace a number of ancient amber trade routes from the shores of the North Sea and the Baltic Sea through northern Europe and on to the Mediterranean (Sarton 1970a). Extensive trade on a smaller scale has been identified for ancient quarries that produced high-quality flint used for making cutting tools (Sarton 1970a). The small island of Kos (Cos) in the Dodecanese of Greece was a major center of Neolithic trade due to its deposits of high-grade obsidian used to make projectile points (Sarton 1970a).

The objects found in collections from this time were increasingly sophisticated and, in some instances, unusual. In Babylon, where extispicy (divination using animal entrails) and, in particular, hepatoscopy (divination based on the liver) were practiced, collections contained clay models of the liver used to teach the art (Sarton 1970a). During his 1903–1906 excavations of a circular building in Heliopolis, Egypt, Ernesto Schiaparelli (1856–1928) of the Museo Egizio (Turin, Italy) unearthed a specimen of a fossil sea urchin from the Eocene (56–34 million years old). Written on the fossil in twelve hieroglyphs was an inscription by a scribe named Tja-nefer stating that the fossil had been found in the south quarry of Sopdu in Egypt in 2000 BCE. Along with the fossil, other objects, including Old Kingdom statues and vases (dating to 2690–2160 BCE), were found, leading to speculation that the round building may have housed a museum or storeroom of some sort (Mayor 2011; McNamara 2010). Five hundred years later in Egypt, Tuthmosis III (1504–1450 BCE) built up an extensive collection of art, antiquities, flora, and fauna from Asia (Lewis 1985) and was said to have once gathered botanical specimens between battles. Tuthmosis III ordered the catalog of his botanical collection to be carved in stone on the wall of a chamber in the temple at Karnak (Rigby and Rigby 1944). After one military campaign he published an inventory of everything that had been seized from the conquered foe, including household goods such as dishes, vases, cooking vessels, knives, objects fashioned of silver and gold, chairs, ivory, and other furniture (Rigby and Rigby 1944). There are many similar accounts of lists of war booty and plunder in ancient collection records.

Amenhotep III (ca. 1386–1353 BCE) of Egypt was an avid collector of rings and gemstones, as well as blue and polychrome enameled cups, drinking bowls, kohl pots, vases (Capart 1926), and blue ceramics (Blom 2002). The tomb of Tutankhamen (1342–1323 BCE) was full of objects, many of which were family heirlooms and relics, as well as 130 walking sticks—Tutankhamen was lame and walked with a cane (Hawass et al. 2010; Rigby and Rigby 1944). Tutankhamen also collected fine ceramics. At shrines to the Egyptian god Set excavated in Qau and Matmar in 1922–1923, archaeologists found three tons of fossil bones, apparently revered as sacred relics. The bones were mostly from hippos, crocodiles, hartebeests, horses, and water buffalo, skeletons of which would have been familiar to the ancient Egyptians. Flinders Petrie (1853–1942) found a similar cache of fossils in Qau tombs the following year (Mayor 2011).

Asian literature from this period does not tell us much directly about objects that were selected for collections but does provide a context for understanding the development of later collecting cultures. The *Rigveda*, one of the earliest known religious texts in any Indo-European language, is a collection of Vedic Sanskrit stories, prayers, and hymns composed from about 1400–1100 BCE in northwest India. The text includes Hindu accounts of the origin of the world and is one of the best sources of information about early Aryan Bronze Age culture and the objects valued in that culture (Roberts and Westad 2013). The *Upanishads*, an important text marking the evolution of a more philosophical religion, dates to about 700 BCE (Roberts and Westad 2013). Classical Hinduism took form during the first millennium BCE, about the same time that Buddhism originated—the religion that would eventually come to dominate Asia (Roberts and Westad 2013). Both Hinduism and Buddhism produced conservative societies that emphasized the anticipation of a spiritual afterlife that was very different from that imagined by the ancient Egyptians, with their emphasis on musealized funerary objects.

The oldest extant written records from China consist of oracle bones that date from the sixteenth to eleventh centuries BCE. Oracle bones were turtle plastrons or the scapulae of oxen that were inscribed with Chinese pictographs. The bones were heated to produce cracks on the reverse side, and the directions and lengths of the resulting cracks were then interpreted in relation to the pictographs (Roberts and Westad 2013). Some oracle bones have survived the passage of time because they were maintained as official archival records.

The first five books of the Hebrew Tanakh, known as the Torah (a combination of history, literature, and theology), were assembled in written form during the tenth century BCE (Voth 2007). Many of the stories in Hebrew literature are strikingly similar to those of Mesopotamia and Egypt, including the account of Noah's flood and Moses floating in a papyrus basket in the Nile (Voth 2007). The biblical account of King Solomon, who ruled ca. 970–931 BCE in Jerusalem, makes reference to his extensive collections, which some nineteenth-century authors characterized as a forerunner of the cabinets of curiosities (Murray 1904). The biblical Book of Kings includes a detailed list of temple objects, including Solomon's accumulation of gold, bronze, fine wood, and precious stones and the objects that were made from them. In addition, the Book of Kings tells the story of Hezekiah (who reigned ca. 715–686 BCE), who showed the collection in his treasure room to envoys from the ruler of Babylon. When Jerusalem was later sacked by the Babylonians, the treasures were seized as war booty and dispersed (see discussion in chapter 5). In the Middle Ages, many European churches claimed to have the actual objects once owned by Solomon or Hezekiah in their collections (Murray 1904; Rigby and Rigby 1944).

GREEK CONCEPTIONS OF THE OBJECT IN
THE *ILIAD* AND THE *ODYSSEY*, CA. 800 BCE

Sometime around 800 BCE, in the Mediterranean world, two rather gory poems about the Trojan War and its aftermath (the *Iliad* and the *Odyssey*) that had long been told and retold as part of the oral tradition were at last written down. These works are significant for a number of reasons, not the least of which is that both were accepted for centuries as accurate histories and both influenced the future development of European cultures (Roberts and Westad 2013). The *Iliad* and the *Odyssey* were long considered to be important sources for teaching morals, ethics, history, oratory, and literature (Dirda 2013). The *Iliad* is a story of warfare, and the *Odyssey* is a story of postwar peace and domestic life, rich in details about travel, merchants, and colonists; both helped standardize Greek language and history (Sarton 1970a). A fair amount is known about public and private collections in this period in the Mediterranean due to extensive archaeological work and surviving written documents.

Exactly who first converted the *Iliad* and the *Odyssey* into stable, written stories is unknown (Roberts and Westad 2013), but it is noteworthy that, by the time the stories appeared in writing, they were describing early Greek societies that had vanished, as power had shifted from monarchs to aristocrats in almost all of the Greek city-states. It is known that the stories had been in the oral tradition for at least four hundred years before they were written down under the pen name of Homer (Voth 2007). Although the focus of both the *Iliad* and the *Odyssey* is on individual heroic action and its consequences, both works show a deep understanding of past history and the importance of the use of historic objects in their narratives (Grethlein 2008), which is reflected in the composition of Greek temple collections.

Specifically, the *Iliad* tells the story of a conflict between King Agamemnon and the warrior Achilles during the last year of a ten-year-long siege of the city of Troy (*Ilium* in Greek) by an alliance of other Greek states. The *Odyssey*, a sequel to the *Iliad*, is the story of the ten-year-long homeward journey of the hero Odysseus after the fall of Troy. Both works contain numerous references to historical objects, including weapons (armor, a belt, a bow, a club, a helmet, a spear, a sword, a shield, and the scepter of Agamemnon) and amphorae, baskets, bathing tubs and tripods, bowls, cups, a discus, drugs, headgear, a lyre, and kraters, many of which have special features or were thought to have special powers (Grethlein 2008). Biographies for several of these objects are included in the stories, including details of their prior history of ownership (museological object provenance). The attention devoted to individual objects is a reflection of the role of the objects in Greek society, particularly the importance placed on object provenance. Several objects serve as major reference points for the reader and anchor the poems in the historic past, in effect serving as mnemonic references by means of the musealization of the objects (Grethlein 2008). For example, in the *Iliad*, the warrior Meriones gives Odysseus a leather helmet. The description of the helmet includes the details that it could be tied on the head over a felt cap and that it was adorned with gleaming white boar tusks, as well as a recitation of the chain of ownership (mostly by theft) from Eleon to Autoclycus to Amphidamas to Molus to Meriones (*Iliad* 10:261–66). Similarly, when Nestor is served Pramnian wine containing grated goat's milk cheese sprinkled with white barley, Hecamede offers the wine in a vessel that is described as gold-plated, with four handles, each on two supports ornamented with pecking doves. The cup is then revealed to be a cup that Nestor had personally brought from Greece (*Iliad* 11:632–35). In book 24 of the *Iliad*, there is a description of the contents of the treasure chamber of Priam, the king of Troy. The high-ceilinged room, paneled in cedar (a wood that was valued both for its beauty and because its oil is a pest repellant), contained chests of fine vestments, gold, tripods, caldrons, and a cup given to Priam by the Thracians.

The detailed object descriptions and histories in the *Illiad* emphasize the importance of associating particular objects with specific persons and places in Greek life. The weapons of heroes that were displayed in Greek temples have similar historic affiliations. The sanctuary of Athena at Phaselis, for example, claimed to exhibit the spear of Achilles, while the temple of Aesculapius at Nicomedia displayed the sword of Memmon (Murray 1904). There is a correlation between the status of weapons displayed in the temples and the numerous references in the *Iliad* to battle wounds and their treatment, such as the removal of arrows, the cleaning of puncture wounds, the use of compresses and bandages, and the application of balms and herbs (Marketos and Androustos 2009). Sarton (1970a) counted descriptions of 147 wounds in the text.

In the *Iliad*, Homer tells how Heracles slew the Monster of Troy, a mighty creature that was said to have arisen from the sea and ravaged the coast of Troy. To appease the monster, the king's daughter, Hesione, had been sent to sacrifice herself to the beast, but Heracles arrived on the scene in time to dispatch the monster and thereby save the princess. The climactic scene in which Heracles kills the Monster of Troy is depicted on a Greek column krater dating to 550 BCE that now resides in the Museum of Fine Arts in Boston. The Monster of Troy was long dismissed as mythic fiction, but a close examination of the image by several paleontologists has revealed that it is a very close match to the skull of an extinct creature. Adrienne Mayor (2011) notes that it is highly significant that the depiction on the krater is clearly that of a skull (albeit with a tongue) rather than a fleshed-out monster, speculating that the image was most likely based on a fossil that was exposed in a weathered outcrop—in other words, the story of the Monster of Troy was substantiated for its believers by the discovery of the fossil remains of extinct animals that resembled descriptions of the monster. Such discoveries are reminders that, whereas we cannot take tales from oral traditions too literally, we must also be careful not to dismiss them outright—such stories can tell us much about the worldviews of the cultures that composed them, how they saw the objects around them, and the objects that they valued enough to musealize.

The *Iliad* and the *Odyssey* are significant in another way that relates to collections and museums—despite their popularity and significance, the full texts of both stories were nearly forgotten for a thousand years after the Greek language died out in western Europe. The tales were only recovered when they were found in a Byzantine manuscript in a monastery collection (Dirda 2013).

SUMMARY

Archaeology provides tantalizing glimpses into the reasons ancient collections were made and evidence of a growing complexity in the processes and rationales for the musealization of objects by collectors. Despite the striking similarities of at least one Babylonian and one Egyptian site to museums and despite the evidences for the exhibition of objects, no direct links can be made from these institutions to modern museums, but they are evidence of a continuous, worldwide culture of collecting and exhibiting objects.

3

———

The Temple of the Muses

The Conjunction of Objects and Knowledge, Classical Antiquity, 700 BCE–400 CE

The Greeks had a significant influence on the cultures of classical antiquity throughout the Mediterranean region (Cunliffe 1987). The distinctive character of classical Greek culture was largely due to the nature and function of Greek religious beliefs and practices, along with their enormously complex pantheon and thousands of mythic stories (Roberts and Westad 2013).

Classical Greece was distinguished by a tradition of support and care for public treasures, supported by the donation of objects to the treasuries at public sanctuaries (temple sites) by private citizens (Ullberg et al. 2002). A treasury was usually a small, one-room templelike building with a roofed porch the width of the building (Bounia 2004). Some treasuries were more elaborate than others, and they varied in size from temple to temple. A temple might have just one treasury or multiple treasuries (twelve treasury buildings were found in Olympia and thirteen at Delphi). The treasury was not itself a temple (a temple contained a cult statue and functioned as a religious center) but an ancillary structure.

Temple treasuries served several purposes. They were places for the display of the spoils of war, the commemoration of military victories, the demonstration of a city's prosperity, evidence of piety on the part of the citizens of a city, sites for celebrations of community wealth, and manifestations of civic pride (Bounia 2004). The concept of the temple treasury has roots in both the mythic past of Greece and the tradition of gift exchange in Greek culture.

Donations to the temple treasuries were indicators of changes in previous collecting habits in the areas of the world influenced by Greek

29

culture—analysis of bronze objects in treasuries between the eleventh and eighth centuries BCE shows that an increase in donations to temple treasuries coincided with a marked decrease in grave goods (Bounia 2004). Other donated objects included sculptures and paintings; objects crafted in gold, silver, and bronze; antique weapons attributed to mythic heroes; votive offerings and other objects with religious or cultural significance; and objects valued because they were unusual (both artificial and natural). The donation of objects for display at Greek temples prefigured the way that relics, religious art, and such wondrous objects as ostrich eggs and griffin claws later came to fill churches and monasteries across Europe during the Middle Ages and the early Renaissance (Pearce 1995; Rigby and Rigby 1944), as discussed in chapter 4.

In addition to their use as donations at temple treasuries, private Greek homes were often decorated with art objects, fossils, precious stones, ceramics, and antiquities (Bazin 1967; Lewis 1985; Mayor 2011).

The oldest reference to the organization of objects in a *pinakothekai* (a temple picture gallery) is a description of the propylaea, or gateway to the Athenian Acropolis, built by Mnesicles in the fifth century BCE (Bazin 1967). In many Greek temples of the classical era, paintings were grouped by schools in the *pinakothekai* (the word is derived from *pinas*, meaning "plank or board," because most of the paintings were on wood and were called *pinakés*). Other objects in the treasuries were also arranged for public viewing and were regularly inventoried by the temple guardians (the *hieropoei*), who were tasked with the care of the treasures and offerings. Objects were exhibited in the *prodomos* (entrance vestibules) or on shelves in the inner chamber, called the naos (Bazin 1967). When large numbers of donations were accumulated, members of the public would be called on to finance the construction of a treasury building (thesaurus) to contain the overflow (Ullberg et al. 2002).

The Greek historian Herodotus (484–425 BCE) recorded several instances of donated objects that were exhibited in temples (Grene 1987). For example, when Gyges (716–678 BCE) became king, he donated six golden bowls, which Herodotus reported "stand in the treasure house of the Corinthians and weigh thirty talents" (Grene 1987:28). To gain the favor of the gods, Croesus (595–ca. 547 BCE) sent gifts to the Temple of the Oracle of Delphi, including a statue of a lion made of gold; "two immensely great mixing bowls, of gold and silver, whereof the golden one stood to the right as you enter the temple, the silver one to the left"; as well as four silver jars; a "statue of a boy with the water running through his hand"; and other objects (Grene 1987:54–55). A golden shield and spear, which Croesus gave to Amphiaraus, were exhibited in the Temple of Ismenian Apollo in Thebes (Grene 1987).

The tradition of the exhibition of public collections was sufficiently widespread in Greek society that special techniques were developed for the protection of the objects. Pausanias the Geographer (d. 180 CE) reported that in the *stoa poikile* (or painted porch) on the north side of the ancient agora (gathering place) in Athens, bronze shields were coated in pitch to prevent them from corroding, and in the Parthenon, large vats of oil were placed at the feet of the gold and ivory *Athena Parthenos* of Phidias to protect it from deterioration in the dry atmosphere (Bazin 1967).

THE TEMPLE OF THE MUSES

The modern concept of the museum as a place where learning and objects are associated is based on an institution in ancient Alexandria called the Temple of the Muses. Although there are no direct links in the form of successively modified institutions evolving from the Temple of the Muses into modern museums, it was the use of objects as sources of knowledge that formed the conceptual basis of museum development beginning in the Renaissance (see chapter 5), when the name *museum* first began to be applied to collections.

The Muses refers to the sister-goddesses of Greek mythology (Findlen 1989; see table 3.1). The modern word *museum* is derived from the Greek word *mouseion*, which means "place of the muses." One of the earliest uses of the word *museum* in English was in an account by George Sandys (1578–1644) of his visit to Alexandria (box 3.1) in which he described "that famous Musaeum founded by Philadelphus" and "that renowned Library" (Sandys 1621:111).

The city of Alexandria was founded by Alexander the Great (356–323 BCE), the conqueror from Macedonia, in April 331 BCE in present-day Egypt. Alexander intended the city to serve as the center of Greek culture

Table 3.1. The Muses

Name	Area of Inspiration	Symbols
Calliope	Epic poetry	Writing tablet and stylus
Clio	History	Laurel wreath, scrolls
Euterpe	Music and elegiac poetry	Aulos (a type of flute)
Thalia	Comedy, pastoral poetry	Comic mask, shepherd's staff
Melpomene	Tragedy	Tragic mask, sword
Terpsichore	Dance and choral song	Lyre
Erato	Lyric poetry	Cithara (a type of lyre), crown of roses
Polyhymnia	Sacred song and sacred poetry	Veil
Urania	Astronomy	Globe and compass

BOX 3.1.
A Visit to Alexandria

The English traveler George Sandys (1578–1644) was born in Bishopthorpe and attended Oxford but began his travels before obtaining his degree. Sandys set out in 1610 on a trip across France, northern Italy, then to Venice, and on through Constantinople to Egypt, Mt. Sinai, Palestine, southern Italy, and Rome. Sandys published his account of this journey, including his visit to Alexandria, in 1621 in a book with the title *A Relation of a Journey begun An. Dom. 1610. Foure Bookes Containing a Description of the Turkish Empire, of Aegypt, of the Holy Land, of the Remote parts of Italy, and lands adjoining.* Sandy's description of Alexandria is as follows:

After *Alexander* had subdued Aegypt, determining to build a Citie that might preserve his memory, and to plant it with *Grecians*; he made election of this Promontory: advised (as it is said) thereunto by *Homer* in a dream, who seemed to pronounce these verses:

An ile there is by surging seas embrac'd
Which men call Pharus, before Aegypt plac'd.

The platform for want of chalke, was laid out with meal; prognosticating thereby her ensuring felicity: drawne in the figure of a *Macedonian* cloak; and afterward walled by *Ptolomy*. The sides stretching out in length contained in diameter three thousand seven hundred paces; those in the latitude a thousand; contracted at the ends by narrow Isthmoses: here bounded with the lake, & there with the sea. The contriver, and overseer of the work was *Dinocrates*. From the gate of the Sunne, unto that of the Moon, on each side of the way stood ranks of pillars: in the midst a spacious Court, led into by a number of streets: insomuch as the people that passed throughout, in some sort did seem to have undertaken a journey. On the left hand of this stood that part of the Citie which was named of Alexander; being as it were a Citie of it selfe, whose beauty did herein differ: for look how far those columnes directly extended in the former, so did they here, but obliquely placed. So that the sight dispersed through multitudes of ways, and ravished with the magnificency thereof, could hardly be satisfied. A wonderfull adorning thereunto were the Fannes, and regall palaces, possessing wel-nigh a fourth part of the Citiy; for every one did strive to adde some ornament as well to the houses of their kings, as to the Temples of their Gods: which stood on the East side of the Citie; adjoyning, and participating one with another. Amongst the which was that famous *Musæum* founded by *Philadelphus*, & endowed with ample revenues: planted with such as were eminent in liberall sciences, drawne tither by rewards, and cherished with favours. He caused the Philosophy of the *Ægyptians* (before alone peculiar to the Priests) to be divulged in Greek for the benefit of students. He procured seventy of the principall learned amongst the *Jews* to translate the Bible, called at this day the Septuagint. And erected that renowned Library furnished with seven hundred thousand volumes, burnt long after by mishap: at that time when *Cæsar* was driven into a narrow exigent by the unlookt for assault of *Achillas*. Renewed, and augmented by the *Romane* Emperors, it flourished until the *Mahometans* subdued *Aegypt*, and subverted all excellencies with the barbarisime. Within a *Serraglio*

called *Somia*, belonging to the Palaces, the *Ptolomies* had the sepultures, together with *Alexander* the great. . . .
  Such was this Queen of Cities and *Metropolis* of *Africa*: but

  Ah how much different is
  That Niobe from this!

who now hath nothing left her but ruines, and those ill witnesses of her perished beauties: declaring rather, that townes as well as men, have their ages and destinies. (Sandys 1621:87–89)

in the region. Dinocrates, who was appointed the city's chief architect, designed Alexandria as an enclave enclosed by more than fifteen kilometers of walls, with streets thirty meters wide (Empereur 2002). Although Alexander did not live to see his city built, it did become the cultural, intellectual, and commercial center that he envisioned.

After he founded the city, Alexander and his army crossed into Asia Minor, defeated the Persians at Issus, continued south to Syria (destroying Tyre along the way) and on to Egypt, then back to Asia to defeat Darius III in 331 BCE at Gaugamela. Alexander and his army then sacked Persepolis, fought their way through Iran, and on into Afghanistan and the Punjab. Alexander returned as far as Babylon before dying of a fever or from drinking a large bowl of bad wine—or perhaps both—in the former palace of Nebuchadnezzar II in June 323 BCE (Roberts and Westad 2013). Tradition says that Alexander's body was either preserved in honey or mummified (although these are not necessarily mutually exclusive) so that it could be brought back to Macedonia for burial (Ransome 1937). However, to ensure the prominence of Alexandria in a post-Alexander world, Ptolemy Soter (one of Alexander's generals) had Alexander's body diverted to Alexandria and installed in a tomb near the royal palaces. There are accounts of a number of Roman officials who later saw the preserved body, including Octavian (63 BCE–14 CE), who had the body lifted out of the sarcophagus so that he could place a gold crown on Alexander's head in 31 BCE, following his victory over the forces of Mark Antony and Cleopatra in the Battle of Actium (Empereur 2002).

Following Alexander's death, his empire quickly fragmented (Roberts and Westad 2013). By 275 BCE, it had been divided into three parts—the Antigonids took control of Greece and Macedonia; the Seleucids ruled most of Asia Minor; and the Ptolemies took over Egypt, southern Syria, Cyrenaica, and Cyprus (Berti and Costa 2009; Sarton 1970a). Ptolemy Soter and his descendants continued to rule in Egypt for three hundred years, until the death of Cleopatra in 30 BCE (Roberts and Westad 2013).

The Muses were the daughters of Zeus (the god of sky and thunder) and Mnemosyne (the goddess of memory). In Greek mythology, the Muses were the personifications of knowledge and the arts. The sisters lived on Mount Helicon and were the attendants of Apollo (the god of prophecy). Their duties included singing at the feasts of the gods on Mount Olympus. Greek artists would typically invoke a Muse by name before beginning creative work. Of the nine muses, seven are devoted to literature and the arts, the other two to astronomy and history (di Pasquale 2005). There were many shrines and temples dedicated to the Muses in Greece, often associated with fountains or natural springs. When the philosopher Pythagoras of Samos (ca. 570–ca. 495 BCE) arrived at Croton to establish his school of mathematics around 530 BCE, he advised the townspeople to build a shrine to the Muses in the center of the city to promote learning and civic harmony.

The Alexandrian Temple of the Muses, which was loosely based on similar institutions in Greece, is best described as a combination of a school of scholars, a research institution, and a library. The Greek word *mouseion* was already associated with other schools, including the Academy of Plato in Athens (see box 3.2). In his description of Plato's academy, the historian George Sarton writes, "We may assume that in his time it already included some buildings, for example, a chapel or museum (a temple to the Muses), perhaps a few chambers for teachers and disciples, and halls for assembly, for lecturing, and for eating together, if only on formal occasions" (Sarton 1970a:398).

An enormous amount of mythology has accumulated around the Temple of the Muses and the Library of Alexandria (collectively called the Musaeum), what took place there, what objects and books were housed there, and the cause of their destruction (Battles 2015). For example, a poem by the Argentine writer Jorge Luis Borges ("Alejandría, 641 A.D.," written in 1977) describes the Caliph Omar of Damascus issuing the order for the library to be burned (which is not true); the plot of a 1988 novel by Clive Cussler (*Treasure*) begins with a Roman named Julius Venator escaping with the treasures of the Library of Alexandria and burying them in a foreign land (which turns out to be Texas). The reality is that reliable contemporary descriptions of the Temple of the Muses and the Library of Alexandria are few, and care must be taken to sift through the many imaginative and conjectural accounts (Berti and Costa 2009) due to what Butler has called the "mytholigisation of Alexandria" (Butler 2007:32).

It is significant that Alexandria was both an Egyptian city and a Greek colony with an ethnically diverse population, so that Ptolemy Soter had to blend the two dominant cultures in order to unite them politically, which supports the idea that the Musaeum was probably an "eclectic hybrid of Egyptian and Greek architectural elements (with Roman bits later added by the conquering Caesars)" (Lee 1997:394). It is known that, in general, Alexandrian architecture and public art were a mixture of

BOX 3.2.
Plato, Forms, and Cabinets of Curiosities

Following the execution of his beloved teacher Socrates (470–399 BCE), Plato (428–347 BCE) established his own school, choosing a location along the river Cephissus that was removed from the crowded streets and marketplaces of Athens (Sarton 1970a). The place Plato chose was surrounded by a wall and included an olive orchard, a park, a grove of trees, and an athletic field. More significantly, the area was associated with the mythic Greek hero Akademos, hence the derivation of the name Academy of Plato.

There are several important links between Plato's contributions to Hellenistic culture and the development of modern museums that are worth noting. Plato's theory of forms or theory of ideas, which held that the objects we see are but mere imperfect and ephemeral representations of ideal archetypes, led to the idea that a universal classification could be developed based on ideal standards and patterns. The concept of an ideal universal classification allowed objects to be understood "in their reality, instead of having to consider only their evanescent appearances," and explained the "law of change and decay" (Sarton 1970a:402). Plato's theory formed the groundwork for identifying marvels to be included in the Renaissance cabinets of curiosities (discussed in chapter 5; see also Daston and Park 2001).

In 368 BCE, a teenage Macedonian student named Aristotle (385–322 BCE) was sent to study with Plato at his academy in Athens. In 343 BCE, Aristotle moved to Pella in central Macedonia to become tutor to the young prince Alexander (who later founded the city of Alexandria, home of the Temple of the Muses). In 335 BCE, Aristotle returned to Athens to establish his own school, called the Lyceum (Sarton 1970a). There is a direct link between the Lyceum and the library of Alexandria—a student of Aristotle named Demetrius of Phalerum (ca. 350–280 BCE) went to Egypt in 307 BCE to serve as director of the library under Ptolemy I and Ptolemy II (Berti and Costa 2009; MacLeod 2000).

While conquering the empires of Persia and India, Alexander sent specimens and descriptions of what he saw to Aristotle. Many of the species described by Aristotle in *Historia Animalium*, including the elephant—first seen by Alexander when he defeated Darius at the Battle of Gaugamela in 331 BCE (French 1994; Yoon 2009)—were based on information from Alexander (Simmons and Snider 2012).

The taxonomic system developed by Aristotle in *Historia Animalium* endured for thousands of years and had a profound impact on the development of European thought. Aristotle organized all the known species of animals (about 450 in all) in a staged progression called the *scala naturae* based on their perceived degree of perfection (and idealized archetype). Variations of Aristotle's organization scheme were the basis for arranging collections of animals in museums until it was eventually supplanted in the mid-eighteenth century. The international rules for naming scientific specimens of plants and animals still make use of type specimens, an etymological reference to the ideal archetypes of Plato.

Greek, Macedonian, and Egyptian styles, flavored with the influences of other cultures with whom the Alexandrians traded (Empereur 2002). The Musaeum's collections included objects of art and natural history. Many important scholars worked at the Musaeum, including Euclid (fl. 300 BCE); the astronomers Aristyllus (fl. ca. 261 BCE) and Timocharis (ca. 320–260 BCE); Eratosthenes of Cyrene (ca. 273–ca. 192 BCE), who calculated the circumference of the Earth; Erasistratus (ca. 304–ca.250 BCE), who studied physiology; and Herophilos of Chalcedon (335–280 BCE), who performed public dissections (Empereur 2002; Sarton 1970a; Watson 2002). One study sums up the importance of the Musaeum in this way:

> The central place of the Alexandrian library in Western cultural memory derives, in our opinion, from a combination of several factors: the foundation project; the connection between the library and the Museum; the capability of the Alexandrian library to generate knowledge, and not only to accumulate it; and its violent and sudden destruction, a symbol of countless similar tragedies that have happened in the course of history. (Berti and Costa 2009:13–14)

One of the few reliable contemporary eyewitness accounts of the Temple of the Muses was written by the geographer and historian Strabo (64/63 BCE–ca. 24 CE), who visited Egypt between 24 and 19 BCE. Strabo's account begins with a description of his arrival at Alexandria by sea, sailing around the small, oblong island of Pharos at the entrance to the harbor (the harbor that so impressed Alexander that he decided to build his city there). A 135-meter-high white stone lighthouse stood on the island of Pharos (Empereur 2002). Strabo tells the story of how, during the planning of the city, the architects ran out of chalk to mark the location of the walls and streets and had to substitute flour, which was considered by those present to be a good omen for the future of the city. The Musaeum complex was part of the royal palaces. Strabo describes the layout as including a public walkway (a *peripatos*), a room furnished with seats (an exedra), and a large dining hall where the temple scholars held their communal meals. The institution was directed by a priest (an epistates) appointed originally by the ruling Ptolemy (but, in Strabo's time, by Caesar). The tombs of the kings and of Alexander were adjacent to the Musaeum; Alexander's body reposed in an alabaster coffin. In Strabo's time, the city of Alexandria had many public and sacred buildings. Because Alexandria held a monopoly on trade for all of Egypt, prices were kept high and made the city rich (Hamilton and Falconer 1903; MacLeod 2000). Another eyewitness account of the Musaeum was written by Strabo's contemporary the Homerian scholar Grammaticus Aristonicus, but the text has not survived—his description is known only from citations by other authors (di Pasquale 2005).

Based on the sources mentioned here, information gleaned from other accounts, and descriptions of similar Greek temples and schools, historians have determined that the institution likely included a shrine to the Muses (the actual *mouseion*) with statues of the goddesses, a bust of Aristotle in a small cloister (or *stodion*), small cells in which the scholars lived, an observatory, a zoo, and a botanical and meditation garden (Gudeman 1894), among other structures (El-Abbadi 1990; MacLeod 2000). As an institution dedicated to the Muses, the museum had the same legal status under Greek law as did Plato's school in Athens (MacLeod 2000). The library itself was comprised of several wings and porticos, with the books stored on shelves (*theke*) along covered walkways. The library staff included both librarians and translators (Empereur 2002; MacLeod 2000). When Ptolemy II (Philadelphus) took charge of the Musaeum around 283 BCE, he encouraged the formation of a community of about thirty to fifty scholars (called a *synodos*) who lived at the museum, were paid a regular salary, were provided room and board, and were exempted from taxes in return for their services (MacLeod 2000).

Exactly what activities took place at the Musaeum is difficult to determine. Historians are divided on whether the scholars taught classes there, exactly how objects were used, and who had access to the library (aside from the institution's own scholars). The library contained a large number of papyrus scrolls (and probably writings on other media as well), which were arranged alphabetically according to author by the librarian Zenedotus (d. 260 BCE) and later were annotated following a system developed by the grammarian Callimachus of Cyrene (d. 240 BCE). Callimachus's system sorted works into classes and subclasses, arranged alphabetically by authors' names within each group (Berti and Costa 2009). Ptolemy II was reputed to have required travelers arriving in Alexandria to surrender any manuscripts in their possession so that they could be copied for the library, often returning the copy but not the original (Battles 2015; Empereur 2002).

The Greek literature of classical antiquity was collected, edited, and corrected to produce the most authentic versions possible at the Temple of the Muses in Alexandria. This literature shows a continual diversification from narrative into stories, songs, poetic forms, and plays. The great tragedies of the fifth century BCE include such works as the *Oresteia* trilogy of Aeschylus (ca. 524–456 BC); *Antigone* by Sophocles (ca. 496–406 BC); and *Medea, Hippolytus,* and *Hecuba* by Euripides (ca. 480–406 BC) that reflect a robust intellectual life and address the often complex relationships between humans and the gods. The narrative literature includes stories of travel, exploration, and war, such as the Trojan War stories of the *Iliad* and the *Odyssey* (discussed in chapter 4), and the stories of Hesiod, Archilochus, and Alcman.

The Musaeum continued to exist throughout the Hellenistic period (Sarton 1970a) and may have been destroyed during the war between Aurelianus and Zenobia of Palmyra, which took place between 270 and 275 CE (di Pasquale 2005). The exact date of the destruction of the Musaeum remains controversial, but it is thought that, by the time Julius Caesar captured Alexandria in 47 BCE, the complex was already in ruins (MacLeod 2000). When the explorer and linguist Richard Francis Burton (1821–1890) arrived in Alexandria in 1877, he speculated about what the city had once been, lamenting, "[I]t is her unlucky fate to be abused by every traveler" (Burton 1878:5).

COLLECTIONS IN LATER MESOPOTAMIA

During the period of classical antiquity, collections continued to be amassed in the Mesopotamian region. In Nineveh, the Assyrian capital on the eastern bank of the Tigris (at one time the largest city in the world), Ashurbanipal (668–627 BCE) established a library that was composed of more than 30,000 clay tablets containing Mesopotamian literature, history, science, and religious works (Rigby and Rigby 1944). These documents were musealized through the processes of cataloging, numbering, and arrangement on shelves, in boxes, and in baskets. The library collection contained both contemporary and historic clay tablets that were used to teach the Sumerian language and writing and to establish Sumerian history (Sarton 1970a). The Babylonian ruler Nebuchadrezzar (605–562 BCE) assembled a large private collection that included antiquities, art, and natural history objects, and Nabonidus (555–539 BCE) was known for his collections of antiquities and natural history objects (Lewis 1985).

A museum-like institution flourished around 530 BCE in the Sumerian city of Uruk. In 1925, British archaeologist Leonard Woolley and his colleagues, excavating the site of a Babylonian palace, found a collection of old temple treasures, including "small figures of animals, stone vases decorated in relief, vases of dark steatite inlaid with red limestone, lapis lazuli and shell, and a quantity of cylinder seals" (Rigby and Rigby 1944:102). Woolley (1935) described the find as including a fragment of a diorite statue with an inscription dating it to 2280 BCE, a clay foundation cone and some tablets from 2000 BCE, and a votive stone mace head from about 2500 BCE. The most significant object was a small clay drum cylinder with an inscription that Woolley translated as "These are copies from bricks found in the ruins of Ur, the work of Bur-Sin king of Ur, which while searching for the ground-plan [of the temple] the Governor of Ur found, and I saw and wrote out for the marvel of the beholders" (Woolley 1935:203–4). Woolley concluded, "The room was a museum of local antiquities maintained by the princess Bel-Shalti-Nanna . . . and in the collection was this clay drum, the earliest museum label known" (Woolley 1935:204). Bel-Shalti-Nanna (also known as Ennigaldi-Nanna) was the daughter of Nabonidus and a priestess of the temple of the moon god Sin at Ur. Other clay documents indicate that some of the objects in the trove had been excavated by Nabonidus. While Woolley was confident that he had found the oldest museum in the world, other scholars are more cautious about the interpretation, characterizing the objects and their identifying label as a private royal collection. In any case, despite the fact that these were labeled, musealized objects, there is no physical or conceptual linkage between them and later museums.

COLLECTIONS IN THE ROMAN EMPIRE

Extensive individual collecting took place during the time of the Roman Empire, but there were still no collecting institutions comparable to modern museums (Pearce 1995). The prevalence of public art prompted one historian to quip, "In short, Rome had no museum *per se* but all Rome was a museum" (Bazin 1967:23). The prevalence of Roman public art led another historian to conclude, "Like the Library and the Museum of Alexandria, Rome was another world, a museum where people collected objects from all over the world. Masterpieces of art, buildings and curiosities were *ornamenta urbis*, their presence signifying the greatness of Rome" (di Pasquale 2005:11). The Forum of Augustus (2 BCE) and the Forum of Trajan (112 CE) became, in effect, national portrait galleries, and in 365 CE, Caracalla ordered decorative statuary installed in the baths (Pearce 1995).

Unfortunately, along with public art comes public vandalism. In 1162 CE, the Roman senate issued a decree prohibiting destruction or mutilation of Trajan's Column (*Colonna Traiana*), which had been erected in 113 CE to commemorate Trajan's victory in the Dacian Wars, one of the earliest attempts to pass a law to preserve a historic monument (Bazin 1967).

Collecting and displaying fossil bones was common in Rome. The fossils (particularly tusks and bones of extinct proboscideans) were usually interpreted as creatures known in regional mythology, including dragons, giants, griffins, and monsters (Mayor 2011). Fossil specimens were actively bought, sold, and traded, with some specimens coming from as far away as modern-day India. First-century Rome was the site of the first significant market for the sale of Egyptian antiquities (Moser 2006), a trade that continued throughout most of museum history. Cicero (107–44 BCE), Mummius (second century BCE), and Verres (120–43 BCE) all assembled extensive collections of art (Pearce 1995). In 31 BCE, the future emperor of Rome, Augustus (63 BCE–14 CE), removed the giant tusks reputed to be from the mythical Calydonian Boar from the Temple of Athena in Tegea (Greece) and took them back to Rome, where they were seen by Ovid (43 BCE–17/18 CE), who compared them to tusks from an Indian elephant. One of the Calydonian tusks was still on exhibit at least two hundred years later, when it was seen by Pausanias (110–ca. 180 CE). After he became emperor, Augustus acquired a great many fossils for his villa on Capri, assembling what was, for all practical purposes, the first paleontological museum (Mayor 2011).

Pliny the Elder (Gaius Plinius Secundus, CE 23–79) produced an impressive literary output concerning Roman life. In his encyclopedic *Naturalis Historia*, Pliny claimed that the first person in Rome to have a collection of precious stones (called a dactyliotheca) was Scaurus, the stepson of Marcus Aemilius Scaurus (ca. 163–89 BCE), an influential Roman politician (Murray 1904). In the third book of his *Naturalis Historia*, Pliny mentioned several other collections and significant objects, including the bones of giants, a hippopotamus, four crocodiles that were exhibited alive in Rome (and later pickled in brine, along with a monkey), and a sow that had given birth to thirty piglets that was pickled in brine and exhibited at Lavinium (also called Latium, about fifty kilometers south of Rome), where it was reportedly seen by Marcus Terentius Varro (116–27 BCE) ten centuries later (Hagen 1876; Langone, Stutz, and Gianopoulos 2006).

There are several depictions of Roman writing materials and how scrolls were stored, such as the wall painting found in Pompeii that now resides in the Museo Archeologico Nazionale di Napoli (National Archaeological Museum in Naples). The painting, which was protected by the fall of ashes when the city was destroyed by the eruption of Vesuvius in CE 79, shows a cylindrical lidded *capsa* containing rolled scrolls standing on end (Diringer 1953). The *capsae* were usually made of wood but sometimes metal and could be locked if important documents were stored inside. A similar container made of wicker or metal, called a *cista*, was sometimes used for storing scrolls and papyrus sheets as well (Smith, Wayte, and Marindin 1890). The satirical Roman poet Juvenal (Decimus Iunius Iuvenalis, d. 130 CE) ridicules his colleague Cordus for being so poor that he must store his scrolls in a *cista* rather than a *capsa* because "analphabetic mice had gnawed their way well into his texts of the great poets" (Juvenal 1974, III:206).

Roman collections were usually exhibited in their owners' homes. A villa owned and decorated by the Roman general and consul Lucius Licinius Lucullus (ca. 114–57 BCE)—and that later became the home of the Medici family—had a library, Lucullus's collection of Greek paintings, and both botanical and zoological gardens (Rigby and Rigby 1944). The poet Martial (Marcus Valerius Martialis, ca. 38–104 CE) produced a series of short, witty satirical poems known as the *Epigrams*, which were published in Rome between 86 and 103 CE. Several objects in collections are mentioned in the *Epigrams*, including a fossil bee and an ant in amber. In one of his poems, Martial described a snake preserved in amber, but the specimen was probably a fake, as many amber inclusions are today (Dahlström and Brost 1996; Rigby and Rigby 1944). In other epigrams, Martial commented on how boring his friend Euctus had become because he was always talking about his historic silver collection, and blasted an acquaintance named Paullus as a vulgar show-off and braggart whose sole purpose in collecting was to attract attention to himself. Then there was a man named Codrus, who was satirized by Juvenal as an impecunious amateur whose meager resources meant he could only afford to collect a few books, cups, and two pieces of sculpture, and Licinus, a rich man so fearful that his collection of sculpture, amber figures, and inlaid furniture would be stolen that he forced his slaves to mount an around-the-clock guard over them (Juvenal 1974, III).

BEYOND THE BLUE HORIZON—
THE WORLD OUTSIDE THE MEDITERRANEAN

Little is known about Indian collections during the period of classical antiquity, but it was a time when a rich written literature developed following a long oral tradition, from at least the fourth century BCE to the fourth century CE, a reflection of the growing diversity and pluralism of Indian society. It is entirely possible that some Asian literature had been recorded in written form earlier and then lost, as early Asian writing was done on materials that do not preserve well, such as lengths of bark strung together with cord and (in China) on split bamboo (Diringer 1953; Rigby and Rigby 1944). The *Bhagavad Gita*, the *Mahabharata*, and the *Ramayana* were all finalized and written down about 400 BCE (Roberts and Westad 2013; Voth 2007). The *Bhagavad Gita* was added to the *Ramayana* in the first century CE. In effect, the *Ramayana* reinforced the strict, unbending hierarchical caste system in Indian society. The *Mahabharata*, which is the longest epic poem in the world, appeared after the *Ramayana* and tells the story of an epic war, supernatural intervention, and love and reflects the then-ongoing cultural evolution on the continent as small cities merged to form larger kingdoms. The stories that constitute the *J taka* are part of a long, interconnected narrative of individual stories that illustrate how karma is carried over from one lifetime to another and presented Buddhism as an alternative to Hinduism (Voth 2007). The stories of the *J taka* were translated into a number of languages (including Greek, Persian, and Arabic) and influenced stories in many other cultures. *The Pañcatantra*, written in

Sanskrit, influenced later works, such as the *One Thousand and One Nights*, the *Decameron*, and *The Canterbury Tales*.

During the period known as Classical China (ca. 1994 BCE–589 CE), Chinese culture developed independently and with amazing continuity due to China's relative geographic remoteness, which kept it insulated from significant outside influence (Roberts and Westad 2013). China was unified in 211 BCE under the Qin dynasty. During the Han dynasty, a universal system of writing was introduced and its use enforced by a government run by a cultural elite. Although most of the wooden structures and art (primarily paintings on silk) from that era have long since disappeared, ceramics, literature, and official records remain. By the year 0, half of the world's population was under the control of either the Roman Empire or the Han dynasty (Roberts and Westad 2013). Paper was being made in China by the second century, and an early form of printing was practiced using paper for stone block rubbing (Murray 2009).

Chinese collections from this period seem to be already formalized, consisting primarily of objects selected based on aesthetic principles. Chinese literature is particularly interesting because of China's cultural isolation (Parrinder 1971). During this period, Chinese literature is primarily composed of lyric poetry and songs about everyday concerns, dating back to about the tenth century (Voth 2007). The sayings of the revered teacher Confucius (551–479 BCE) were recorded in writing after his death as *The Analects of Confucius*. The Confucian canon, commonly called the *Five Classics* (composed of *Classics of Poetry*, the *Book of Documents*, the *Book of Rites*, the *I Ching*, and *Spring and Autumn Annals*) was composed about 1000 BCE. These writings, with their emphasis on balance, reason, and duty, were an important influence on the development of Chinese culture, as were the works of Chuang Chou (ca. 369–286 BCE), one of the founders of Taoism, which emphasized individual thinking while seeking harmony with all things (Voth 2007). The philosophical emphasis on ethics and ideals is reflected in the composition of early Chinese collections, which included extensive archives and objects perceived as artistic and valuable treasures (Rigby and Rigby 1944). Significantly, Chinese collecting practices did not include collections based on wonder, as did early collections in Europe (see chapter 5).

Far less is known about the Americas during this period due to a lack of written records comparable to those from the Mesopotamian and the Mediterranean regions. The oldest known writing in the Americas is an Olmec inscription on the Mojarra Stela from Río Acula in southeastern Mexico, which dates to 143 CE. Writing in the Americas was used primarily in making calendars and inscribing messages on monuments, not for bookkeeping, as it was in the Old World. In the Americas, other means of tracking inventory (e.g., knot records, such as quipus) were already in use before writing was developed (Fischer 2001). Objects selected for grave goods varied widely from culture to culture in the Americas, from the mainly utilitarian objects among the Mound Builders of eastern North America (Milner 2004) to the elaborate musealized objects found in the tombs of many Andean cultures (Engel 1976).

SUMMARY

At the close of the period of classical antiquity, the influence of the Christian church in Europe was growing rapidly. The first monastic communities were founded in the second century as the Roman Catholic Church rose to dominance in the West and the Byzantine or Orthodox Church in the East (Murray 2009). The resulting shift in European societies to the church as the center of learning and knowledge preservation was accompanied by changes in the content of collections and the perceptions of the objects in them, particularly the role of religious organizations as collection depositories and places of exhibition, as well as the motivations of collectors for acquiring and donating objects.

4

—◦◦◦—

The Power of Objects
Medieval Collections, 400–1400

The name *medieval* (from the Latin *medium*, or "middle") refers to the period from the fifth to the fifteenth century in Europe, after the collapse of the western Roman Empire and before the beginning of the Renaissance. This time period is also known as the Middle Ages or the Dark Ages.

In this chapter, collecting and collections worldwide between the years 400 to 1400 are discussed. During this time span, Europe settled into a period of cultural quietude, but from 700 to 900, the cultures of Tang China, the Islamic caliphate, Mayan Mesoamerica, the Inca Empire in the Andes, and many others around the world all flourished.

Medieval Europe was not isolated, as is demonstrated by the objects in collections (particularly in the British Museum) that found their way to Europe during this period (MacGregor 2011). From about the year 800 on, travelers, pilgrims, merchants, and soldiers brought objects and ideas back to Europe from Africa, the Middle East, and Asia, while Scandinavian Vikings traded from Greenland to Central Asia. An extensive maritime economic network of trade and transport eventually connected diverse cultures from Africa, the Middle East, and Asia (MacGregor 2011). In the early Middle Ages, European Christian scholars sought rare manuscripts in the book markets of the Islamic-controlled Iberian cities of Toledo and Córdoba; later, books and manuscripts came to Europe from Islamic regions as war booty (Battles 2015).

Before the medieval era drew to a close, belief in the powers of musealized objects had intensified due their increasingly direct associations with religious beliefs and institutions and due to the motivations for collecting the objects, particularly in the traditions of Christianity, Buddhism, Islam, and some of the religions of African and American cultures. The idea that an inanimate object possesses some sort of supernatural power is probably as old as humanity itself—human cultural history is also a history of idols and sacrifices, of belief that groves of trees or mountaintops were sources of divine energy, of credence given to healing waters and magic stones, or that superhuman strength could be endowed by special weapons or armor. The use of relics and icons in the early Christian church reinforced these ideas in medieval Europe and extended to the belief that the power of objects could be transferred to the owners of the objects (Pearce 1992). By the end of the Middle Ages, the belief in the power of objects was widespread in European cultures.

THE MIDDLE AGES IN EUROPE

The medieval era in Europe is popularly called the Dark Ages in reference to the decline of cultural achievement, learning, and economies that generally occurred throughout western Europe, but it was also a time when private and institutional collections began to diversify as trade and travel to and from Europe increased. When the new king of France, Charlemagne (742–821), established his capital at Aachen, he hired an English theologian and scholar named Alcuin of York (ca. 735–804) to build his royal library and collection (Rigby and Rigby 1944). Unfortunately, along with objects, a few undesirable things were also imported, including a plague-causing pathogen now known as *Yersinia pestis*, which killed somewhere between 75 and 200 million people as the Black Death swept through Europe between 1346 and 1353, as well as large numbers of people across much of Asia (Biddle 1995; Cohn 2002; Langer 1964).

During the latter part of the eighth century and into the early ninth century, there was an initial expansion in the number of church and monastic libraries and collections in Europe, but from the end of the ninth century until well into the thirteenth century, a combination of civil conflicts, fire, and theft resulted in an overall net decrease in the number of books and objects in these collections (Rigby and Rigby 1944).

The latter part of the Middle Ages in Europe was distinguished by a series of military invasions and other incursions into the Middle East that were inspired by charismatic preachers and sanctioned by the Catholic Church. Pilgrims and soldiers alike poured out of Europe in an attempt to liberate the areas perceived as the Holy Land (the regions associated with biblical history) from Islamic control. These expeditions, generally known as the Crusades, had a profound effect on the development of European societies and institutions, and there remain many visible reminders of this

Figure 4.1.   Moat and walls of a crusader fortress in Caesaria, Israel.

period across Europe and the Middle East in the form of buildings, monuments, and symbols (figure 4.1).

It has been noted that "[c]rusading sacralized the lands it attacked or conquered" due to the emphasis on recovering Christian heritage from the infidels (Tyerman 2007:141). In the same sense that the Holy Land was sacralized by the Crusades, the relics and other objects brought back to Europe by returning crusaders, pilgrims, and travelers were musealized in church and monastic treasuries and in a few private collections (Frazer 1986; Rigby and Rigby 1944). Organizing a crusader force was a complex undertaking, requiring personal, political, social, and financial coordination and planning (Tyerman 2007), so it is not surprising that crusaders brought back spoils of war to have something to show for their efforts. The most desired trophies were religious relics or other holy objects that the crusaders could bestow on a local church to enhance personal social standing and demonstrate the depth of their devotion. In 1821, Jacques Albin Simon Collin de Plancy (1793–1881) compiled a three-volume inventory of relics and miraculous images in European church treasuries, many of which had been donated by returning crusaders (Collin de Plancy 1821). The Cathedral of Milan (Italy) contained objects that were believed to have once belonged to the biblical personages of Daniel, Jonas, and Abraham; the church treasury in Durham (England) exhibited part of the tree under which Abraham was supposed to have met the three angels, as well as a piece of Moses's rod; the Abbey of St. Denis (France) had in its treasury a gold-and-jewel-encrusted drinking cup that had belonged to Solomon himself (Murray 1904).

The Crusades encompassed dozens of organized military excursions between 1095 and about 1300. The larger of these efforts are now identified by numbers, but many smaller military actions occurred as well (Tyerman 2007). The First Crusade was launched in 1095 and lasted until 1099, culminating with the liberation of Jerusalem, during which the city was pillaged, mosques were plundered, and numerous citizens massacred. The Second Crusade (1145 to 1149) also had Jerusalem as its goal, but it was a military disaster for the European invaders. In 1187, as the Arab Caliphate was slipping into decline, the Islamic leader Saladin rallied his troops to seize power in Egypt, united the scattered Muslim forces, and recaptured Jerusalem. This triggered the Third Crusade, which lasted from 1188 to 1192 (Roberts and Westad 2013). The European forces of the Third Crusade failed to reach Jerusalem due to heavy losses and supply problems. The Fourth Crusade (1198–1204) was diverted for political reasons to Constantinople. Because of the desire to return home with something of value in hand, the "lure of the unique richness of treasure houses of Christian relics at Constantinople acted as a spur to its destruction in 1204," despite the fact that at the time Constantinople was a Christian enclave and the capital of the Byzantine Empire (Tyerman 2007:137). One reminder of this crusade is that the bronze horses known as the *Triumphal Quadriga* that once adorned the Hippodrome of Constantinople were carried away by crusaders and installed at St. Mark's Basilica in Venice (Lewis 1985).

Further military excursions and Crusades took place between 1213 and 1291 (Roberts and Westad 2013; Tyerman 2007). By the time of the Hundred Years War (1337–1453), the objects brought back by veterans of the Crusades had become cherished heirlooms and treasured church displays. Many of these objects are listed in the inventories of medieval church treasuries (Frazer 1986; Lindauer 2010), where they were valued because an "object donated to a treasury generated both heavenly rewards and earthly commemoration" (Ackley 2014:5).

One side effect of the Crusades was that trading posts were established in the Middle East in the twelfth and thirteenth centuries, which resulted in a significant expansion of economic markets in Europe and an increase in the importation of rare silks, porcelains, and other objects (Ayers 1985:260). During the Middle Ages, Europe remained largely a cultural importer, unable to match such achievements as the architecture of the Mediterranean classical period, the pointed Arabic arch, and Arabic scientific advances or to produce textiles and ceramics as fine as those that were imported from other countries (Roberts and Westad 2013). The influence of foreign cultures was often reflected in the imported objects displayed in religious institutions.

It was widely believed in Europe that the bodies of some saints were incorruptible. In some instances, this belief may have been due to confusion between the actual body of the saint and the simulated life-size figures that often decorated the reliquaries (Cruz 1977). A brisk trade in saintly bodies and body parts developed as religious institutions sought to enhance their standing with the faithful by acquiring relics. In addition to incorruptible bodies, all manner of holy objects were traded and sold widely (see box 4.1), both by religious organizations and individual collectors, and greatly valued in collections because of the belief that the veneration of relics facilitated a special communion with God because they retained some of the saint's religious attributes (Lindauer 2010). One of the largest collections of relics in medieval Europe was at the Abbey of St. Denis near Paris (Mauriès 2002).

Before the establishment of universities in Europe, the church was the center of intellectual life, the custodian of education and knowledge, and as a result, collecting was largely confined to religious institutions. The collected objects most often became part of the church treasuries (Bazin 1967; Mauriès 2002; Pearce 1995). The term *church treasury* is derived from the Greek word *thesaurus*, referring to the temple treasures of classical Greece. The majority of objects in medieval church treasuries were Eucharist vessels (chalices, patens, and pyxides), secondary liturgical objects (censers, crosses, crosiers, flabella, lamps, and situlas), service books, reliquaries, religious art, and icons (Frazer 1986). However, the collections also included historic objects, classical statuary and ceramics, bones of giants, tongues of giant snakes, eggs of griffins, and other rare and unusual things. The carapace of a giant tortoise adorned the porch of the Cathedral of Merseburg (Goode 1889; Murray 1904), bones of antediluvian beasts were exhibited at Saint Kilian's Church in Heilbronn, and visitors to the cathedral in Brunswick could see a griffin's claw, personally brought back from Palestine by Duke Henry the Lion. It is easy to dismiss such claims today, but understanding the mythical and religious associations of objects sheds light on the worldview of people who collected them. For example, in the All Souls' Church (Schlosskirche) in Wittenberg, "on whose doors Luther affixed his famous theses—two whale ribs were suspended, when Faber wrote in 1717, which were said to have been brought from the Holy Land, but which in fact belonged to a whale thrown up on the shores of the Baltic" (Murray 1904:9–10). How and why the ribs of a Baltic whale were believed to be those of the great fish that swallowed Jonah is not known, but considering that most people in Wittenberg had likely never seen a whale (and quite possibly never even heard of whales) and the fact that the ribs were displayed at the church makes such a belief more understandable.

BOX 4.1.
Relics Sacred and Profane

The veneration of bodies of the dead and objects considered sacred is a very old tradition, probably originating with the first humans who buried grave goods (mortuary sacrifices) and established rituals when burying their dead (James 1962). Such practices are widespread in world cultures. The venerated human bodies and body parts are usually referred to as relics (derived from the Latin *reliquiae*, meaning "remains"). When Siddhērtha Guatama (the Buddha) died in 483 BCE, his body was cremated and the ashes and remaining pieces of hair, teeth, bone, and fingernails were distributed among his followers to be housed in small shrines called stupas (figure 4.2). Buddhists who visit a stupa circumambulate clockwise around the shrine as a demonstration of devotion and respect (Hitchcock and Esposito 2004). Two hairs from the prophet Mohammed are kept in a reliquary inside the Dome of the Rock in Jerusalem, and his cloak is kept in the Kerqa Sharif (Shrine of the Cloak) at the central mosque in Kandahar, Afghanistan. The bodies of deceased Inca rulers were mummified and used in religious rituals (Kendall 1973), the embalmed body of Vladimir Lenin is on public display in a shrine in Red Square in Moscow

Figure 4.2. Buddhist stupas at Wat Phra Mahathat, Nakhon Si Thammarat, Thailand.

(Zbarsky and Hutchinson 1997), and an eternal flame burns at the grave of John F. Kennedy in Arlington National Cemetery in Virginia.

Perhaps the best-known relics are those preserved in medieval-era churches in Europe. Although just when the Christian practice of veneration of relics originated is not known, it was widespread by the fourth century—by that time, relics were commonly housed in ornate silver or gold reliquaries decorated with precious stones, nacre, and ivory (Cruz 1984; Lindauer 2010). By the eleventh and twelfth centuries, devotion to saints (and hence to their relics) was nearly universal in the church, along with a concurrent emphasis on the historicity of the gospels (Tyerman 2007). The Catholic Church categorizes relics in three classes: first-class relics are either bodies or body parts of saints; second-class relics (also called contact relics) are objects sanctified by close association with a saint (e.g., clothing or other objects); third-class relics are objects believed to have been touched by a saint (Blom 2002; Cruz 1984).

Some of the objects in the medieval church collections were quite fantastic. A hair from the beard of Noah was exhibited at Corbie Abbey, and a goblet of rock crystal from Solomon's temple could be seen at St. Denis (both in France). A bone from the very whale that swallowed Jonah was exhibited in the Cathedral of Halberstadt, Germany. Several European churches had griffin's claws (usually antelope horns), including the church of St. Michael in Hildesheim and two other churches near Helmstadt (Murray 1904). The body of St. Agatha (who died in 251 CE) was separated into several pieces. Her arms, legs, and breasts were "preserved in a glass case in an incorrupt condition, although rather dried and dark after more than seventeen hundred years," while her skull and other major body parts are enclosed in an effigy wearing a jeweled crown in a church in Catania, Sicily (Cruz 1977:49). The body of St. Zita (patroness of domestic workers) is on exhibit in a glass case in the Basilica of St. Frediano in Lucca, Italy (Cruz 1977:47). Several churches have made competing claims to such objects as the crown of thorns, the chalice used at the last supper, and the foreskin of Jesus (called the Holy Prepuce). Other churches have claimed incorrupt hosts, holy tears, and drops of holy blood. Perhaps the most famous Christian relic of all is the Shroud of Turin, which the faithful believe was the burial cloth that the body of Jesus was wrapped in (and which now bears his image). The authenticity of the Shroud of Turin has been the subject of numerous inconclusive investigations over the centuries (Cruz 1984).

Not all relics are sacred. Galileo's middle finger is displayed in the Museo Galileo in Florence (formerly the *Istituto e Museo di Storia della Scienza*) in an egg-shaped glass container decorated in gold (the finger was removed in 1737 when Galileo's body was exhumed). In Victorian England, locks of hair from one's beloved were treasured keepsakes, often woven into jewelry—Charlotte Brontë had an amethyst bracelet made with woven locks of hair from her sisters Emily and Anne (Lutz 2015). The arm of Mexican president Alvaro Obregón (1880–1928) was displayed in a jar of alcohol in La Bombilla Park in Mexico City from 1935 until 1999 (when it was either stolen or removed from view), and the National Museum of Health and Medicine in Silver Spring, Maryland, displays bone fragments from Abraham Lincoln's skull.

The preservation and display of relics and unusual objects in the medieval churches was similar to practices in the Greek temples (discussed in chapter 3), and their veneration has precedence in the way the Greeks attributed historical or mythological significance to temple objects (Murray 1904; Pearce 1995; Rigby and Rigby 1944). The practice of suspending unusual natural objects from the ceilings of churches became increasingly common in Europe through the fifteenth century, "when ostrich eggs and whale ribs were joined by meteorites and, most notably, crocodiles" in many churches and cathedrals (Daston and Park 2001:86).

Toward the end of the Middle Ages, the number of private collections in Europe began to slowly increase. For example, Jean de Berry (1340–1416), the brother of King Charles V of France, was known for his extensive collection of illuminated manuscripts, but he also possessed an ostrich egg, exotic snail shells, seven boars' tusks, the molar of a giant, the jaw of a serpent, a coconut (an unusual object in medieval France), porcupine quills, pieces of red coral, the skin of a white bear, and three unicorn horns (Daston and Park 2001).

THE INFLUENCE OF ISLAM, 400–1400

After the collapse of the Roman Empire, during the period from about 800 to 1300, while Europe was in decline, there was a great flourishing of philosophy, medicine, and scientific thought in the newly ascendant Muslim world, particularly in Baghdad (present-day Iraq) and Córdoba (present-day Spain). Stable societies, created by the ruling caliphs, enabled a massive translation project to convert hundreds of Greek texts (including the works of Aristotle, Euclid, Galen, and Plato) into Arabic (Langone, Stutz, and Gianopoulos 2006). By the end of the eighth century, Baghdad was a center of world learning (Battles 2015).

The prophet Mohammed (ca. 570–632 CE) spent twenty-three years (from 609 to 632) receiving the Quran by divine inspiration and reciting it to his followers so that they could write it down (the name *Quran* means "recitation" in Arabic). The influence of the Quran on Arabic culture cannot be underestimated—it was equivalent to the impact of Luther's translation of the Bible on the German language or the King James Version of the Bible on the English language (Roberts and Westad 2013:340). Some of the earliest Muslim scribes wrote down the verses of the Quran as they were received from Mohammed on materials as diverse as bones, wooden tablets, and date palm leaves (Diringer 1953; Nasrallah 2011).

Under Mohammed's influence, the institution of the caliphate expanded. The caliphate is a form of Islamic government in which the ruler is both a religious leader and head of state. As the power of the caliphate grew, belief in Islam began to spread due to the increased reach of Muslim traders, explorers, and soldiers (Roberts and Westad 2013). Between the years 623 and 1100, through a combination of military conquests, newly established trade routes, and missionary activities, Islam spread along the northern coast of Africa, up to Constantinople, throughout much of southern Europe, to Sicily, across the Iberian Peninsula, and into central Asia. This expansion gave Muslim scholars access to the libraries and books of the Byzantine Empire (the heirs of classical Greek and Roman culture). Many copies of Byzantine manuscripts were made and circulated as they were translated from Greek, Latin, Persian, and Sanskrit into Arabic by Muslim scholars, who greatly admired books and learning. Under the Umayyad Caliphate, the arts flourished, books became more numerous and more widely available, and the number of libraries increased (Battles 2015). Public libraries were created in major cities throughout the Muslim world, with books in circulation in codex form, and many mosques developed libraries (Murray 2009). There were seventy libraries in Islamic Spain prior to 1085 (Battles 2015). Several key aspects of Western book culture were developed in Arabic countries—papermaking was learned from the Chinese; the art of making a codex (a book consisting of bound sheets with covers) was learned from the Amharic scribes of Ethiopia and quickly replaced scrolls; and Islamic calligraphers and illustrators made books that were both functional and beautiful and thus more desirable in collections (Battles 2015).

Later, during the twelfth and thirteenth centuries, when Christian and Islamic cultures intermingled in Italy and Spain, the Greek works preserved in Arabic were translated into Latin, the lingua franca of Europe. The new Latin translations were read widely and traded through communication channels among church scholars and alchemists. Of particular interest were manuscripts dealing with astrology, astronomy, mathematics, and cartography. This dissemination of Arabic scholarship produced a new appreciation of the works of classical antiquity across Europe (Roberts and Westad 2013).

An Islamic collecting tradition arose based on the concept of waqf, or property that is given for the public good (Lewis 1985; Nigosian 2004). The concept of waqf has much in common with the donations at Greek temples and crusader gifts to European churches. Waqf practices included depositing gifts at tombs of the martyrs, such as the Shah-Abdol-Azim shrine in Rey (Iran) or the tomb of Massouma-Ghom (Fatema Mae'sume) in the Persian city of Qom (Bazin 1967:34).

Islamic Influence in Europe

As a result of trade and other interactions, the church treasuries in many parts of Europe acquired such objects as carved ivory, inlaid metalwork, rock crystal, enameled glass, semiprecious stones, weapons (particularly daggers and Ottoman guns), and copper bowls. Textiles were particularly valued by European collectors, especially silks and (from the fifteenth century on) carpets (Raby 1985). Goblets made of rock crystal and enameled glass were often converted to liturgical use. Such exotic materials as herbs and medicinal clay (terra Lemnia from the island of Lemnos in the Ottoman Empire) were valued for their healing properties (Raby 1985). In the late Middle Ages, papermaking technology from China was introduced to Europe from Arabia (Murray 2009), replacing the more expensive parchment (made from animal hide) during the 1300s and 1400s (Fischer 2001). The design and manufacture of such machine-work objects as clocks and automatons was highly advanced in the Islamic countries, and these mechanical devices were much desired by European collectors. The water-powered automatic clocks of thirteenth-century Europe were crude compared to their counterparts in the Islamic regions (Daston and Park 2001).

COLLECTIONS IN ASIA, 400–1400

Chinese cultural development followed a markedly independent trajectory due to the relative remoteness of China from other cultural influences, which made trade with China more desirable (Roberts and Westad 2013). The Silk Road trade routes between China and the Mediterranean were at their peak of activity between the years 500 and 800, as Europe was slowly sinking into decline (Roberts and Westad 2013). The silk trade routes also connected China with the emerging Islamic caliphate governments (MacGregor 2011). Still, China remained relatively isolated and free from military invasion by outsiders, despite the collapse of the empire into a series of independent states in 220 CE.

As Chinese culture expanded southward from the Yellow River to the Yangzi River, Buddhism became the majority religion in the empire. Buddhist missionaries began penetrating China along the silk trade routes. In 581, the Chinese independent states were united once again under Emperor Wen of the Sui dynasty to form a new Imperial China. By 650, Imperial China was using paper money, a concept that would not reach Europe for hundreds of years (Roberts and Westad 2013). Emperor Hui Tsung (northern Sung dynasty, 960–1127) assembled an extensive royal collection, and a scholar named Wang Fu prepared a catalog of it between 1119 and 1125 called *Illustrations of the Ancient Objects in Hsüan-Ho Hall*. The catalog occupied 30 volumes and documented more than 10,000 objects, including antiquities, jade sculptures, official and private seals, tripods, stone drums, bronze vessels, calligraphy, and 6,396 paintings by 231 painters (Rigby and Rigby 1944). The collection was later destroyed when Chin Tartars sacked the Chinese capital.

The spread of Buddhism by missionaries traveling the silk trade routes had a notable impact on Asian collecting traditions. In contrast to later Christian missionaries, who generally arrived in the company of an aggressive, colonizing military force intent to impose their own cultural systems, Buddhist missionaries were wandering monks and merchants who adapted their religious beliefs to the prevailing cultures (Barwise and White 2002). Based on evidence of Buddhist images, the religion was spread throughout southeast Asia beginning in the fourth century BCE. The use of image-based evidence to track missionary activity is ironic because, for the first six hundred years after his death, there were no direct portrayals of the Buddha. Instead, symbols were used to represent him (a wheel, footprints, or an empty throne), despite the fact that the body of the Buddha had been musealized immediately after his death (see box 4.1). The first images of the Buddha were made in northern India and were soon followed by the appearance of other Buddhist objects, including begging bowls and the *japa mala*, a string of 108 beads used to count mantras, chants, and prayers that was adopted from Hinduism (Barwise and White 2002; Dechen 2004).

Japan was at the very end of most of the Asian trade routes and was relatively isolated (even from neighboring China) for an extended period (MacGregor 2011). In Japan, as in many other places in the world at this time, collections were associated with temples and religious shrines (Bazin 1967:34). What is considered by some historians to be the oldest continuously functioning museum in the world was founded during the eighth century BCE in Japan—the Shōsō-in at the Tōdai Temple in Nara. Although the wooden building has been regularly rebuilt over the centuries, it is still considered a continuously functioning original structure by Japanese standards. The Emperor Shōmu (724–749) compiled the collection that is still preserved in the Shōsō-in in an *azekura*-style log structure with a raised floor (Bazin 1967). The collection, consisting of objects from as far away as Greece, Persia, and central Asia, includes manuscripts, paintings, weapons, musical instruments, lacquer objects, textiles, pottery, metalwork, and glass (Rigby and Rigby 1944). The collection was donated by the Empress Kōmyō (701–760) in 756 in memory of her husband. The Shōsō-in collection presently contains about 9,000 objects.

AFRICA AND THE AMERICAS, 400–1400

Little is known about African and American collections prior to 1400 CE, due in large part to a lack of written records and the disruption of the transmission of history in the oral tradition as a result of the violence, disease, and plundering that rapidly followed European contact.

The oldest writing system in the Americas was developed by the Olmec culture in southeastern Mexico prior to 143 CE (Fischer 2001).

Unfortunately, most pre-1400 American writing and inventory systems (e.g., the system of quipus in the Andes, which used knots in strings for inventory purposes) can no longer be interpreted, and most of the written or graphic documents encountered by Europeans were destroyed. The Spanish spent a full century after the conquest confiscating and burning almost all of the Mesoamerican texts they could find, believing them to be profane documents (Battles 2015).

When the Spanish conquistador Hernán Cortés (1485–1547) and his men reached the heart of the Aztec Empire in the autumn of 1519, they found an astoundingly modern and well-kept botanical garden and a zoological park. The zoo was located adjacent to the palace of Montezuma in Tenochtitlán on an island in the middle of Lake Texcoco in what is now Mexico City (Dembeck 1965). The collection housed hundreds of specimens, including jaguars, pumas, venomous snakes and boa constrictors, fish, birds, and many species not native to the area, including a bison. In addition to the animals, there was a collection of deformed human beings also kept in cages. The zoo and its inhabitants were destroyed during the siege of the city in 1521 (Dembeck 1965).

LITERATURE OF THE MIDDLE AGES

Literacy was rare during the medieval period, and printing had not yet been developed in Europe, which greatly limited the production and circulation of written materials (Roberts and Westad 2013). Early medieval literature was predominantly religious in nature, consisting mostly of theological works and hymns. An example is the *Divina Commedia* (*Divine Comedy*) by Dante Alighieri (1265–1321), written between 1308 and 1321. The *Divina Commedia* is an epic poem presenting an allegorical vision of the medieval worldview of heaven, hell, and purgatory. The poem looks back in history to the intellectual leadership of the Roman poet Virgil, who serves as a guide through the ethical categories of Aristotle (Voth 2007).

Toward the latter part of the Middle Ages, there was a slow growth in secular and mystical literature (particularly alchemical writings) and travel narratives. Travel literature varied from imaginative texts, such as those attributed to the mythical Prester John around 1165 and Sir John Mandeville between 1357 and 1371, to the travel books about Asia penned by Marco Polo (1254–1324) and William of Rubruck (ca. 1220–1293) (Sprague de Camp and Ley 1952).

The common language throughout most of Europe was Latin in the areas controlled by the Roman Catholic Church, with Greek more common in areas influenced by the Eastern Orthodox Church (churches and monasteries being the only significant sources of formal education).

During this time, silent reading gradually replaced the long tradition of reading aloud, as literacy rates slowly began to climb—St. Augustine (354–430) wrote that he was amazed the first time he saw his teacher, Aurelius Ambrose (ca. 340–397), reading to himself without speaking the words aloud (Fischer 2001).

Beowulf was first recorded in writing around 700 by an anonymous Anglo-Saxon poet after circulating for years as oral tradition. *Beowulf* is the earliest known Old English poem and is considered a foundational work of English literature. The story of *Beowulf* is set in Scandinavia in the late fifth century in a period when there were numerous invasions of Britain by Anglo-Saxon and Scandinavian peoples. The hero (Beowulf) slays a monster named Grendel and thus becomes king. Toward the end of his life, Beowulf's kingdom is threatened by a fierce dragon that guards a buried treasure. The dragon's treasure is the collection of a long-dead king who buried the objects when he realized that he could not keep them with him in the afterlife. Beowulf sallies forth to slay the dragon but is mortally wounded during the battle (Chickering 2005). After he dies, Beowulf's body is cremated on a funeral pyre and buried along with the decayed remnants of the treasure in a mound of dirt and stones. The story is significant for its portrayal of the deterioration of a collection despite the meaning, power, and value of the objects in it—previous accounts of collections rarely addressed the material decomposition of objects deemed important enough to be in collections.

From the eleventh century onward, the influence of the Crusades introduced new themes into secular European literature, particularly heroic narratives, nobility, chivalry, and courtly love. The *Canterbury Tales* by Geoffrey Chaucer is a collection of interconnected stories composed at the end of the fourteenth century and written in standard Middle English, which was the language of everyday life in England. The stories that make up the work involve a group of pilgrims on a journey to the shrine of St. Thomas Becket in the Canterbury Cathedral. The tales are told by the pilgrims as part of a storytelling contest. The late-fourteenth-century tale *Sir Gawain and the Green Knight* is a long alliterative narrative poem with a richness of text and refined language that stands in marked contrast to the everyday language of Chaucer's *Canterbury Tales* (Stone 1964). The story recounts the chivalrous and loyal actions of Sir Gawain, one of King Arthur's Knights of the Round Table.

In matters of science and philosophy, medieval European scholars looked back to the Greeks of the classical era, predominantly Aristotle (384–322 BCE). Aristotle's *scala naturae* enforced the belief that all living organisms were made by special creation and that they could be arranged in a progression from less perfect to more perfect, culminating with human beings. This idea exerted enormous influence on the way the world was understood for thousands of years, and in particular, the concept appealed to medieval scholars in both Europe and the Muslim world, as it demonstrated what was thought to be the "fundamental unity and order of nature" (Sarton 1970b:535). The structure of the *scala naturae* was used by Pliny (23–79 CE) in his *Naturalis Historia* and later by the unknown compilers of the influential *Physiologus* in Alexandria. The *Physiologus* is important as the forerunner of the medieval bestiaries, which presented the natural world from a theological perspective (Langone, Stutz, and Gianopoulos 2006; Payne 1990). Although the bestiaries of the Middle Ages have been described as consisting primarily of "zany pictures, bizarre zoology and religious parables," they also contain "gems of acute observation in attempts to understand and convey how things actually are" (Henderson 2013:xi) and were fundamental to the later development of the collections in the cabinets of curiosities (see chapter 5).

While Europe was looking back, scholars in the Islamic regions were producing new and creative literature and writings about science. Between the eighth and fourteenth centuries, during the rule of the caliphates, stories from Arabia, Egypt, India, Mesopotamia, and Persia were collected and translated into Arabic over the course of many centuries to produce what is now known in English as *One Thousand and One Nights* or the *Arabian Nights*. The work was not available in a European language until the French translation of 1704 by Antoine Galland. The French and later English translations greatly influenced European ideas about Islamic countries and cultures. The *Arabian Nights* is a series of interconnected stories that, although culled from many cultures and time periods, are unified by a storyteller named Scheherazade, who relates the tales to her husband, Shahrayar (Voth 2007). The diverse collection demonstrates the extensive cultural and object exchanges taking place outside of Europe, which later helped make Europeans aware of the larger world around them.

SUMMARY

During the period from 400 to 1400, collecting continued to be a near-universal human activity but with new rationales for the musealization of objects. Both in European cultures and in other world cultures, the acquisition and deposition of objects at religious sites often had spiritual implications based on the belief that objects have power. The next chapter considers how increasing trade with the rest of the world and technological improvements that made long-distance travel easier brought growth and diversification to collections, new significance to the musealization of objects, and the birth of the first real museums.

5

———✦✦✦———

Of Cabinets and Kings
Renaissance Collections, 1400–1600

It was during the Renaissance, when collecting objects became fashionable as a social activity and as an intellectual pursuit for individuals, that a collection first began to be called a museum—or more typically, a *musaeum*, an intentional reference to the ancient Temple of the Muses in Alexandria (Findlen 2004). In Europe, new models of knowledge were constructed to organize and classify the influx of strange objects and unknown plants and animals arriving from the New World and other previously unexplored areas (Nieto Olarte 2013), and a new spirit of creativity began to reshape art, literature, and music. Despite their advances in the arts and learning, however, Renaissance Europeans were still credulous about the world beyond their borders, having little knowledge of geography and lacking a history that adequately prepared them for the shock of the new (Wood 2000). Consider Christopher Columbus (1450–1506), an experienced mariner and navigator who obtained the sponsorship of the Spanish crown to search for a new route to Asia. Columbus departed Spain on August 3, 1492, and reached the Bahamas on October 12 of the same year. Despite his discovery of strange lands and people, Columbus did not realize that he had landed in a continental area unknown to Europe. Columbus made three more voyages to the Americas (in 1493, 1498, and 1502), during which he enslaved native peoples against the wishes of the Spanish crown, failed to establish a thriving colony, and brought back numerous objects that found their way into European cabinets of curiosities. Nevertheless, when he died in 1506, Columbus still believed that he reached Asia (Bergreen 2011). In the assessment of some historians, the greatest accomplishment of Columbus was not establishing contact with the Americas but finding a safe round-trip navigational route between the Americas and Europe that allowed further exploration and contact (Nieto Olarte 2013).

Much of the world underwent wrenching changes between the years 1400 and 1600 that were beneficial for some cultures but disastrous for others (Roberts and Westad 2013). These changes included the alteration of human migration patterns, the advent of new technologies, increased world trade, and economic developments (particularly in European societies). The trend of continuous cultural differentiation that had dominated human migration since prehistory was altered to become primarily the exportation of a single dominant culture (European) throughout much of the world. Rapid advances in technology, particularly in the design and construction of oceangoing ships and navigational aids, made long-distance travel from one place to another easier, faster, and safer. As a result, there was a hitherto unimagined increase in international trade, as new routes of exchange were established, linking cultures that had previously been remote or unknown to each other. Coupled with an expansion and diversification of domestic market economies and banking, the increase in world trade gave rise to a new European middle class that had sufficient disposable income to purchase the newly available commodities and rarities, as well as the leisure time to enjoy them. All of these changes together contributed to an explosion in private collecting activity, particularly among the wealthy (Blom 2002). In short, during the sixteenth century, unprecedented transformations brought about the first period of globalization (Nieto Olarte 2013).

The more direct oceanic trade routes that were established beginning in the fifteenth century between Europe and the Far East replaced the long and often difficult overland routes that had been used since Roman times. Portuguese mariners explored far into the Indian Ocean, ousting the Muslim traders from Malacca (present-day Malaysia) in 1511 (Ayers 1985) and initiating new exchanges between Portugal and India and between Spain and the Americas (Nieto Olarte 2013). Sometime after 1504, the Portuguese made contact with Chinese ships in the Indian Ocean. The Chinese ships were a startling four to five times larger than the vessels used by the Portuguese or by Columbus and were more technically advanced, with superior compasses and stern rudders (Wood 2000). The extent of worldwide exploration, conquest, and colonization throughout the Renaissance meant that, by about 1800, the European nations and Russia combined could claim more than half of the land surface of the Earth—although in reality, they were only in control of about a third of the land surface (Roberts and Westad 2013).

The successful European colonization of such diverse places as the Americas, South Africa, and China required not just improvements in

European shipbuilding and navigational technology but also government patronage and private investment in exploration and colonization. Successful trans-Atlantic travel required the perfection of the astrolabe and the cross-staff for determining latitude (both invented by the ancient Greeks and used by the Arabs in medieval times but only introduced to Renaissance Europe though the spread of Arabic manuscripts), the magnetic compass, the preparation of accurate astronomical tables, and the manufacture of reliable clocks (Derry and Williams 1961; Nieto Olarte 2013; Roberts and Westad 2013).

Advanced metallurgical knowledge, described in *De la Pirotechnia* (*The Arts of Fire*), published in 1540 by Vannoccio Biringuicco (1480–1539), and *De re Metallica* (*On the Nature of Metals*), published in 1556 by Georgius Agricola (Georg Bauer, 1494–1555), gave Europeans the distinct advantage of superior weapons, which enabled relatively small European military forces to conquer and dominate the larger armies of other cultures. The close links between governments, business interests, and Christian missionary activities combined to enable Europeans to conquer, colonize, and exploit many foreign lands (Roberts and Westad 2013).

A number of other technological innovations contributed to changes in collecting activities, how collection objects were ordered and classified, and how they were preserved and stored. Among these innovations were advances in glassmaking technology, an increase in the quality and production of paper, printing with movable type, an increase in literacy rates, and improvements in indoor lighting (Derry and Williams 1961).

EUROPEAN RENAISSANCE

Although there is no definitive moment marking the end of the medieval era or the beginning of the Renaissance, in retrospect the contrast between the two periods is stark (Roberts and Westad 2013). In fact, the metamorphosis from the medieval to the Renaissance was dispersed about Europe chronologically, geographically, and culturally (Roberts and Westad 2013). The Renaissance in Europe was a time of both looking back and looking forward (box 5.1). The rediscovery and reinterpretation of the writings of many Greek and Latin authors of antiquity produced a new appreciation for the accomplishments and knowledge of the ancients and spurred innovation, creativity, and curiosity about lands beyond Europe, all of which affected collecting practices. Whereas medieval collections had been primarily repositories of objects representing wealth and power, the growing collections of the European Renaissance were microcosms of the macrocosm, distillations of the universe, places of study where the wonders of art and nature could be exhibited and admired (Daston and

BOX 5.1.
Ancient Wisdom, Modern Knowledge

The Renaissance was a time of transition between the authority of the ancients and the new methods of inquiry of the moderns (Jones 1961). As newly recovered works of philosophers and scientists became available, Renaissance scholars looked back to the classical Greek authors as revered sources of knowledge and the arts, although they were reading these authors largely in translations from Arabic into Latin—the first Greek grammar wasn't published in Europe until 1497 (Roberts and Westad 2013). One scholar observed, "Dazzled by the recovered light of the past, the Elizabethans so invested the ancients with the robes of authority that the latter became oracles, to question which bordered upon sacrilege" (Jones 1961:9). Indeed, the ideas of Aristotle dominated much of medieval theology and continued to dominate Renaissance science until observation and experimentation became established.

Reverence for ancient authority was clearly evident in early Renaissance writings about medicine, including in the herbals. Medieval European philosophy taught that the whole of the universe was divinely designed for the comfort and use of human beings, thus it was believed that every herb could be used to treat a specific aliment and that plants themselves had no other purpose (Jones 1961).

As the Renaissance progressed, a number of people, including Francis Bacon (1561–1626), came to believe that science and experimentation should be used to determine when the ancients were right, not sacred tradition. Although it took some time for his influence to be felt, Bacon emphasized starting without assumptions and using experimentation and observation to establish facts before theorizing. In his book *Novum Organum* (*New Organon*, 1620), Bacon proposed a reorganization of all knowledge, arguing that "science is neither philosophy nor humanism . . . but a process of discovery that leads to the accumulation of knowledge" (Langone, Stutz, and Gianopoulos 2006:251). This idea that a new science was to come from the ability of humans to develop a rational, intellectual understanding of the world based on the use of observation and invention led to the founding of several universities that rejected the condemnation in medieval ecclesiastical teachings of curiosity as a vice (Lindauer 2010).

As the scientific spirit of the Renaissance grew, there was an explosion of collecting activities, particularly in the second half of the sixteenth century, aimed at gathering objects together to both explore and represent the natural world (Blom 2002). Bacon's emphasis on observation gave justification to collecting and studying objects, led to the establishment of the collection of the Royal Society, and was key to converting cabinets of curiosities into modern science collections.

Park 2001; Lindauer 2010). The collections demonstrated and enhanced the prestige of their collectors based on the principle that "in creating a microcosm of the universe, intellectual power over the whole, the macrocosm, could be displayed" (Pearce 2010:17).

Renaissance collectors focused on unusual objects, the evidence of rare phenomena, anything counterintuitive or unexplained, and whatever objects were "astounding by their unfamiliarity" (Daston and Park 2001:23). Collectors rationalized the acquisition of such objects by using the *doctrine of magnificence* (derived from Aristotle's *Ethics*) to justify the expenses associated with their superior aesthetic taste (Lindauer 2010). Collectors referred to the objects they coveted as marvels, curiosities, and wonders.

The period from 1500 to 1600 brought about a new appreciation for ancient art and objects. Coupled with an unprecedented increase in the exchange of objects from around the world and fueled by trade and a growing culture of consumption, private collections grew and diversified (Keating and Markey 2011). The economic practices of pawning and credit increased the circulation of collectible objects. This trade in objects, in turn, strengthened the connections between collectors (Clark 2013). As time went by, interest in collecting increased until it "permeated seventeenth century English culture" (Swann 2001:1) as well as that of much of the rest of Europe (Findlen 1998). When the first Spanish ship returned from Mexico to Spain in 1519, its cargo of American featherwork, stone carvings, tools, weapons, plant and animal specimens, gold and silver objects, and jewelry was quickly acquired by members of the royalty for their cabinets and by members of the clergy for the papal collections (Yaya 2008). As more ships brought goods from the Americas and other far-flung places, commercial object dealers opened shops all over Europe (Yaya 2008).

With the increase in collecting activity during the Renaissance, a new, more comprehensive form of documentation of collections began, driven by the need to keep track of objects in the collections. Medieval collections were sometimes inventoried, but these inventories were simple listings indicating little interest in classification or in documenting the relationships among the objects (although some inventories included information on the monetary or prestige value of selected objects). The monetary value of medieval collections was important because many church collections were used as cash reserves. It has been suggested that the typical European medieval collection, compared to collections of the Renaissance, was "not a *musaeum* but a *thesaurus*" or treasury (Daston and Park 2001:74). The collection catalog, however, was an invention of the late-sixteenth-century Renaissance in response to the need to organize and classify new learning. Catalogs provided an interpretation or analysis of the collection, not just a listing of the contents (Yaya 2008).

Published catalogs rapidly evolved from spare documents into elaborate illustrated books that provided proof of a new level of status for the collector (Findlen 1994). The catalogs served scholarly purposes as well as practical purposes by establishing the importance of a collection and providing a basis for estimating its value. Collectors "imbued things with value and significance, manipulating and contesting their meaning over time," with the result that museum objects were attributed varied meanings and values as collectors and visitors perceived objects in different ways (Alberti 2005:561). In addition, the catalogs were often the basis for study of a collection and the relationships between the objects (Keating and Markey 2011).

ORGANIZATION AND CLASSIFICATION

The period from 1550 to 1700 in Europe has been dubbed "The Age of the Marvelous." The period was characterized by an "intense fascination with the marvelous, with those things or events that were unusual, unexpected, exotic, extraordinary, or rare" (Kenseth 1991:25). The Age of the Marvelous was shaped by the confluence of medieval beliefs and the new discoveries coming to Europe. Things marvelous were investigated and expressed in a variety of ways, including art, music, and literature, and in the organizational schemes in the cabinets of curiosities. Making cabinets of curiosities became a social craze among the European elite and fostered a network of relationships among collectors and hence between families, dynasties, and alliances, as well as patronage, gift and mercantile exchange networks, and scholarly connections (Meadow 2013). These networks enabled "[d]iscussions of the reciprocal relationships between art and nature" to take place "in the intimacy of private collections where the virtuosity of *artificialia* competed side by side with the perfection of a work of nature" (Yaya 2008:175). By the end of the Renaissance, collections made for social prestige and tradition were giving way to collections made in a spirit of inquiry, for the enjoyment of private study, and for the advancement of knowledge (Lewis 1985).

The emergence of private cabinets of curiosities, in marked contrast to the medieval court and church treasuries, was the product of the intellectual and economic ferment of the Renaissance, including the need to organize and classify new knowledge (Yaya 2008). Since the sixteenth century, collectors had organized their collections in ways that promoted the transmission of knowledge (Schulz 1994), but as the collections of the cabinets of curiosities expanded, increasingly elaborate classification schemes were developed to give order to the objects, although the "arrangement of the collections seems to have been highly idiosyncratic.

There were probably as many different classification schemes as there were individual collectors" (Pyenson and Sheets-Pyenson 1999:127). Printed books from this period shed some light on how marvels were categorized and classified as supernatural objects (*miracula*, sublimely mysterious miracles and transcendent divine interventions), natural objects (*naturalia*, the odd wonders of nature—mythic, monstrous, and real), and artificial objects (*artificialia*) (Kenseth 1991). In their analysis of Renaissance collections, Keating and Markey (2011) show that the catalogs generally follow a similar structure. The catalog begins with a preface naming the collector (or owner) of the collection and its location, followed by the date that the catalog was prepared and the name of the author (or cataloger). The names of witnesses who could attest to the validity of the catalog might be mentioned as well, before the section describing the objects in the collection. Some of the catalogs, particularly those with an emphasis on natural history collections, document a moment in the evolution of intellectual history that illustrates the "watershed between medievalism and humanism," with their systematic organization and detailed specimen descriptions (Wittlen 1970:40).

The catalogs vary widely in their organization and in the complexity of their classification schemes. Although many of the collections may not seem to modern eyes to have been organized, they were, and their organizational structure provides a unique perspective on the collector's worldview. Sometimes all that linked the objects were unknown assumptions on the part of the collectors. On occasion, exhibition strategies and catalog representations intentionally subverted the boundaries between familiar categories, with some objects being located on the margins between categories (Daston and Park 2001). For example, a rhinoceros horn covered in goldwork and gems was not only monetarily valuable, it was also rare, finely crafted, and strange (Daston and Park 2001). There was much debate over the nature of coral—was it an animal, a plant, or a mineral (Bredekamp 1995; Mauriès 2002)? In Greek mythology, red coral was a plant that had been stained with the blood dripping from the severed head of Medusa. Pliny thought that coral turned as hard as stone as soon as it was touched by a human hand. In some folk traditions, coral was thought to avert the effects of the evil eye. Other popular objects were so ambiguous that it was difficult to determine whether they were natural or created by humans, such as ornately formed stones shaped like human organs or images found in the grain of wood.

Europeans were completely baffled by many of the objects, animals, and plants arriving in Europe for their cabinets of curiosities. In many instances, the collectors had only parts to work with, such as shards or a few teeth, a horn or tusk, claws or feathers, perhaps pieces of skin or a partial skeleton (Olmi 1985). The first tree sloths to reach Europe were thought to be monkeys and were therefore illustrated sitting upright rather than hanging from a tree limb by their long claws. Armadillos were initially classified as turtles because they had hard outer shells. Birds of paradise were especially valued for their exotic plumage and the myths surrounding them. Sailors typically skinned the birds, inserted a stick into the head to hold the skin rigid, then removed the legs (because they were difficult to prevent from decaying), and dried the bird skins (often smoking them) to preserve them for the long trip back to Europe (George 1985). As a result, a legend grew in Europe that the bird of paradise never stopped flying. It was widely believed that chicks hatched from eggs balanced on the back of the flying male (Simmons and Snider 2012). In assessing this period, one historian writes,

> *El anhelo de un paraíso en la Tierra contrasta con el temor de un mundo desconocido. La tensión entre el temor a lo desconocido y la ilusión del paraíso terrenal se percibe en la descripción del ave del paraíso, monstruosa y bella al mismo tiempo.*

> The longing for an Earthly paradise contrasts with the fear of an unknown world. The tension between the fear of the unknown and the illusion of Earthly paradise is perceived in the description of the bird of paradise, which is monstrous and beautiful at the same time. (Nieto Olarte 2013:226)

In most of the catalogs, the rationale for how objects were grouped and associated is not provided, so the distinctions between categories are not always clear. In some instances, objects are misidentified, which contributes to further confusion in trying to parse out categorical criteria. Table 5.1 provides a selection of classification categories from catalogs beginning in the early 1400s, with the simple division into *mirabilia* (finite marvels) and *miracula* (infinite or divine marvels) and *artificialia* (artificial objects) and *naturalia* (objects from nature). By the late 1400s, other categories appeared, such as *antiquitas* (antiquities). Some collections were organized using more closely defined categories. For example, after visiting Gessner's cabinet of curiosities (discussed here), Johannes Kentmann (1518–1574), a German naturalist and physician from Torgau, cataloged his collection of 1,600 mineral specimens in 26 categories based on Agricola's *De re Metallica* (1556). Kentmann's classification was published by Gessner in 1565 (Murray 1904).

Toward the end of the Renaissance, collections and classification schemes had become sufficiently sophisticated that in 1565 Samuel von Quiccheberg (1529–1567), the librarian for the Duke of Bavaria (Albrecht V), wrote a book on collection organization. Quiccheberg's book, *Inscriptiones; vel, tituli theatric amplissimi* (*Inscriptions; or, Titles of the Most Ample Theater*) is now recognized as the first museological treatise concerning the systematic organization of collections (Robertson 2013; Smith 2008),

Table 5.1.   General Collection Classification Schemes, 1400–1823

Date	Categories	Use
Early 1400s	*Mirabilia* (finite marvels) *Miracula* (infinite or divine marvels)	Wunderkammern, Kunstkammern, Cabinets of Curiosities
Mid-1400s	*Artificialia* *Naturalia*	
Late 1400s	*Artificialia* *Naturalia* *Antiquitas*	
1565	Material glorifying the founder Handcrafts from antiquity Natural specimens Technical and cultural objects Paintings and sacred objects	Samuel von Quicchebert
1655	Minerals Plants Animals Ethnographic objects	Olaus Worm
1656	Birds, eggs, and nests Fourfooted beasts Fish Shell creatures *Insecta* and *Serpentes* Rocks and minerals Outlandish fruits Mechanical objects Variety of rarities Warlike instruments Garments and ornaments Utensils and housewares *Numismata* Medals *Hortus* (garden plants)	John Tradescant
1664	Mathematical and physical instruments, metal ores, asbestos, gems, figured stones, magnets and lodestones, *pietra fungifera* Fossil remains Zoological specimens Products of the vegetable kingdom Ethnographic objects Weapons Archaeological objects European craft objects Musical instruments Books, prints, drawings, and codices Paintings, statues, and medals	Lodovico Settala, Manfredo Settala

(continued)

Table 5.1. (*continued*)

Date	Categories	Use
1679	Objects from mines Growing things Animals Works of art	Jan Swammerdam
1714	Natural history Things sacred and superstitious Artificial rarities Apparatus (philosophical, mathematical, anatomical, surgical, and chemical) Coins and medals	Michael Bernhard Valentini
1727	*Naturalia* *Artificialia* *Curiosa*	Caspar Neikelius
1759	Manuscripts, medals, and coins Natural and artificial productions Printed books	British Museum
1814	Manuscripts, medals, and coins Natural and artificial productions Printed books Antiquities and art	British Museum
1823	Ancient relics Arms Dresses and implements of half-civilized nations Rarities (gifts, memorials, amulets, curious works of art) Pictures Books and manuscripts Zoological specimens	Ashmolean Museum at Oxford

Sources: Aimi, de Michele, and Merandotti 1985; Hafstein 2003; Lindauer 2010.

but it was more of a procedural manual than a conceptual approach (Meadow 2013). Quiccheberg, who had traveled widely in Europe to visit cabinets of curiosities (including Aldrovandi's museum), intended for his book to be a practical how-to guide—for this reason, he used the word *theater* in its architectural rather than its metaphorical sense (Meadow 2013). The book likely found a ready audience, as collecting had become a common practice among merchants, lawyers, apothecaries, and royalty, involving considerable sums of money spent on objects for the collections (Meadow 2013).

In Quiccheberg's conception, a cabinet of curiosities should promote the collecting of objects and their research and display and serve as a site for education in the arts, crafts, and sciences (Robertson 2013). Quiccheberg believed that establishing a collection was a form of scholarship that produced knowledge (Meadow 2013). In particular, Quiccheberg thought of collecting as "part of a new conception of philosophy that viewed knowledge as active, productive, and based on nature" (Smith 2008:116) and thereby gave the owner of a cabinet of curiosities a way to access knowledge outside of written texts (Robertson 2013). Quiccheberg recognized that the juxtaposition of objects and the processes of categorizing objects in groups enhanced the value of each object and the knowledge that could be gained from the objects.

The book consists of six thematically related texts. The first, "Inscriptions, or Titles," presents a system of five numbered classes of objects, each with ten or eleven subclasses that Quiccheberg calls inscriptions (see table 5.2). The classes and inscriptions were intended to include anything that a collector might want to acquire. The second section concerns "Museums, Workshops, and Storerooms," which Quiccheberg describes as utilitarian spaces housing workrooms, collection storage and display areas, and spaces for collection study and research (table 5.3). The third section is devoted to Quiccheberg's recommendations and advice for establishing a collection, followed by a section on "Digressions and Clarifications" that provides more details about the inscription categories.

The last two sections of the book are "Exemplars for the Reader" (a list of established collectors and scholars, along with notes about their social ranking and families) and "End of the Theater," which is a collection of biblical texts that Quiccheberg believed pertained to collecting, along with several poems. Among the exemplars mentioned by Quiccheberg are the Temple of Solomon and Hezekiah's treasury, which he believed demonstrated that "wisdom, honor, peace, and prosperity will result from establishing Kunst- and Wunderkammern" (Meadow 2013:34). The biblical accounts cited by Quiccheberg describe the dimensions of the Temple of Solomon and the materials used in its construction (e.g., cedar walls and ceilings, which, it is interesting to note, would have acted to control pests but at the cost of a high concentration of volatile acids) and the temple decorations, including figures covered in gold leaf (1 Kings 6:1–38 and 7:1–51). The treasury of Hezekiah is described on the occasion when the king received visitors from Babylon and "shewed them all the house of his precious things, the silver, and the gold, and the spices, and the precious ointment, and all the house of his armour, and all that was found in his treasures: there was nothing in his house, nor in all his dominion, that Hezekiah shewed them not" (2 Kings 20:13). However, in 2 Kings 20:14–17, the prophet Isaiah warns Hezekiah that his collection will be seized and dispersed by invaders—which indeed happened (Schulz 1994:179).

Table 5.2. Quiccheberg's Categories, 1565

Class	Inscription	Notes
First	Inscription 1	Panels (painted, sculpted, etc.) depicting sacred history
	Inscription 2	Genealogy of the founder of the museum
	Inscription 3	Portraits of the museum's founder
	Inscription 4	Maps, general and scientific
	Inscription 5	Illustrations of cities of Europe and the Holy Roman Empire
	Inscription 6	Military excursions and conflicts
	Inscription 7	Public spectacles and festivals
	Inscription 8	Grand paintings of animals
	Inscription 9	Architectural models
	Inscription 10	Scale models of machines
Second	Inscription 1	Statues of prominent people, divinity, and animals
	Inscription 2	Artisanal metal crafts
	Inscription 3	Artisanal crafts other than metal
	Inscription 4	Ingenious objects worthy of admiration
	Inscription 5	Foreign objects
	Inscription 6	Measures and weights
	Inscription 7	Ancient and contemporary coins
	Inscription 8	Portraits resembling coins
	Inscription 9	Symbolic objects resembling coins
	Inscription 10	Tiny gold ornaments
	Inscription 11	Engraved copper artifacts
Third	Inscription 1	Marvelous and rare animals
	Inscription 2	Animals cast from metal, plaster, clay, or other materials
	Inscription 3	Memorable parts of animals (horns, beaks, teeth, bezoars, etc.)
	Inscription 4	Skeletons
	Inscription 5	Seeds, fruit, vegetables, grains, and roots
	Inscription 6	Herbs, flowers, branches and boughs, bark, wood, and roots
	Inscription 7	Metals and ores
	Inscription 8	Gems and precious stones
	Inscription 9	Distinctive stones
	Inscription 10	Colors and pigments
	Inscription 11	Earthen materials and liquids
Fourth	Inscription 1	Musical instruments
	Inscription 2	Mathematical and navigational instruments
	Inscription 3	Writing and painting instruments and materials
	Inscription 4	Instruments used to lift, move, or break objects
	Inscription 5	Instruments for workshops and laboratories
	Inscription 6	Surgical and anatomical instruments
	Inscription 7	Hunting and fishing equipment
	Inscription 8	Equipment or games
	Inscription 9	Weapons of other nations and unusual weapons
	Inscription 10	Foreign garb
	Inscription 11	Rarer and durable garments and costumes

Table 5.2. **(continued)**

Class	Inscription	Notes
Fifth	Inscription 1	Oil paintings by eminent artists
	Inscription 2	Watercolors by distinguished painters
	Inscription 3	Prints
	Inscription 4	Tables of sacred and secular classifications, historical catalogs
	Inscription 5	Genealogies
	Inscription 6	Images of eminent and famous men
	Inscription 7	Coats of arms
	Inscription 8	Tapestries and embroidered hangings
	Inscription 9	Aphorisms and gnomae (ethical aphorisms)
	Inscription 10	Containers for storing objects

Source: Meadow and Robertson 2013.

Table 5.3. **Quiccheberg's Museums, Workshops, and Storerooms, 1565**

Category	Classification
Library	Theological
	Juridical
	Medical
	Historical
	Philosophical, dialectical, and magical
	Mathematical and astrological
	Literary
	Poetry, sacred and profane
	Musical
	Grammatical
Workshops	Print
	Turner's equipment
	Pharmacy or apothecary
	Foundry
Museums and closets	For exhibition or storage

Source: Meadow and Robertson 2013.

CABINETS OF CURIOSITIES

During the Renaissance, the emphasis in collecting shifted from accumulating hoards of rare and valuable objects to assembling collections that helped interpret the world and reflected the collector's erudition and sophistication. The new admiration for the culture, architecture, and monuments of classical antiquity prompted a series of private excavations of archaeological sites in Rome by eager collectors between 1450 and 1550. Coins and medals were particularly sought after—the Venetian collector Benedetto Dandolo is reputed to have assembled the first comprehensive

Renaissance coin collection (Murray 1904). Collectors wanted to obtain relics from the classical past because they thought that the physical objects provided unmediated access to antiquity, unlike the manuscripts that had been copied and probably corrupted by medieval scribes (Stenhouse 2014).

It was at this juncture that the first cabinets of curiosities appeared in Europe (Mauriès 2002). The cabinet of curiosities went by many names, including *museo, teatro, microcosm, gallery, gazophylacium, study, wonder cabinet, memory theater, Kunstkammer*—derived from *Kunst* (art) and *Kammer* (room or chamber)—*Wunderkammer* (wonder room), *Schatzkammer* (treasure room), *studiolo*, and *cabinet de curieux* (Findlen 1994; Lindauer 2010; Mauriès 2002; Pearce 1995). Several historians have attempted to parse these terms into discrete categorical units based on the physical spaces they described, what objects were in them, and how they were used, but consensus has been difficult to achieve due to overlapping meanings and contradictory usage. In general, a *Kunstkammer* was a chamber of artifice or chamber of art, as was a *Schatzkammer* (Robertson 2013). A *Wunderkammer* was a chamber of wonders or a curiosity cabinet (Blom 2002; Mauriès 2002; Robertson 2013). The word *Rustkammer* was used to describe collections of armor (Robertson 2013). A *gazophylacium* was a place where valuable objects were stored.

The word *museum* was used in the fifteenth century in reference to the encyclopedic nature of the Medici collection (Lewis 1992)—it was first recorded in an English-language work in 1615. The word *gallery* is derived from the name of the long, narrow corridors in the Medici palaces where the treasures were exhibited. The word *collector* wasn't used until 1582 and then only to refer to a literary compiler (Swann 2001). Not all authors used the terms so precisely. Later in the Renaissance, the meanings of *Wunderkammer* and *Kunstkammer* seemed to merge (Mauriès 2002). The name *studiolo* (*estudes* in French) was often applied to the chambers that held antiquities, gemstones, sculptures, and other treasures of the rich in Italy and is derived from the word for *study*, meaning a "place where the owners would retreat to study their collections"—the distinction between the medieval church treasuries and the new *studioli* was the privacy inherent in the concept of the latter (Blom 2002).

The physical form of these collections varied from actual cabinets to rooms to entire wings of palaces, as the cabinets of curiosities were owned by royal families, rulers, government officials, physicians, clerics, scholars, lawyers, and apothecaries (Findlen 2000; Lindauer 2010). Collectors ranged from the nobility to the middle class (Yaya 2008). Exhibiting a cabinet of curiosities in one's home soon became an important means of expressing (or sometimes increasing) prestige and social standing throughout Europe, with collectors linked through individual contacts and the circulation of manuscripts, handbooks, and other literature (Tribby 1992).

Some of the best-known, most widely read periodicals (including *Mercure de France* and *Journal des savants* in France and *Giornale dei letterati* in Italy) published accounts of travelers' visits to private collections, further reinforcing the social networks among collectors (Tribby 1992).

As with the treasure troves or caches of relics of the medieval era, the objects in the cabinets of curiosities were signs and tokens of power, invested with political import to affirm the authority of the owner (Mauriès 2002). The contents of the cabinets of curiosities almost defy description, as most any object might become part of a collection, either because it was unusual or because it was believed to be special. Francis Bacon (1561–1626) described cabinets of curiosities as containing "whatsoever the hand of man by exquisite art or engine has made rare in stuff, form, or motion; whatsoever singularity, chance and the shuffle of things hath produced; whatsoever Nature has wrought in things that want life and may be kept" (Bacon 1688:35).

Objects commonly found in the cabinets of curiosities included such things as dried animals, seashells, unicorn horns (narwhal teeth), snake stones (see box 5.2), giants' bones (elephant bones or fossil remains of extinct pachyderms), Egyptian mummies, tongues of giant snakes (fossil shark teeth), holy relics (see box 5.3), works of art, and ethnographic objects from Asia or Africa. In part, such objects were collected in response to the "veneration of the rare, the unusual, the wonderful and the miraculous" (Whitehead 1970:51) that permeated the Renaissance, but more important, the collections of the cabinets of curiosities were seen as confirming the existence of a divine order in the world. As Mauriès notes, "One of the true raisons d'être behind the growth of cabinets of curiosities was a restless desire to establish a continuity between art and nature. Thus they demonstrate the existence of a supreme unifying principle" (Mauriès 2002:35–43). According to the authors of a study of marvels, "During the heyday of the *Wunderkammern* in the late sixteenth and early seventeenth centuries, the ancient opposition between art and nature first blurred and then dissolved in natural philosophy, most notably in the works of Francis Bacon, René Descartes, and their many followers" (Daston and Park 2001:260). The cabinet of natural curiosities owned by Antonio Giganti (1535–1598), who served as secretary to the bishop of Bologna, was organized to reflect what were presumed to be the inherent, harmonious relationships that were found in nature and thus demonstrated the glory of the divine creation (Lindauer 2010).

Cabinets of curiosities, particularly those owned by apothecaries, were likely to contain healing stones or mummy dust, which were valued for their use in the practice of medicine and alchemy (since medieval times, mummy dust had been used to stop bleeding, heal bruises and fractures, and relieve convulsions), or objects treasured because of the powers they

BOX 5.2.
Snake Stones

Many cabinets of curiosities included snake stones, also known as vipers' stones, black stones, and serpent stones. Snake stones (figure 5.1) were named for their resemblance to a coiled snake (Hooper-Greenhill 1992). Snake stones were variously believed to prevent snakebite or to cure snakebite; some were also attributed with the power to cure rabies.

Figure 5.1. Snake stone.

Snake stones are fossils of marine invertebrates known as ammonites (fossil cephalopods about 400 to 66 million years old). The name *ammonite* is derived from the fossil's resemblance to the *Cornu Ammonis* (Ammon's horn) of an Egyptian deity who was depicted with a human's body and a ram's head. Coins struck to commemorate Alexander the Great showed him in profile with a horn of Ammon as confirmation of his status as a semideity.

Snake stones and other fossils were valued in alchemy because they were thought to be formed in the ground by the conjunction of two pure salts and thus could be used as essences (pure substances) in the recipe for the philosopher's stone that would transform base metals into precious metals. The belief that the fossils were formed by pure salts was an outgrowth of Aristotle's idea that minerals and fossils were formed by exhalations. According to Aristotle, fuliginous exhalations produced fossils, ochre, sulfur, and vermillion, while vaporous exhalations produced metals (Murray 1904).

The snake stone shown in figure 5.1 is a fossil cephalopod that lived some-time between the late Devonian and the Cretaceous periods, about 400 million to 66 million years ago, in what is now Villa de Leyva, Colombia. The animal lived in the outer chamber of the shell; the inner chambers were filled with water and air for buoyancy.

BOX 5.3.
Relics and the Protestant Reformation

During the Middle Ages in Europe, collections of relics, art, and other valuable objects were common in church treasuries. Many of the objects in these collections were sacred or were thought to have miraculous powers; others were curiosities interpreted as evidence of the divine nature of creation. These collections were guarded in secured spaces and exhibited to the public, presaging collection storage and exhibition in museums (Lindauer 2010; Pomian 1990).

On October 21, 1517, an Augustinian monk named Martin Luther (1483–1546), who was concerned about corrupt practices in the Catholic Church, posted a document (written in Latin) that he had titled *Disputatio pro declaratione virtutis indulgentiarum* ("Disputation on the Power and Efficacy of Indulgences") on the large wooden door of the castle church in Wittenberg, Germany, as was the custom in scholarly disputation at the time (Roberts and Westad 2013). To ensure that his document was read, Luther also sent a copy to the archbishop in Mainz, who sent it on to Rome along with a request that Luther's religious order forbid him from continuing to preach on this topic. Nevertheless, Luther's essay was soon translated into German and was widely circulated among the public. Although Luther's religious order abandoned him, his university did not (Roberts and Westad 2013). Luther's missive triggered what came to be known as the Protestant Reformation, which had far-ranging religious, social, and political impacts as it led to the decline in importance of the Catholic Church in daily life (Roberts and Westad 2013).

The secularizing influence of the Protestants on the veneration of holy relics coincided with the increased importation of unusual and exotic objects to Europe from the New World, Asia, and other far-flung sources, which contributed to the growth and diversification of private collections (MacGregor 1983). As a result of the undermining of institutional church authority and the subsequent social revolution that took place throughout most of Europe, the Catholic Church was displaced as the place where most collections were deposited in Renaissance Europe, and some church collections were secularized. For example, a 127-kilogram meteorite plummeted through the sky on November 7, 1492, landing in a wheat field just outside of the walls of Ensisheim, France. The fireball it created was seen 150 kilometers away, with

(continued)

BOX 5.3.
(continued)

the result that the event was widely interpreted as a portent or omen (Marvin 1992). For many years, the meteorite was exhibited in the local parish church, but because of the fame of the meteorite, parts of it were chipped off and distributed around Europe. One piece was sent to Cardinal Piccolomini at the Vatican, the Emperor Maximilian chipped off a piece for Archduke Sigismund, and fragments were exhibited in the public library in Colmar and the Musée National d'Histoire Naturelle in Paris (Murray 1904). The meteorite was described in 1565 by one of the most famous keepers and catalogers of a cabinet of curiosities, Conrad Gessner (1516–1565), in his book *De Rerum Fossilium*. The Musée de la Régence in Ensisheim (France) still exhibits the remains of the meteorite.

Although the Protestant Reformation split the Western Christian church into two rival factions and triggered major religious wars (MacGregor 2011), it did not put an end to the collecting of relics. Phillip II of Spain (1527–1598) accumulated a collection of more than 7,000 holy relics, including 10 entire bodies, 144 heads, 306 limbs (arms and legs), bones, and other body parts, as well as secondary relics and fragments of the true cross and the crown of thorns encased in a gold and silver setting studded with gemstones (Blom 2002). However, the "quest for collections waned after the 1618 outbreak of the Thirty Years War, a religious war between Protestants and Catholics in the Holy Roman Empire that extended into a political war that involved most of Europe" (Lindauer 2010:723).

were believed to possess (Moser 2006). In the sixteenth century, Egyptian antiquities became very popular in collections, in part because they were easy to acquire (Moser 2006).

The cabinet of Rudolph II (1552–1612), emperor of Hapsburg, reflected his interests as both a collector of curiosities and an alchemist, which was not an unusual combination (Blom 2002). Lorenzo the Magnificent (1449–1492), a member of the Medici family of Florence (see box 5.4), had a highly valued unicorn horn (narwhal tooth) in his collection. Unicorn horns were believed to sweat in the presence of poison and were thus useful for a member of the very political Medici family (Murray 1904). Cosimo de Medici (1519–1574) was able to acquire objects from South America for his collections, as well as objects from Africa, India, China, and Japan, along with a number of natural history specimens (MacGregor 1983). Hooper-Greenhill points out that the development and exhibition of the Medici collections was based on the use of "[w]ealth, patronage, and the use of the past" to glorify the members of the Medici family through the role of magic and occult cosmology in giving power to ob-

BOX 5.4.
The Medici Dynasty

In her perceptive study *Museums and the Shaping of Knowledge*, Eileen Hooper-Greenhill provides a detailed analysis of the development of the collections of the Medici dynasty through several generations as they created what has been called the "first museum of Europe." The Medici were a family of bankers and merchants, part of the emerging merchant class who rose to a new status in Italian Renaissance society.

Cosimo de Medici (1389–1464) amassed a large fortune and commissioned a new palace in the Via Largo in Florence in 1444. The palace was successively occupied by his son Piero de Medici (1419–1469) and grandson Lorenzo de Medici (1448–1492). The palace set a new standard in Florence with its interior and exterior decorations and use of space (Hooper-Greenhill 1992).

Piero de Medici dedicated a room in the palace with high, vaulted ceilings and majolica tiles as his personal *scrittoio*, or studio, in which he kept his books and collection of images, effigies, precious stones, jewels, and other objects, which he was known to spend large amounts of time studying (Hooper-Greenhill 1992). In the 1570s, another Medici, Francesco I (1541–1587), created a *studiolo* (a small room without windows, lined with cabinets, cupboards, and paintings) for objects that he believed demonstrated the hierarchical order of art and nature (Pearce 1995).

The wealth and power of the Medici family grew along with that of the city of Florence throughout the fifteenth century. The Medici collection reached its zenith with Lorenzo the Magnificent, who was a poet, scholar, and patron to several important Renaissance artists, helping them secure important commissions. Lorenzo employed agents to help build his library and a workshop in which books were copied and added greatly to the Medici family collections.

The family collections eventually wound up in the *Galleria degli Uffizi* (Uffizi Gallery), built in the late 1500s by the Medici family as offices for Florentine magistrates. The museum was opened to the public in 1769.

jects, such that the power of the Medici family was a reflection of the power of the objects they possessed (Hooper-Greenhill 1992:65). The Medici collections were opened to the public at the Uffizi Palace in 1582, then bequeathed to the state of Tuscany in 1743 (Lewis 1985).

Among the other well-known Renaissance cabinets of curiosities were those of a tailor-turned-artist named Francesco Squarcione (ca. 1395–1468) of Padua, who assembled a collection of art from ancient Greece and Rome that he used to establish a school for artists (Bazin 1967:43). The first pope to make significant collections while in office was Pietro Barbo (1417–1471), from Venice, who was named Pope Paul II in 1464. The pope's collection of art and antiquities, housed at

Palazzo San Marco (now Palazzo Venezia), included gems, cameos, coins, bronzes, tapestries, and paintings (Bazin 1967). One of the artists who studied the Squarcione collection was a painter and collector of Roman archaeological artifacts named Andrea Mantegna (ca. 1431–1506). Mantegna's collection, kept in his house in Mantua after 1460, was visited by Lorenzo de Medici (Bazin 1967).

In response to the humanist movement, during the late fifteenth century and into the sixteenth century, many small towns in Italy took steps to preserve Roman antiquities as public art by exhibiting statues and other objects; by incorporating stones, inscriptions, and other relics into new building construction; and by protecting ruins (Stenhouse 2014). In some instances, citizen groups also protected Roman works from outsiders who wished to take them away for their own collections, and some municipalities enacted laws that forbade the removal of antiques (Stenhouse 2014).

King Matthias I (Matthias Corvinus, 1443–1490) of Hungary maintained a cabinet that featured paintings and Roman antiquities. A collection of Benin ivories and Chinese paintings was amassed by Ferdinand of Tirol (1529–1595; Lewis 1985). Paolo Giovio's (1482–1552) cabinet was centered around his collection of portraits of great men, while the Grimani family's collection featured archaeological artifacts in Venice. In England, Sir Robert Cotton (1570–1631) maintained a collection of illuminated manuscripts. The first herbarium collection was made by Luca Ghini (1490–1556) in Padua, Italy. Ghini is credited with inventing the practice of pressing and drying plants and then attaching them to paper sheets, called a *hortus siccus*, or dry garden (Lewis 1992; Pavord 2005). Many Renaissance collectors were apothecaries, thus there were important links between dry plant collections, medicinal gardens, and the medical professions (Findlen 1994). What is considered the oldest botanical garden in Europe was established in 1590 by Charles de l'Écluse (1526–1609), better known as Carolus Clusius, at the University of Leiden. Clusius was asked by the university administration to start a *hortus medicus* (medicinal garden) for use by the medical school, but he instead initiated a *hortus academicus*, or true botanical garden (van der Veen 2001), that is now known as the Hortus Botanicus (figure 5.2).

In Italy, more than 250 natural history collections were recorded in the sixteenth century (Lewis 1985) and another 100 in Amsterdam between 1600 and 1740. In Holland, the cabinets of curiosities were sufficiently well known that there were dollhouses made with miniature cabinets of curiosities as part of their furnishings (Blom 2002). The English traveler John Evelyn (1620–1706) described his visit to the greatly admired cabinet of the family of Carlo Ruzzini (1554–1644) in Venice in 1645 (see box 5.5). The extensive Ruzzini collection included 66 marble statues, 84 marble

Figure 5.2. The Hortus Botanicus in Leiden.

fragments, 3,600 medals and medallions, and 120 paintings among its treasures and could still be seen as late as 1750 (Pomian 1990).

Two of the best known collectors of natural history specimens in the Renaissance were Ulisse Aldrovandi (box 5.6) and Konrad Gessner (1516–1565). Gessner, from Zurich, published an arrangement of all known animal species according to the *scala naturae* of Aristotle in his great opus, *Historia animalium* (3,500 pages in 4 folio volumes). After he died of the plague at the age of forty-nine, Gessner's collections were acquired by Felix Potter (1536–1614), then passed to the Naturhistorisches Museum in Basle, where some of the specimens are still extant (Lewis 1992).

As one historian states, "Accumulation, definition, classification: such was the threefold aim of the earliest cabinets of curiosities" (Mauriès 2002:25). All three can be seen in several images of Renaissance cabinets of curiosities, which provide a glimpse into the contents of the collections, organizational schemes, and exhibition styles. One of these is the collection of Francesco Calzolari (1522–1609), who, like many owners of cabinets of curiosities in the Renaissance, was an apothecary (figure 5.3). The catalog of Calzolari's collection, *Musaeum Calceolarium*, was published in Verona in 1622 (Mauriès 2002). The primary motivation for most apoth-

BOX 5.5.
The Cabinet of Carlo Ruzzini, from the Diary of John Evelyn

When the English traveler John Evelyn (1620–1706), a fellow of the Royal Society, visited Italy from 1644 to 1646, he kept a detailed diary. While on this journey, Evelyn purchased four unusual anatomical preparations that he sent back to England: a spinal cord and nerves; an aorta and arteries; the vagi and sympathetic nerves and veins of the lungs and liver; and a preparation showing the distribution of the veins in the body. All four of these preparations had been tediously dissected from cadavers, carefully positioned on flat pine boards, dried, and then glued to the boards and coated in varnish. This preparation technique was then unknown in England, and the specimens created a stir among physicians and medical students alike when they reached London. Known today as the Evelyn Tables, they are the oldest known anatomical preparations in Europe and are in the collection of the Hunterian Museum in London. I saw them on exhibit at the Hunterian Museum in 2010, and even by today's standards, they are spectacular preparations.

Among the many places Evelyn visited was the famous cabinet of Carlo Ruzzini (1554–1644). Evelyn wrote the following description in his diary (he refers to Ruzzini as Signor Rugini):

29th September, 1645. Michaelmas day, I went with my Lord Mowbray (eldest son to the Earl of Arundel, and a most worthy person) to see the collection of a noble Venetian, Signor Rugini. He has a stately palace, richly furnished with statues and heads of Roman Emperors, all placed in an ample room. In the next, was a cabinet of medals, both Latin and Greek, with divers curious shells and two fair pearls in two of them; but, above all, he abounded in things petrified, walnuts, eggs in which the yoke rattled, a pear, a piece of beef with the bones in it, a whole hedgehog, a plaice on a wooden trencher turned into stone and very perfect, charcoal, a morsel of cork yet retaining its levity, sponges, and a piece of taffety part rolled up, with innumerable more. In another cabinet, supported by twelve pillars of oriental agate, and railed about with crystal, he showed us several noble intáglios of agate, especially a head of Tiberius, a woman in a bath with her dog, some rare cornelians, onyxes, crystals, etc., in one of which was a drop of water not congealed, but moving up and down, when shaken; above all, a diamond which had a very fair ruby growing in it; divers pieces of amber, wherein were several insects, in particular one cut like a heart that contained in it a salamander without the least defect, and many pieces of mosaic. The fabric of this cabinet was very ingenious, set thick with agates, turquoises, and other precious stones, in the midst of which was an antique of a dog in stone scratching his ear, very rarely cut, and comparable to the greatest curiosity I had ever seen of that kind for the accurateness of the work. The next chamber had a bedstead all inlaid with agates, crystals, cornelians, lazuli, etc., esteemed worth 16,000 crowns, but, for the most part, the bedsteads in Italy are of forged iron gilded, since it is impossible to keep the wooden ones from the cimices. (Quoted in Bray 1901:211–12)

BOX 5.6.
Aldrovandi, Master Cataloger

Ulisse Aldrovandi (1522–1605) was an exceptional individual but also emblematic of many of the Renaissance savants—his natural curiosity led him to acquire large collections, which he studied and wrote about at great length. Born into a noble family (his father, Count Teseo Aldrovandi, was a lawyer who served as secretary of the senate of Bologna), Aldrovandi studied in Padua, Pisa, and Bologna. After earning degrees in medicine and philosophy in 1553, Aldrovandi taught logic and philosophy (and later natural sciences) at the University of Bologna.

Aldrovandi was arrested in 1549 at the age of twenty-six and charged with heresy for advocating the antitrinitarian beliefs of Camillo Renato. Aldrovandi denied the allegations but was nevertheless sent to Rome for trial, where he spent ten months under house arrest. The charges against Aldrovandi were ultimately dropped, but while awaiting judgment, his interest in natural history intensified (Baucon 2008). Once free from confinement, Aldrovandi returned to Bologna and organized several plant-collecting expeditions between 1551 and 1554. Aldrovandi himself collected at least 4,760 botanical specimens, which are now preserved and mounted as dry plants attached to paper sheets that are sewn into bound volumes. In 1568, Aldrovandi established a medicinal botanical garden, the Orto Botanico dell'Università di Bologna.

Aldrovandi wrote numerous books and manuscripts, most published posthumously, including seventeen volumes documenting his collections, which he described as a *Teatro della Natura* (*Theater of Nature*). Aldrovandi's works served as the standard zoological, botanical, and paleontological references for centuries. Meticulous about the details of his burgeoning collection in his cabinet of curiosity, Aldrovandi even prepared a *Catalogus virorum qui vistarunt Musaeum nostrum* (*Catalog of the Museum and Its Visitors*), in which he classified the people who came to see his collections, organizing them according to their geographical origin and social status (Mauriès 2002). An analysis of the catalog reveals that Aldrovandi's visitors included scholars (57.4 percent); members of the clergy (16.6 percent); royalty (10.2 percent); physicians (6.0 percent); civil servants (5.3 percent); professors (3.0 percent); and antiquarians, painters, poets, and jewelers (1.5 percent; Findlen 1994).

One of Aldrovandi's many innovations was his extensive use of illustrations (Baucon 2008; Bauer, Ceregato, and Delfino 2013). An example of how Aldrovandi integrated illustrations, specimens, and other information can be found in the story of his dragon. A somewhat "fearsome dragon" was brought to Aldrovandi in Bologna on May 13, 1572 (Findlen 1994:17). The beast, which had appeared suddenly in the road outside of the city, frightening a team of oxen, had been clubbed to death by a terrified peasant. The occurrence of the dragon caused quite a stir because it appeared on the very day

(*continued*)

BOX 5.6.
(continued)

that Pope Gregory XIII (a relative of Aldrovandi) was to be ordained. Once the dragon specimen was safely in his collection, Aldrovandi summoned an artist to make a drawing of the animal. Later, Aldrovandi carefully described the specimen in his book on dragons (*Serpentum et Draconum Historiae*, 1640) and included a woodcut of it that was prepared from the drawing.

Given that Aldrovandi was a careful and cautious observer and collector, when he saw the dragon, what did he think he was looking at, and what happened to the specimen? A recent analysis (Senter, Hill, and Moton 2013) has revealed that, in fact, the dragon was a fake, composed of the body of a grass snake, the torso of a European perch, and the front legs of a toad. The authors of the study argued that Aldrovandi knew the specimen was a chimera, but for complex political reasons, he avoided saying so directly (although his description of the dragon included hints that he knew all along it was a fake). The only preservation technique then available was dehydration (Simmons and Snider 2012), but unfortunately, dry organic specimens are susceptible to deterioration and attack from pests, so the dragon has not survived—in fact, only a small number of the natural history specimens in Aldrovandi's collection are still with us. For example, a recently published study determined that only nineteen of Aldrovandi's herpetological specimens exist today—all dry preparations, and curiously, some of them are also faked chimeras, as was the dragon (Bauer, Ceregato, and Delfino 2013).

An inventory from 1557 shows the Aldrovandi collection to have contained about 13,000 natural history specimens at that time (Blom 2002). The collection had grown to 18,000 by 1595, including 11,000 specimens of animals, fruits, and vegetables; 7,000 plants dried and pasted into 16 volumes of herbaria; 8,000 tempera illustrations; and 14 cupboards full of woodblock illustrations (Olmi 1985; Simmons and Snider 2012). By 1600, it had surpassed 20,000 specimens. Aldrovandi valued pictorial representations both as a way to compensate for the lack of specimens of some species in his collection and to supplement descriptions in his written texts. Aldrovandi's collection emphasized *naturalia* but included antiquarian objects and ethnographic objects, as listed in a catalog, *Index alphabeticus rerum omnium naturalium in musaeo appensacrum incipiendo a trabe prima*, published in 1587 (Laurencich-Minelli 1985:20).

Antonio Giganti (1535–1598) was a contemporary of Aldrovandi who also maintained a diverse collection. A 1586 inventory of Giganti's collection includes mention of a picture gallery, natural history specimens, ethnographic objects, archaeological specimens, philological objects, and other materials. The ethnographic objects were chiefly from the East Indies and West Indies, Turkey, and North America. The objects of *naturalia* and *artificialia* were intermingled and arranged for maximum use of space and aesthetic symmetry rather than in a classification based on a specific system of order (Laurencich-

Minelli 1985). Aldrovandi and Giganti were colleagues who maintained a close relationship based primarily on their mutual collecting interests. The two traded advice as well as objects, and Aldrovandi made frequent use of objects in Giganti's collection in his writing (Laurencich-Minelli 1985).

In his will of 1603, Aldrovandi bequeathed his collection and library to the senate of Bologna. In 1617, the collection was transferred to the Palazzo Pubblico and arranged in six rooms, with a full-time keeper in charge (Laurencich-Minelli 1985). The collection amassed by Ferdinando Cospi (1606–1683) was added in 1660. In 1742, the two combined museums were relocated to the Istituto delle Scienze (Institute of Sciences; Tribby 1992).

ecaries in collecting was to acquire specimens of plants, minerals, and animals (plants were often cultivated in medicinal gardens) that could be used to treat the sick (Pomian 1990). Like most of the collecting apothecaries, Calzolari used his collection for research on medications. When the collection was inherited by his son, Francesco Calzolari the younger, the collection became better known for its curiosities rather than its pharmaceutical research value. The woodcut of Calzolari's collection shows a

Figure 5.3.   The cabinet of curiosities of Calzolari, 1622. *Source:* Francesco Calzolari, "Musaeum Calceolarium" (Verona, 1622); unknown artist.

crowded room with stuffed and dried creatures hanging from the ceiling, mounted specimens sitting atop cabinets, and shelves and drawers seemingly crammed with objects.

Ferrante Imperato (1525–1625), a Naples apothecary, published a collection catalog entitled *Dell'Historia Naturale* in 1599. The image of Imperato's collection (figure 5.4) has been described as the "first known image of a didactic study collection" (Moser 2006:15). Imperato is believed to have emphasized an aesthetic presentation of his collection, which suggests that a great deal of effort was devoted to the impact of the exhibition on the audience. In figure 5.4, several of the drawers and cupboards are shown opened, to reveal the objects that are stored in them. One of the figures (thought to be Imperato or his son) is indicating the creatures arranged on the ceiling to three visitors, while two small dogs gambol about the floor. The image shows a rare specimen of an armadillo, frogs, and lizards intermixed with marine specimens; neatly arranged books; numerous types of containers for specimens; and, of course, a crocodile hanging from the ceiling. Crocodiles were popular in the cabinets of curiosities because of their extravagant size and monstrous appearance and because they were enigmatic dwellers of both land and water (Davenne

Figure 5.4.   The cabinet of curiosities of Imperato, 1599. *Source:* Ferrante Imperato, *Dell'Historia Naturale* (Naples, 1599); anonymous, for Ferrante Imperato.

and Fleurent 2012). On the top shelf on the left-hand side of the image is a stuffed pelican, mounted so that it is "in the act of opening its breast with its beak in order to resuscitate its dead young with its own blood. Such was the influence of secular tradition that the symbol of man's redemption through Christ's blood, taken straight from the pages of the *Physiologus*, appears in and is even classified within the natural history museum" (Olmi 1985:10). According to Moser, in this and similar representations of Renaissance cabinets, the "tension between didactic organization and aesthetic presentation, which was to become a preoccupying concern of early museums, was manifested at the earliest stages in the creation of knowledge-based collections" (Moser 2006:15).

An image of the cabinet of another apothecary, Basilius Besler (1561–1629), appeared on the title page of a book, *Fasciculus rariorum et aspectu dignorum varii generis*, published in Nuremberg in 1616 (figure 5.5). The image is significant for being one of the first to show labels on the storage containers (Moser 2006). In addition to being a collector, Besler was in charge of botanical gardens at Eichstätt. The image appears to show more specimens from the Americas than previous illustrations of cabinets had shown (Moser 2006:25).

The ability to organize and retrieve large amounts of information is fundamental to the establishment of the modern museum, and in this

Figure 5.5. The cabinet of curiosities of Besler, 1616. *Source:* Basilius Besler, "Fasciculus Rariorum" (1616); engraved by Hans Troschel the Younger after Peter Isselburg's design.

period, we can find several examples of the forerunner of many modern organization systems, the card file. The card file has been described as a "universal discrete machine" used for processing and storing information because, unlike a scroll or codex book, the information in a card file is inscribed on mobile carriers (the individual cards), which allows it to be arranged and rearranged in different ordering systems (Krajewski 2011:3). The first true card file in a library did not appear until around 1780, but Gessner was one of the first to describe the use of a card catalog to organize information related to his museum and library, using slips of paper that he cut and pasted for later mounting in book form. Slips of paper for card files were later cut to uniform size and organized in boxes, and later still, information was written on playing card blanks (Krajewski 2011).

Near the end of the Renaissance, the first purpose-built museum building was probably constructed, although there is disagreement among historians as to which edifice should claim the title. What is considered by many historians to be the oldest purpose-built museum is the building known as the Mint (Münzhof) in Munich, Germany. The structure was designed by Wilhelm Egkl and constructed between 1563 and 1567 to exhibit the paintings of Wilhelm IV and Albrecht V (Lewis 1992), but it also housed the Bavarian mint from 1809 to 1983. Another claim comes from a structure built by Archduke Ferdinand for his collection at Schloss Ambras in 1573. Ferdinand commissioned a complex of buildings that, "for the first time in the history of post-antiquity architecture, was designed specifically for the purpose of housing a collection" (Bredekamp 1995:30–31). Three of the buildings were for arms and armor, another held a *Kunstkammer* that consisted of twenty display cases, and all of the rooms were connected (Scheiches 1985). The collection was inventoried in 1596 immediately after the death of Ferdinand, and a catalog of it was prepared in 1601 (Scheiches 1985).

ELSEWHERE IN THE WORLD

The history of Africa, the Americas, Arabia, and Asia has been described as having "moved to rhythms very different from those operating" in Europe, even though Islam gained a foothold in much of Africa, followed by European traders (Roberts and Westad 2013:469). The period from roughly 1450 to 1650 marked the emergence of the first modern global economy, as Europeans ventured down the coast of western Africa, into the Indian Ocean, and across the Atlantic to the Americas. In 1602, the Dutch East India Company began trade between the Far East and Europe, making it the first multinational company (MacGregor 2011).

Portuguese traders managed to establish themselves in China (in Macao) in 1557, with the Jesuits arriving not long after. By 1602, an Italian Jesuit named Matteo Ricci (1552–1610) had managed to learn Chinese in Macao and gain entry to the Ming court. The Jesuits presented gifts of European mechanical toys and clocks for the Chinese imperial collections, and their scientific and cosmological knowledge was of interest to Chinese intellectuals (Roberts and Westad 2013).

On December 31, 1600, by means of a royal charter, the British East India Company (a joint-stock company with investments from wealthy aristocrats and merchants) was founded to develop commercial opportunities in Asia—it would go on to field its own army and handle half of the world's trade as the British Empire grew in India (Roberts and Westad 2013:541). From 1550 to 1700, Eurasia was dominated by three great Islamic powers after Zahir ud din Muhammad Babur (1483–1530) established the Mughal dynasty on the Indian subcontinent between 1520 and 1530—Ottoman Turkey, Safavid Iran, and Mughal India (MacGregor 2011; Roberts and Westad 2013).

The expansion of European cultures across the world was accomplished with greater ease in some areas than in others. The conquest and colonization of the Americas, despite the enormous loss of life and cultural disruption to those living on the American continent, was comparatively swift and easy for the European conquerors. The cornerstone for the first Catholic cathedral in the Americas was laid in 1523 in Santo Domingo, where the first university was established in 1538. The first printing press in the Americas went into operation in Mexico City in 1539 (Roberts and Westad 2013).

Although Hernán Cortés (1485–1547) did not find anything resembling a museum when he conquered Mexico (1518–1520), he did find a very large related institution (a zoological garden). Both Cortés and Francisco Pizarro (1478–1541), who conquered the Inca Empire in the Andes of Peru (1531–1533), found extensive displays of public art, including finely made gold and silver objects. The Americas rapidly became a source of products that increased European wealth to undreamed-of levels. The primary exports from the New World included corn (maize), fish, fruit, fur, gold, indigo, potatoes, salt, silver, sugar and molasses (introduced to the Americas from Asia by Europeans), sweet potatoes, timber (particularly hardwoods), and tobacco. The primary Old World exports to the New World included chickens, manufactured goods, pigs, sheep, and slaves from Africa (Roberts and Westad 2013). Many of the newly imported materials were acquired by wealthy collectors (particularly members of royalty), who hired skilled artisans to use them to create new and spectacular objects for their collections.

Unlike Asia and Africa, the Americas quickly became more culturally European, particularly through the influence of the Spanish, the Portuguese, and the English. Although linguistically distinct, all three of these cultures "offered edited versions of the same text" (Roberts and Westad 2013:657). In large part because of this Westernization of American cultures, the museum concept arrived much sooner in the Americas and was more readily adapted to local cultural needs than in African, Arabian, or Asian cultures (see chapter 7).

LITERATURE

During the Renaissance, private libraries grew as an intense reading culture developed with the rediscovery of ancient writings, even before books became plentiful with the introduction of printing with movable type (Battles 2015). In 1455, Johannes Gutenberg published the first book in Europe printed with movable type. Printing caught on quickly (box 5.7). By 1500, at least 35,000 separate editions of books had been published—in total, an estimated 15 to 20 million individual books (Roberts and Westad 2013).

A novel written by Miguel Cervantes (1547–1616) called *El Ingenioso Hidalgo don Quixote de la Mancha* (*The Ingenious Gentleman Don Quixote of La Mancha*) denotes a significant change in literature—it is a story that reflects the real world rather than the heroics of the ancient heroes or the romances of the Middle Ages (Voth 2007). In the story, Cervantes tells his readers that the brain of the protagonist (Alonso Quixano) has become dry from reading too many medieval romances.

The exploration, subjugation, and exploitation of the Americas influenced a number of literary works, including Shakespeare's *The Tempest* (Wood 2000). The novel *Utopia* by Thomas More (1478–1535), published in Latin in 1516, contrasts a contentious European society with the peace and order of an imagined ideal native society in the Americas. In a similar vein, Michel Eyquem de Montaigne (1533–1592) wrote an essay comparing European society to that of the noble savages of the New World and found European society lacking.

BOX 5.7.
Movable Type and Peripatetic Catalogs

The first printed collection catalogs were published in the sixteenth century. Unlike handwritten catalogs, printed catalogs could be widely circulated to fellow collectors, dealers in collection objects, travelers, and government officials (Hafstein 2003). Published catalogs and books about their collections were often used by collectors to pay tribute to patrons, as they were the most effective way to record the activities that gave value to the collection, particularly the acquisition and trading of objects (Findlen 1994).

Printing with movable type was one of the technologies that had widespread, profound effects on many areas of culture and society. Ink had been applied to the raised surface of a wood block (called relief printing) to make multiple copies of a single block of wood since before the ninth century in China (Chappell 1970). Movable ceramic type had been known in China since around 1040 CE, and by the fourteenth century, metal movable type was in production and use in both China and Korea (Fischer 2001; Murray 2009). However, there was no direct transfer of this technology, so the invention of printing with movable type in Europe was an independent event.

Johannes Gutenberg (ca. 1394–1468) from Mainz (Germany) is generally credited with the invention of movable type in Europe sometime in the 1440s, although there is some evidence that Dutch printers may have been the first. However, the quality of Gutenberg's work was markedly superior to other printers of his day. Gutenberg is best known for his production of a two-column, forty-two-line Bible printed between 1450 and 1455 (Chappell 1970). The key to success for Gutenberg was figuring out how to cast metal type from molds in the form of sturdy, uniform letters. Printing also requires good-quality, inexpensive paper that can be produced in quantity. Paper was invented by the Chinese in the second century (Chappell 1970) using native plant fibers, including mulberry and bamboo. The fibers were beaten into a pulp, then spread evenly on a cloth to dry. Papermaking technology reached Europe in 1085 when a mill opened in Játiva, Spain, producing paper made from linen fibers (Chappell 1970).

Movable type could be easily combined with woodcuts to print text and illustrations together. As a result, during the last few decades of the fifteenth century and the first few decades of the sixteenth century, the production of woodcuts reached a new level of excellence in the hands of such artists as Albrecht Dürer (1471–1528; Chappell 1970).

The growth of the printing industry was explosive. Between 1450 and 1470, printshops opened in at least fourteen cities. By 1480, there were more than 100 printshops in Europe, and by 1500, there were more than 1,100 printshops in 200 cities, which had by then printed 12 million books (Chappell 1970). By one estimate, at least 40,000 book editions had been published by

(*continued*)

BOX 5.7.
(continued)

the start of the sixteenth century (Murray 2009). Printing presses began operating in Turkey in 1503, in Romania by 1508, in Greece in 1515, in Mexico in 1534, in India in 1556, and in Japan in 1590. The first printing press in the American colonies was set up in 1638 in Cambridge, Massachusetts (Chappell 1970). The first book printed in the Americas was a bilingual Spanish and Nahuatl edition of a book of religious instruction printed in Mexico City. The first Bible printed in English North America was an Algonquian edition in 1663 (Murray 2009).

In 1565, Johannes Kentmann (1518–1574) of Torgau published a catalog of 1,600 rock and mineral specimens that were organized based on the classification of rocks and minerals in *De re metallica* (1556) by Georgius Agricola (1494–1555; Murray 1904).

In 1681, a physician named Nehemiah Grew (1641–1712) prepared a detailed catalog of the collection of the Royal Society, published under the title *Musaeum Regalis Societatis: or, a Catalogue and Description of the Natural and Artificial Rarities Belonging to the Royal Society, and Preserved at Gresham College*. The catalog includes woodcut illustrations of many of the specimens. A 1691 catalog printed in English, the *Catalogue of all the cheifest Rarities in the Publick Theater and Anatomie-Hall of the University of Leyden*, includes listings for shoes and sandals from Russia, Siam, and Egypt; the skin of a man dressed as parchment; a "drinking cup [made] of the skull of a Moor killed in the beleaguering of Haerlem" (Schuyl 1723:9); Chinese paper; Egyptian mummies; a Roman lamp believed to be capable of burning eternally; a "Hand of a Meermaide presented by Prince Mauritz" (Schuyl 1723:7); and a one-hundred-year-old mushroom (Murray 1904).

SUMMARY

At the start of the Renaissance in 1400, Europeans still thought that Jerusalem was the center of a world consisting of three continents—Europe, Asia, and Africa. Despite the fact that the Vikings had crossed the Atlantic four hundred years earlier (reaching what is now Canada from their Greenland colony), the technologies that would ultimately lead to the great era of European exploration of the world were just beginning to be developed. Before the century was over, the combination of long-range navigation skills, the use of the compass and astrolabe, and the invention of the sternpost rudder and improved rigging gave European ships the maneuverability and reliability needed for great voyages of exploration. The increased exploration brought to Europe undreamed-of riches, unfamiliar objects made by new arts and crafts, and unknown species of plants and animals that were eagerly purchased by the growing class of private collectors for their cabinets of curiosities. Using these collections to try to comprehend the world around them led to attempts to develop comprehensive systems for classifying the products of nature and objects made by human ingenuity. Toward the end of the Renaissance, as the philosophical underpinnings of the cabinets of curiosity began to shift toward rationalism, many of the collections were transformed through processes of consolidation or expansion and opened to the public, becoming the first modern museums. From this collecting, studying, and classifying, the modern museum arose in the years of the Enlightenment that followed, and with this change came the fragmentation of collections into such specializations as art, history, and science museums.

6

—⟨⟨⟩⟩—

The Museum Enlightened,
1600–1800

The Age of Enlightenment coincided with the beginnings of the scientific revolution in the early 1600s. It was a time when ideas about
science, reason, liberty, and progress dominated much of Europe. China
underwent a similar period in the Qing dynasty (beginning in the mid-
1600s), when literature and traditional art forms (particularly painting
and calligraphy) flourished and technology advanced during a long time
span of Confucian influence (Ying-Hsing 1966).

The Enlightenment was a period of aggressive imperial expansion by
many European countries and the time when the unspeakable horror
known as the Atlantic slave trade reached is height (MacGregor 2011).
Between the sixteenth and nineteenth centuries, more than 13 million
Africans were forcibly captured, removed from their homelands, and enslaved in European colonies around the world (McMillan 2002).

There were many advances in learning during the Enlightenment
brought about by the introduction of new methodologies, such as empiricism, experimentation, and inductive methods of reasoning, as well as the
institutionalization of science through the formation of the first scientific
organizations. At this time of the emergence of modernity, the making
of collections—the accumulation, classification, study, arrangement, and
display of material objects—was crucial to the examination of the role of
humans in the universe (Pearce 2010). The display of objects in collections
became a "strategic practice that aimed to both impart messages and create a visual effect" because "both the individual objects and the display as
a whole functioned as sources of information, collections being intended
to communicate on a number of levels" (Moser 2006:31). The exhibition of

objects was no longer limited to churches and cabinets of curiosities. The coffeehouses cropping up in England and elsewhere not only provided friendly venues for the discussion of new ideas but often hosted exhibitions of collections (Wittlin 1970). By 1739, there were more than five hundred coffeehouses just in London (Cuno 2011). It was during this time that the first modern menageries appeared in Europe, housing animals that were intended to be observed and studied rather than to be used for fighting or as tokens of power by the wealthy (Baratay and Hardouin-Fugier 2002), and a time when botanical gardens were established in cities across Europe (Pyenson and Sheets-Pyenson 1999).

During the Enlightenment, European cites grew in size, as workers moved from the rural countryside into urban areas, seeking new economic opportunities. The expanding industrialized sector required better-educated workers, which resulted in higher rates of literacy among the general public (literacy had previously been the privilege of the upper classes). Although literacy is difficult to define and to gauge in this period of history, evidence from signatures in parish registers and other documents has enabled scholars to make some reasonable estimates of literacy rates. In England, about 30 percent of males were literate in the 1640s, and about 65 percent were literate by the 1750s (as were about 35 to 40 percent of females). In France, between 1686 and 1690, the estimated literacy rates were 29 percent for males and 14 percent for females; by 1786 to 1790, the rates were 48 percent and 27 percent, respectively. Literacy rates were probably similar in Germany (Melton 2001). Among the factors contributing to the increase in literacy rates were better access to schools (mostly run by religious organizations) and the circulation of inexpensive printed Bibles and other books (the first authorized, widely distributed English-language translation of the Bible, the King James Version, was issued in 1611).

THE DIVERSIFICATION OF MUSEUMS

In the growing cities, improvements in public transportation made it easier for people to move about, and factory work gave people more regular hours than did farm labor. In this atmosphere, in the late eighteenth century, a "new public institution came into being—the Museum—which both reflected and fostered changing ways of life" (Wittlin 1970:81). As the modern museum emerged, the practice of collecting shifted from a focus on the strange and the unusual to emphasize objects that were more representative of the finest the world had to offer (Bennett 1995). The idea of the intentional collecting of the ordinary was still more than two hundred years in the future.

Collections became more encyclopedic and expansive as "human curiosity began directing itself away from the mystical, hidden world of the microcosm and toward the empirically knowable macrocosm" (Pyenson and Sheets-Pyenson 1999:127). It was a time when scientific notions and systematized methods were beginning to be applied to understand both nature and culture, when Francis Bacon (1561–1626) applied inductive empiricism to the cataloging of knowledge, and when René Descartes (1596–1650) rationalized (but failed to reconcile) science and religion, developments that were reflected in the nature of collections as museums diversified (Jones 1961).

As the modern museum emerged from the Renaissance cabinets of curiosities, collections became more specialized, eventually diverging into many types that, for the sake of comparison, can be grouped into three broad categories: art, history, and science museums (table 6.1). These categories are based on the nature and the use of the objects in the collections. During the Renaissance, exhibition had been the primary use of collections, but this changed with the development of the modern museum, as new and more sophisticated ways were found to use objects to understand the world. The three collection categories in table 6.1 are intentionally broad and generalized for the purposes of understanding the divergence of museums—some collection objects could be classified into two or all three of the categories (e.g., a carefully crafted jade axe

Table 6.1. The Nature of Museum Collections

Type of Museum Collection	Art	History (historic sites, halls of fame, and science and technology centers)	Science (research-based natural history and anthropology collections)
Nature of the Collection	Aesthetic	Documentary	Systematic
Nature of the Collection Objects	Reflective	Interpretive	Representative
Material Composition of Objects	Artificial	Artificial	Natural
Primary Use of Objects	Exhibition	Documentation	Research
Amount of Interpretation in Exhibition	Low	Medium to high	High
Relative Number of Objects	Small	Medium	Large
Value of Collection Objects Relative to Nature of Collection	High	Low	High
Value of Diminishing Subsets of Collection Objects	Increases	Increases	Decreases

might be categorized as a work of art for its aesthetic appeal, as a historical artifact for its cultural associations, or as a scientific specimen as a type
of metamorphic rock).

Art collections generally contain objects that are acquired primarily
(though not exclusively) to be exhibited or studied for their aesthetic
properties. These are objects of a reflective nature, given the subjectivity
of aesthetic principles and decisions and the dependence of aesthetics
on interpretation of sensory perceptions. Most objects in art collections
are composed predominantly of artificial materials (which includes processed natural materials, such as dyes, pastes, and sculpted stone).

The objects in history collections are documents of human actions
and activities or are used to interpret human actions and activities, thus
they are documentary and interpretive in nature. This category includes
objects associated with historic houses and historic sites, objects in the
collections of hall of fame–type institutions (e.g., the Rock-and-Roll Hall
of Fame in Cleveland or the Ruhmeshalle in Munich), and science and
technology centers (which use objects primarily as teaching tools). The
objects in history collections are preserved for their documentary and
interpretive nature relative to persons, places, chronological events, and
scientific or technological principles. History collection objects are primarily (though not exclusively) composed of artificial materials (including processed natural materials).

The objects in science collections are primarily objects and specimens
acquired as selections from nature that are used primarily for research,
thus these collections are systematic and representative in nature. In the
Renaissance cabinets of curiosities, the rare and the unusual were the
most highly valued objects in collections of *naturalia*, so such things as a
two-headed calf or a stone shaped like a kidney were considered appropriate objects to acquire. Beginning in the Enlightenment, changes in the
interpretation of nature meant that objects that were representative of the
variety of things found in the natural world became more valuable than
those that were exceptional and unusual.

There are, of course, specimens in science collections that are primarily aesthetic or documentary (e.g., the magnificent display of African
elephants in the Akeley Hall of Mammals in the American Museum of
Natural History), and there are objects in art and history collections that
are used for research—the categories in table 6.1 are intentionally generalized for purposes of broad comparison.

The differences in the nature of the collections, the objects in them,
and the primary use of collection objects are reflected in the amount of
interpretation of the objects when they are exhibited. Generally speaking, objects in art museums are presented with minimal interpretation—
although, since the beginning of the Enlightenment, many collections

have continued to be arranged for exhibition by artist, chronology, or school of art, the amount of information on exhibit labels is usually limited to the title and date of the work and the name of the artist. By contrast, in the exhibits of a history museum, the amount of information provided on an exhibit label is much greater and usually establishes the chronological and historic significance of the object, often providing other information as well. In a science museum, exhibit labels are very detailed, usually with extensive interpretation regarding the ecology and evolutionary history of a species represented by the specimen.

Institutional specialization of museums produced other differences in collections that are reflected in table 6.1. The refined aesthetic decisions employed to select objects for art collections resulted in collections that were finely winnowed from a broad artistic output to just those objects most valued for their aesthetic qualities, hence art collections generally are small in terms of the number of objects compared to history collections or science collections. Science collections are generally much larger than art or history collections, in part because the majority of the objects in science collections are much smaller (therefore require fewer resources to store) than the objects in art and history collections and because many more objects are needed to be representative of nature and for scientific research than are needed for the primarily aesthetic and reflective uses of objects in art collections or the primarily documentary and interpretive uses of objects in history collections.

Related to the size of the collection is the characteristic of the value of the objects relative to the nature of the collection. This value is high in an art museum because the objects are obtained primarily for purposes of exhibition. In a history museum, this value is lower because the collection is primarily documentary in nature. Most historical research, even in history museums, is not object-based (although there has been a recent increase in interest in object-based research, as discussed in chapter 9). In science museums, the value of the objects relative to the nature of the collections is high because the collections are used for the research that produces the information used to interpret the specimens.

Another aspect of relative collection size is the value of individual objects as members of a subset of the larger set that comprises the entire collection (Simmons and Muñoz-Saba 2003). The objects in art museum collections are generally valued higher if they are unique rather than one of a series (e.g., there is only one *Mona Lisa*, and it has a much higher relative value than any one of the more than six thousand terra-cotta warriors of Qin Shi Huang). Similarly, in a history museum, one-of-a-kind objects or objects that have a unique historic association are more highly valued than are series of similar objects (e.g., there is only one *Spirit of St. Louis* airplane, which has a higher relative value than any other monoplane built in the 1920s). By contrast, a single, unique specimen or archaeological artifact in a science collection has much less relative value than does a series of specimens of similar plants or animals or a series of archaeological artifacts used in research because accurate interpretation of these objects depends primarily on comparisons to similar objects (e.g., a single specimen of an unknown frog has limited value, but if it is part of a series of similar specimens, then the species it belongs to can be identified or named, its variation and relationships can be evaluated, and its ecology can be studied). Thus, the value of diminishing subsets of collection objects increases in art and history collections but decreases in science collections (see table 6.1).

During the Enlightenment, the ascent of a new class of affluent merchants and bankers (which came about as the result of the increasingly important role of mercantilism in national economies) and a corresponding decline in royal patronage systems across Europe worked together to increase public involvement in collections. From about 1760 on, the social forces instigated by the Industrial Revolution began to increase public interest in science, technology, and the arts, so that by the beginning of the nineteenth century in Europe, museums were recognized for their role in communicating nationalism and a sense of shared history (Lewis 1992). As we see in chapter 7, this rapidly brought about the emergence of the modern museum. So many new museums were founded during the nineteenth century across Europe that it is often called the Golden Age of Museums. Objects of art—particularly paintings and sculptures—began to be viewed as a means to educate the public as well as a way to instill a sense of morality that would make the populace more accepting of government by enlightened rulers. As a result, many private collections were converted to state property and became public museums (Bjurström 1993). By the eighteenth century, the museum concept was well established in both the institutional and public domains (Findlen 1994), and exhibitions were valued because "they expressed ideas and concepts that when articulated through the medium of display became more comprehensible" (Moser 2006:31). Before the nineteenth century was over, nearly every country in western Europe had opened a comprehensive national museum.

The cultural and civic changes brought about by the Enlightenment did not progress evenly across Europe. For example, by 1789, the pace of social change in Great Britain and the Netherlands was proceeding much faster than in the rest of Europe, where the questioning of traditional values and systems had barely begun. Although in many societies the Renaissance worship of the classical past was fading fast, as late as 1800, parts of Europe still espoused ideas about society and politics that were similar to those of the previous four hundred years, particularly in terms of societal organization and governance, and many people believed that history would continue more or less as it had always done (Roberts and Westad 2013).

ENLIGHTENMENT MUSEUMS

During the latter part of the Renaissance, cabinets of curiosities mediated between public space and private space, as collections were acquired and studied by private collectors but exhibited to visitors who shared newly created knowledge (Findlen 1994). Museums became significant cultural institutions (Findlen 1994)—there were at least seventy collections in Venice and surrounding towns by the end of the seventeenth century (Pomian 1990). Museums had become sufficiently important that, in his treatise on educational travel, Francis Bacon recommended visiting cabinets of curiosities and provided a list of the most important ones to see (Bredekamp 1995; see box 6.1). There were plenty of cabinets of curiosities for the traveler to choose from. Michael Bernhard Valentini (1657–1729), a German physician and collector, listed 658 collections (many with published catalogs) in an appendix to his 1714 book *Museorum Museum* (Pearce 1995).

One indication of the social significance of collecting was the shifting trends in what was acquired. An analysis of 723 collections in Paris revealed that between 1700 and 1720, some 39 percent of the collectors were interested in medals, nearly to the exclusion of all other objects, but by 1750, only 8 percent of collectors were seeking medals (Pomian 1990). During this same time span, interest in natural history specimens increased from 15 percent of collections to nearly 40 percent (Pomian 1990).

In the eighteenth century, the flowering of Enlightenment ideals, the encyclopedic spirit of inquiry, and a desire for exotic objects all influenced the growth of museum collections (Lewis 1985). For example, the objects brought back from North America by Jacques Cartier (1491–1557) on his three voyages of exploration were responsible for sparking the interest of the French royal court in collecting exotic ethnographic materials (MacGregor 1983). An interesting glimpse of the sorts of objects available to collectors comes from an advertisement by a returning seaman who was trying to locate his traveling trunk, which had been stolen after his ship docked in port. The advertisement was placed in the *Amsterdamse Courant* on October 11, 1695, promising a reward for the return of the chest, which contained porcelain objects, ornamental vases, birds' nests, a bow and arrow, an ivory box with silver ornaments, a writing box from Japan, a tea table, and some exotic textiles, probably all intended for sale to supplement the sailor's meager pay (Blom 2002). In the seventeenth century,

BOX 6.1.
Francis Bacon's Travel Tips

The English philosopher, scientist, and statesman Francis Bacon, Viscount St. Alban (1561–1626), wrote a series of influential essays on various topics. In one essay entitled "Of Travaile" ("Of Travel"), Bacon recommends travel, study, and keeping a journal for both young people and mature adults as a means of gaining knowledge and experience of the world. Bacon's list of places that should not be missed while traveling includes archaeological ruins, cabinets of curiosities, and collections of rarities:

Travaile, in the younger Sort, is a Part of Education; In the Elder a Part of Experience. He that *travaileth* into a Country, before he hath some Entrance into the Language, goeth to *Schoole*, and not to *Travaile*. That Young Men travaile under some Tutor or grave Servant, I allow well; So that he be such a one that hath the Language, and hath been in the Country before; whereby he may be able to tell them what Things are worthy to be seen in the Country where they goe, what Acquaintances they are to seeke, what Exercises or discipline the Place yeeldeth; for else young Men shall goe hooded, and look abroad little. It is a strange Thing, that in Sea voyages, where there is nothing to be seene but Sky and Sea, Men should make Diaries; but in *Land-Travaile*, wherein so much is to be observed, for the most part they omit it; As if Chance were fitter to be registered than Observation. Let Diaries, therefore, be brought in use. The Things to be seene and observed are: The Courts of Princes, specially when they give Audience to Ambassadours; the Courts of Justice, while they sit and heare Causes; And so of Consistories Ecclesiasticke: The Churches and Monasteries, with the Monuments which are therein extant: The Wals and Fortifications of Cities and Townes; And so the Havens & Harbours: Antiquities, and Ruines: Libraries: Colledges, Disputations, and Lectures, where any are: Shipping and Navies: Houses, and Gardens of State and Pleasure, neare great Cities: Armories: Arsenals: Magazens: Exchanges: Burses; Ware-houses: Exercises of Horseman-ship; Fencing, Trayning of Soldiers; and the like: Comedies; Such wherunto the better Sort of persons doe resort; Treasuries of Jewels, and Robes; Cabinets, and Rarities: And, to conclude, whatsoever is memorable in the Places; where they goe. (quoted in Kiernan 1995:56–57)

From the essay "Of Travaile" in *The Essayes or Counsels, Civill and Morall, of Francis Bacon, lo Verulam, Viscount St. Alban*, printed by John Haviland for Hanna Barret, London, in 1625.

shops could be found in many European cities, including Amsterdam, Lisbon, London, Paris, and Rome, that catered to collectors by selling both authentic and inauthentic rarities—everything from dried animals to ethnographic artifacts to ceramics, pictures, plaster casts, jewelry and precious stones, sculptures, deformed fetuses, and thousands of other objects and fakes (MacGregor 1983). The faking of collectible objects is probably as old as collecting itself (Bruhns and Kelker 2010). Some collectors were able to utilize personal connections to acquire particularly spectacular objects, such as John Tradescant the Elder and John Tradescant the Younger (father and son), who took advantage of their connections to both royalty and the British government to enlarge their collections, and Athanasius Kircher, who was supplied with exotic objects by his fellow Jesuits serving abroad as missionaries (MacGregor 1983).

Athanasius Kircher (1602–1680) was a polymath Jesuit priest who taught in Rome at the Collegio Romano, where he assembled one of the best-known, most influential collections at the close of the era of cabinets of curiosities and birth of the modern museum. Kircher's museum (figure 6.1) featured vaulted ceilings, large exhibition galleries, and objects displayed on pedestals in imitation of many royal palace collection spaces. While it was judiciously decorated with busts and obelisks, the museum did not have the overcrowded appearance of many cabinets of curiosities, such that a "major new convention has been introduced to the didactic study collections, with the space within which the objects were arranged asserting itself as a central component in the overall display strategy" (Moser 2006:30). Kircher closely studied the objects in his collection and believed that he had managed to interpret the inscriptions on several Egyptian obelisks (although this would later be proven to be incorrect). A catalog of Kircher's collection was published

Figure 6.1.   Das Kircher-Museum im Collegium Romanum. Abb. in "Turris Babel" (Amsterdam, ca. 1679). *Source:* Book scan of Alexander Roos, *Alchemie & Mystik*, 576 S., Köln u.a.; unknown artist.

in 1678, but within a century of Kircher's death, a "new generation of scholars invalidated the premise of the humanist encyclopedia of nature and, with it, the museums that contained this knowledge," so that Kircher's collections, too, are now mostly gone (Findlen 1994:393). No doubt a contributing factor to the loss of Kircher's collections was the inadequate preservation technologies of the period.

The Tradescant Ark

The first public museum in England was the result of the near-obsessive collecting activities of John Tradescant the Elder (ca. 1570–1638) and his son, John Tradescant the Younger (1608–1662). Their collection was particularly popular with the public, despite the fact that at the time there were many other collections in London competing for attention (MacGregor 1983). London had expanded significantly to become an important center of commerce and culture. In 1550, the population of London was estimated to be about 50,000, but by 1600, it had grown to more than 200,000 to become the largest city in Europe (Harkness 2007).

The Tradescants lived in South Lambeth (now part of greater London). Both father and son were gardeners with connections to many wealthy clients, royalty, and government officials. Both Tradescants traveled widely in search of new plants (and objects for their collection) to bring back to England. Tradescant the Elder journeyed through the Low Countries, Russia, the Levant, Algiers, and France; Tradescant the Younger went to the colony in Virginia (Potter 2006). Among the plant species that they brought back and acclimatized to England were horse chestnuts, lilacs, plane trees, larches, acacias, tulip trees, and the Virginia creeper (Blom 2002; Potter 2006).

The Tradescants made good use of their connections to amass an extensive collection, which they exhibited (for an entrance fee) in Lambeth. The Tradescant collection was called the Ark to emphasize its worldwide scope (Potter 2006). Tradescant the Elder enlisted the help of the secretary of the admiralty in 1625 by asking that British sailors be instructed to bring back objects "that be Rare or Not knowne to us," as well as "Any thing that Is strang" (quoted in Swann 2001:31). Over time, the Tradescants acquired an astonishing variety of objects both mundane and unusual, including "Cloven and hairy-tongued Lizards" and "A natural Dragon, above two inches long" (Tradescant 1656:6), "Divers sorts of Ambers (with Flyes, Spiders, naturall)" (Tradescant 1656:36); an "Indian lip-stone which they wear in the lip" and "Halfe a Hasle-nut with 70 pieces of housholdstuffe" inside it (Tradescant 1656:37); an "Indian Idol made of Feathers, in shape of a Dog" (Tradescant 1656:42); a piece of "Stone of Saint *John Baptists* Tombe" and a piece of the "Stone of *Diana's*

Tomb" (Tradescant 1656:43); "Hat-bands of Porcupine Quills beaten flat and dyde" (Tradescant 1656:49); "Napkins made from the rinds of trees" and a "Variety of Chains, made of the teeth of serpents and wilde beasts, which the Indians weare" (Tradescant 1656:51); and a "Turkish toothbrush" and "Gurgolets to poure water into their mouthes without touching it" (Tradescant 1656:53).

The Tradescant Catalog

After his father's death in 1638, Tradescant the Younger continued to develop the collection. As the fame of the Ark spread, numerous accounts of it were written by visitors. By this time, collection catalogs had become their own literary genre that interpreted the objects of a collection (Swann 2001), so Tradescant sought the services of Elias Ashmole (1617–1692), a lawyer interested in astrology and alchemy, and his friend Thomas Wharton (1614–1673) to help catalog the collections. Ashmole already had a reputation as a cataloger based on his work on royal collections (Swann 2001). The catalog was not an easy task to complete, as the objects included natural history specimens, precious stones, weapons, coins, carvings, paintings, medallions, and other treasures from all over the known world. In addition to the magnitude of the task, Tradescant the Younger had not had an easy time of it—among other setbacks, his nineteen-year-old son had recently died.

The completed catalog, which was published in 1656, includes an introduction by Tradescant the Younger, followed by the listings of the objects in the collection written (at least primarily) by Ashmole, a list of Tradescant plants based on two previous lists compiled by Tradescant the Elder, and a list of the collection's benefactors. A two-page section following the introduction with the title of "A view of the whole" summarizes the catalog's classification system but with some minor, though interesting, differences with the catalog's categories (table 6.2).

In his introduction to the catalog *Musaeum Tradescantianum: or, A Collection of Rarities. Preserved at South-Lambert neer London by John Tradescant,* Tradescant writes,

> To the Ingenious Reader. For some *reasons* I apprehend myself engaged to give an account of *two* things, that refer to the ensuing piece: The one, for not *publishing* this *Catalogue* untill now: The other, of the *mode* & *manner* thereof, being partly Latine, and partly English.
>
> About three yeares agoe, (by the perswasion of some *friends*) I was resolved to take a *Catalogue* of those *Rarities* and *Curiosities* which my *Father* had acidulously *collected,* and my *selfe* with continued diligence have *augmented,* & hitherto *preserved* together: They then pressed me with that Argument, *That the enumeration of these Rarities, (being more for variety than any*

Table 6.2. Organization of the Tradescant Collection, 1656

A View of the Whole	Catalog Listing
1-Birds with their egges, beaks, feathers, clawes, spurres	I-Some kindes of Birds their Egges, Beaks, Feathers, Clawes, and Spurres (pages 1–4)
	1-Egges 2-Beaks, or Heads 3-Feathers 4-Clawes 5-Whole Birds
2-Fourfooted beasts with some of their hides, hornes, and hoofs	II-Fourfooted Beasts, with some Hides, Hornes, Hoofs (pages 5–7) Animalia quadrup. I digit. vivipera
	1-fera 2-semifera Digitata ovipara Quadrup. Soliped Quadrup. bifulsa
3-Diverse sorts of strange fish's	III-Some Fishes and their parts (pages 8–9) Animalia squatilia
	1-Sanguinea
4-Shell-creatures, whereof some are called Mollia, some Crustacea, others Testacea, of these, are both univalvia, and bivalvia	IV-Aquatilia exsanguinea Testacea (pages 10–14)
5-Several sorts of Insects, terrestrial (anelytra, coleoptera, aptera, apoda)	V-Insecta & serpentes (pages 14–17)
6-Mineralls and those of neare nature with them as Earths, Coralls, Salts, Bitumens, Petrified things, choicer Stones, Gemmes	VI-Fosilia (pages 17–34) 1-Metallica [and Metallica factitia] 2-Terrae 3-Succi concreti macri 4-Succi concreti pingues 5-Lapides selectiores 6-Materie petrificatae 7-Gemmae
7-Outlandish Fruits from both the Indies, with seeds, Gummes, roots, Woods, and divers Ingredients Medicinall, and for the Art of Dying	VII-Fructus Exotici (pages 34–36) Materialls of Dyers and Painters 1-For Blacks 2-For Yellowes 3-For Reds 4-For Blewes 5-For White

Table 6.2. *(continued)*

A View of the Whole	Catalog Listing
8-Mechanicks, choice pieces in Carvings, Turnings, Paintings	VII-Mechanick artificiall Works in Carvings, Turnings, Sewings and Paintings (pages 36–41)
9-Other variety of Rarities	VIII-Variety of Rarities (pages 42–44)
10-Warlike Instruments, European, Indian, &c.	IX-Warlike Instruments (pages 44–46)
11-Garments, Habits, Vests, Ornaments	X-Garments, Vestures, Habits, Ornaments (pages 47–51)
12-Utensils, and Housholdstuffe	X-Utensils (pages 52–55)
13-Numismata, Coynes ancient and modern, both gold, silver, and copper, Hebrew, Greeke, Roman, both Imperial and Consular	XI-Nomismata (pages 56–66) Aurea Moderna Moneta Aurea Nomismata Hebraica Nomismata Graca Nomismata Romana secunda Familia Nomismata Imperatorum
14-Medalls, gold, silver, copper, and lead	XIV-Medalls (pages 66–72) Gold Silver Copper and Lead Several sorts of Modern Moneyes from most Countries in Europe Moneys from beleaguered Cities, &c.
15-*Hortus Tradescantianus* 16-An enumeration of his Plants, Shrubs, and Trees both in English and Latine	XV-Catalogus *Plantarum in Horto* Johannis Tredescanti, *nascentium* (pages 73–178)
16-A Catalogue of his Benefactors	Principall Benefactors to the precent Collection (pages 179–193)

one place known in Europe *could afford) would be an honour to our Nation and a benefit to such ingenious persons as would become further enquirers into the various modes of Natures admirable works, and the curious Imitators thereof:* I readily yeilded to the thing so urged, and with the assistance of two worthy *friends* (well acquainted with my design,) we then began it, and many *examinations* of the *materialls* themselves, & their *agreements* with several Authors *compared,* a *Draught* was made, which they gave into my hands to examine over. Presently thereupon my *onely Sonn dyed,* one of my *Friends* fell very *sick* for about *a yeare* and my *other Friend* by unhappy *Law-suits* much disturbed. Upon these accidents that *first Draught* lay neglected *in my hand* another year. Afterward my said Friends call again upon me, and the design of *Printing* a-new contrivead, onely the prefixed Pictures were not ready and I found my kinde friend Mr. Hollar then engaged for about tenne Moneths, for whole hand to finish the Plates, I was necessarily constrained to stayt until this time. (Tradescant 1656:22–26)

The Dunghill Caper

After the death of Tradescant the Younger, Ashmole began a series of lawsuits and legal maneuvers to obtain control of the Tradescant collection, even though the widow, Hester Pookes Tradescant (ca. 1608–1678), resisted his attempts. Swann demonstrates that the "relationship between collecting, cataloguing, and personal prestige in Ashmole's quest for enhanced status becomes most evident in his attempt to gain ownership of the Tradescant collection" (Swann 2001:44). In 1674, Ashmole moved into the house next door to Hester Tradescant. Among other annoyances, Ashmole sued Hester Tradescant over a dunghill that was piled against a common wall in Tradescant's backyard that Ashmole claimed allowed thieves to enter his property and rob him. Finally, early one morning in 1678, Hester Tradescant was found drowned in a shallow lake on the grounds of her Lambeth property, and with her death, Ashmole was able to take full possession of the collection (Swann 2001). Ashmole donated the Tradescant collection to Oxford University as the Ashmolean collection on the condition that Oxford provide a proper home for it. The Ashmolean Museum at Oxford, which opened in 1683, established the pattern for modern university museums with space for exhibition, collection storage, and offices for the teaching staff associated with the university (Boylan 1999).

It has been noted that "Tradescant's rarities were not top-of-the-range collecting items; they were amusing, interesting, or exotic pieces about which it was possible to tell stories" (Pearce 2010:17), and there were many other comparable cabinets of curiosities in London and throughout Europe at the time (MacGregor 1983). Nevertheless, the collection was extremely popular and influential when on exhibit, both at South

Lambeth and later at Oxford, in large part because of the widely read catalog and numerous descriptions by visitors. A close examination of the Tradescant catalog reveals other reasons this collection was so popular, as it exhibited not just the expected rare and unusual but also several natural history specimens that confronted common myths of the era (see box 6.2). Other factors contributing to the popularity of the Tradescant collection include its size, accessibility, and the family's connections to the ruling elite of England. The catalog of the collection was published on the cusp of the great transition between the Renaissance cabinets of curiosities and modern museums.

BOX 6.2.
A Closer Look at the Tradescant Catalog

The catalog of the Tradescant collection was published under the title *Musaeum Tradescantianum: or, A Collection of Rarities. Preserved at South-Lambeth neer London by John Tradescant*. Following the introduction, a section titled "A view of the whole" summarizes the catalog's classification system but differs slightly from the catalog categories (see table 6.2). The catalog proper takes up 193 pages. Because the catalog was produced at a crucial time of transition between the cabinets of curiosities and the emergence of the modern museum, it bears examining closely.

The first section (on birds and their associated parts) is a fairly straightforward alphabetical listing that occupies four pages of text. Under the subheading of bird "Egges," one specimen is referred to as a "Cassawary, or Emeu," with the citation, "*vide Aldrov*: p. 542," a reference to Aldrovandi, who published three volumes on birds between 1599 and 1603. At the time Tradescant's catalog was written, Aldrovandi was still widely recognized as the best authority on world natural history. Both the cassowary and the emu are large flightless birds native to Australia (the cassowary is also found in New Guinea). *Emeu* is the Dutch spelling of *emu*, but at this point in time, very few specimens of either species had reached Europe, so there was still much confusion about the identity of the emu and the cassowary. Aldrovandi's knowledge of the birds came from an account of a live cassowary that was brought to Europe by a Dutch expedition led by Cornelis de Houtman (1565–1599) to Java between 1595 and 1597 (Lai 2013). Although Aldrovandi did not see the specimen himself, he did include the species in his book based on the published reports of the expedition. The next entry under "Egges" is "Crocodiles." Unlike most reptile eggs, which are soft and leathery, the eggs of crocodilians have thick, hard shells, so the grouping of crocodile eggs with bird eggs is not all that unusual, particularly considering how little was known about crocodiles in Europe at the time. The third curious listing under the heading of "Egges" is for "Easter

(continued)

BOX 6.2.
(continued)

Egges of the Patriarchs of *Jerusalem*," which is probably a reference to ostrich eggs that had been painted red and decorated with a cross or other Christian symbols, a craft that dates back to the early Christians of Mesopotamia and is mentioned in Catholic literature as early as 1610.

The next subheading is "Beaks, or Heads," which also lists the "Cassawary, or Emeu." No explanation is provided for how the specimens were prepared, but presumably they were either dried skins of birds or possibly mounted specimens (although taxidermy was then in its infancy). The next entry is for a "Griffin," which is a mythical animal, followed by a pelican, a shoveler (a type of duck), and "thirty other several forrain sorts, not found in any Author," an indication of the frustration that the identification of unknown species caused the European naturalists.

The next subsection is "Feathers," which has several more alphabetically listed birds, including "Two feathers of the Phoenix tayle." The phoenix was another mythical bird, although sometimes the name was also applied to birds of paradise (discussed below).

The "Clawes" subheading begins with "The claw of the bird Rock; who, as Authors report, is able to trusse an Elephant." This entry combines an old legend with a new biological reality. The roc is a giant flying bird of Arabic folklore, but the elephant bird (*Aepyornis maximus*) was a giant flightless bird (more than ten feet tall) that lived on Madagascar until becoming extinct in the seventeenth or eighteenth century. Sailors, reasonably enough, often confounded the legend of the roc with the actual elephant bird. Also in this section is a listing for "A legge and claw of the Cassaway or Emeu that dyed at S. James's, Westminster," which may (or may not) be the source of the egg and head (more on the St. James menagerie below).

The bird names under the "Whole Birds" subheading are not listed in alphabetical order but include "Batts." Bats are mammals, but their inclusion with birds was not unusual in classifications of this era. Bats are also included with birds in the Bible (Leviticus 11:19). There is an entry for a "Dodar, from the Island Mauritius; it is not able to flie being so big." The dodar refers to the dodo (*Raphus cucullatus*), a large flightless bird that is native to the island of Mauritius. The dodo became extinct following contact with Europeans. The first mention of the dodo in Western literature was in 1598; the last recorded sighting of a live dodo in the wild was in 1662. It is, in fact, the first species documented to have been driven to extinction by the actions of human beings. The head and neck of the Tradescant specimen ended up at the Ashmolean Museum. The dodo later became an icon of English literature thanks to its appearance in Lewis Carroll's *Alice in Wonderland* (Potter 2006).

The listing of various "Birds of Paradise, or Manucodiata; whereof are diverse sorts, some with, some without leggs" is significant. The bird of paradise was also known as the manucodiata, which is derived from the Malay name for the birds, *manute-dewata,* meaning "the bird of the gods." This is a family (Paradisaeidae) of forty-one species of beautiful birds, some with extraordinarily long tail feathers, that are native to New Guinea and Australia. Specimens were typically preserved without legs, provoking the legend that the birds flew constantly and never landed (see chapter 5). What was different about the Tradescant specimens is that some of them did have their legs, thus refuting the endless flying myth (the first bird of paradise specimens to arrive in Europe with their legs still attached had been denounced as fakes).

Near the end of the bird list are "Barnacles, four sorts" which refers to an avian vertebrate rather than the marine invertebrate of the same name. The barnacle goose was a staple of the medieval bestiaries (Payne 1990), a bird believed to hatch from barnacles growing on trees overhanging the water.

The catalog listings for the "Cassaway or Emeu that dyed at S. James's, Westminester" and "A Does head and horns, from Saint *James*'s Parke neer London" emphasize the Tradescants' connections to the royal family and high government officials, which enabled them to acquire several exotic animals that had once been maintained alive in English menageries. St. James's Park in Westminster (central London) was originally marshland purchased by Henry VIII in 1532, then drained and landscaped in 1603 by James I. The park long included a royal menagerie of exotic animals.

The category of "Fourfooted Beasts, with some Hides, Hornes, Hoofs" distinguishes between *fera* (wild) animals and some *semifera* (semiwild) species and also uses some of the Latin categories of Aldrovandi and others. The names in this section are not in alphabetical order, but it is unclear if they were listed following a system or just randomly. The listing includes a "Hares head, with rough horns three inches long." European hares with horns were recorded and illustrated in a number of publications at this time. The horn is actually a tumor that is the result of a viral infection and is the source of the legend of the famous *wolpertinger* of Bavaria and the jackalope of the American southwest (Fenner, McAuslan, and Mims 1974).

The category of "Some Fishes and their parts" includes whales, which is not unusual as whales (which are mammals) were commonly thought to be fishes. The story of the prophet Jonah in the King James Version of the Bible (first published in 1611) specifically states that Jonah was swallowed by a "great fish" (Jonah 1:17), although popularly the animal that God prepared was almost always referred to and depicted as a whale, and in Matthew 12:40 it is referred to as a whale. In Sūrah 37:142 of the Quran, the animal that swallowed Jonah is called a "big fish" or "great fish."

Listed among the fishes (just after the whales) is a specimen referred to as *Unicornum marinum* (marine unicorn), referring to a unicorn's horn. For centuries, the elongeated, helical upper-left canine of the narwhal (*Monodon monoceros*) had been valued in collections as a unicorn horn. Tradescant's recording of the unicorn horn as belonging to a marine animal debunks the unicorn myth (MacGregor 1983).

(continued)

BOX 6.2.
(continued)

The listings for the fourth category, the "Shell-creatures," are well organized and consist mostly of Latin names, an indication of how common seashells had become in collections and how widely recognized certain forms
were. Curiously, section 5 is listed simply as insects in the introduction but
is "Insecta & Serpentes" in the catalog and does, in fact, include a short list
of snakes and snakelike animals in alphabetical order, following the alphabetical list of insects. Presumably these species are listed here because they
were not recognized as quadrupeds ("Fourfooted beasts"). Several of the
snake names are still in use today. Included in the list is the amphisbaena, a
legless relative of snakes and lizards but also a creature often mythologized
in medieval bestiaries. Real amphisbaenians have blunt tails about the same
size and shape as their heads, but the mythical amphisbaena had a head
on each end of its body. The Tradescant catalog list includes a caecilian,
which is a snakelike, legless amphibian found only in the tropics, and an
"Anguis Aeseulapii, Ova, sceleton" which is possibly a mixed-up entry. The
anguis, or slow-worm (genus *Anguis*), is a legless lizard. *Aeseulapii* refers
to Aesculapius' snake (*Zamenis longissimus*), a nonvenomous snake of the
family Colubridae. Both the anguis and Aesculapius' snakes are found across
Europe and into Asia, so it is curious that these two would be confused
in the catalog. *Ova* refers to an egg (slow-worms give birth to live young;
Aesculapius' snakes lay eggs), and *sceleton* to a skeleton of one or the other.
The name of Aesculapius' snake is a reference to the classical god of healing (*Asclepius* in Greek, *Aesculapius* in Latin). It is Aesculapius' snake that is
depicted entwined around the staff that Aesculapius carries that has become
a modern-day symbol of the medical profession.

Section 6 includes minerals, rocks, corals, salts, bitumen, petrified things,
and gemstones, all referred to simply as "Fosilia" (things from the ground) in
the catalog but divided more neatly into categories. Included in this section
are mummia and lapis bezoar. Mummia could be either a resinous substance
(a tree sap) used to prepare mummies (MacGregor 1983) or asphaltum (a natu-
rally occurring form of petroleum), which was also used to prepare mummies.
Lapis Bezoar orientalis and *occidentalis* are bezoar stones, a common object
in the collections of cabinets of curiosities and long believed to be antidotes
to poison. A bezoar can be either a gastrolith (a stomach stone) or a hardened
hairball found in the stomach of an animal. Bezoars were highly valued and
sold throughout Europe. Section 7 is called "Outlandish Fruits" in the introduction and "Fructus Exotici" (exotic fruits) in the catalog proper. Included in
this category are substances used for five colors of dye.

The numbering in the catalog goes awry with section 8, mechanical devices, carvings, and paintings, as this section is also numbered 7 in the catalog.

Things that don't seem to fit anywhere else are clumped together in section 9 of the introduction (section 8 of the catalog) as "Other variety of Rarities." Section 10 of the introduction and section 9 of the catalog are "Warlike Instruments," sections 11, 12, and 13 of the introduction correspond to sections 10 (which is repeated) and 11 of the catalog. The numbers again match with section 14, medals and coins.

A surprising number of the original ethnographic objects from the Tradescant collection have survived the passage of time. Although these take up only ten pages in the catalog, there were objects from every continent then known in the collection (MacGregor 1983).

The longest section of the catalog is section 15, the "*Hortus Tradescantianus*" or "Tradescant's Garden," which occupies pages 73 to 178 of the text. As might be expected from professional gardeners who explored the world for new plants, this section is a very orderly listing of plants by their then-generally-recognized compound Latin names, followed by an English name for many species. Although Latin names for plants were already widely used in Europe, they were far from standardized—in many instances, the name itself was a detailed description of the plant, such as *Plantago foliis ovato-lanceolatis pubescentibus spica cylindrical scapo tereti* for the hoary plantain, now known as *Plantago media* (Pavord 2005). This would radically change in another hundred years, when Linnaeus published his system of Latin binomials for plants in *Species plantarum* in 1753.

The last section of the catalog is a listing of Tradescant's benefactors—this list, too, is neatly ordered and hierarchical, beginning with the king and queen and progressing through dukes and duchesses to the archbishop, earls, lords and ladies, knights, captains, and then people without titles.

The Tradescants' birds of paradise (with and without legs); the barnacles from which barnacle geese were thought to arise; the confusion over the identity of the cassowary and the emu; mixing crocodile eggs with bird eggs; listing the claw of a roc but also a dodo; and not being sure how to classify snakes, amphisbaenians, slow-worms, and caecilians, much less bezoars tell us much about this period of history. It was a time of both expanding knowledge and confusion—the voyages of exploration that opened the world to Europeans also brought down many long-held beliefs and cherished systems of order. The catalog entries discussed here allow us to glimpse a time when the existence of creatures of folklore and legend was being affirmed or disproven, a time when a millennium of knowledge was being turned on its head, largely from the close study of museum collections. A full discussion of the extant objects and specimens from the Tradescant collection now in the Ashmolean Museum at Oxford University can be found in MacGregor (1983).

THE THEATRUM ANATOMICUM

Built in 1594, the Theatrum Anatomicum at the University of Leiden was a lecture hall where dissections of human cadavers took place under the watchful eyes of physicians, medical students, and the paying public (Huisman 2009). The anatomy theater also served as an exhibition area for the university medical museum (Schumacher 2007). According to a 1617 inventory, the collection then consisted of about 16,500 objects from all over the world, including 300 ethnographic artifacts, 150 writing implements, 8,700 marine products, 130 antiquities (including Egyptian artifacts), 230 parts of animals, 250 relics and biblical *naturalia*, 1,900 fruits and seeds, 230 mineral specimens, 1,300 coins, and 3 mummies.

Beginning in 1691, several editions of a catalog of the collection were published under the title *A Catalogue of all the cheifest Rarities in the Publick Theater and Anatomie-Hall of the University of Leyden.* Among the objects listed are "The Sceleton of a Scheep-stealer from Haarlem" and "The Sceleton of a Woman called *Catharine* of *Hamburg*, strangled for theft" (Schuyl 1723:5); "The Sceleton of an Asse upon which sit's a Woman that Killed her Daughter's Child" (Schuyl 1723:4); "The Sceleton of a Man, sitting upon an Ox executed for Stealling Cattle" and "The Sceleton of a Lepus Marinus a Fish comonly swimming in the midst of the Sea, and casting Snot out of it's mouth" (Schuyl 1723:5); and "Five Sorts of Colours, of Man's Skin in Frames" (Schuyl 1723:13). The general public was admitted to the theater in the summer months, when classes were not in session—two skeletons would be placed on the dissecting table, symbolizing Adam and Eve and the consequences of original sin (MacGregor 1983).

OTHER NOTABLE COLLECTIONS

In 1693, the English scientist and traveler John Ray (1627–1705) wrote a book about his European journey that includes a description of a cabinet of curiosities, "That of seignior *Mapheus Cusanus* an apothecary, wherein were shewn us many ancient *Aegyptian* idols, taken out of the mummies, divers sorts of petrified shells, petrified cheese, cinnamon, spunge and mushromes" (Ray 1693:186). A beautiful example of the artistic and intellectual complexity of some of the late Renaissance–style cabinets of curiosities is an actual cabinet given to King Gustavus Adolphus of Sweden by a group of Lutherans from Augsburg in 1632 (Daston and Park 2001). The design and production of the cabinet had been supervised by a local merchant and collector named Philipp Hainhofer (1578–1647). The cabinet itself was made of ebony and oak, inlaid inside and out with gemstones, paintings on enamel and marble, mother of pearl, and exotic wood. Many of the objects inside the cabinet were hidden behind secret doors or in secret compartments. The objects in the cabinet included a gold goblet, shells and corals, a music box, a nautilus shell covered in silver decorations, mathematical instruments, a mummified monkey hand, and dozens of other wonders.

FROM CABINETS OF CURIOSITIES TO THE BRITISH MUSEUM

An even larger and more impressive collection than the Tradescant Ark was assembled by Sir Hans Sloane (1660–1753), a doctor who spent time in Jamaica as personal physician to the island's governor. While in Jamaica, Sloane began acquiring botanical specimens, returning to England with eight hundred species of plants. Sloane continued his collecting activities, including the purchase of the collections of others. Among the many collections Sloane acquired was that of apothecary and collector James Petiver (ca. 1665–1718), known for his wide correspondence and printed instructions for travelers who collected for him (Stearns 1953). Sloane kept adding objects until his collections were encyclopedic in scope (Swann 2001). A summary of the Sloane collection as of 1725 (twenty years before he ceased active collecting) is provided in table 6.3. Sloane's collection and library were purchased by the British government after his death in 1753, using funds from a lottery—the Sloane collection was to became the core of the British Museum (Murray 1904).

The British Museum was founded by an act of Parliament in June 1753 with the purchase of the Sloane collection and two additional libraries—the Harleian Library and that of Sir Robert Cotton. A third book collection (the Royal Library) was added in 1757. The inclusion of the library in the museum is significant, as the British Museum was a new, national museum open to the public and with a broad collecting mission that set a standard that many other countries tried to emulate. The library was considered a fundamental research tool necessary to make full use of the collections.

The museum opened its doors to the public in January 1759 in a seventeenth-century London mansion named Montagu House (on the site of the present museum). The collections began to expand, particularly as British voyages of exploration made their way around the world. From the outset, the museum was intended to be both for the public and for scholars. The emphasis on a wide range of collections was in keeping with Enlightenment ideals (Cuno 2011; Lewis 1985).

Early descriptions of the museum refer to the collection of antiquities being mixed up and ill-sorted, but this may have been in part due to the

Table 6.3.   The Collection of Sir Hans Sloane Based on the 1725 Inventory

Category	Number of Objects
Earths, bitumens, metals, minerals, stones, fossils	5,497
Corals	804
Vegetables and vegetable substances	8,226
Dried plants	200
Insects	3,824
Shells	3,753
Echini crustacea, fishes, etc.	1,939
Birds	568
Eggs	185
Quadrupeds and their parts	1,195
Vipers and serpents	345
Humana	507
Miscellaneous objects, natural and artificial	1,169
Things relating to customs of ancient times or antiquities, urns, instruments, etc.	302
Large seals	81
Pictures, many relating to natural history	319
Mathematical instruments	54
Large vessels, handles, and other things made of agats, jaspes, cornelians, christals, besides many camel and seals, *excisa* and *incisa*	441
Coins and medals, ancient and modern	20,228
Books in miniature or colors, with drawings of plants, etc., and various natural and artificial curiosities	136
Books of prints	580
Volumes of manuscripts, the greater part of them relating to physick and natural history, travels, etc.	2,666
Books on medicine, natural history, chemistry, anatomy, etc.	40,000

Source: Murray 1904.

limitations of using an old mansion for a museum. The first Egyptian antiquities in the British Museum collections were among the objects acquired with the Sloane collection. For many decades thereafter, the Egyptian collection (including a mummy) and a selection of natural curiosities were the first things a visitor to the museum saw when entering the first exhibit gallery (Moser 2006). It was not until the early 1800s that the British Museum began to acquire more significant Egyptian artifacts, including inscriptions, papyri, sculptures, and hieroglyphs. For many years the museum contained more artifacts from ancient Rome than it did from ancient Egypt, which may have been due to audience interests or, more likely, to the ease with which Roman objects could be obtained and shipped to England compared to Egyptian objects. However, this soon changed, and between 1759 and 1880, the acquisition and display of artifacts redefined the British public's perception of ancient Egypt, particularly through a series of five major exhibitions of the British Museum Egyptian collections that constructed "distinct identities for ancient Egypt" through compelling stories (Moser 2006:217).

Museum Wormianum

Perhaps the best-known cabinet of curiosities of the late Renaissance was one that belonged a physician and teacher named Ole (Olaus) Worm (1588–1654) of Copenhagen. The fame of the Worm cabinet is largely due to the wide distribution of a woodcut depicting the collection that appeared in his catalog *Museum Wormianum* in 1655 (figure 6.2). Worm studied in Germany and Switzerland and visited several cabinets of curiosities, including those of Ferrante Imperato (1525–1625) in Naples in 1609 and Bernard Paludanus (Berend Ten Brocke, 1550–1633) in the Netherlands in 1610. Worm later corresponded and sometimes traded specimens with scholars throughout Europe (Hafstein 2003; MacGregor 1983).

Worm was a physician and teacher who received his medical degree in 1611. For his dissertation, he compiled an extensive catalog of diseases and their cures (Hafstein 2003), demonstrating his propensity for organization and categorizing. Worm probably began building his collection,

Figure 6.2. The Museum Wormianum, 1655. *Source: Museum Wormianum* (1655); Smithsonian Institution Libraries.

which he confined to *naturalia* and ethnographic artifacts, in 1620 (Findlen 2000; Mauriès 2002). In letters to fellow collectors, Worm explained that his collection was made for the purpose of increasing knowledge. Worm particularly wanted visitors to his museum "to touch with their own hands and see with their own eyes so that they may themselves judge how that which is said fits with the things, and can acquire a more intimate knowledge of them all" (quoted in Hafstein 2003:7). Worm used his collections to teach his students, and his catalog descriptions often noted how the specimens could be used medicinally (Neverov 1985).

The depiction of the Worm collection in the woodcut shows how the use of symmetry and patterned effect had become a convention of exhibition practice by the mid-1600s (Moser 2006). In the Worm museum, we can see neat labels, a number of ethnographic objects (bows and arrows, kayaks and paddles, sealskin clothing, spears, musical instruments), and many natural history specimens (all preserved dry but including taxidermy preparations, turtle shells, skulls, horns, antlers, shells, rocks and minerals, and an armadillo). There is a narwhal tooth in a window recess, significant because Worm had refuted the claim that it was a unicorn's horn in 1638. Although there are specimens dangling from the ceiling, the room is not as crowded as were many other cabinets of curiosities from the same period. There is a close relationship between the arrangement of objects in the image and in Worm's catalog (Moser 2006). In cabinets of this era, objects of *naturalia* were usually organized based on principles derived from Pliny the Elder's *Naturalis Historia* (which had been rediscovered by Renaissance scholars) or based on their raw materials, form, or function (Yaya 2008). The depiction of Worm's museum in the woodcut is considered to be very accurate based on the number of identifiable objects that can be seen in it (Moser 2006). After Worm's death, his collection was purchased by King Frederic II (1609–1670) and integrated into his own Museum Regium, which in turn was eventually dispersed to other museums in Copenhagen (Dahlbom 2009; Gundestrup 1985).

The production and circulation of collection catalogs enabled Worm and other early Enlightenment collectors to display their objects to a wider audience than had been available to their predecessors (Hafstein 2003). Worm's catalog, for example, went through three editions, beginning with a simple inventory in 1642. In 1645, Worm published a revised inventory, and he spent the last few years of his life working on a full account of the collection, which was published posthumously in 1655 as *Museum Wormianum* (Hafstein 2003). The catalog sorts the collection into the categories of minerals (Book I); plants (Book II); animals, including man (Book III); and *artificiosis*, or things made by humans (Book IV; see table 5.1). The objects of *artificialia* are grouped according to the natural materials from which they are made—earth, stone, metal, and glass, on through objects made from plants, furs, bones, and shells. Worm discusses malformed fetuses, a tooth from a giant, and a giant skull in the last chapter of Book III but includes mummies with minerals in Book I (Hafstein 2003).

Other Notable Cabinets

In 1679, an Amsterdam lawyer named Jan Swammerdam (1637–1680) cataloged the collection of a *Wunderkammer* that had been largely assembled by his father, an apothecary named Jacob Swammerdam (1606–1678). The collection was about one-third natural history specimens, one-third artificial curiosities, and one-third coins (MacGregor 1983). Swammerdam divided the objects into four categories in the catalog (table 5.1).

In 1650, Nicolas Grollier de Servière (1596–1689), a French inventor, assembled a collection of models and ornately turned wooden objects that he had made; the museum was opened one day each week to the public (Bredekamp 1995). The exhibits included models of siege engines, floating bridges, pumps, and clocks that operated by balls rolling down inclines or spiral tracks. After his death, Grollier de Servière's son and grandson continued to exhibit the collection for several decades.

Lodovico Settala (1550–1633) was a physician who established a cabinet of curiosities in Milan. His son Manfredo Settala (1600–1680) took charge of the collection and became one of the great collectors of seventeenth-century Europe. A seven-volume catalog of the collection was published in 1666 and in two subsequent editions. The Settala collection was organized in eleven categories (table 5.1). An illustration of the collection (figure 6.3) shows a large, well-ordered, and sophisticated exhibition design that has been described as highly decorative and patterned (Moser 2006). Collection

Figure 6.3. The cabinet of curiosities of Settala, 1666. *Source:* Manfredo Settala, "Museo o Galeria" (1666); unknown artist.

objects were exhibited in glass-fronted boxes, atop the boxes, and hanging from the ceiling. Although the space was crowded, as typical of Renaissance collections, it was much more linear in its arrangement, with a mixture of natural and artificial objects intermingled throughout.

The catalog of the Ferdinando Cospi (1606–1686) collection in Bologna was written by Lorenzo Legati (d. 1675) and published in 1677 (Olmi 1985). The catalog grouped collection objects into the categories of (1) terrestrial and flying animals, (2) aquatic animals, (3) ancient and modern artificial devices, (4) ancient coins and medals, and (5) figures of ancient gods, although the museum itself was not arranged using these categories (Laurencich-Minelli 1985). Cospi, who collected mostly natural history and archaeological objects, held a diplomatic post as a representative of the Grand Duke Ferdinando II and later as a senator. In 1657, the Cospi museum was transferred to two rooms in the Palazzo Pubblico in Bologna (Laurencich-Minelli 1985). Cospi dedicated his collection to the Senate of Bologna in 1660 and published a five-volume catalog of its contents (two volumes for the natural history objects, three for the archaeological objects) seventeen years later. An image of his collection (figure 6.4) published in the catalog references the medieval scholar Dante Alighieri (1265–1321) by showing a bust of him on the top shelf in the very center of the image. A dwarf named Sebastiano Biavati is shown apparently giving a tour of the collection and holding an Egyptian sculpture. Biavati

Figure 6.4. The Cospi collection, 1677. *Source:* Ferdinando Cospi, "The Collection of Natural Curiosities of Ferdinando Cospi (1601–1686), with Cospi to the Right and the Dwarf Sebastiano Biavati" (ca. 1658); unknown artist.

was both an employee of Cospi (serving as tour guide and caretaker of the objects) and one of the exhibits in the collection. The collection arrangement, like that of Settala (figure 6.3), contains fewer objects per unit space than earlier depictions of cabinets of curiosities and a more artistic arrangement of the objects.

After being received by the Senate of Bologna, Cospi's collection was combined with that of Ulisse Aldrovandi (see box 5.6) in 1743 in the Academy of Sciences of the Bologna Institute. Unlike Aldrovandi, neither Cospi nor Settala were scientists, yet they both invested heavily in collecting natural history specimens.

The image of the collection of Levinus Vincent (1658–1727), a wealthy textile merchant in Amsterdam, published in *Wondertooneel der Nature* (1706) reveals several changes taking place in collections (figure 6.5). One of these is the depiction of specimens preserved in jars of alcohol (which can be seen on the left side of the illustration), a technique discovered in 1664 but at the time not yet widely used due to the expense of glass jars and alcohol (Simmons 2014). The preserved specimens include both animals and malformed human fetuses. On the right side of the illustration are paintings or possibly textile samples. Levinus arranged his specimens of coral in the form of a park with trees and shrubs, acknowledging the

Figure 6.5. The Vincent collection, 1706. *Source:* Levinus Vincent, *Wondertooneel der Nature*—A Cabinet of Curiosities or *Wunderkammern* in Holland (1706–1715); Universities of Strasbourg.

uncertainty as to whether coral was an animal or a plant (Rigby and Rigby 1944). Of perhaps greater interest is the layout of the museum, with high shelves for the objects (mostly *naturalia* and ethnographic objects) fronted by long tables covered in cloth, around which a large crowd of visitors examines objects from the collection, all neatly housed in trays. In the lower right-hand corner, a young boy appears to be assisting some of the visitors. The visitors include not just stylish Europeans but also two men wearing turbans and robes in the lower left-hand corner.

The images of the Cospi, Settala, and Vincent collections demonstrate how these collections served the twin functions of education and entertainment and were arranged and exhibited aesthetically as if they were works of art (Moser 2006). This was a time when many collections still contained objects of art, history, and science intermingled. Even when collectors began to specialize, their collections were usually exhibited in carefully structured aesthetic displays. A scientist named Luigi Ferdinando Marsigli (1658–1730) in Bologna began assembling a collection in 1690 as a *Kunstkammer* with minerals, plant and animal specimens, ancient art, and automatons. As time went by, the nature of Marsigli's collection changed to become more scientific and research oriented, so he converted his house to hold his collection, a research library, and a laboratory. In 1712, Marsigli donated the collection, library, and laboratory to Bologna University, where it became the Istituto delle Scienze (Bredekamp 1995).

There are several other collections from this era that shed light on this crucial juncture as the modern museum emerged from the cabinet of curiosities. Among the more fascinating is the collection of the Archduke Ferdinand of Tyrol (1529–1595), which occupied eighteen cabinets. Although Ferdinand is best known as an art collector, his cabinet also contained gold and silver plate, bronzes, ironwork, coins, minerals, alabaster, corals, porcelain, glass, ivory, musical instruments, arms and armor, woodcarving, saints, and historical paintings (MacGregor 1983). Ferdinand's collection was housed in a purpose-built building constructed between 1572 and 1583 at Schloss Ambras Innsbruck, where it is still exhibited. In 1671, the city of Basel created a municipal museum to exhibit a collection inherited from Basilius Amerbach (1533–1591) that included drawings, paintings, sculpture, and medals. The Amerbach family had previously exhibited the collection in a special gallery at their house for select visitors (MacGregor 1983). One of the best collections of medals in Europe (as well as Roman and Egyptian antiquities, Indian clothing and weapons, dried animals and shells, and a "Sea-mans Skin") was that of Francesco Angeloni (ca. 1575–1652; MacGregor 1983:73).

When Andrea Mantova Benavides (ca. 1632–1711) inventoried the collection he had inherited from his grandfather in the mid-1600s, he found that the contents included a weeping crocodile, a piece of watermelon turned into stone on Mount Carmel by St. Benedict, giant teeth and bones, and a unicorn's horn (Pomian 1990). By this time, such objects were fast falling out of favor. When Antonio Vallisnieri (1661–1730), a professor at the University of Padua, acquired a faked basilisk specimen made from a ray—an object that earlier collectors had accepted at face value as authentic—Vallisnieri decided to keep the specimen to make his visitors aware of similar deceptions in other collections (Pomian 1990). The English traveler John Evelyn (see chapter 5), a fellow of the Royal Society, described a French collector who arranged his butterfly specimens in the form of a tapestry (Rigby and Rigby 1944).

By the late 1600s, keeping a traditional cabinet of curiosities was rapidly going out of fashion. Pierre Borel (1620–1671), a French chemist and botanist who considered his cabinet of curiosities to be a microcosm of the universe, recorded sixty-three cabinets similar to his in France and forty-four in twenty-eight other countries (Pomian 1990:47). Despite the fact that there were so many of these cabinets that they constituted an "important socio-cultural phenomenon," by 1750, very few of them were left (Pomian 1990:48), but more modern museum collections were appearing.

In Germany between 1709 and 1714, a government official named Johann Wilhelm II (1658–1716) built a dedicated building for his collection of paintings next to his house, Schloss Bensberg, in Dusseldorf (Bjurström 1993). In 1756, the collection was reorganized by a painter and art collector named Lambert Krahe (1712–1790). In his reorganization of the collection, Krahe transferred what he considered to be the less desirable paintings to Wilhelm's residence to serve as decorations. The remaining works were arranged in three galleries in a new style to reduce crowding. Krahe positioned what he deemed to be the most significant works at eye level, with the larger, lesser works arrayed above them, thus retaining the spirit of Baroque exhibition style while still reducing the amount of art on each wall to make for more relaxed viewing (Bjurström 1993). Krahe's arrangement was influential in much of Europe over the next few decades.

Two significant collectors of scientifically based cabinets of curiosities were Albertus Seba (1665–1736) and Frederik Ruysch (1638–1731), both of Amsterdam. Seba was an apothecary with a passionate interest in natural history. Through judicious trading, purchases, and a habit of meeting incoming ships at the port in Amsterdam, he built up a large and well-known collection of natural history specimens that he sold in its entirety to Peter the Great of Russia in 1716. Seba then built up a second extensive collection, which became the basis for his four-volume, fully illustrated collection catalog, which he began publishing in 1734 (Müsch 2001). The catalog, *Locupletissimi rerum naturalium thesauri accurata descriptio* (*Accurate Description of the Very Rich Thesaurus of the Principal and Rarest Natural*

Objects), is better known simply as Seba's *Thesaurus*. The last two volumes were published after Seba's death (in 1758 and 1765).

Seba's *Thesaurus* was the last great pre-Linnaean collection-based natural history work using premodern scientific nomenclature. Linnaeus, in fact, visited the collection at least twice and cited Seba's specimens and illustrations 284 times in his new classification system (Willmann and Rust 2001). Although the text of Seba's work is rarely cited today, the detailed illustrations from the 446 plates of the four volumes are frequently reprinted, incorporated into new artwork, reproduced as calendars, and referred to by taxonomists. Seba's *Thesaurus* sits squarely at the intersection of art and science, intentionally appealing to both. As was customary, the catalog was sold by subscription, with black-and-white plates that purchasers could hire an artist to hand-color, which provided added value to the work, although it resulted in sometimes fanciful color renditions of specimens and objects. One artist named J. Fortuÿn apparently had access to Seba's collection, as he specialized in coloring the Seba plates, signing his work (Müsch 2001). What is significant is that, to support the extraordinary cost of producing such catalogs, it was necessary to design them in a way that would appeal to collectors of both art and natural history (Simmons and Snider 2012).

Seba was instrumental in helping Ruysch arrange the sale of his collection to Peter the Great as well. Ruysch was an anatomist who developed secret methods to prepare astoundingly lifelike preparations of the human body (Cole 1921, 1944). Ruysch's preparations varied from fluid-preserved specimens to allegorical tableaus created with dried human body parts. In addition to his well-known anatomical museum, which was open to the public two days a week, Ruysch worked as a physician and anatomist.

THE EVOLUTION OF THE MODERN MUSEUM

In the eighteenth century in the Venetian Republic, public collections began to be seen as coherent collections "rather than as decorative elements," and thus they "began to benefit from the protection of the authorities" (Pomian 1990:192). As discussed in chapter 5, during the Renaissance, the classification of objects in cabinets of curiosities became increasingly complex, with the addition of new categories and attempts to find linkages between categories (see table 5.1). It is important to keep in mind that, although the Renaissance catalogs and depictions of collection arrangements might "initially seem chaotic, with items crammed on shelves and hung from walls and ceilings, they were thoughtfully arranged 'documents' that were designed to demonstrate the diversity of life on earth" (Moser 2006:31) and to demonstrate the products of human creativity. As one museologist sums up the period, "From a place of amateur delight, the museum was turned into a temple of human genius" (Maroević 1998:47).

Natural History Collections

By 1700, the *naturalia*-based cabinets of curiosities had largely been replaced by the first institutions with the characteristics of modern natural history museums, which turned away from their Renaissance fixation on the rare and the strange to emphasize the similarities among kinds of plants and animals, as comparison and classification became the new tools of scientific exploration (Pearce 2010). The use by Linnaeus of several private collections, particularly those of George Clifford III (1685–1760) and Albertus Seba (1665–1736), for the preparation of *Systema Naturae* (in 1735) and *Species Plantarum* (in 1753) greatly influenced the systematic arrangement of all collections and helped diminish the emphasis on the unusual (Wittlin 1970).

The various new classification schemes proposed for natural history collections affected the way that specimens were displayed and interpreted. Moser (2006) identifies several new exhibition strategies that emerged in this period, including the use of all the available space to exhibit as many specimens as possible to make comparisons between species easier; the use of symmetry and patterns in exhibit design to emphasize affinities between species; the use of labels (and sometimes trained guides) for visitors (the increasing use of labeling after 1700 demonstrated the new focus on the classification of species and the use of exhibits to convey knowledge); the use of innovative architectural designs, including lighting and exhibit furniture, to enhance the visual impact of the collection for the viewer; and the designation of some specimens as iconic exhibition focal points.

The influx of specimens of new species had a major impact on European natural history collections. George (1985) found 1,657 identifiable specimens listed in the catalogs of 13 cabinets from the seventeenth century (table 6.4). More than half of the specimens (57.8 percent) were of European origin, with specimens also from Africa (10.1 percent), Asia (13.0 percent), and the Americas (19.1 percent). The influence of specimen-preservation technology (Simmons and Snider 2012) is also reflected in table 6.4. For most of the seventeenth century, the predominant means of preserving natural history specimens was dehydration. Mammals, birds, and insects—which can all be easily dehydrated—together make up 61.9 percent of the specimens in the catalogs.

Table 6.4.   Specimens in Cabinets of Natural History

Animal	Africa	Asia	Europe	Americas	Total	Percent
Mammals	55	51	215	60	381	23.0
Birds	25	80	122	61	288	17.4
Reptiles	59	39	118	79	295	17.8
Fish	17	21	239	60	337	20.3
Insects	12	24	264	56	356	21.5
Total	168	215	958	316	1,657	100.0
Percent	10.1	13.0	57.8	19.1	100	—

Source: George 1985.

Armadillos, which are found only in the Americas, were the most popular animals in the collections, listed in ten of the thirteen catalogs (76.9 percent). The armadillo was strange in appearance; its hard, scaly covering made it easy to dehydrate in a relatively lifelike form; and it did not look like any other animal then known to European collectors. However, it was probably the similarity of most North American and European animals that accounts, at least in part, for why there are so few other North American animals in the collections (George 1985). Other common specimens in the catalogs include antlers and horns of various animals and the skin, bones, or tusks of hippopotamuses and elephants, which were impressive for their size (George 1985). The bird of paradise was the most popular bird specimen listed in the catalogs (see chapter 5 and box 6.2), along with cassowary casques, legs, eggs, and feathers. Almost all of the collections had crocodile skins and dried chameleons in them. Half the collections had turtle carapaces.

Among the most prized animals were the very strange flying lizards (*Draco*) from Asia—only two cabinets had specimens of them. James Petiver (ca. 1665–1718) was known to have at least two alcohol-preserved specimens of flying lizards in his collection (George 1985), writing, "This wonderful Animal entire and very curiously preserved in Spirits was given me by my Honoured and Worthy Friend Mr. Charlton. Another of the same I also received lately from Madam Herman at Leyden" (Petiver 1695–1703:19). Nine of the collections had sawfish scales; several had trunkfish and puffer fish. Half of the collections contained rhinoceros beetles, king crabs, and scarab beetles. The rarest specimens were butterflies, which are hard to preserve properly and difficult to maintain due to their fragility, susceptibility to pests, and tendency to fade when left exposed to light (George 1985). Among the reptile specimens were stuffed lizards of the thick-skinned genus *Uromastyx*, which can be seen in the illustrations of the Besler (figure 5.5) and Calzolari (figure 5.3) cabinets.

An example of how sailors came to have so many specimens to sell when they reached ports in Europe can be found in the autobiography of the English buccaneer and bird enthusiast William Dampier (1651–1715), who casually remarked that, during a stop on Bouton Island in 1687, "Here our Men bought also abundance of Crockadores, and fine large Parakites, curiously coloured, and some of them the finest I ever saw" (Dampier 1927:308). This was the manner in which many objects and specimens were obtained for museums during this era—sailors taking advantage of port calls in exotic locations to purchase specimens (or living animals that could be made into specimens) from local people. The birds purchased were later identified as sulfur-crested cockatoos and parakeets (George 1985).

The Louvre and Other Art Museums

The Louvre Museum (Paris) is widely regarded as the first great national museum of art (Alexander and Alexander 2008). Art exhibitions began at the Louvre Palace in 1750, when Louis XV (1710–1774) decided to display ninety-six works of art from the royal collection. In 1765, in the ninth volume of his *Encyclopédie ou Dictionnaire raisonné des sciences, des arts et des métiers, par une Société de Gens de lettres*, Denis Diderot (1713–1784) proposed creating a museum at the Louvre Palace that would be based on the *Mouseion* of Alexandria, a modern temple of the arts and sciences, combining collections with communities of scholars. Diderot's plan was never carried out, but the Louvre did eventually become a museum (Lewis 1985; Wittlin 1970).

The present Louvre Museum is a product of the French Revolution that, in 1793, declared that the Cabinet du Roi and the Cabinet d'Histoire Naturelle were the property of the French people, not the king, and chose the name *muséum* for them and other public collections, as the word *muséum* evoked ancient Alexandria (in all its glory) and implied intellectual achievement and monumental architecture (Lee 1997). The next question was, What should be in the museum's collections in addition to the royal treasures? Napoléon Bonaparte (1769–1821) appointed Dominique Vivant Denon (1747–1825) director general of museums and head of the Louvre, which he renamed Musée Napoléon in 1802. Denon had established his reputation by accompanying Napoléon's army on its Egyptian campaign as part of the scientific and technical corps of the Institut d'Égypte (Blom 2002). Napoléon set out to fill his new museum with objects abducted from other collections, beginning with Egyptian objects but also pieces taken from across Italy (Blom 2002). Denon arranged the objects in the new museum "according to art-historical ideas and methodology, not randomly or purely according to the curator's tastes, as had been the case before. He focused on chronology, on national schools and on the evolution of styles. The *grand système* of the natural sciences had communicated itself to the display of artistic work" (Blom 2002:118). In 1793, the museum exhibited 537 paintings, hung floor to ceiling on the walls, and 184 other objects on tables in the center of the gallery (Alexander and Alexander 2008). Many of the looted Italian works were returned after the defeat of Napoléon by the British at Waterloo.

The Luxembourg Gallery was established in 1750 in four rooms of the Luxembourg Palace and was open free to the public two days each week (McClellan 1993). After the museum opened, a new classification system was gradually instituted that was inspired by the hierarchical scientific nomenclature of Linnaeus and Buffon (see following discussion) and identified works of art by school and, within each school, by chronology (McClellan 1993). This was a crucial change in the organizational structure of the collection that profoundly altered the pedagogic purpose of the museum— the previous arrangement had been based on a comparison of the aesthetic qualities of the paintings, but the new system aimed to teach visitors about the history of art based on a series of great masters and regional traditions rather than based on the artistic quality of the works (McClellan 1993).

In 1779, Christian von Mechel (1737–1817) reorganized the Belvedere Palace (in Vienna) "according to the chronological principle and art schools, stressing the educational character of the exhibition, not the pleasure it provides" (Maroević 1998:47), in effect making it a "visible history of art" (Holdengräber 1987:111). In 1756, Wilhelm Lambert Krähe (1712–1790) arranged the Düsseldorf Gallery in the "first thematic arrangement according to artists and schools" (Maroević 1998:47). In the Stallburg Museum, "pictures were cut into such shapes as would form a continuous wall covering, and would fit the shapes of doors" (Wittlin 1970:85).

The Royal Society

The Royal Society of London for Improving Natural Knowledge was founded on November 28, 1660, by a small group of men who had been meeting at Gresham College in London to discuss science and philosophy. The new organization gained royal approval in 1663 and adopted the motto *Nullius in verba* ("Take no one's word for it"). The group established a cabinet or repository of collections, housed at Gresham College, and began collecting shortly thereafter (Stimpson 1948). Robert Hooke (1635–1703) was named keeper of the repository. The founders of the society believed that developing a comprehensive collection of objects was crucial to their plans for the "systematic reform of knowledge" (Hunter 1985:165).

The collections assembled by scientific societies and other institutions in the seventeenth and eighteenth centuries are important because of their intermediate position between private collections and public museums (Hunter 1985). In addition, the institutional collections had a potential for longevity that private collections did not have—private collections were typically sold and dispersed following the deaths of their owners. Indeed, the Royal Society announced in its *Philosophical Transactions* in October 1666 that donors could rest assured that their collections would be preserved by the society "probably much better and safer than in their own private Cabinets" (quoted in Hunter 1985:159). Among the early donors to the collection was John Wilkins (1614–1672), who contributed a large collection of natural rarities in 1663 (Hunter 1985). Wilkins was the author of several influential works, including *An Essay Towards a Real Character, And a Philosophical Language* (1668), in which he attempted to establish a universal classification of objects by means of a universal language (Jones 1961).

An indication of how quickly collecting and nature of collections were changing was that in 1668 the society had to institute a rule that all donations must first be reviewed by the society's president "for fear of lodging unknownly ballads and buffooneries in these scoffing times" (quoted in Stimpson 1948:90). The society had no wish to have its collection cluttered with fakes, frauds, or useless specimens. Nevertheless, when the collection was cataloged by Nehemiah Grew (1641–1712) in 1681 (figure 6.6), among the many scientific specimens and objects, he also recorded a "HUMANE SKULL cover'd all over with the Skin. Having been buried,

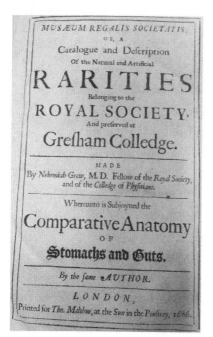

Figure 6.6. Title page of the 1686 reprint of the catalog of rarities belonging to the Royal Society and preserved at Gresham College. *Source:* Biodiversity Heritage Library.

as is probable, in some Limy, or other like soil, by which it was tann'd or turn'd into a kind of Leather" (Grew 1681:7), "A piece of a BONE voided by Sir *W. Throgmorton* with his Urine" (Grew 1681:9), a "WEESLE-HEADED ARMADILLO" (Grew 1681:19), and "Skin on ye Buttock of a Rhinoceros" (Grew 1681:tab. 2). Although these may seem to be useless specimens to a modern reader, for a curious resident of London in the 1680s, they were things rarely (if ever) before seen. In Grew's defense it should be noted that all of these entries are accompanied by extensive commentary on their significance. For example, of the "weesle-headed armadillo," Grew remarked, "I find this species no where describ'd" and proceeds with a detailed description of the specimen (Grew 1681:19).

The problem of the odd and the unusual in collections would continue for years, in part because objects such as these were in collections largely because they were expected to be. One hundred years later (in 1871), the curator of the Ashmolean Museum, John Henry Parker, explained, "I do not wish to exclude curiosities. . . . [T]hey attract people, and when they are brought hither by curiosity, they may stop to learn something better; they may want to know something of the history of the curiosities they have come to see" (Murray 1904:204), an argument that is still invoked by museum curators to justify the acquisition of outrageous objects not in keeping with their museum's mission.

The Royal Society wished to make its collection as complete as possible, so Nehemiah Grew's catalog stressed the inclusion of the common things as well as the rare (Pearce 2010) and positioned its holdings within a complex classification scheme that included humans with animals (table 6.5). Grew's catalog ran 450 pages and listed the names of 83 donors to the collection (Stimpson 1948). The collections were later transferred to the British Museum.

During the second half of the eighteenth century, as systematic approaches to learning began to come into dominance, museum collections came to be valued far more for the order of the objects in their collections than for their rarity—it was a time when scholars were searching for universal systems of order and universal languages (Maroević 1998). Some of these classification schemes were more successful than others, such as the first truly universal classification system developed by the Swede Carl Linnaeus (1707–1778) beginning in 1735; the zoogeographical classification schemes of Georges-Louis Leclerc Buffon (1707–1788) in 1761 and 1766; and the earliest comprehensive evolutionary theory to show linkages between categories, proposed by Jean-Baptiste Pierre Antoine de Monet, Chevalier de Lamarck (1744–1829) in 1809 (George 1985). This emphasis on order led to more complex and detailed classification systems in museums as older classification schemes were replaced by new systems based on ideas about scientific classification that differentiated objects rather than unifying them (Hooper-Greenhill 1989).

Table 6.5. Organization of the Catalog of the Royal Society, 1681

Part	Sections	Chapters
Part I. Of Animals	1. Of Humane Rarities	
	2. Of Quadrupeds	1. Of Viviparous; and particularly of Multisidous Quadrupeds
		2. Of Bisidons, and Solidipedous Quadrupeds
		3. Of Oviparous Quadrupeds
	3. Of Serpents	
	4. Of Birds	1. Of Land-Fowles
		2. Of Water-Fowles; particularly of the Cloven Footed
		3. Of Palmipeds or Web-Footed
		4. Of their Eggs and Nests
	5. Of Fishes	1. Of Viviparous Fishes
		2. Of Oviparous Fishes; particularly such as are Not-Scal'd.
		3. Of Scaled Fishes
		4. Of Exanguious Fishes
	6. Of Shells	1. Of Shells Whirled and single
		2. Of Shells Double and Multiple. To which are subjoyned 7. Schemes comprehending them all
	7. Of Insects	1. Of Insects with Naked Wings
		2. Of Insects with Sheathed Wings
		3. Of Creeping Insects
Part II. Of Plants	1. Of Trees	1. Of Weeds, Branches, and Leaves
		2. Of Fruits; particularly such as are of the Apple, Pear, and Plum Kinds
		3. Of Calibashes; and some other like Fruits
		4. Of Nuts, and divers other like Fruits
		5. Of Berries, cones, Lobes, and some other Parts of Trees
	2. Of Shrubs and Arborescent Plants	1. Of Shrubs, chiefly
		2. Of Arborescent Plants
	3. Of Herbs	1. Of Stalks and Roots
		2. Of Fruits
		3. Of Seeds

(continued)

Table 6.5. (*continued*)

Part	Sections	Chapters
Part II. Of Plants (*continued*)	4. Of Mosses, Mushrooms, & Together with some Appendents to Plants	
	4. Of Sea Plants	1. Of Sea Shrubs
		2. Of other Sea Plants; and of Sponges
Part III. Of Minerals	1. Of Stones	1. Of Animal Bodies petrified and such like
		2. Of Vegetable Bodies petrified; and Stones like them
		3. Of Corals, and other like Marine Productions
		4. Of Gems
		5. Of other Stones Regular
		6. Of Stones Irregular
	2. Of Metalls	1. Of Gold, Silver, and Copper
		2. Of Tin, Lead, and Iron
		3. Of Antimony, Mercury, and other Metallick Bodies
	3. Of Mineral Principles	1. Of Salts
	2. Of Ambar and other sulphurs	
	3. Of Earths	
Part IV. Of Artificial Matters	1. Of things relating to Chymistry, and to other Parts of Natural Philosophy	
	2. Of things relating to Mathematicks; and some Mechanicks	
	3. Chiefly, of Mechanicks	
	4. Of Coyns, and other matters relating to Antiquity	
Appendix	Of some Plants, and other Particulars	
Index	Of some Medicines	
List	Of those who have contributed to this Musaeum	

Table 6.5. (*continued*)

Part	Sections	Chapters
Of the Anatomical Part	1. Of the Stomachs and Guts of six Carnivorous Quadrupeds, sc. a Weesle, Fitchet, Polecat, Cat, Dog, and Fox	
	2. Of the Mole, which seems to feed on Insects, as also of the Urchan, Squiril, and Rat; chiefly frugivorous	
	3. Of a Rabbit, Horse, and Pig; both frugivorous and graminivorous	
	4. Of a Sheep, and Calf, chiefly graminiviorus	
	5. Of the Uses of the Gulets of Quadrupeds	
	6. Of the Uses of the Stomachs of Quadrupeds	
	7. Of the Uses of the Guts of Quadrupeds	
	8. Of the Stomachs and Guts of Birds	
	9. Of their Uses	
	10. Of the Stomachs and Guts of Fishes	

Source: Grew 1686.

THE BEGINNINGS OF MUSEOLOGY

As the number of museums grew across Europe, in 1727, a museum object dealer in Hamburg named Kaspar Friedrich Jenequel published a book called *Museographica Oder Anleitung zum rechten Begriff und nützlicher Anlegung der Museorum oder Raritäten-Kammern* (*Museographica or Guide to the Correct Concept and Useful Application of the Museum or Chamber of Rarities*) using the pen name Caspar Neikelius. The *Museographica* is considered to be the first museological work (Holdengräber 1987; Schulz 1994), as it provides advice concerning acquisitions, classification problems, and collection care. Neikelius suggests putting a table in the center of each room, "where things brought from the repository could be studied" to minimize handling and accidents, and recommends that museum objects be stored in dry conditions and kept out of direct sunlight and that museums have an accession book and a catalog (quoted in Hooper-Greenhill 1992:144). Neikelius's book is the first to discuss the difference in viewing objects clustered in a small room (e.g., as in a cabinet of curiosities) compared to those displayed in a large room, specifically in a long exhibition hall derived from the *grande salle* of French medieval chateaux (Holdengräber 1987). As late as 1759, the organization of the British Museum reflected Neikelius's divisions of knowledge, with its collections divided into three departments—manuscripts, medals, and coins; natural and artificial productions; and printed books (table 5.1).

In 1753, David Hultman published *Instructio Musei Rerum Naturalium*, in which he recommends that a museum building be made of brick (to be fire resistant) and be longer than wide with north-facing windows for good lighting (Murray 1904).

Despite the appearance of these books, collection care in some museums during this period was still not terribly good. One historian wrote that, as late as the 1840s, William Swainson compared the storerooms of the British Museum "with the catacombs at Palermo, each of which was apparently opened once a year to determine how much decay had occurred and to deposit fresh material" (Whitehead 1970:56).

THE PUBLIC MUSEUM AND THE PUBLIC

One of the distinguishing features of modern museums is that they are public museums, but in truth, many early modern museums were open only to a narrow sector of the populace until well into the nineteenth century. In an era before labels and signage, many visitors found these museums to be an "alien land in which people were addressed by a visual equivalent of several tongues unknown to them and issuing simultaneous messages" (Wittlin 1970:118). Deciding who should be allowed inside the museums, once they became popular attractions in the seventeenth century, varied widely. Marcello Malpighi (1628–1694) was concerned with the proper demeanor of visitors, declaring that ideal visitors were those who could understand the experience and conduct themselves with "'judicious curiosity,' rather than an unbridled appetite for wonder" (Findlen 1994:29). It was not uncommon to impose restrictions on potential visitors, such as requiring them to either wait for a special occasion when the institution would be open or to apply in advance for admission. Despite the Enlightenment spirit of the times, most museum visits were social rather than autodidactic (Maroević 1998). When the German historian Gebhard Friedrich August Wendeborn (1742–1811) visited London in 1785, he complained that visitors to the British Museum had to submit their credentials and then wait anywhere from several days to several months for an admission ticket to the museum. Some applicants were turned down entirely. If awarded, the admission ticket only entitled the visitor to participate in a guided group tour. Object labels were scarce, the British Museum guides did not provide much information, and the tours were rushed. The general public was admitted to the museum on just four days a week (Monday through Thursday), except on days reserved for students of the royal academy (Wittlin 1970).

THE FURTHER DIVERSIFICATION
OF THE CABINETS OF CURIOSITIES

Toward the end of the Enlightenment, as museums continued to become specialized institutions, they focused increasingly in particular areas, such as art, ethnography, history, technology, and natural history. As they specialized, their schemes for classifying their collections also diverged (tables 5.1 and 6.1).

There was eventually some unity in the classification schemes used in natural history collections, despite the chaos that initially surrounded the identification and names of the many new plant and animal species pouring in from previously unknown parts of the world. The resolution came in the second half of the eighteenth century with the system of standardized scientific names in a hierarchical classification scheme proposed by a Swedish naturalist named Carl Linnaeus (1707–1778; Blunt 2001). Modern botanical nomenclature began in 1753 with the publication of *Systema Plantarum* and modern zoological nomenclature in 1758 with the publication of the tenth edition of *Systema Naturae*. Among Linnaeus's innovations was the establishment of a simple binomen for each species—a two-word, Latinized name for each kind of plant and animal. This efficient classification system rapidly became the organizing principle for natural history collections and created a universal language for biologists. A usable equivalent taxonomy for cataloging human-made objects did not appear until 1978 (Chenhall 1978), although other systems of near-universal classification had been proposed earlier, such as the Dewey decimal system (which categorized library materials in ten major classes) in 1876, the Universal Decimal Classification (published in Europe in 1895), and the Library of Congress system (1897).

Among the specialized museums founded in this period was the Museo Sacro (the first of the Vatican Museums), which opened in Rome in 1756 (Alexander 1979). The Uffizi Gallery in Florence was opened to the public in 1769 with Giuseppe Querci (d. 1773) appointed as its first gallery director. The pictures in the gallery were arranged and labeled by artist and subject in 1795 (Bjurström 1993). The Pio-Clementino Museum, widely considered to be the first museum devoted exclusively to art, opened in 1773. The Hermitage Museum, established in St. Petersburg in 1764, exhibited the last of the significant royal collections to be displayed to the public. In Spain, Charles III brought together works of art and natural history for a new museum in 1785, which became the Prado in 1819 (Lewis 1992).

THE EXPORTATION OF THE MUSEUM CONCEPT

The concept of the museum as a conjunction of objects and learning was born in Hellenistic Alexandria, nurtured in Renaissance Europe, and refined during the Enlightenment, as modern museums evolved. The museum concept was exported from Europe beginning in the 1700s and eventually spread around the world. One of the earliest instances of the export of the museum model occurred when Peter the Great took the museum ideal from Europe to czarist Russia.

Peter the Great (Peter Alexeyevich, 1672–1725), czar of Russia, made his first trip to Europe in 1697–1698 and wrote numerous letters about his travels and his acquisition of objects for a planned cabinet of curiosities (Neverov 1985). Among the objects he acquired was a numismatic collection compiled by Simon Schynvoet (1652–1727) in Amsterdam and a collection of Asian objects that had been compiled by Bernard Paludanus (1550–1633), which eventually became part of the Asiatic Museum in St. Petersburg (Murray 1904). When the Russian capital was moved from Moscow to St. Petersburg in 1714, what Peter the Great called his *Kunstkamera* was established in the summer palace as the first public museum in Russia, officially opened in 1719 (Neverov 1985). The czar made a second journey to Europe in 1716–1717, returning with collections of natural history and human anatomical specimens purchased from Albertus Seba and Frederik Ruysch in Amsterdam and many other objects. Not content with the collections he had amassed, Peter mounted his own collecting expedition to Siberia and sent his personal librarian, Johann Schumacher (1690–1761), to visit European museums and obtain more objects and books for the royal collections (Neverov 1985).

Peter the Great devoted considerable attention and resources to developing his collections, which he saw as crucial to his Enlightenment-inspired reforms. In many ways, his museum was a look back to the cabinets of curiosities of the Renaissance (particularly with his penchant for rare and unusual objects), but in other ways, it was a modern museum for Russia. The extensive collections included European art, Asian art, archaeological and ethnographic artifacts, coins and medals, natural history specimens, precious stones, live exhibits of unusual human beings, and preserved human body parts (Murray 1904; Neverov 1985). In 1724, the collection was placed under the direction of the Russian Academy of Sciences (founded in 1724 by a fiat of Peter the Great) and was divided into three categories, which were reflective of the Renaissance cabinets: (1) *naturalia* (rarities of nature), (2) rarities executed by art, and (3) antiquities.

Although Peter the Great was in many ways a reformer and progressive thinker, embracing several of the ideals of the Enlightenment (including the value of science for improving human society) in his efforts to bring modernity to Russia, he remained an absolute and at times ruthless monarch (Roberts and Westad 2013). Neverov relates the story of Princess Yekaterina Romanovna Vorontsova-Dashkova (1743–1810), a close friend of Empress Catherine the Great, who during the 1780s

> came all of a sudden upon two glass jars which, she discovered, held, preserved in spirits, the heads of the executed lovers of Peter I and his consort, Mary Hamilton, and Willem Mons. Peter, not content with forcing Catherine to be present at her lover's execution, apparently ordered the jar with his head to be placed in her apartments. Princess Dashkov and Catherine remarked on the wonderful preservation of the two beautiful young faces, still striking after the passage of fifty years. (Neverov 1985:58)

Mary Hamilton (d. 1719) was a lady-in-waiting for Catherine I and a mistress of Peter the Great; Willem Mons (1688–1724) was a personal adjutant to Peter the Great—both were beheaded after running afoul of the czar.

In 1728, Peter the Great's collection was moved to a new building (although the building was not completed until 1734), and in the 1730s, plans were made for a complete catalog of the collection, which was eventually published in Latin in 1741. A devastating fire in 1747 destroyed a good part of the collection (Neverov 1985).

The first museum in the Americas was established by the Charleston Library Society in 1773 in Charleston, South Carolina. Modeled on the European museum concept, its mission was "to collect materials for a full and accurate natural history of South Carolina," but donations included objects from as far away as Surinam and Hawaii (Alexander and Alexander 2008:61). Only members of the library society could see the collections until it was opened to the public in 1824. The collection was moved to the College of Charleston in 1850 and then incorporated as the Charleston Museum in 1915 (Alexander and Alexander 2008).

Another significant museum was opened in Philadelphia in 1782 by Swiss-born Pierre Eugène Du Simitière (ca. 1736–1784), an artist and naturalist (Orosz 1985). Du Simitière's *Curio Cabinet* included an extensive collection of plants and animals (mostly from the West Indies), Indian and African antiquities, a collection of colonial-era newspapers, books, and two thousand prints and drawings (Alexander and Alexander 2008; Levey 1951). Beginning in 1782, the museum was advertised in the Philadelphia newspapers to attract patrons. The museum closed after Du Simitière's death in 1784, and the collection was sold at public auction in thirty-six lots in 1785 (Levey 1951).

The American painter and naturalist Charles Willson Peale (1741–1827) is responsible for establishing the first public museum in the United States in 1785 in his home in Philadelphia after purchasing most of Du

Simitière's specimens (Goode 1889; Miller 1979; Murray 1904). Peale, who wholeheartedly embraced the Enlightenment ideals of intellectual freedom and tolerance, based his museum on the European concept, with the democratic notion of providing instruction and entertainment to all visitors who paid the entrance fee (Alderson 1992; Alexander and Alexander 2008). Peale's ideal was to make his museum a place for "rational amusement" (Alexander 1992:19). At this pivotal moment in the development of museums, and despite the diversification that was affecting many European museums, Peale worked assiduously to integrate art and science in his exhibits, displaying paintings by himself and his sons intermixed with taxidermy mounts, fossils, ethnographic objects, and sometimes live animals. In 1786, Peale announced that he was arranging his museum according to the newly established taxonomic principles of Linnaeus. In 1794, when the museum outgrew the available space in his house, Peale moved it to the American Philosophical Society (figure 6.7) and then in 1802 to the Long Room of Independence Hall in Philadelphia, which he was allowed to use rent-free (Alexander and Alexander 2008).

Not only was this a crucial moment for museum development in the fledgling United States, it was also an important time for the development of an American scientific enterprise (Dugatkin 2009), and the two are closely linked. The distinguished French naturalist Count Georges-Louis Leclerc Buffon (1707–1788) had invoked the theory of degeneracy in volume 5 of his majestic, six-thousand-page *Histoire Naturelle Générale et Particulière* (1766) to argue that species in North America were smaller

Figure 6.7.   The American Philosophical Society Hall, Philadelphia.

and more feeble than those of the Old World due to living in a cold, damp climate. Furthermore, Buffon claimed that the offspring of domesticated animals imported to North America were also smaller than those of the Old World, and Native American people were smaller and degenerate. Thomas Jefferson (1743–1826) responded to Buffon in his book *Notes on the State of Virginia* in 1781 by offering evidence that proved Buffon was incorrect (Dugatkin 2009). It was in this atmosphere that in 1801 the American Philosophical Society financed Peale's expedition to Ulster County, New York, to excavate a mastodon skeleton (Alexander and Alexander 2008). The fossil provided further proof that North American animals were not smaller and weaker than those of the Old World but that many species were, in fact, larger. Peale mounted the mastodon fossil in front of a painted background in his museum. It can be seen in Peale's 1822 self-portrait *The Artist in His Museum* at the Philadelphia Academy of the Arts.

LITERATURE IN THE ENLIGHTENMENT

During the Enlightenment, literature became a means of disseminating knowledge, as literacy rates rose in most of Europe. Typical of the early part of this period is the work of the French playwright Molière (Jean Baptiste Poquelin, 1622–1673), with its satire, verisimilitude, classical character types, and sense of decorum. Molière's plays include *The High-Brow Ladies, The Imaginary Invalid, Tartuffe, The Miser,* and *The Misanthrope.* Later theatrical works, such as William Congreve's *The Way of the World* (1700), and novels (a relatively new literary form) were particularly important with their expressions of individuality and values based on reason and empirical evidence, such as Daniel Defoe's *Robinson Crusoe,* which was published in 1719 and marks the beginning of realistic fiction (Voth 2007). The adventures of the fictional protagonist parallel some of the most significant events of the time period—Crusoe goes to sea against his parents' wishes (an expression of individuality), is captured and made a slave, escapes and journeys to newly colonized Brazil, then joins a slaving expedition to Africa but is shipwrecked on the way. As Crusoe is establishing himself on his castaway's island, he makes a careful enumeration of the objects he salvages from the ship—objects that he both needs to navigate his new world and forms attachments to as a way of clinging to his distant culture (Rogers 1932). Reading the original text of *Robinson Crusoe* reveals many variant spellings of common words, which has a parallel in the classification of objects in collections. In the early decades of the Enlightenment, neither English spelling and grammar nor classification systems had been standardized, but by the close of the Enlightenment, the standardization of both was well under way.

SUMMARY

The Enlightenment was a period of great change in much of the world, particularly as Europeans became more aware of lands, flora and fauna, and cultures that were previously unknown to them. However, changes in perception and knowledge of the world often came slowly. In 1515, the Dutch artist Albrecht Dürer (1471–1528) cut a woodblock image of a rhinoceros that was destined to become very famous. Prints made from Dürer's woodblock were widely circulated (more than 900,000 impressions were made from it), and the image was repeatedly copied for well over one hundred years (Simmons and Snider 2012). Although several collections contained pieces of a rhinoceros, no collection had an entire animal. The catalog of the Tradescant collection (1656) lists a rhinoceros horn, jaw, and vertebrae, as well as an oval goblet carved from rhino horn, and the 1681 catalog of the collection of the Royal Society of London includes an illustration of its specimen of a piece of "Skin on ye Buttock of a Rhinoceros" (Grew 1681:tab 2). Nevertheless, most people in Europe did not have the opportunity to see a live rhinoceros until a female Indian rhinoceros named Clara went on tour between 1741 and 1758 (Ridley 2004). The objects in museum collections were crucial resources for understanding expanding horizons, for providing a means to categorize, and for absorbing new knowledge (Findlen 1994).

7

═══◈◈◈═══

Emergence of the Modern Museum, 1800–1900

The modern museum that emerged in Europe has roots deep in the inherent human need to collect objects. It evolved from caches of prehistoric grave goods through temple hoards and troves of kings' treasures to become the cabinets of curiosities that provided order to understand the chaos of the world. Modern museums appeared in Europe at a time when the collecting and exhibition of cultural and natural objects had become fashionable in both private homes and public institutions (Moser 2006).

The modern zoological park took shape about the same time, with many European zoos following the general pattern established by the redesign of the menagerie at the Jardin des Plantes in Paris that was implemented by Étienne Geoffroy Saint-Hilaire (1772–1844) and Frédéric Cuvier (1773–1838) in the early 1800s, who made winding paths and larger, more natural animal enclosures in a garden setting (Baratay and Hardouin-Fugier 2002). After midcentury, efficient steam heating systems and inexpensive plate glass led to an increase in greenhouses and conservatories associated with botanical gardens, zoological parks, museums, and the homes of the wealthy—Charles Darwin (1809–1882) had a heated greenhouse built at his home in 1863 in which he grew hundreds of plants for his experiments (Browne 2002). There is a typical conservatory from this era in the gardens at the Horniman Museum in London, built in 1894 (figure 7.1).

Over the course of the nineteenth century, modern museums became increasingly specialized and diversified, as many national museums were founded and the museum concept was successfully exported worldwide (table 7.1). This flowering of museums was not without controversies—some of the new institutions were poorly managed, some had substandard

Figure 7.1.   The 1894 Conservatory at the Horniman Museum, London.

collections, and more than a few exhibited inauthentic objects. Controversies sometimes arose from the way collections were obtained. Although the purchase of the Phigalian marbles in 1815 and the Elgin marbles in 1816 established the reputation of the British Museum as a repository of antiquities, the acquisition of the Elgin marbles was contentious at the time and remains so today (see box 7.1). As with any human endeavor, what was collected varied with time, fashion, and the whims of curators. When the British Museum first began collecting Egyptian materials,

> [o]bjects valued as documents of art or as evidence of history were not sought after. . . . [I]t was not until the 1820s that items like papyri and sculptures with inscriptions or hieroglyphs were widely demanded by collectors. Thus the museum's first collection of Egyptian antiquities was not valuable or significant in an aesthetic or archaeological sense, but rather can be described as constituting a miscellaneous assortment of curious items. (Moser 2006:43)

By the 1830s, Egyptian artifacts had become better known and more desirable in collections, to the point that unwrapping an Egyptian mummy was occasionally a Victorian parlor entertainment (Brier 1994). As a result of the surge of interest in authentic and documented Egyptian objects, many Cairo-based European consuls expanded their excavation programs in Egypt, resulting in more European museums and private collectors acquiring ancient Egyptian collections, particularly museums in Florence, Turin, Paris, and Rome.

Table 7.1. Founding Dates for Some Representative Museums

Date	Name and Location
1506	Musei Vaticani, Rome (Italy)
1523	Grimani Gallery, Venice (Italy)
1567	Wilhelm IV and Albrecht V collection in the Mint, Munich (Germany)
1573	Collection of Archduke Ferdinand at Schloss Ambras (Germany)
1581	Galleria degli Uffizi, Florence (Italy)
	Medici collection opened at Uffizi Palace, Florence (Italy)
1594	Theatrum Anatomicum (University of Leiden), Leiden (The Netherlands)
1620	Museum Wormianum, Copenhagen (Denmark)
1625	Tradescant's Ark, London (England)
1626	Jardin des Plantes, Paris (France)
1663	Royal Society of London for Improving Natural Knowledge, London (England)
1671	Amerbach Cabinet, Basel (Switzerland)
1677	Ashmolean Museum, Oxford (England)
1694	Musée des Beaux-Arts et d'Archéologie, Besançon (France)
1717	Kunstkammer, St. Petersburg (Russia)
1734	Musei Capitolini, Rome (Italy)
1749	Palazzo dei Conservatori, Rome (Italy)
1750	Luxembourg Gallery (Luxembourg)
1752	Museo Nacional de Ciencias Naturales, Madrid (Spain)
1756	Museo Sacro, Rome (Italy)
1759	British Museum, London (England)
1764	State Hermitage Museum, St. Petersburg (Russia)
1773	Charleston Library Society Cabinet, Charleston (United States)
	Museum of the History of Riga and Navigation, Riga (Latvia)
	Pio Clemente Museum, Rome (Italy)
1778	Central Museum of Indonesian Culture (Batavia Society for Art and Science), Jakarta (Indonesia)
1781	Belvedere Palace, Vienna (Austria)
1782	Du Simitière's Curio Cabinet, Philadelphia (United States)
1784	Indian Museum, Kolcata (India)
	Accademia Gallery (Galleria dell'Accademia di Firenze), Florence (Italy)
1785	Museo del Prado, Madrid (Spain)
1786	Peale Museum, Philadelphia (United States)
1790	Museo de Historia Natural, Mexico City (Mexico)
1791	Massachusetts Historical Society, Boston (United States)
1793	The Louvre, Paris (France)
1795	Rijksmuseum, The Hague (The Netherlands)
1796	Czartoryski Museum, Krakow (Poland)
1801	East India Museum, London (England)
1802	National Museum (now Hungarian National Museum), Budapest (Hungary)
1807	Museum de Nordiske Oldsager, Copenhagen (Denmark)
1814	Asiatic Society of Bengal, Kolcata (India)
1815	Museu Nacional, Rio de Janeiro (Brazil)
1816	Museu Nacional de Belas Artes, Rio de Janeiro (Brazil)

(continued)

Table 7.1. *(continued)*

Date	Name and Location
1818	Moravské Múzeum, Brno (Czech Republic)
1822	Pictou Academy, Pictou (Canada)
1823	Museo Nacional, Bogotá (Colombia)
	Museo del País (Museo Nacional), Buenos Aires (Argentina)
	Raffles Museum and Library, Singapore (Singapore)
1824	National Gallery, London (England)
1825	Iziko South African Museum, Cape Town (South Africa)
1827	Australian Museum, Sydney (Australia)
1829	National Archaeological Museum, Athens (Greece)
1830	Altes Museum, Berlin (Germany)
	Museo Nacional, Santiago (Chile)
1831	Rumyantzev Museum, Moscow (Russia)
1835	Egyptian Museum, Cairo (Egypt)
1836	Alte Pinakothek, Munich (Germany)
1837	Museo Nacional, Montevideo (Uruguay)
	National Museum of Ethnology, Leiden (The Netherlands)
	Sir John Soane Museum, London (England)
1841	Nelson Provincial Museum, Stoke (New Zealand)
1842	Ancanthe Museum, Hobart (Australia)
	Wadsworth Atheneum, Hartford (United States)
1843	National Museum of Canada, Ottawa (Canada)
1846	Smithsonian Institution, Washington, DC (United States)
1850	Hasbrouck House, Newburgh (United States)
1852	Victoria and Albert Museum (was South Kensington Museum), London (England)
1853	Auckland Institute and Museum, Auckland (New Zealand)
1854	National Museum of Victoria, Melbourne (Australia)
1855	Neues Museum, Berlin (Germany)
	Queensland Museum, Brisbane (Australia)
	Royal Ontario Museum, Toronto (Canada)
1856	Lahore Museum, Lahore (Pakistan)
1858	University of Iowa Museum of Natural History, Iowa City (United States)
1859	The Louis Agassiz Museum of Comparative Zoology, Cambridge (United States)
1860	Mount Vernon, Fairfax County (United States)
1861	National Gallery of Victoria, Melbourne (Australia)
1862	Museo Nacional de Guayaquil (Ecuador)
1865	Museum of New Zealand Te Papa Tongarewa, Wellington (New Zealand)
1866	Museu Paraense Emilio Goeldi, Belém (Brazil)
1869	American Museum of Natural History, New York City (United States)
1870	Metropolitan Museum of Art, New York City (United States)
	Museum of Fine Arts, Boston (United States)
1871	National Museum of Nature and Science, Tokyo (Japan)
1872	Museo de Historia Natural de la Plata, Buenos Aires (Argentina)
	National Museum, Tokyo (Japan)
1873	Nordiska Museet, Stockholm (Sweden)

Table 7.1. (*continued*)

Date	Name and Location
1874	Grand Palace Collections (now National Museum), Bangkok (Thailand)
	Philadelphia Zoological Park, Philadelphia (United States)
1875	Indian Museum, Kolkata (India)
1876	Nationalgalerie, Berlin (Germany)
1877	Sri Lanka National Museum, Colombo (Sri Lanka)
1879	Art Institute of Chicago, Chicago (United States)
	Musée National des Arts Asiatiques Guimet, Paris (France)
1880	National Gallery of Canada, Ottawa (Canada)
1881	The Natural History Museum (was British Museum, Natural History), London (England)
1884	Hancock Museum (now Great North Museum: Hancock), Newcastle upon Tyne (England)
	Pitt Rivers Museum, Oxford (England)
1885	Museu de Historia Natural de São Paulo, São Paulo (Brazil)
1887	Museo Nacional, San José (Costa Rica)
	University of Pennsylvania Museum of Archaeology and Anthropology, Philadelphia (United States)
1888	Musée Alaoui (now National Museum), Tunis (Tunisia)
	Sarawak State Museum, Kuching (Malaysia)
1889	Brooklyn Children's Museum, Brooklyn (United States)
	L. C. Bates Museum, Hinckley (United States)
	National Zoological Park, Washington, DC (United States)
1891	Kunsthistorisches Museum, Vienna (Austria)
	Museo de Geologia, Lima (Peru)
	Skansen Museum, Stockholm (Sweden)
1892	Danmarks Nationalmuseum, Copenhagen (Denmark)
	National Archaeological Museum, Sofia (Bulgaria)
1894	The Field Museum, Chicago (United States)
	National Museum of Natural History, Sofia (Bulgaria)
1895	Geographical and Geological Museum, São Paulo (Brazil)
1896	Fogg Museum (Harvard University), Cambridge (United States)
	Rova of Antananarivo, Antananarivo (Madagascar)
1899	Bronx Zoo (New York Zoological Society), New York City (United States)
1901	Horniman Museum and Gardens, London (England)
	National Museum, Bulawayo (Zimbabwe)
1903	Deutsches Museum, Munich (Germany)
	Galleria Borghese, Rome (Italy)
	Museum of Islamic Art, Cairo (Egypt)
1904	Kaiser Friedrich Museum of Western Art (Bode Museum), Berlin (Germany)
	Prince of Wales Museum (now Chhatrapatī Shivaji Mahārāj Vastu Saṅgrahālay), Mumbai (India)
1905	Nant'ung Museum, Kangsu (China)
1906	National Ethnographic Museum, Sofia (Bulgaria)
	Peshāwar Museum, Peshāwar (Pakistan)
	Wilberforce House, Hull (England)

(continued)

Table 7.1. (*continued*)

Date	Name and Location
1908	Coptic Museum, Cairo (Egypt)
	Uganda Museum, Kampala (Uganda)
1909	National Museum of Kenya, Nairobi (Kenya)
	Newark Museum, Newark (United States)
1910	Musée Océanographique, Monaco-Ville (Monaco)
	Museo Nacional de Arqueología, Historia, y Etnología (now Museo de Antropología), Mexico City (Mexico)
1912	Openluchtmuseum, Arnhem (The Netherlands)
	Pushkin Museum, Moscow (Russia)
1913	Dr. Alvaro de Castro Museum, Maputo (Mozambique)
1915	Dar Batha Museum, Fez (Morocco)
1916	Mercer Museum, Doylestown (United States)
1918	Museo de Historia Natural de la Universidad de San Marcos, Lima (Peru)
1919	Museo Nacional de Bellas Artes, Havana (Cuba)
	Red Castle Archaeological Museum, Tripoli (Libya)
1925	Barnes Foundation, Philadelphia (United States)
1926	Colonial Williamsburg (United States)
	National Science Museum, Seoul (Korea)
1927	University of Santo Tomas Museum of Arts and Sciences, Manila (Philippines)
1929	Greenfield Village and Edison Institute (now The Henry Ford), Dearborn (United States)
	Museum of Modern Art, New York City (United States)
1930	Pergamon Museum (Pergamonmuseum), Berlin (Germany)
1933	Barbados Museum and Historical Society (Barbados)
	Museum of Science and Industry, Chicago (United States)
1936	Central Lenin Museum, Moscow (Russia)
1937	Ashutosh Museum of Indian Art, Kolkata (India)
	Museé National des Arts et Traditions Populaires, Paris (France)
	National Gallery of Art, Washington, DC (United States)
	Palais de la Découverte, Paris (France)
1942	National Art Gallery, Sofia (Bulgaria)
1949	Calico Museum of Textiles, Ahmedabad (India)
	National Museum of India, New Delhi (India)
1951	National Gandhi Museum, New Delhi (India)
1953	Yad Vashem, Jerusalem (Israel)
1954	National Gallery of Modern Art, New Delhi (India)
1956	National Handicrafts and Handlooms Museum, New Delhi (India)
1957	National Gallery of Zimbabwe, Harare (Zimbabwe)
1959	Birla Industrial and Technological Museum, Kolkata (India)
	Guggenheim Museum, New York City (United States)
1962	House of Slaves (Maison des Esclaves), Gorée Island (Senegal)
	Nagoya City Science Museum, Nagoya (Japan)
	Raja Dinkar Kelkar Museum, Pune (India)
1964	Museo Nacional de Antropología, Mexico City (Mexico)
	Nehru Memorial Museum and Library, New Delhi (India)

Table 7.1. *(continued)*

Date	Name and Location
1968	Ontario Science Center, Ottawa (Canada)
	The Exploratorium, San Francisco (United States)
1971	Nakhon Si Thammarat National Museum, Nakhon Si Thammarat (Thailand)
1973	Museo del Hombre Dominicano, Santo Domingo (Dominican Republic)
1975	International Marionette Museum, Palermo (Italy)
1977	Singapore Science Centre, Singapore (Singapore)
1979	Écomusée du Val de Bièvre, Fresnes (France)
	Makah Cultural and Research Center, Neah Bay (United States)
	Musée et Centre Régional d'Interprétation de la Haute-Beauce, Saint-Évariste-de-Forsyth, Ontario (Canada)
	National Science Centre for Education, Bangkok (Thailand)
1981	Vechaar Utensils Museum, Ahmedabad (India)
1983	Rock and Roll Hall of Fame, Cleveland (United States)
1984	Ecomuseu Municipal do Seixal, Seixal (Portugal)
1985	The Nanjing Massacre Memorial Hall, Nanjing (China)
	Ekomuseum Bergslagen, Bergslagen (Sweden)
1986	Musée d'Orsay, Paris (France)
	National Museum of Natural Science, Taichung (Taiwan)
1988	China Science and Technology Museum, Beijing (China)
	Museum of Jurassic Technology, Culver City (United States)
1989	Vitra Design Museum, Weil am Rhein (Germany)
1990	Kiasma Museum of Contemporary Art, Helsinki (Finland)
	Musée Les Abattoirs, Toulouse (France)
	Vasa Museum (Vasamuseet), Stockholm (Sweden)
1991	Hong Kong Science Museum, Hong Kong (China)
1992	Museo Nacional Reina Sofía, Madrid (Spain)
1993	Carré d'Art, Nîmes (France)
1994	Bagatti Valsecchi Museum, Milan (Italy)
1996	John Heinz Pittsburgh Regional History Center, Pittsburgh (United States)
	National Science Centre, Kuala Lumpur (Malaysia)
1997	Centre Georges Pompidou, Paris (France)
	Deutsche Guggenheim, Berlin (Germany)
	Getty Center, Los Angeles (United States)
	Guggenheim, Bilbao (Spain)
	Museum of Marrakech, Marrakech (Morocco)
	Nelson Mandela National Museum, Mthatha (South Africa)
1998	Ciudad de las Artes y las Ciencias, Valencia (Spain)
1999	El Museo de los Niños Abasto, Buenos Aires (Argentina)
2000	Lwandle Migrant Labour Museum, Lwandle (South Africa)
	Tate Modern, London (England)
2001	Jewish Museum (Jüdisches Museum), Berlin (Germany)
	Museo de Arte Latinoamericano de Buenos Aires, Buenos Aires (Argentina)
2002	Instituto Ricardo Brennand, Recife (Brazil)
	Museo d'Arte Moderna e Contemporanea di Trento e Rovereto (Italy)
2003	Alexandria National Museum, Alexandria (Egypt)

(continued)

Table 7.1. *(continued)*

Date	Name and Location
2004	The Museum of World Culture, Gothenburg (Sweden)
2006	Ben M'sik Community Museum, Casablanca (Morocco)
	Inhotim, Brumadinho (Brazil)
	Mercedes-Benz Museum, Stuttgart (Germany)
	Musée du Quai Branly, Paris (France)
2007	Creation Museum, Petersburg (United States)
2009	Acropolis Museum, Athens (Greece)
2011	Museo Memorial de la Resistencia Dominicana, Santo Domingo (Dominican Republic)
	National September 11 Memorial and Museum, New York City (United States)
2012	Children's Civilization and Creativity Museum, Cairo (Egypt)

The 1800s were marked by profound and often rapid changes that shaped society and its museums. It was a time when most European countries and the United States were "transformed from agricultural to industrial economies" (MacGregor 2011:593). At the start of the century, in 1800, land transportation was limited to walking or the use of wheeled vehicles pulled by draft animals. Just eleven years later, the first practical steam locomotive began operating in England, and by the close of the century, there were more than 350,000 miles of railroad track worldwide. When the first photograph (a view through the window of a house in Le Gras, France) was taken by Joseph Nicéphore Niépce (1765–1833) in 1826, the image required an exposure of more than eight hours and could not be duplicated. Less than fifty years later, in 1872, Charles Darwin (1809–1882) became one of the first scientists to use mechanically reproduced photographs to illustrate a scientific publication—his book *On the Expression of the Emotions in Man and Animals* (Browne 2002). During the 1800s, Great Britain become the largest colonial empire the world had ever seen, at the same time that Karl Marx (1818–1883) was writing *Das Kapital* (1867) in the Reading Room of the British Museum (Roberts and Westad 2013). In 1800, the phlogiston theory (which had dominated chemistry since the late 1600s) had just been disproved, paving the way for the first periodic table of the elements arranged by atomic weight to be published in 1869 by Dmitri Mendeleev (1834–1907; Partington 1957). Many in Europe, particularly in England, assumed that indefinite improvement in the future was possible.

The possible future was made clear for Londoners in 1851, when the Crystal Palace Exposition opened in Hyde Park. The exposition was effectively the first world's fair, designed to demonstrate the power and influence of England on the world stage. The name for the exposition came from the building it was housed in, which was unlike any structure previ-

BOX 7.1.
Losing One's Marbles

The case of the Elgin marbles is one of the most famous, oft-debated, and ultimately vexing museum legal and ethical problem. Thomas Bruce (1766–1841), the 7th Earl of Elgin and the 11th Earl of Kincardine, was named Great Britain's ambassador to Constantinople in 1798, a rather unglamorous posting that Elgin sought because of his lifelong interest in art and antiquities. To pursue his interests in Greek art, Elgin hired a crew of artists to make drawings of structures and plaster casts of marble statuary, inscriptions, and building features among the ruins in Athens. At the time, Athens was under the control of the Ottoman Empire. The Ottoman government had made it illegal to remove parts of ancient buildings in an attempt to thwart the thriving trade in classical antiquities, which were much desired in European collections. Despite this law, bits of buildings and statues were routinely broken off and sold. Elgin later asserted that, while in Athens in 1801, he had obtained permission to remove marbles and export them to England, which he felt was imperative because they were deteriorating badly in situ. Elgin wrote that he believed the Greeks did not deserve to have the marbles and, in fact, considered them worthless. Elgin believed he had a divine calling to preserve the antiquities in England.

Between 1801 and 1812, Elgin had workmen remove approximately 247 feet of the frieze and 17 figures from the Parthenon, as well as pieces from the Acropolis, the Erechtheion, the Propylaia, and the Temple of Athena Nike. The marbles were shipped to England, where they were exhibited by Elgin's mother at her Park Lane estate before Elgin returned to England in 1805. Several influential people thought it was wrong of Elgin to remove the marbles, including several writers. In order to increase her income (the Elgin family seemed to be always in debt), Elgin's mother held a series of events in conjunction with the marbles, for which admission was charged. At one point, a well-known prizefighter was hired to pose nude among the sculptures for two hours so paying guests could compare his anatomy to that of the figures depicted in the marbles. A London newspaper reported that several gentlemen paid to attend the event. This led to several boxing matches being held at Park Lane, with the marbles as the backdrop. At least two writers who visited the exhibit at Park Lane wrote poems about the marbles, John Keats (1795–1821)—the most famous being "Ode to a Grecian Urn"—and Lord Byron (George Gordon Byron, 1788–1824), who, in the second canto of "Childe Harold's Pilgrimage," railed against Elgin for taking the marbles.

By 1806, Elgin himself was deeply in debt (to the tune of £74,000, the equivalent today of about $2 million) and also embroiled in a controversial and costly divorce, so he decided to sell the marbles to the British government. In a hearing before the Select Committee of the House of Commons on the Earl of Elgin's Collection in 1816, several experts were consulted to try to

(continued)

BOX 7.1.
(continued)

determine the value of the collection based on the quality of the marbles as works of art and the dates of their creation. The expert opinions ranged from priceless to worthless (with a few witnesses claiming the marbles were fakes). Elgin was asked for the documentation of his permission to collect and export the marbles. Although he was unable to produce the requested original documents, Elgin pointed out that the marbles were removed openly by local workers (all paid by Elgin) under the supervision of the Constantinople authorities and that he was far from the only collector exporting marbles and other antiquities from Athens at the time. Elgin reiterated his opinion that, had he left the marbles in place, they would have either deteriorated or been removed by other collectors. After consideration of whether Elgin might have bribed officials to obtain the marbles, contemplation of the benefit of the marbles to the study of the arts in England, and finally questioning Elgin's motives in collecting the marbles in the first place, the vote to purchase the marbles went eighty-two for, thirty against. After further deliberation, the British government offered Elgin £24,000 for the marbles (although collecting and shipping them to England had cost him £74,000). In 1816, the marbles were purchased for £34,000, and Elgin was named a trustee of the British Museum.

Sources: Jackson 1992; Moser 2006; Nagel 2005; Siegel 2008.

ously seen in Europe—a cast-iron-and-plate-glass structure that enclosed 92,000 square meters of space, soaring 39 meters in height. More than 100,000 objects from around the world were displayed in 4 groups (raw materials, machinery, manufactures, and fine arts). During the year that the exposition was open, it had more than 6 million visitors (Camin 2007).

After the exposition closed, several of the displayed collections and some of the proceeds were used to start the Museum of Manufactures at Marlborough House, which opened in 1852, administered by the Department of Practical Art of the Board of Trade (Goodwin 1990). In 1853, the museum was renamed the Museum of Ornamental Art, and later it was relocated to South Kensington, where it became the South Kensington Museum, which opened in 1857 (Siegel 2008). Because the new museum was intended to be a fine art museum based on the European model, "[g]reater emphasis was placed upon collecting artefacts of European culture and British art; even contemporary art or manufactured design took second place as far as the interests of the Museum were concerned" (Goodwin 1990:10). There was much debate about the purpose of the museum and what it should collect, centered around the dichotomy of whether the collection should be based on the intrinsic physical properties of objects, their materials, how they were made, and their craftsmanship or based on the extrinsic surrounding culture and the aesthetic of a particular period. Henry Cole (1808–1882)—an inventor, civil servant, and innovator in commerce and education who is credited with inventing the commercial Christmas card in 1843—thought that the purpose of the museum should be learning and inspiration. Cole was appointed to the Royal Commission for the Exhibition of 1851 and used that role to improve science and art education in the United Kingdom. Cole served as general superintendent of the Department of Practical Art, which enabled him to be instrumental in developing the museum and moving it to South Kensington. Cole then served as the first director of the museum (from 1857 to 1873). These experiences led Cole to believe that "it was a duty of Governments to involve themselves in public education and support for science and art" (Goodwin 1990:45). In an address Cole presented in 1857 concerning the functions of the Science and Art Department of the museum, he stated, "The working man comes to this Museum" (quoted in Siegel 2008:246). In 1899, the name of the institution was changed to the Victoria and Albert Museum. Today, the museum's collections contain more than 4.5 million objects of decorative arts and design.

A somewhat similar pattern to the establishment of the Victoria and Albert Museum brought the Field Museum in Chicago into being (figure 7.2). The Field Museum was founded to preserve some of the exhibits from

Figure 7.2. The Field Museum, Chicago.

the 1893 World's Columbian Exposition. Henry Ward Putnam (1839–1915) began advocating for a postfair museum in 1890 (before the exposition opened), which attracted the attention of several philanthropists who wanted to show off Chicago as an important world center (Brinkman 2009). The intention was to establish a museum that would serve as a memorial of the World's Columbian Exposition by including art, archaeology, science, and history, although in 1905, the museum's scope was restricted to anthropology, botany, geology, and zoology (Brinkman 2009). The primary financial backing for the new museum came from a businessman named Marshall Field (1834–1906), who was not at all interested in natural history but changed his mind about underwriting the museum after being persuaded that it would give his name a special immortality (Brinkman 2009). The new Field Museum opened in 1894.

Throughout the nineteenth century, collections continued to flow into European museums from the exploration, exploitation, and colonization of other continents and islands. The East India Museum opened in 1801 at the offices of the East India Company (a commercial joint-stock company) on Leadenhall Street in London. When the Government of India Act was passed in 1853 (which kept East India under the administration of the East India Company in trust for the British Crown), the control of the museum passed to the India Office of the British government, and the museum was reopened in Fife House between 1861 and 1868. The museum's collections began to be absorbed into the South Kensington Museum about 1875. Between 1879 and 1880, the collections were divided between the South Kensington Museum and the British Museum (Siegel 2008). A greater influx of Asian objects began showing up in European museums after the Opium War (between China and Britain) opened China to more Western trade in 1839 and as a result of the US Navy forcing Japan to engage in trade with foreigners in 1851 (Roberts and Westad 2013).

Pomian (1990) identified four patterns in the formation of European museums between 1800 and 1900, using Venice as a model: (1) Traditional museums grew from collections in church treasuries that were opened to the public and metamorphosed into museums during the nineteenth century; (2) palace collections (e.g., the Uffizi Gallery) became museums following a pattern similar to the church treasury collections; (3) teaching collections at educational establishments developed into public museums; and (4) museums were formed from collections purchased by an institution, such as the Modern Art Gallery in Venice or the British Museum.

Another pattern that would become fairly common in England and the United States was that of the wealthy private individual who left a personal collection to become a public museum, such as the architect Sir John Soane (1753–1837). Soane's neoclassical-style house, filled to overflowing with his architectural drawings and models; prints and paintings; Greek,

Roman, and Egyptian antiquities; and medieval objects, was established as a museum by an act of the British Parliament in 1833 that took effect upon Soane's death in 1837. The act provided for the appointment of a board of trustees for the collection and two staff members, a curator and an inspectress. The alterations to the Soane collection can be followed through a series of descriptions of the museum that were published, beginning with the first version prepared by Soane himself in 1830, which went through eleven editions between 1830 and 1930. In 1955, *A New Description of Sir John Soane's Museum* was published in an all-new edition that followed Soane's original plan (but no longer relied on the original text) and went through several editions, the twelfth appearing in 2014 (Summerhorn 1984). The regular appearance of these accounts presents an unusual opportunity to trace the chronology of how the collection was exhibited in detail.

Museum growth and development is closely correlated with literacy, which increased in much of the world between 1800 and 1900. Book prices generally fell about midcentury, after the publishing industry became increasingly mechanized and the paper tax in England was repealed in 1860 (Lutz 2015). The estimated world literacy rate nearly doubled, from about 12 percent in 1800 to about 21 percent in 1900 (Roser 2015), but literacy rates were much higher in some regions than others. By the mid-nineteenth century, an estimated half of Europeans were literate, with the highest levels of literacy in England and the Netherlands (Roberts and Westad 2013). For example, in Britain, the literacy rate rose from about 54 percent in 1800 to about 68 percent in 1900. Over the same time period, the literacy rate in France went from 35 percent to 75 percent, in Germany from 50 percent to 73 percent, in Italy from 23 percent to 48 percent, and in the Netherlands from 88 percent to 92 percent (Roser 2015). In the United States, the literacy rate among those of European descent went from about 60 percent to more than 80 percent between 1800 and 1900, aided by the development of public libraries. In 1875, there were only 188 public libraries in the United States, but by 1886, there were more than 600 (Murray 2009:182). During this period of time, museums were widely seen as institutions integral to raising the level of education of the public. In the United States, the assistant director of the Smithsonian made the bold statement, "The museum of the future of this democratic land should be adapted to the needs of the mechanic, the factory operator, the day-laborer, the salesman, and the clerk, as much as to those of the professional man and the man of leisure" (Goode 1889:263). In Great Britain, the increase in museums was helped by the rise of the popular press, which itself grew enormously thanks to the introduction of less-expensive means for the reproduction of illustrations and the end of the paper tax (Siegel 2008).

THE "NEW MUSEUM IDEA"

The rapidly rising middle class in Victorian England was very fond of objects—people tended to crowd their homes with them to the point that the "objects that pack Victorian parlors—aquariums, terrariums, globes, books, and beetle collections among them—might seem to make bourgeois life into a collector's paradise, an alternative to ever quitting the home" (Plotz 2008:1), but this seeming clutter of objects was a physical sign of financial success and a means of autodidacticism, of engaging in wholesome self-improving activities. At the beginning of the nineteenth century, museums were portrayed as places of amusement, but by the end of the century, they had come to be seen as primarily educational institutions. The popularity of art museums came about due to a combination of the "rise of academic art history, new aesthetic theories, and the development of democracy. Once high art moved from churches, temples, and princely collections into the public space of the museum, visitors needed to be educated" (Carrier 2006:4). In the latter part of the 1800s, the "new museum idea" that there should be a separation of study collections from exhibition collections became dominant (Pyenson and Sheets-Pyenson 1999):

> The issues at stake here are posed most clearly by the debates regarding whether or not collections might be separated into two parts: one for research purposes and the other for public display. Richard Owen [1804–1892] had proved recalcitrantly opposed to this during his period as Director of the Natural History collections at the British Museum as well as, later, founding-Director of the Museum of Natural History when it moved to its own premises. . . . It was [John] Edward Gray [1800–1875], the Keeper of Zoology at the British Museum, and Owen's subordinate, who was the first to suggest [it], in 1858. (Bennett 1995:41)

In the United States, Louis Agassiz at Harvard (1807–1873) tried "to reconcile the two functions of research and popular pedagogy" in his institution by maintaining just one collection, all of it on exhibit (Bennett 1995:41), but in 1878, the collections of the Museum of Comparative Zoology were also divided. The new museum idea was vigorously championed by Owen's successor at the British Museum (Natural History), William Henry Flower (1831–1899) beginning in 1884 (Flower 1898). Flower believed that it was the role of the curator to make the separations, identify significant objects for exhibition, and prepare their labels (Bennett 1995). In 1889, George Brown Goode reported that, at the Smithsonian Institution in the United States, the "collections are divided into two great classes: the exhibition series, which constitutes the educational portion of the museum, and is exposed to public view, with all possible accessories for public entertainment and instruction; and the study series, which is kept in the scientific laboratories, and is rarely examined except by professional investigators" (Goode 1889:265).

The new museum idea brought significant changes to the way that museums exhibited their collections. The challenge to the principles of display in the previous generation's cabinets of curiosities "came from the changing focus of natural history displays which . . . came increasingly to accord priority of attention to the normal, the commonplace and the close-at-hand at the expense of the exceptional and the exotic. This shift of emphasis was . . . simultaneously epistemic and utilitarian. It was the product of new principles of scientific rationality" (Bennett 1995:41). Until the end of the 1800s, most museums had all (or almost all) of the objects in their collections on display in closely arranged arrays in neatly ordered cases. Paintings and drawings were hung on walls to maximize the use of space, with two, three, or even four paintings crowded one above the other. At a time when mass media presentations of the wider world were largely limited to written descriptions, this style of exhibition was popular with the public, as it gave them the opportunity to see a lot of objects in a relatively small space. It was a time when museums were perceived as places to come and see new and different things, institutions that continued to help people make sense of the chaos in the world.

THE PUBLIC IN THE PUBLIC MUSEUM

At the beginning of the nineteenth century, public museums were not necessarily easy for the public to access or even open to all of the public. As late as 1785, the British Museum still required potential visitors to apply in advance for admission tickets (Carrier 2006), and even in the early 1800s, the museum was "difficult to visit, particularly for any member of the working classes, due to the hours it kept and the mode in which its collections could be viewed—the notoriously rushed tour that followed on the required prior reservation" (Siegel 2008:7). Although the Louvre was opened to the public in August 1793 as the old regime faded, signaling that the art that had once been the private property of privileged monarchs was now available to everyone (Carrier 2006), in reality, the change took time to be adopted. The British Museum established rules that prohibited the admission of children under eight years of age and required visitors to not touch anything, not speak too loudly, and to not be obtrusive. The House of Commons formed a Select Committee on National Monuments and Works of Art in 1841 to address a variety of issues related to public access to public institutions, including how dirty the objects on display became and how they were

Table 7.2. Visitors to the British Museum, 1807–1840

Year	Number of Visitors
1807	13,046
1814	33,074
1818	63,253
1821	91,151
1824	112,840
1825	127,643
1826	123,302
1827	79,131
1828	81,228
1829	68,101
1830	71,336
1831	99,712
1832	147,896
1833	210,495
1834	237,366
1835	289,104
1836	383,147
1837	321,151
1838	266,008
1839	280,850
1840	247,929

Source: Siegel 2008.

cleaned, how much damage was occurring to the collections, whether public institutions should be open on Sundays, and whether working-class crowds caused more problems than other groups of visitors (Siegel 2008). For most of the century, the labeling of objects on exhibit was minimal—it was recommended that visitors purchase the 240-page guidebook *A Synopsis of the Contents of the British Museum* (Siegel 2008). Nevertheless, the numbers of visitors to the British Museum grew steadily between 1807, when 13,046 visitors came to the museum, and 1839, when there were 280,850 visitors (table 7.2). The National Gallery, which was founded in 1824, went from 130,000 visitors in 1835 to an amazing 768,244 visitors five years later in 1840 (Siegel 2008).

Most editions of the guidebook for Sir John Soane's Museum in London include the set of ten "General Regulations" for visitors inside the back cover, which includes requirements that each visitor sign the visitor's book, that visitors leave "sticks, umbrellas, cases and parcels" (Summerhorn 1984:cover) with the attendant at the entrance, that visitors who wished to sketch in the museum not impede other visitors, and that visitors under the age of fourteen be accompanied by an adult (Summerhorn 1984).

The factors contributing to the growth in the number of museums and in museum attendance by the public were complex and interrelated. These included the more obvious factors, such as the aura of egalitarianism and democratic culture in the wake of the French Revolution and the emerging market economy in Europe that resulted in a redistribution of wealth, giving the rising middle class more discretionary spending power (Carrier 2006); the corresponding rise in literacy rates, and a shift in population from rural to urban areas in many European countries. Some of the less-obvious factors included the development of reliable and affordable indoor gas lighting, lower prices for plate glass, improvements in public transportation that made it easier for people to get to museums, and the prominence of new aesthetic theories in the arts and architecture. The growing interest in museums was manifested in many new ways, including the circulation of portable museum exhibits to schools, which in turn boosted family visits to museums (Lewis 1985; Wittlin 1970). Other factors included greater accessibility of museums—by the end of the 1800s, more American museums were open on Sundays, had low admission or free admission, and had special programs for children than did British museums (Wittlin 1970). In 1855, the South Kensington Museum in London established a Circulation Department to send portable exhibits to schools (Wittlin 1970). In 1912, the German Museum of Applied and Commercial Arts (Deutsches Museum für Kunst in Handel und Gewerbe) in Hagen sent fifty exhibits to forty-two towns (Wittlin 1970). In the United States, the ratio of automobiles to house museums in 1895 was 20:40, but by 1910, there were 500,000 cars for every 100 house museums (Wittlin 1970). The expansion of the railroads in the United States meant that trains could be used to circulate agricultural exhibits in rural areas by the end of the nineteenth century (Wittlin 1970).

The period from 1800 to 1900 was a time of creation of national museums. In England, the National Gallery was founded in 1824 to exhibit British culture, which many have interpreted as an expression of the country's confidence as a world power. The National Museum of Budapest played a role in the independence struggle in Hungary, as it was on the steps of the museum that the poet Sándor Petőfi (1823–1849) read his famous "Up, ye Magyars!" poem to launch the Hungarian revolution in March 1848 (Wittlin 1970). The National Museum of Prague, founded in 1818 with a collection emphasizing the natural sciences in the district of Bohemia, was, by the 1830s, developing into a distinct national cultural unit and expanding the diversity of its collection. The Smithsonian Institution in the United States was founded in 1846 (discussed in this chapter). A number of private art collections of both old masters and British art opened to visitors on a regular basis in London between 1800 and 1820 (McClellan 1993).

The centuries-long quests for universal classification schemes finally bore fruit in several areas between 1800 and 1900. The hierarchical system for the classification of plants and animals proposed by Linnaeus in the previous century (chapter 6) was, for all practical purposes, universally adopted by the time that *On the Origin of Species* was published by Charles Darwin in 1859 (box 7.2). Darwin's theory of evolution gave even more weight to the Linnaean system by providing an explanation for biodiversity. For library materials, the Dewey decimal classification (also called the Dewey decimal system) was published by Melvil Dewey (1851–1931) in 1876 in a four-page pamphlet. Dewey's revolutionary idea grouped library materials into ten classes, each class having ten divisions, each division further divided into ten sections, with up to a thousand topics (Murray 2009). The advent of the Dewey decimal system not only helped librarians organize and classify the materials they cared for, but it also provided a much more efficient means of physically managing the collection, as it introduced the concepts of relative location and relative indexing, which allowed newly acquired materials to be added to the collection based on subject and without having to do massive rearrangements of the storage array or maintain a complicated index to storage locations (previously most libraries had assigned permanent shelf locations to books in the order that they were acquired). Systems for the classification of the contents of art and history museums were further refined, although none achieved the universality of the Linnaean and Dewey systems.

Reforms launched in response to social problems related to the rise of industrialization contributed to the development of many municipal and regional museums, more than one hundred new museums in the United Kingdom, and at least fifty new museums in Germany (Lewis 1985). In 1820, there were still very few museums in the British Isles, but there were more than four hundred by the end of the nineteenth century and the start of World War I (Siegel 2008). This is not to say that all of the museums were as good as they should be. Complaining about the state of provincial museums, Edward Forbes (1815–1854) wrote,

> When a naturalist goes from one country into another, his first inquiry is for local collections. He is anxious to see authentic and full cabinets of the productions of the region he is visiting. He wishes, moreover, if possible, to study them apart—not mingled up with general or miscellaneous collections—and distinctly arranged with special reference to the region they illustrate. For all that concerns the whole world or the general affinities of objects, he seeks the greatest national collections, such as the British Museum, the Jardin des Plantes, the Royal Museums at Berlin and Vienna. But that which relates to the particular country he is exploring, he expects to find in a special department of the national museum, or in some separate establishment, the purpose of which is, in a scientific sense, patriotic and limited. So

BOX 7.2.
The Darwin Effect

The near-universal acceptance of Linnaean hierarchical classification in the nineteenth century is a rather odd confluence of a system designed by a creationist used to classify the products of evolution and a testimony to the strength of a good organizational system. Carl Linnaeus (1707–1778) was a deeply religious individual who believed that he had been divinely appointed to classify the products of creation (Blunt 2001; Schmitz, Uddenberg, and Östensson 2007). As discussed in chapter 6, the Linnaean binomial scientific name brought much-needed order to a confusion of plant and animal names, despite the fact that many of Linnaeus's groupings of species were artificial (Linnaeus sometimes thought species were related based on their superficial resemblance alone). Linnaeus believed in the divine creation of species and the validity of Aristotle's *scala naturae* and based his system on the philosophical idea of Plato's theory of forms (box 3.2).

Despite the profound effect that Darwin's ideas had on biological thought and the recognition that related species are descendants of a common ancestor, the basic structure of the Linnaean nomenclatural system was retained, although the system was substantially revised and amplified after Charles Darwin, particularly with the formation of international rules regulated by elected commissions for zoology beginning in 1895 and botany in 1930 (Mayr 1969, 1982; Melville 1995; Nicolson 1991).

In the century after the publication of Linnaeus's work and before the publication of Darwin's *On the Origin of Species* in 1859, natural history collections were typological, meaning that only one or two specimens of a species were considered sufficient to represent the species. As a result, collections tended to be relatively small, and there was much trading of specimens among museums. Darwin's theory of natural selection prompted a fundamental revolution in the biological sciences and our understanding of the origin and diversity of life on Earth and how species are related, which in turn had far-reaching effects on how specimens were collected, preserved, and exhibited. Prior to the publication of Darwin's work, animal and plant species were believed to be created, immutable entities, hence natural history museum collections would have only one or two representative specimens of each species. Most natural history museums featured comprehensive synoptic displays, with the organisms arranged according to the prevailing version of Aristotle's *scala naturae*, the continuous chain of life from most lowly to most advanced forms. Darwin's theory demonstrated that the evolution of life was not a continuous advancement of perfection but rather a diverse branching in response to natural selection (called descent with modification), and to understand this, it was necessary to study the variation within species. To study variation, many specimens of each species were needed from throughout the

(*continued*)

BOX 7.2.
(continued)

species' geographic range, not just the one or two that had served for decades when the typological philosophy had underpinned biology (Whitehead 1971). Furthermore, a "scientific rationale for active collecting . . . became compelling, as taxonomic practices became more exacting and dependent on large series collections" (Kohler 2006:111). In the late 1880s and 1890s, many natural history museums began sponsoring their own expeditions rather than purchasing collections from commercial collectors as they had done in the past. With this change, a new pattern emerged so that the "history of collecting in the last two hundred years is one of continual intensification: from the geographically extensive and serendipitous collecting of the age of exploration and empire; to the extensive and intensive methods of the age of survey; and to local and highly intensive collecting in the age of ecology" (Kohler 2006:270).

The growth of the natural history collections at the British Museum led a number of British scientists, including Darwin, to petition the government in 1866 to officially separate the natural history collections from the British Museum. The collections were moved to a new purpose-built building in South Kensington in 1881 (figure 7.3), but natural history was to remain a department of the British Museum until 1963, when it became independent

Figure 7.3. The Natural History Museum, London.

with its own board of trustees. The institution's name was changed to the Natural History Museum in 1992, and today it is the world's largest natural history museum, with more than 70 million specimens, housed both in the original building and in two specialized collection storage facilities, Darwin Centre I and Darwin Centre II (Simmons 2013).

Darwin himself had collected many specimens on his five-year voyage aboard the *Beagle*, and after his return to England, he made extensive use of museum specimens from around the world during the decade he spent studying more than 10,000 specimens of barnacles (Anderson and Lowe 2010). Had Darwin relied solely on museum collections, he would not have found the evidence to support his theory of natural selection due to the insufficient number of specimens of each species then in collections. Both Darwin and the codiscoverer of descent with modification, Alfred Russel Wallace (1823–1913), formed their initial ideas about evolution while working in the field with the vast abundance of living things.

One of the great advantages of the Linnaean system was the ease with which a natural history collection could be put in order anywhere in the world. In effect, the system of scientific nomenclature gave scientists a universal language to communicate about species diversity. Arguably Darwin's biggest impact on museums was the realization that many specimens of each species were needed in collections in order to understand the range of variability within and between species, thus after Darwin, natural history collections became extremely large, as many specimens of each species were retained. Darwin's theory of evolution gave natural history museums not just a system for putting collections in order but also a motivation to seek more specimens to better understand biodiversity.

also with the students of history and antiquities; they are often disappointed, and in the end find what they require here and there, bit by bit, in the cabinets of private individuals. In like manner, when the inquirer goes from one province to another, from one country to another, he first seeks for local collections. In almost every town of any size or consequence, he finds a public museum; but how often does he find any part of that museum devoted to the illustration of the productions of the district? The very feature which of all others would give interest and value to the collection, which would render it most useful for teaching purposes, has in most instances been omitted, or so treated as to be altogether useless. Unfortunately, not a few country museums are little better than raree-shows. They contain an incongruous accumulation of things curious, or supposed to be curious, heaped together in disorderly piles, or neatly spread out with ingenious disregard of their relations. The only label attached to nine out of ten is, "Presented by Mr and Mrs So-and-so"; the object of the presentation having been, either to cherish a glow of generous self-satisfaction in the bosom of the donor, or to get rid— under the semblance of doing a good action—of rubbish that had once been prized but latterly had stood in the way. (quoted in Siegel 2008:259)

In 1882, the British economist W. Stanley Jevons (1835–1882) published an essay entitled "The Use and Abuse of Museums," in which he offers a critique of the museum phenomenon, writing, "It is a remarkable fact that, although public Museums have existed in this country for more than a century and a quarter, and there are now a very great number of Museums of one sort or another, hardly anything has been written about their general principles of management and economy" (quoted in Siegel 2008:283). Jevons proposed a classification of museums into six categories, while admitting that there would be some institutions that overlapped from one category into another:

1. Standard National Museums
2. Popular Museums
3. Provincial Museums
4. Special Museums (formed for particular purposes, such as the Monetary Museum at the Paris Mint)
5. Educational Museums (at colleges and schools)
6. Private Museums

Among Jevons's complaints were that far too many people used museums just to "promenade" and that "[m]any go to a public Museum just as they take a walk, without thought or care as to what they are going to see" and that it was easy to measure museum attendance but much more difficult to measure museum learning (Siegel 2008:284). Jevons also believed that museums exhibited too many objects and that there was too little time to learn from them. Although Jevons liked the idea of museums, he also thought that

> [a]s with the books of a public library, so in the case of public Museums, the utility of each specimen is greatly multiplied with regard to the multitude of persons who may inspect it. But the utility of each inspection is vastly less than that which arises from private possession of a suitable specimen which can be kept near at hand or be studied at any moment, handled, experimented and reflected upon,

which led him to conclude, "The whole British Museum accordingly will not teach a youth as much as he will learn by collecting a few fossils or a few minerals, *in situ* if possible, and taking them home to examine and read and think about" (Siegel 2008:289).

SPECIALIZATION

The nineteenth century was the first period of major specialization of museums. Prior to this point in time, most collections were diverse (with a few notable exceptions that contained mostly art), but museums were just beginning to diversify and specialize. During the period 1800–1900, a much wider array of institutions that gave more attention to the presentation of particular kinds of objects began to appear.

It was during this century that restorations and re-creations of historic building interiors became increasingly popular. In 1830, the Altes Museum in Berlin opened with its collection arranged to serve as a "visual history of art from its beginnings" (Holdengräber 1987:111), corresponding with Hegel's lectures on aesthetics in the late 1820s, which "provided the intellectual framework for the historic hangings of the new public museum" in accordance with Hegel's belief that paintings could only be understood in a historic arrangement (Carrier 2006:13). The Alte Pinakothek in Munich, which opened in 1836, had gallery spaces designed to protect the art that was on exhibit from fire, dust, and vibration and had north-facing windows for light and moderate heat in the winter (Lewis 1992). One of the first ethnology museums opened in Leiden in 1837 (Zubiaur Carreño 2004), the first historic-house museums appeared in Europe and the United States, and the first open-air or living museum was founded near Oslo, Norway, in 1881. Arthur Hazelius started the Skansen open-air museum on Djurgården Island in Stockholm in 1891 to portray the preindustrial rural life of Sweden. The first mobile museum, developed to serve schoolchildren, was started in Liverpool, England, in 1884 (Zubiaur Carreño 2004).

An archaeologist at the University of Pennsylvania named Henry Chapman Mercer (1856–1930), who traveled extensively in Europe between 1881 and 1889, became concerned about the effects of industrialization on craftsmen and their trades. In response, he founded the Moravian Pottery and Tile Works in 1889 (a museum in which artisans continue to make decorative tiles by hand) and the Mercer Museum in 1916 (to preserve the tools of preindustrial American trades), both located in Doylestown, Pennsylvania. The historic environment museum complex known as Colonial Williamsburg was established in the United States in 1926 (Alexander 1979; Lewis 1992). The Henry Ford Greenfield Village museum opened in Dearborn, Michigan, in 1928. The predominance of history museums, particularly historic-house museums, in the United States has been explained as the result of an abundance of local and regional historical societies, beginning with the Massachusetts Historical Society, which was founded in Boston in 1791 (Lewis 1992).

Some of the diversification of museums into specialized institutions came with the breakup of larger museums into more specialized departments and, in some cases, larger institutions splitting into more than one museum. In an 1858 review of several government reports on the British Museum, Elizabeth Eastlake wrote,

To congregate under one roof the productions of nature, art, science, and literature, might be proper at the commencement of the institution, when the contributions in each department were few, and the whole together only constituted a Museum of very moderate dimensions; but the question is entirely different now that every collection is made as far as possible complete, and has thus assumed colossal proportions. (Siegel 2008:220)

In 1836, the British Museum was organized into three main departments: Printed Books (which included prints and engravings), Manuscripts (which included coins, medals, and drawings), and Natural and Artificial Productions (which included antiquities and natural curiosities), with some minor variations (Siegel 2008; table 5.1). Additions to the collections prompted the addition of other departments, including Antiquities and Art (which included prints, drawings, coins, and medals) and Botany. Prints and Drawings later became a separate department, and Natural History was divided into two departments, Geology (which included paleontology and mineralogy) and Zoology. In 1861, the Department of Oriental Antiquities and Ethnography was split into three separate units with the creation of two new departments, Greek and Roman Antiquities and Coins and Medals. In 1866, the Department of Oriental Antiquities was redefined as Egyptian and Assyrian objects, with British and Mediaeval Antiquities becoming a separate department, along with Ethnographic collections (Murray 1904; Wittlin 1970). Between 1880 and 1883, the natural science collections were moved from Bloomsbury to Kensington to become the British Museum (Natural History), then still a department of the British Museum but now the Natural History Museum (figure 7.3).

During this era, many museums attempted to present foreign material culture in an accurate, scientific manner; however, their presentations were often undermined by cultural biases and the prevalent belief that foreign cultures were examples of stages in a progressive development from primitive to advanced (Wittlin 1970). One of the most prominent persons promoting this idea was the self-taught anthropologist Augustus Henry Lane-Fox Pitt Rivers (1827–1900), who amassed an enormous personal anthropological collection while serving as an officer in the British army in various overseas posts. Pitt Rivers began collecting the objects in 1851 that ultimately became his own Ethnographical Museum, which opened at Bethnal Green in 1874. In stark contrast to the cabinets of curiosities of the past, Pitt Rivers focused on common, everyday expressions of material culture, although he also believed that his collection illustrated progressive stages in the development of civilization (Wittlin 1970). In 1875, Pitt Rivers stressed that his collections of "ordinary and typical specimens, rather than rare objects, have been selected and arranged in sequence, so as to trace, as far as practicable, the successions of ideas by which the minds of men in a primitive condition of culture have progressed from the simple to the complex, and from the homogenous to the heterogeneous" (quoted in Blom 2002:123). In a statement provided to Oxford University, Pitt Rivers wrote, "The specimens, *Ethnological* and *Prehistoric*, are arranged with a view to demonstrate, either actually or hypothetically, the development and continuity of the material arts from the simpler to the more complex form" (quoted in Murray 1904:243). In 1884, Pitt Rivers donated more than 20,000 ethnographic objects to Oxford University.

NATURAL HISTORY MUSEUMS

The most significant changes in collection organization, structure, and function took place in natural history museums. During the first three-quarters of the century, natural history was seen as an appropriate, uplifting hobby for the middle class, for men, women, and children (Barber 1980; Merrill 1989), with a corresponding increase in public interest in natural history museums, zoological parks, and botanic gardens. The study of natural history was widely accepted as a pious hobby for Christians who wished to better understand divine creation. Many Victorian families had newly fashionable aquariums or terrariums in their parlors containing live plants and animals or participated in collecting everything from rocks and fossils to ferns, insects, and bird eggs (Thwaite 2002). Dozens of magazines for natural history hobbyists were published in the Victorian era, filled with ads for the purchase or trade of specimens and collection-related equipment and furniture (Allen 1994). To support this commercial trade, professional field collectors searched the world over for specimens. The codiscoverer of the theory of evolution, Alfred Russel Wallace (1823–1913), was among many naturalists who financed decades of scientific work and exploration by selling specimens through his London agent (Berry 2002).

With the publication in 1859 of *On the Origin of Species* by Charles Darwin (1809–1882), things began to change as a different view of nature came to be understood by the public. The long-cherished ideal of the harmony of Eden had been replaced by the complex struggle for survival of the fittest. By the end of the century, natural history as a general hobby was in decline, while the scientific study of natural history as a profession was on the rise (Allen 1994; Barber 1980). The effect on museums, particularly natural history museums, was what has been called "museological Darwinism" in which all objects, "even specimens of archaeology or crafts were to be arranged as a consultative library of objects progressively subdivided into orders and genera" (Wittlin 1970:135).

The nineteenth century was when the habitat diorama came into its own—the depiction of animals in nature that became the staple of exhibitions in natural history museums (Wonders 1993). Preserved animals had been posed with background paintings beginning in the eighteenth century (e.g., in the Peale Museum in Philadelphia and in various places in Europe), but the diorama emerged from the combination of advanced, highly accurate taxidermy and botanical preservation; realistic perspective background paintings (often depicting actual scenes in nature); and scientific accuracy in the presented scene, all blended seamlessly with a realistic foreground, presenting the animals and plants as a momentary glimpse of life in the real world. Dioramas range from those that present accurate animal behavior and life history to those that present the animals accurately but in an artificial arrangement (e.g., the inclusion of male, female, and young of a species as a family group when, in fact, the species does not live in nature in such family groups). Good dioramas are works of both art and science, although they are not always recognized as such (Quinn 2006). The development of the nineteenth-century habitat diorama was made possible by advances in taxidermy, a better understanding of anatomy and the relationship of animals to their habitats, the availability of pesticides (particularly arsenic and mercuric chloride), inexpensive clear plate glass, and greatly improved electric indoor lighting. Particularly at a time when full-color depictions or films of animals in nature were not available in mass media, habitat dioramas proved to be extremely popular with museum visitors. By the mid-nineteenth century, commercial taxidermy suppliers and commercially prepared dioramas were common across Europe and North America.

The growth in natural history collections could have a negative effect on collections. In an 1835 report on testimony before the House of Commons concerning the British Museum and the fate of the original collections purchased from Hans Sloane in 1753 and those given by Joseph Banks in the 1780s, it was reported that:

> Mr. König, in his evidence before the Committee of the House of Commons, states in answer to a question as to the condition of the entomological collection: "When I came to the Museum most of those objects were in an advanced state of decomposition. Dr. Shaw had a burning every year; he called them his cremations." On his being asked, "Is there one single insect specimen remaining of the 5394 which were presented by Sir Hans Sloane?" he replies, "I should think not." Again the same witness stated that he did not think there was one specimen left of Sir Joseph Bank's collection of birds. He adds, "I know there was a considerable number of bottles which contained birds, partly in spirits of wine, partly dry, consisting of skins merely. They were transferred with other objects, chiefly of comparative anatomy, to the College of Surgeons, but they wished to have the bottles, otherwise they probably would not have taken them." (Siegel 2008:222)

RESEARCH IN MUSEUMS

In the second half of the nineteenth century, museums came to be seen not just as educational institutions but also as producers of original research. Particularly at this time in the United States, universities were primarily finishing schools, not centers of knowledge creation, so museums "assumed intellectual leadership because they fostered original research through the careful and systematic way they dealt with their objects" (Conn 1998:16). One of the first scientific expeditions in the United States was launched by the Peale Museum of Philadelphia in 1801 (see chapter 6) and is portrayed in a painting by Charles Willson Peale, *The Exhumation of the Mastodon,* painted in the period 1806–1808 (the painting is now in the Baltimore City Life Museum). Furthermore, museums presented the results of their research to the public, unlike universities, which were accessible only to the elite. In their exhibitions and programs, "[i]n matters of interpretation, of using museums as mediators between research and general education, museums in the United States were on the way to becoming innovators" before the end of the century (Wittlin 1970:135).

THE MUSEUM CONCEPT EXPORTED

Despite its European origins, the concept of the modern museum was successfully exported to many other parts of the world through trade and colonialism (Lewis 1992). The result was a burst of growth in museums in Latin America and Asia in the 1800s and in Africa in the early 1900s (table 7.1). Colonial museums were modeled on the European modern museum concept and (at least initially) dependent on the colonial power for their establishment, senior staff, and direction. Colonial museums focused on regional collections that were acquired in the service of the colonial power as examples of natural and raw materials and locally crafted trade goods (Bhatti 2012; Sheets-Pyenson 1988). A colonial museum typically had a small staff relative to its European counterparts, with native workers only in low-level assistant positions (Sheets-Pyenson 1988). Many of the colonial museums later evolved into significant national museums and were used as instruments to define postcolonial nationality and citizenship. Figure 7.4 provides a comparison of the generalized pattern of evolution of the museum concept in European and European-based cultural settings (e.g., the United States or Argentina) compared to the evolution of the museum concept in non-European cultures in which museums were decolonized before being transformed into institutions reflecting national cultures (Bhatti 2012; Cummins 1994; Morales-Moreno 1994). In South

Generalized pattern of museum development in European or European-based cultural settings:

Generalized pattern of exported European model in non-European-based cultural settings:

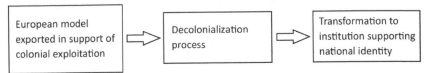

Figure 7.4. Comparison of generalized patterns of evolution of museums.

America and Asia, the "emergence of the nation-state, the public, and the public museum in the late eighteenth century, were intimately bound together" (Macdonald 2003:1). The postcolonial reinterpretations of museum collections defined nationality in a way often distinct from other nations and cultures, as discussed further in chapter 8 (Cummins 1994; Macdonald 2003; Morales-Moreno 1994).

As museums were exported from Europe into the rest of the world, they began to diverge from the European model (a process that, as discussed in the next chapter, has redefined museums in many parts of the world). In some instances, the divergence of museums was related to their legal organization. In the majority of Europe and Canada, most museums were established by local, regional, or national government agencies, while in some countries, there were centralized state museum systems, as in France and later in the former Soviet Union (Lewis 1992). Museum development was different in the United States, where most new museums were established by individuals or small groups working at the local level, resulting in museums that often reflected their founders' diverse interests and social backgrounds (Wittlin 1970). The change in museums from being privately owned to being public institutions had significant impacts on the way collections were shaped, in large part because:

[w]hile the nature of a private collection is limited only by the resources, aspirations, and opportunities of an individual who may acquire, sell, or rearrange holdings at will, the public museum is always of necessity a compromise shaped by competing interests as well as the practical constraints including the characteristics of objects acquired through gift or purchase, the architecture of structures built or redesigned to accommodate particular collections, and competition for funding from other quarters. (Siegel 2008:xii)

The first museums in South America included the National Museum of Brazil (Museu Nacional), founded in 1815 as a colonial museum in Rio de Janeiro to exhibit a collection of paintings from King Dom João VI (1769–1826) of Portugal and to stimulate research on the region's flora and fauna (Lewis 1992), and the National Museum of Colombia (Museo Nacional de Colombia), founded in 1823 in Bogotá. In Asia, the Asiatic Society of Bengal opened a museum in 1814 in Calcutta to exhibit primarily natural products of the region, which became the Indian Museum in 1875 (Punja 1991). By contrast, the National Museum of Bangkok (the first public history museum in Thailand) was not a colonial museum but was founded in 1874 by Phra Bat Somdet Phra Poraminthra Maha Chulalongkorn (1853–1910), who reigned as King Rama V (Chongkol 1999). The first museum on the African continent was the South African Museum, founded in Cape Town in 1825 (Lewis 1992).

As discussed in chapter 6, most of the early museums in the United States were focused on natural history (although notably the Peale museum started with a combination of art and natural history). One explanation for this is that "[n]atural history exhibits had priority in the orientation of the citizens in the new country; they contained directions to available natural resources. Art mattered less" (Wittlin 1970:116), but a more nuanced explanation is that natural history specimens were easy to collect and far less expensive to obtain than importing the European art and classical artifacts that then dominated European museums. This is supported by the fact that the first major art museums in the New World included large numbers of casts of classical statuary and architecture—the casts were useful both for public exhibit and for teaching art and art history (see box 7.3).

In August 1814, Rembrandt Peale (1778–1860), one of the sons of Charles Willson Peale (see chapter 6), opened a new museum in Baltimore in what is considered to be the first purpose-built permanent museum building in the United States (Brennan 1992). Peale's Baltimore Museum and Gallery of Paintings contained displays similar to those of the original Peale museum but also objects of local interest. After the British navy shelled the port of Baltimore in September 1814 (during the War of 1812), the museum exhibited British bombs and cannonballs. The Baltimore Peale museum closed in 1830, and eventually the Philadelphia museum closed as well when confronted with the same problems that many museums face today—inadequate funding, inability to maintain a sufficient paying audience, and lack of new exhibitions to attract more paying visitors. The extensive Peale collections were sold at auction in 1858 (Miller 1979).

An American merchant named John Pintard (1759–1844) and the Tammany Society (a New York political organization) opened a museum

BOX 7.3.
The Past Is Cast

Plaster casts of ancient statuary have long been a staple of collections. In the mid-sixteenth century, an Italian artist named Francesco Primaticcio (1504–1570) was hired by Francis I (1494–1547) of France to make copies of statues that the king admired in the collection of the Belvedere Courtyard in Rome that had been assembled by Pope Julius II (1443–1513; Born 2002). Primaticcio made the molds of twelve statues on site in Rome, then shipped the molds to France, where the copies of ten of the statues were cast in bronze in 1543 for the Royal Château de Fontainebleau. Primaticcio's molds were used repeatedly for the next two centuries—Thomas Jefferson (1743–1826) owned three casts made from the molds.

Although plaster casts of statues were exhibited in museums across Europe, they were particularly important for the new United States, which lacked the traditions and classical art collections of the Old World. Between 1874 and 1905, plaster casts of classical statuary became the "central attractions of American museums" (Born 2002:8). Casts were inexpensive but highly accurate depictions of the original statuary and were frequently purchased or exchanged by museums, used not just for exhibit but also for detailed study by students of art and art history.

The Boston Athenaeum, founded in 1807 as an independent library and cultural institution, set out to become a repository of fine art in the New World. The Athenaeum acquired its first plaster casts in 1822, and an art gallery was added to the institution in 1827. The plaster casts proved to be very popular:

> The Museum of Fine Arts in Copley Square . . . opened in 1876 with twenty-five casts from the Athenaeum, fifty cases of casts imported from England and thirty architectural casts of the Alhambra that had been exhibited at the Pennsylvania Centennial Exhibition. A case of fig leaves was also procured and attached "decently and in haste," per order of Dr. Bigelow, Professor of Surgery, Harvard University. (Born 2002:9)

By 1879, the Museum of Fine Arts was exhibiting 614 casts and by 1890 had acquired 777 casts, the third-largest collection in the world, topped only by the Königliches Museum (now known as the Altes Museum) in Berlin and the Strasbourg University Museum (Born 2002). Plaster cast collections were started at the Philadelphia Academy of Fine Arts in 1805, at Yale University in 1869, at the Corcoran Gallery in 1876, and also at universities across the country, including Brown, Columbia, Cornell, Dartmouth, Harvard, Mount Holyoke, and Princeton. By 1894, the Metropolitan Museum of Art had more than two thousand casts. The J. F. Slater Memorial Museum in Norwich, Connecticut, opened in 1895 with a large collection of casts that are still on exhibit.

During the early decades of the twentieth century, casts fell out of favor as museums in the United States began to receive contributions from wealthy individuals eager to collect and donate original European art and classical archaeological artifacts—the influx of original works soon displaced the casts in many museums (Born 2002). Plaster casts fell into aesthetic disfavor as well. Matthew Stewart Pritchard (1865–1936) of the Museum of Fine Arts in Boston argued for their removal, calling plaster casts the equivalent of player pianos, "mechanical vulgarities that substitute for music" (quoted in Born 2002:10). Some museums kept a few plaster casts for educational purposes, but most were simply sledge-hammered into dust and dumped. This is unfortunate because the plaster casts were an art form themselves, with some studios well known and well respected for the accuracy and aesthetic appeal of their casts, and of course, not every museum could afford actual marble statues even if there had been enough on the market to go around. In an era when few representations of classical statuary were available, the life-size replicas were extremely important as educational objects and still have an important role to play in teaching art and art history.

One of the few North American universities to retain and exhibit its collection of casts is the University of Kansas, home of the Wilcox Classical Museum. The museum was founded in 1888 with the acquisition of five casts (Venus de Milo, figures from the Parthenon, and the Emperor Augustus) from the studios of P. Caproni and Sons in Boston, well-known and widely respected dealers in casts for university and museum collections (Grant 1966). The present collection includes not just the beautifully preserved plaster casts but original artifacts, inscriptions, and coins as well, serving as both a modern educational institution and a way to understand the cultural values of our nineteenth-century ancestors.

called the American Museum in New York City in 1781. The museum consisted initially of one room of exhibits (including a stuffed bison and an eighteen-foot-long snake from South America, along with Chinese artifacts) with another room containing live animal displays. In 1809, the American Museum collection was sold to a retired seaman named John Scudder (1775–1821), who reopened it as Scudder's American Museum in 1810, adding oddities he acquired from fellow mariners to the collection (Wallace 1959). A number of prominent visitors called at the Scudder museum, including Alexis de Tocqueville (1805–1859) in 1831 to see the assemblage of objects and a trained dog named Apollo who played cards and dominoes (Wallace 1959). In addition to exhibits, the museum included a lecture room and an experimental laboratory and hosted occasional music performances (Haberly 1959).

In 1841, a Connecticut-born entrepreneur named Phineas Taylor "P. T." Barnum (1810–1891) purchased Scudder's American Museum and reopened it on New Year's Day in 1842. At that time, the museum was run-down and neglected, with shabby exhibits that included several cracked and fading panoramas; scale models of Dublin, Paris, and Jeru-salem; several creaking automatons; a variety of tired stuffed animals; paintings of famous Americans; and the arm of a pirate named Tom Trouble (Wallace 1959). Over the years, Barnum added more attractions (such as a working model of Niagara Falls) and several other collections to his museum, including objects he purchased from the Peale collection or imported from Europe, as well as a live orangutan. At its height, Bar-num's American Museum exhibited more than 600,000 objects, including living human giants, dwarfs, and people from exotic cultures, all with little regard for accuracy or decorum (Betts 1959; Pitman 1999; Wallace 1959). In one of the many hoaxes that Barnum perpetrated against a gull-ible public, he purchased a specimen of a "feejee mermade" in 1842 and put it on display in his museum—tripling his revenues in the process (Kohlstedt 1992). When ticket sales declined, Barnum sent the mermaid specimen on tour, taking care to alert scientists and teachers throughout the United States in advance of its exhibition in the hopes that they would protest the local showing and denounce the mermaid as an obvious fake, which always boosted ticket sales. One reporter described the mermaid specimen (which was made from the torso and head of a monkey sewn onto the body of a fish) as an "ugly dried-up, block-looking, and diminu-tive specimen about three feet long. Its mouth was open, its tail turned over, and its arms thrown up, giving it the appearance of having died in great agony" (quoted in Kohlstedt 1992:34). After losing, then regaining, his museum through bad investments, then losing it again in two disas-trous fires in 1865 and 1868, Barnum decided to take his show on the road and gave up the museum business to became a circus owner in 1870 (Betts 1959; Wallace 1959).

What has been described as the "first art museum of any standing" in the United States, the Wadsworth Atheneum, was founded in Hartford in 1842 and is the oldest continuously operating art museum in the country (Lewis 1992:13). In 1936, the donation of an estate by an English scientist named James Smithson (1765–1829) was accepted by the Congress of the United States to be used "to found in Washington, under the name of the Smithsonian Institution, an Establishment for the increase & diffusion of knowledge among men" (True 1934:223). After eight years of haggling, Congress voted in 1846 to establish a museum as the best way for knowl-edge to be increased and diffused. The original museum building, affec-tionately known as the Castle, is still used as the Smithsonian Institution headquarters in Washington, DC (figure 7.5). By 1860, it was estimated that the United States had at least 327 museums (Wittlin 1970).

Figure 7.5. The Castle, headquarters of the Smithsonian Institution, Washington, DC.

THE DEVELOPMENT OF THE MUSEUM PROFESSION

Despite the proliferation of museums during the nineteenth century, there was as yet no real museum profession. Most museums employed one or more self-trained or university-trained curators along with a staff of poorly educated and poorly paid, nearly anonymous assistants who learned whatever they needed to know on the job. The academic training of those who were educated was usually in a discipline related to the collection they worked with, so there was little or no critical examination of museums, museum operations, or their role in society. Coupled with the apprenticeship system for training assistants, there were few opportunities or perspectives for introducing new ideas into museum work (Lewis 1985). Nevertheless, a few significant museological texts were published during the 1800s (Lorente 2012), including

- *Zur Geschichte der Sammlungen für Wissenschaft und Kunst in Deutschland* (*History of Art and Science Collections in Germany*), published in 1837 by Gustav Klemm (1802–1867), director of the Royal Library in Dresden;

- *Les Musées d'Europe: Guide et Memento de l'Artiste et du Voyageur* (*The Museums of Europe: A Guide and Memento for the Artist and Traveler*), published in six volumes in 1869 by Louis Viardot (1800–1883) in Paris;
- *Los Museos de España* (*The Museums of Spain*), published in Madrid in 1875 by the painter and writer Ceferino Araujo Sánchez (1824–1897);
- *Museums and Art Galleries*, published by Thomas Greenwood (1851–1980) in London in 1888;
- *The Principles of Museum Administration*, published by George Brown Goode (1851–1896) in 1895 in Washington, DC; and
- *Vychova v Museologii* (*Education in Museology*), published by archaeologist and museologist Kliment Čermák (1852–1917) in 1901 in Prague.

Toward the end of the century, George Brown Goode stated, "It is proper that there be laboratories and professional libraries for the development of the experts who are to organize, arrange, and explain the museum" (Goode 1889:263), but it would not be until well into the next century that the training of museum personnel began to be taken seriously.

LITERATURE

Much of the world literature produced between 1800 and 1900 reflects societies in the throes of change, caught between old imperial traditions and revolutionary movements destined to overturn imperial rulers, both in Europe and in Asia (Puchner et al. 2012). This tension produced many works questioning the validity of old cultural traditions and searching for ways to cope with new influences (e.g., the penetration of European cultures into parts of Asia that had previously been more or less isolated and the dramatic cultural upheavals resulting from the conquest of the New World by Old World forces). In Europe, by the end of the 1800s, much literature addressed the changes brought about by increasing globalism, the industrial revolution, and the resulting upheaval of previous ways of living, particularly the population shifts from rural to urban areas.

Johann Wolfgang von Goethe (1749–1832) and his best-known work *Faust* (part 1, published in 1806) have been described as an author and a literary work that are emblematic of the ending of the Age of Enlightenment (Voth 2007). Goethe was a polymath, with accomplishments in science, art, and government, as well as in literature, whose retelling of the sixteenth-century legend modeled on the biblical book of Job addresses the merits of creation. In Goethe's version, Faust is a scholar and alchemist bored with conventional knowledge and searching for transcendent knowledge.

With rapidly rising rates of literacy and the wide availability of books, reading novels (usually serialized in magazines) became a very popular pastime in Victorian England and throughout the rest of the English-speaking world. Even before book prices declined midcentury, there was a thriving used-book market, many readers joined for-profit subscription libraries, and reading aloud in the home was common (Lutz 2015). Far more literature was available at this time than ever before in history, thanks to technological advances in printing and distribution and lower paper costs. Coupled with the rising literacy rate, a new reading public was forming (Goldhill 2011).

A popular writer of the era, Sir Walter Scott (1771–1832), author of the Waverly novels (which include *Ivanhoe*, 1820), was also a collector who lined the walls of his home, Abbotsford, with real objects related to his fiction. One authority on Victorian life describes Scott as the "inventor of tradition, finding history in things, 'the lord of the buried past.' With the cabinet of bizarrely interconnected knickknacks in the library of well-thumbed books, you might just imagine Scott the antiquarian tour guide of local and national history holding forth, with wry passion, about his writer's things, his collection" (Goldhill 2011:36).

The works of Charles Dickens (1812–1870), the three Brontë sisters (Charlotte, 1816–1855; Emily, 1818–1848; and Anne, 1820–1849), George Eliot (Mary Ann Evans, 1819–1880), William Thackeray (1811–1863), and Thomas Hardy (1840–1928) were very popular. Emily Brontë's *Wuthering Heights* (1847) reflects the repudiation of Enlightenment values (reason, empiricism, conforming to societal norms) in popular literature and the introduction of romanticism (intuition, subjectivity, emotion, the supernatural), along with a new type of romantic hero, the volatile Heathcliff (Voth 2007). At the very end of the nineteenth century, romanticism in literature gave way to naturalism, which dealt more directly with real-life situations. Reflecting the Victorians' fondness for possessions, English novels from about 1830 to 1870 frequently featured objects represented as endowed simultaneously with sentimental and monetary value, often problematically (Plotz 2008).

A popular writer of the late nineteenth century was Abraham "Bram" Stoker (1847–1912), best known for his tales of horror, many of which exemplified museum-related themes of the era, with reference to dark and mysterious locales and exotic objects in plots set primarily in Great Britain. Stoker's 1903 novel *The Jewel of Seven Stars* centers around a private collection of Egyptian artifacts and mummies, recalling Victorian Egyptomania. The epistolary novel *Dracula* has been called the first modern English novel because of its references to Victorian technologies (many of which aided the growth of museums), including typewriting, stenography, dictation machines, newspaper clippings, telegrams, photography, and rapid international shipping and rail transport (Wicke 1992).

Charles Darwin's first book, *The Voyage of the Beagle* (published in 1839), is a narrative of the five years he spent traveling around the world and collecting specimens (which led to his development of the theory of evolution). The book was a best-seller, going through several editions, including an illustrated version in 1890. Darwin's book was eagerly received by a Victorian audience that had a growing appetite for scientific travel writing.

Although Mark Twain (Samuel Langhorne Clemens, 1835–1910) is best known today as a novelist and humorist, he also wrote several best-selling travel books. In his chronicle of an 1867 tour of Europe and the Holy Land (*The Innocents Abroad; or, The New Pilgrim's Progress*, 1869), Twain expressed his dismay and outrage at the souvenir-hunting activities of his fellow American passengers, who frequently went ashore armed with hammers and chisels (their actions were not unusual at the time). At the site of the Battle of Malakoff in Sevastopol on the Crimean Peninsula, Twain reported, "[E]veryone went relic hunting," returning to the cruise ship with cannonballs, artillery shell fragments, and even bones (most of the travelers were disappointed to discover that the bones were of mules and oxen, not fallen soldiers). Twain described how one passenger turned his stateroom into a "museum of worthless trumpery" and labeled a piece of a horse jaw as a "Fragment of a Russian General" (Twain 1869:385). In Syria, Twain's fellow passengers engaged in collecting "fragments of sculptured marbles and breaking ornaments from the interior work of the Mosques," only to have their treasures confiscated by a government official (Twain 1869:430). In Palestine, Twain reported with evident disgust, "The incorrigible pilgrims have come in with their pockets full of specimens broken from the ruins. I wish this vandalism could be stopped" (Twain 1869:471). Such objects as those collected by Twain's companions frequently found their way into local history museums once the travelers returned home.

The increased popularity of literature in the Victorian era created a new phenomenon—visits to the homes, haunts, and graves of famous authors (Goldhill 2011; Lutz 2015). Readers wanted to see the place where writers worked, take in the scenes that inspired them, and touch the objects that the creators of their beloved fiction had touched—and if possible, carry away souvenirs for their home collections.

SUMMARY

The first modern, comprehensive treatment of museums and museology was published in a three-volume work in 1904 by a Scottish archaeologist and bibliophile named David Murray (1842–1928) under the title *Museums, Their History and Their Use: With a Bibliography and List of Museums in the United Kingdom.* Murray's delightful text overflows with facts and anecdotes and is at times a witty treatment of the history, development, and purposes of museums through the end of the nineteenth century. Murray reveals that William Henry Flower thought that the modern museum could be distinguished from its antecedents by its "specialization and classification" and that scientist and educator Thomas Henry Huxley (1825–1895) described the museum as a "consultative library of objects" (Murray 1904:231). Murray himself then offers the idea that the "lesson of the museum is the importance of order and method. These are what give scientific value to the collection. It was the want of these that made the old museums comparatively worthless" (Murray 1904:236). While, as we have seen, the old museums were far from worthless, Murray, Huxley, and Flower were all essentially correct in their characterizations of the modern museum in the nineteenth century.

The historian Germaine Bazin (1901–1990) called the period from 1789 to 1900 the "Age of Museums" (Siegel 2008:3), and in many ways, it was, as museums proliferated and diversified throughout a rapidly changing world. The changes were so significant that "[b]y the end of the nineteenth century . . . a world once regulated by specific separate cultures was on a new course. Its destiny was now to be continuing and accelerating transformation" (Roberts and Westad 2013:701). In this environment, it is not surprising that the institution of the modern museum so quickly captured the public imagination and became a "socially sanctioned gathering place" (Siegel 2008:4). The century ended on a note of optimism, at least as far as the future of museums went, with George Brown Goode of the Smithsonian opining,

> The museum-idea is much broader than it was fifty or even twenty-five years ago. The museum of to-day is no longer a chance assemblage of curiosities, but rather a series of objects selected with reference to their value to investigators, or their possibilities for public enlightenment. The museum of the future may be made one of the chief agencies of the higher civilization. (Goode 1889:263)

8

—◦◦◦—

Museums in a World
Gone Awry, 1900–1970

Although the nineteenth century had been a time of rapid transformations, for the most part, the changes had occurred in an ordered and
somewhat predictable manner. Colonies had expanded along with world
trade, and new technologies had accelerated improvements in transportation and communication, as the process of globalization affected cultures
around the world. Throughout Europe, as the 1800s drew to a close,
industrialization had essentially brought an end to modes of living that
were based on the rhythms of nature, overturning the patterns that had
shaped human beings for millennia. For the most part, workers now did
the same tasks year-round, labored in shifts, and building interiors were
illuminated by artificial light (Roberts and Westad 2013).

The changes that occurred in the world during the century that began
in 1900 were chaotic and disruptive and occurred with a suddenness
and at a pace previously unknown—as if the world had gone awry.
Almost every aspect of life was affected, from food production to governance, from gender roles to life span, from the duration and nature
of the workday to how leisure time was spent. Literacy increased, the
mechanization of agriculture enabled fewer farmers to produce more
food, and urban centers expanded while rural populations shrank. The
pace of industrialization was driven by higher-quality but less-expensive metals (particularly iron), aided by richer fuels (especially coal) and
new energy sources (Roberts and Westad 2013). Just how much and how
rapidly the world was changing at the turn of the century is illustrated
by a comparison of communication technologies used by two presidents
of the United States. During the 1893–1897 term of Grover Cleveland

(1837–1908), the White House had just one telephone (the operator went off duty each day at 6 p.m.), and Cleveland had a single secretary who wrote out the presidential correspondence in longhand. Just a few years later, during the 1901–1909 terms of Theodore Roosevelt (1858–1919), the White House had several telephones, a score of stenographers to take dictation, and a pool of typists to handle the president's correspondence (Wershler-Henry 2005).

In 1900, there were three basic spheres of influence in the world. One sphere was Old Europe, now prosperous after three centuries of growth in wealth and population, which absorbed and consumed most of the world's export goods. A second sphere of influence encompassed the regions where European cultures had been transplanted—North and South America, Australia and New Zealand, and South Africa, which shared much of the wealth, standards, and Christianity of Old Europe. The third sphere was composed of the rest of the world, primarily Asia, Oceania, and Africa (Roberts and Westad 2013).

In 1900, the world population was 1,640,000,000; by the end of the century, it had grown to 6,070,581,000. Many significant demographic shifts occurred with this growth. The percentage of the world's population living in Africa went from 8 percent to 15 percent, while the percentage in Asia grew from 57 percent to 60 percent. Meanwhile, the percentage in Europe declined from 24 percent in 1900 to 11 percent in 2000, while the percent of world population of the United States and Canada kept steady at about 5 percent. The population of Central and South America and the Caribbean accounted for about 9 percent and Australasia and Oceania for less than 1 percent (Roberts and Westad 2013).

INCREASE AND EXPANSION

In 1900, people of European descent dominated most of the world through a system of colonies and complex trade exchanges, but as the century went on, the power of colonial governments rapidly eroded or was completely overturned. The twentieth century saw the end of British imperial power, which had reached its height in North America with British ownership of Canada and the thirteen colonies in 1763 (Roberts and Westad 2013). The Ottoman Empire had almost disappeared in Europe and Africa, as Europe became the center of world trade in the late nineteenth century. Along with dominating world trade, Europeans exported their cultures and customs, so that a "remarkable aspect of the European cultural hegemony is how quickly other peoples responded to it, creating amalgams of their own cultures and foreign imports" (Roberts and Westad 2013:791). An example of this adoption and modification of a cultural import is the evolution of the European museum concept. The pace of museum growth worldwide accelerated after 1900, with new museums often shaped to meet the needs of the diverse cultures that adopted them. Although some historians have called the 1800s the "Century of History" because "museums were flooded to the point of overflowing with products created by all kinds of human endeavor, by all peoples of all periods" (Bazin 1967:7), as we shall see, the title is arguably more appropriate for museums of the twentieth century. For example, history museums and historic sites account for more than half of the museums in the United States (AAM 1994; IMLS 2014a). Only 4 percent of museums in the United States were in existence before 1900, 75 percent of current museums were founded after 1950, and 40 percent were founded after 1970 (Pitman 1999). The increase in the number and variety of museums worldwide prompted the founding of the International Council of Museums (ICOM) in 1946.

Between 1860 and 1914, the number of museums in the United States nearly doubled, from 327 to about 600 (Wittlin 1970). In 1928, the American Association of Museums estimated that there were 1,400 museums in the United States that attracted 32 million visits annually, which was the equivalent of about 25 percent of the population (Schwarzer 2006). The 1960 edition of the *World Book Encyclopedia* reported that the United States then had more than 2,400 museums, including art, history, natural history, science and industry, children's, trailside, and general museums. The average annual museum attendance in the United States had reached nearly 50 million people by 1944; by 1998, there were more than 10,000 museums in the United States, with 856 million visitors per year. The number of museums in Great Britain went from 59 in 1860 to 354 in 1914 and by 1970 to about 2,500. Germany had 179 museums in the early twentieth century and about 6,000 by 1970.

A number of technological developments initiated just before the First World War affected museum development, including the availability of safe and efficient indoor lighting and new methods to produce large sheets of polished plate glass, which allowed museums to make bigger display cases than had previously been possible (Pearce 1992). The first commercially successful typewriters had become available in 1873, followed in 1935 by electric typewriters. Typewriters made museum documentation much faster and more accurate, but by the 1980s, typewriters began to rapidly disappear, replaced by desktop computers and printers (Wershler-Henry 2005). These technological innovations coincided with population shifts to urban centers, which meant more visitors for museums and a growing emphasis on the development of community museums (Lewis 1992). As rural populations moved into the cities, new jobs were created for women as typists, secretaries, telephone operators, factory workers, store assistants, teachers, and museum assistants and educators (see box 8.1), almost none of which had existed in the

BOX 8.1.
Mr. Frisky, Docents, and Choo-Choos

Toward the end of the nineteenth century, as museums began to separate their collections into objects for study and those for exhibition, they came to be increasingly seen as educational institutions. In the early 1900s, the first formal training programs for museum educators were established in the United States. In 1889, George Brown Goode of the Smithsonian had published a pivotal paper, "Museum-History and Museums of History," in which he criticized the public side of museums for being too trivial while also arguing that museums catered too much to scholars and scientists. Professional museum educators were seen as the means to make museums more educational for the public, in effect bridging the gap.

Education was then, as now, hotly debated, and into the heat of the debate strode John Dewey (1859–1952), a philosopher with an intense interest in museums. In his book *Democracy and Education* (1916), Dewey hypothesized that experience is not an isolated sensory act, that a response to a stimulus is influenced by previous knowledge and experience, and that the response itself influences future actions and learning. In museums, this means that the engagement of the visitor with the content of the museum (a process of making personal connections to the museum experiences) is crucial for learning. Dewey criticized art museums as "primarily the product of the capitalist urge to flaunt wealth," which resulted in the fine arts becoming "separated from the rest of life and cloistered in selected, inaccessible places" that did not provide opportunities for active engagement (quoted in Hein 2012:48). Dewey thought other kinds of museums were better as places of social learning.

In 1902, a former biology teacher named Anna Billings Gallup (1872–1956) was hired at the Brooklyn Children's Museum as a curatorial assistant. As she rose through the ranks to become curator and then curator-in-chief, Gallup developed several innovative educational programs, including one that allowed children who demonstrated an interest in learning to borrow selected museum objects to take home and study at their leisure.

At the Newark Museum, John Cotton Dana (1856–1929) initiated several innovations, including designing exhibits with broad popular appeal, exhibiting crafts as art, loaning objects to public schools, establishing a junior museum and branch museums in public libraries, and instituting teacher-training courses at college campuses. Dana liked to refer to his museum as an "institute of visual instruction," while categorizing most other institutions as mere "grazing museums" (quoted in Alexander 1996:391). Dana hired Louise Connolly (1862–1927) in 1912 as an educational advisor. Connolly, who had earned a master's degree and written textbooks while working full time as a teacher, was a feminist and suffragette and was not reluctant to do whatever was necessary to promote museum education. Dana sent Connolly on a trip west to visit sixty museums to find out what they were doing about education. Connolly became a very popular lecturer, at one point touring the country in the company of Mr. Frisky, a stuffed squirrel, to present museum programs. It was Connolly who trained the museum educators, most of them former teachers, for the Newark Museum.

Benjamin Ives Gilman (1852–1933), the secretary of the Boston Museum of Fine Arts from 1893 to 1925, thought that the visitor's museum experience should be mainly aesthetic. He once wrote, "A museum of science is in essence a school; a museum of art is in essence a temple" (quoted in Hein 2012:125). Gilman supported museum education by hiring museum educators, establishing lecture rooms, publishing an educational handbook, and instituting educational tours. In 1907, Gilman began using the word *docents* for educators in the museum, borrowing the German academic term to avoid calling them instructors or educators. In 1917, he classified museum workers into three categories: administrative, curatorial, and educational. Gilman carried out some of the first visitor studies and coined the term *visitor fatigue* to describe the phenomenon of overstimulation experienced by some museum visitors.

By 1932, an estimated 15 percent of American museums had organized educational programs, and by 1938, museum educators were using well-developed teaching methods and special programs developed for museums. The American Association of Museums formed its first Committee on Education in 1942.

The real beginnings of research in museum education were in the 1920s and 1930s, with studies that focused on such issues as museum layout and the number of objects that should be used in exhibits and, later on, museum visitors, what they were learning, and how they learned. In 1949, the visitor research pioneer Alma Stephanie Wittlin (1899–1990) published the results of her scientific observations of the reactions of people to the presentation of objects in exhibits in England.

During the late 1950s and through the 1960s, there was a shift in visitor expectations, with many people now coming to museums for social outings, for fun, or just to pass their leisure time. Some curators were appalled at this, as they felt it trivialized their work if the visitors were not there to become educated in a strict, more formal sense. Nevertheless, between 1952 and 1962, gross attendance at museums in the United States doubled, and by 1960, 79 percent of museums had some kind of organized educational programming.

The 1970s were a time when many museum professionals began to advocate using showier display methods to cater to a generation of visitors who had been raised with mass media, primarily television and movies. Museums tried enhancing the visitor experience with all sorts of things, including films; slide projectors; sound systems; and, by the end of the decade, computer terminals. There was, of course, opposition, with one author cautioning, "The curator should not prostitute his institution by transforming it into an amusement center full of 'fun-house' gimmicks in an attempt to win the interest of all potential

(continued)

BOX 8.1.
(continued)

visitors" (quoted in Roberts 1997:39). In a 1974 article entitled "The Icing Is Good but the Cake Is Rotten," a museum planner named Joseph Shannon complained, "By taking aboard the 'concept' exhibition and consequently the audio visual as a primary technique to achieve 'relevance,' museums . . . are going to hell on a psychedelic choo-choo" (Shannon 1974:30).

In 1973, the American Association of Museums created its first standing professional committee on education (the Museum Education Roundtable) and in 1981 began publishing the *Journal of Museum Education*. By this time, the old arguments about popularization versus scholarship had evolved into new arguments about entertainment versus education, but it was finally realized that education and entertainment were not necessarily mutually exclusive. In 1975, Mihaly Csikszentmihalyi pointed out in *Beyond Boredom and Anxiety* that playful, enjoyable and fun events evoked in people the optimal conditions for learning. Csikszentmihalyi called it "flow" (Csikszentmihalyi 1975:11).

By the late 1970s, visitor studies were a standard tool for evaluating and improving educational programs and exhibits, and they began to focus more on how people learn in museum settings (see box 9.2).

Sources: Csikszentmihalyi 1975; Dewey 1916; Goode 1889; Hein 2006, 2012.

century before. Other changes altered gender roles, including the availability of reliable contraception after 1914 and innovations that made women's traditional roles somewhat easier, such as piped indoor water, gas and electric heating and lighting, better shops, more diverse food options, better food preservation, and the invention of detergents to replace soap. By midcentury, the people of North America, the United Kingdom, Scandinavia, and a good part of industrialized Europe had life expectancies that were two or three times those of their medieval ancestors, and more women were in the workforce outside of the home (Roberts and Westad 2013).

By 1900, there was a new crisis facing museums in several European countries—lack of space for their ever-growing collections. Consider the example of Frederick John Horniman (1835–1906), who, after inheriting his father's tea business, used his personal wealth to amass a collection of about 30,000 objects. As the collection grew, he realized that he needed a place to exhibit it all, so the Horniman Museum and Gardens was opened in London in 1901. By the end of the century, the museum's collection had grown from 30,000 to more than 350,000 objects. In some cases, the rate of collection growth was out of control. The most extreme example of a collector during this era is Henry Solomon Wellcome (1853–1936), an American who made a fortune with a pharmaceutical company and became a naturalized British citizen in 1910 (Larson 2009). Not only did Wellcome travel extensively to collect, he hired scores of agents to scour the world for objects for him. Eventually, Wellcome accumulated more than one million objects that were stored in various warehouses around London. Although initially interested in assembling a collection of artifacts related to the development of medicine, Wellcome's combination of inquisitiveness and acquisitiveness soon led him to collect many other kinds of objects, as well. After Wellcome's death, it took more than forty years to consolidate and reduce the collection to a reasonable size (most of it was sold at auction) in order to establish the Wellcome Trust Centre for the History of Medicine and the Wellcome Library.

Distressed by the rates of collection growth in many institutions, the British Egyptologist William Matthew Flinders Petrie (1852–1942) proposed a unique solution: a large, off-site storage facility that would be shared by the big London museums and would streamline not just storage but also the slow processes of registration and access to collections (Podgorny 2012). Petrie wrote,

> At the end of a century which has so rapidly and greatly changed our very conceptions of the nature of knowledge, and our standpoint for seeing both man and his world, it is well to loosen our old ideas somewhat, and look at things with fresh eyes, so as not to be in bondage to conditions that have already passed away. No one would now think of writing a scientific or historical book on the lines of treatises of 1800 or even 1850. And if that be true of the formal presentation of our new knowledge, how much more is it true of the nature of the materials and evidence on which our books are built. (Petrie 1900:525)

Petrie's idea was to construct a series of free-standing, one-story, unadorned, purpose-built, fire-resistant buildings to be named "Sloane Galleries" in honor of Sir Hans Sloane (1660–1753), whose collections were the foundation of the British Museum. The facility would be located on a square-mile tract of land outside of London that was served by a railroad line. Over the coming decades, the tract of land would be gradually filled in by more buildings as more space was needed. The area would be planted with shade trees to moderate the environment, each building equipped with skylights to save money on lighting, and quicklime would be used to control relative humidity inside of storage cabinets. The slow pace of collection registration and cataloging would be accelerated through the use of a promising new technology, photo documentation. Instead of the standard method whereby content experts laboriously wrote out a description of each object, close-up photographs would be prepared and affixed to catalog cards. Petrie naïvely imagined that Sloane Galleries would suffice for the London museums for the next one hundred years (Simmons 2013).

Although Petrie's essay drew intense interest when it was published, was awarded a silver medal by the Royal Society of Arts ("Medals" 1900), and was reprinted several times in museum publications in other European countries and the United States, nothing more came of it. The scheme was perhaps too radical, required too much cooperation among museums, or was simply badly timed.

THE WORLD AT WAR

The dominant events of the nineteenth century included two world wars, the Russian revolution, and the Great Depression in the United States and Europe. The First World War (1914–1918) was fought over a much larger geographic area than previous conflicts and had shockingly high casualties as a result of new weapons technology with greater killing power. In *The Face of Battle*, military historian John Keegan points out that the history of battles from Agincourt (1415) to the Somme (1916) is one of using military tactics developed for the previous war against new weapons technology developed for the current war, resulting in disastrously mounting death tolls with each conflict (Keegan 1976). The battle of the Somme resulted in more than 1 million casualties, and the tally for World War I in total was more than 38 million casualties. During and after World War I, European museums became essentially dormant, and museum growth and expansion in the United States also slowed markedly as the Western world slid into a prolonged period of economic doldrums (Wittlin 1970). Worldwide gross domestic product (GDP) fell by more than 15 percent. The Great Depression in the United States and Europe lasted from 1929 until the late 1930s.

The outbreak of World War II (1939–1945) marked the end of the European Age. The first truly global war (with the majority of countries in the world involved in it in one way or another) and its aftermath closed the Soviet Union to European influence and shifted the order of world dominance, bringing massive destruction to most of Europe and new empires to both the United States and the Soviet Union (Roberts and Westad 2013). European museums were profoundly affected, particularly those in the Axis powers of Germany, Italy, and Japan. In Fascist Italy, museums were recognized for their ability to educate the masses, but it was a "special kind of education, a subordination of interests to a single master idea: Italy's political mission to regain the position of a world empire, as dictated by the destiny of Rome" (Wittlin 1970:148). As a result, this "infatuation of the fascist Italians with quantity as a measure of grandeur" led to rapid but poorly planned growth in many museum collections (Wittlin 1970:148). In Nazi Germany, Hitler's rise to power brought several changes to the country's museums, including the removal of what the Nazi Party considered to be degenerate modern art, some of which was destroyed, some of which was hidden away in storage until after the war. In museums in Germany, Jewish staff members were discharged from their jobs, and art was seized in the wake of German conquests across Europe. Ironically, "[i]f Hitler and Goering had not been interested in the arts, Nazi art looting would certainly not have been a war priority; it would not have happened in the methodical manner and on the overwhelming scale it did in Occupied Europe" (Feliciano 1997:4).

German museum workers met at a conference in Mainz in 1933 and resolved that "their first duty was to be true servants of their epoch—of an epoch dictating that 'museums should with all their powers contribute to the shaping of an amorphous mass of population into a nation'" (Wittlin 1970:148). Two types of museums that were promoted during this effort were the *Heimatmuseum*, or homeland museum, and the *Heeresmuseum*, or military museum (Wittlin 1970). More than 2,000 *Heimatmuseen* were created in Germany under the Third Reich (Lewis 1992). The *Heimatmuseum* is considered by many to be the forerunner of the ecomuseum, although as part of a government propaganda program, the "scientific basis" behind the museum's concept "involved distorting science, and in particular . . . natural science, with a view to demonstrating the superiority of the Aryan race" (Cruz-Ramirez 1985:242). Nevertheless, the *Heimatmuseum* was a new museological approach that responded to local community needs by considering popular culture, the relationship between individuals and their environment, and the idea of the museum as an active part of education. Once rid of the politically induced distortions, the model of the *Heimatmuseum* was seen as a way to focus on local history and community, leading to the development of the ecomuseum in France in the 1970s, as discussed in chapter 9 (Cruz-Ramirez 1985).

During World War II, many museums were damaged by bombing or military incursions, and many objects were destroyed. In the course of the postwar Soviet occupation of parts of Eastern Europe, still more museum objects were confiscated (Alexander and Alexander 2008). In Berlin, Museum Island (actually a peninsula formed by the confluence of the Spree and the Kupfergraben Rivers) was the location of several significant museums, including the Altes Museum (founded in 1830 and containing antiquities and modern paintings), the Neues Museum (founded in 1855 to exhibit Egyptian artifacts and European antiques), the Nationalgalerie (founded in 1876 and specializing in modern German art), the Kaiser Friedrich Museum of Western Art (now named the Bode Museum), and the Pergamon Museum (which held Near Eastern and German art). When

Berlin was partitioned at the end of the war, Museum Island became part of the territory on the East German side (Alexander and Alexander 2008).

World War II resulted in a hitherto unimagined number of casualties—more than 60 million dead and massive destruction of infrastructure across much of Europe and parts of Asia. In the aftermath of the conflict, the United Nations was founded in October 1945 in San Francisco. In the decades after the war, the standard of living in most of the world rose, particularly in the United States, which experienced an economic boom and associated increases in wealth and leisure time for workers. This change affected museum attendance, leading to a "period of remarkable achievement for museums" (Lewis 1985:484) that was marked by new types of institutions, such as outdoor museums and the restoration of many historic buildings. It was a time when museums became widely recognized as both educational facilities and destinations for leisure activities.

MUSEUMS, THE RUSSIAN REVOLUTION, AND THE SOVIET UNION

In Russia in 1914, less than 10 percent of the population lived in towns, and only 3 million out of a population of 30 million worked in industry (Roberts and Westad 2013). The Russian revolution of 1917 led to the rise of the Soviet Union (Union of Soviet Socialist Republics) in the early 1920s. This "period of revolutionary social change offered unprecedented opportunities for a reform of the public museum" in the Soviet countries, as museums were used "as aids in the struggle for a reorganization of society" (Wittlin 1970:144).

As early as 1917, a Central Office for the Care of Objects of Art and Archaeology was established by the Soviet government, which extended its control to museums in 1921. At the time, there were three basic types of collections in the Soviet Union. First, the extensive holdings of the few large institutions were transformed from treasure hoards into exhibits that had more significant meaning in such large state museums as the Hermitage and the Rumyantzev Museum of Russian Art. A second group of museums was composed of collections in numerous smaller institutions that had been organized by private societies, primarily collections of natural science specimens and ethnographic and archaeological artifacts. These collections sorely lacked funding and became state museums under control of the central museum authority, along with the third group, which was composed of private collections that were rapidly nationalized (Wittlin 1970). In 1917, it was estimated that the Soviet Union had 122 museums, but that number had grown to 738 by 1934 and to more than

900 by the 1960s, thanks to the establishment of both regional museums and museums focused on communicating ideas about public health, technology, and the history of the revolution. Soviet museology took its own course as the European museum concept was adapted to the needs of the new society. For example, rather than exhibiting paintings in the strict chronological order that had become widespread in European museums, the "new Russian museology called for a different set of criteria in the Hermitage. The guiding principle was to regard all objects which were human products, be they tools, pottery, paintings, or machines, as records of human existence under certain conditions of society—'slave owning,' 'feudal,' 'capitalistic,' or otherwise" (Wittlin 1970:145). When the Central Lenin Museum was founded in Moscow in 1936, it was described in an article in *Pravda* as a "new powerful propaganda weapon for Leninism" (quoted in Lewis 1992:16). Museums in Eastern Europe in general did not fare well during World War II—at least 114 museums were either completely plundered or partially destroyed in the war (Wittlin 1970).

The development of museums in Bulgaria has been studied with respect to the use of museums to define nationality, given that the "main task Bulgarian museums had during the first 40 years of the 20th century was catching up with European museological achievements" (Petrovka-Campbell 2010:175). The National Archaeological Museum was founded in 1892, the Natural History Institutes in 1894, the National Ethnological Museum in 1906, and the National Art Gallery in 1942. Immediately after World War II, museums in Bulgaria were considered archaic and conservative and were heavily criticized by intellectuals. However, during the late 1940s, museums came to be seen as institutions of "great utility serving the needs of the Bulgarian communist party" (Petrovka-Campbell 2010:175), resulting in several changes, such as removing class-related interpretations and close regulation by the government Communist Party. Between 1956 and 1990, the number of state-funded museums and art galleries in Bulgaria grew from 98 to 230.

INDIA'S POSTCOLONIAL MUSEUMS

An instructive example of the internationalization of the European museum concept can be found in the history of museums in India, a former British colony. The first museums in India were established by the British as part of an assessment and promotion of the economic potential of the continent. These early institutions emulated European museums, and the

[d]econtextualized Indian objects fed the colonial imagination's variously constructed images of India's antiquity, ethnology, geology, natural history,

trade, and art. One must also realize that this visualizing practice simultaneously reflected an image of the colonials themselves, so that collecting impulses and museum displays revealed the colonizer's mindset in their exhibitionary constructions, which were trying to possess the Other through objects. (Bhatti 2012:79)

It was significant that the "collections could be classified to evince any objectified order of reality," a concept that was central to European exhibition practices (Bhatti 2012:79).

The first significant museum on the continent was the Indian Museum, established by the Asiatic Society (in effect, on behalf of the British government) in Calcutta (now Kolkata) in 1875 in a Victorian-style building designed by a British architect (Punja 1991). The National Museum of India in New Delhi was established in 1949 following the return of a successful exhibition of Indian art and objects that had been sent to London in 1947 for an exhibition at the Royal Academy (Punja 1991).

There are many factors that influenced museums in India after they were introduced by the British, including the overthrow of colonial rule and changing economic patterns, but the shaping of museums by the dominant cultures of India was critical. As one Indian museologist said, "There are . . . striking differences between museums in India and those in the West. In India, for many of the museum-going public, the items on display are still part of their living tradition. Images of deities—their iconography readily recognizable—may even be viewed as objects of reverence rather than examples of high art" (Swallow 1991:12). Because the more utilitarian objects in Indian museums are familiar to the vast majority of the people, the local visitors often don't need extensive labels, explanations from guides, or other didactic aids, unlike the foreign visitors to the museums (Swallow 1991). Other aspects of cultural influence include the fact that Indian museums draw on more than five thousand years of continuous cultural history, and Indian art developed its own aesthetic principles independent of those of European, Middle Eastern, or Chinese art (Punja 1991). For example, the Vechaar Utensils Museum in Ahmedabad was founded by Surendra Patel in 1981 to exhibit the evolution of Indian metal utensils over five thousand years of Indian history. The objects it contains range from the purely utilitarian to ornately crafted metalwork (Punja 1991).

Following independence in 1947 and partition into two separate countries (India and Pakistan), many other cultural changes occurred that had direct impacts on the museums on the continent. Most of the maharajas in India lost their large estates, and in the process, "family collections of art treasures, archives and memorabilia are in some cases housed in part of a former palace . . . later set up as a public museum" (Punja 1991:21). Since independence, the population of India has become increasingly urban (although the population is still nearly 70 percent rural). In this environment of change, the "expanding middle class, with its colonial hangover, turned its eyes to Western Europe and America for cultural inspiration," as new museums were established and existing museums began to change under the influence of small groups of urban intellectuals, government agencies, and universities, some of which wanted to continue the British tradition, some of which sought change (Punja 1991:73). As might be expected with an imported institution, the architecture of Indian museums varies widely, from early-European-influenced designs (particularly those museums built during the Victorian era) to traditional Indian designs and, for newer museums, modern Indian architecture (Swallow 1991).

Nationalism followed by independence honed a greater interest in Indian culture generally and, in particular, among the more educated upper classes, which in turn inspired a new movement of private collecting that in several instances led to the establishment of pioneering museums (Punja 1991). The development of several of these institutions is reflective of the precolonial and postcolonial museum patterns around the world (see box 8.2). An example of a family collection is the art assembled by Sir Ratan Tata and Sir Dorab Tata and donated in 1921 and 1933, respectively, as the Tata Collection at the Prince of Wales Museum in Bombay (now Mumbai). The museum itself had been founded in 1904 by several prominent citizens of Bombay to commemorate a visit by the Prince of Wales (the future King George V) to the city. The original museum building was completed in 1915 but used as a military hospital in the First World War and after, until 1920, when it was returned to its originally intended function. The museum is now the Chhatrapatī Shivaji Mahārāj Vastu Saṅgrahālay and contains collections of Indian art, archaeology, and natural history.

The Ashutosh Museum of Indian Art, located on the campus of the University of Calcutta in Kolkata, was established in 1937 as the first public museum at an Indian university. The Calico Museum of Textiles in Ahmedabad in western India was founded shortly after independence in 1949 by an industrialist named Gautam Sarabhai and his sister, Gira Sarabhai, to promote the then-flourishing textile industry in Ahmedabad. The museum was originally housed at the Calico Mills but was moved to Sarabhai House in Shahibaug in 1983. The collections include royal court textiles from the Mughal rulers from the fifteenth century, regional embroidery, tie-dyed textiles, religious objects, furniture, crafts, and miniatures. The museum collection is used by students and instructors from the National Institute of Design in Ahmedabad.

Another family origin museum is the Raja Dinkar Kelkar Museum in Pune, which began with a collection assembled by Dr. Dinkar G. Kelkar

190 Chapter 8

BOX 8.2.
The Translated Museum

The concept of the modern museum was exported from Europe first to its colonies, then to other areas of the world (see figure 7.4). At first, these museums reflected the European ideal of cultural representation, but before the end of the Victorian era, many of them began to change, shaped by the societies that they served. Although the most profound evolution of museums in non-European cultures has occurred within the last half-century or so (as discussed in chapter 9), it is important to examine the initial adoption of the museum model and the forces that began to reshape it. A fascinating, detailed, and insightful case study has been developed by Shaila Bhatti in *Translating Museums: A Counterhistory of South Asian Museology* (2012), which is briefly summarized here, based on the idea that the postcolonial desire for self-representation is "politically rationalized by the need to consolidate and construct cultural icons that visualize and interpret the nation's ideology, identity, and . . . 'development of civilization' within which the nation can be chronologically situated" (Bhatti 2012: 84) through complex processes that are not linear or singular but ambiguous.

The Lahore Museum was founded by the British colonial government in 1856 in Punjab as part of a network of museums throughout India connected to the Calcutta-based Asiatic Society. The society's first museum began in 1796 as a repository for the "relicts and curiosities" collected by its members and travelers to the region (Bhatti 2012:51). The colonial government had a specific agenda for the Lahore Museum, one common to colonial museums worldwide—the museum was to "benefit the colonist's progress in terms of knowledge acquisition and trade advancement" by acting as a center for the collection, organization, and exhibition of "material knowledge of local culture and economic products" that would increase the colony's wealth and display its economic potential (Bhatti 2012:22). In the mid-1800s, museums were seen as practical necessities for ordering, classifying, and mapping objects into "visible knowledge" resources (Bhatti 2012:52). By 1857, there were 12 museums in India and 105 by 1935, within a hierarchy that had the Indian Museum at the apex and provincial, district, specialists, and private museums ranked below.

The organization and classification of the collections in the new Lahore Museum were directly based on the successful South Kensington Museum model (discussed in chapter 7), using similar systematic categories of collection objects. In the 1870s, a trained museum worker was hired—John Lockwood Kipling (1837–1911) had been a designer and modeler at the South Kensington Museum from 1861 until 1865, before taking a job as an art teacher at a school in Bombay. Kipling, who embraced the ideals of the Arts and Crafts movement, believed that the Indian art schools were "vehicles of a kind of cultural imperialism in which misplaced models of western art were imposed on Indian students to the detriment of any training whatsoever in native techniques" (quoted in Bhatti 2012:22). In 1875, Kipling moved to Lahore to serve as both head of a new government art school and curator of the Lahore Museum. Kipling strove to integrate the art school and museum, while helping transform the museum "from a material archive into an active institution implicated in craft reform and art education in India" (Bhatti 2012:60). Under Kipling's direction, the museum not only exhibited examples of the region's art and craft trade products but also added collections of antiquities, archaeological artifacts, coins, natural history specimens, and portraits. In 1912, Kipling's son, the writer Rudyard Kipling (1865–1936), popularized the local nickname of the Lahore Museum, *Ajaib-Ghar* (Wonder House) in his book *Kim*. In her study of the Lahore Museum, Bhatti points out the irony that "[a]lthough this enduring image of the museum as a 'wonder house' is popular among the public, it also remains a source of tension between the museum and visitors in South Asia, since this image contests both institutional authority and desired identity based on the Eurocentric museum model" (Bhatti 2012:24–25).

The evolution of the Lahore Museum followed a pattern common with colonial museums, starting out as an institution of the East India Company, then becoming a provincial museum directed from London, then a public-oriented modern museum following partition in 1947 (when 40 percent of the collections were repatriated to India), and finally the museum's rebirth as a decolonialized national museum for Pakistan (figure 7.4). Kipling retired in 1898, and in the 1920s, changes were made in the museum "to offer a more edifying experience" for visitors, including the deaccession of redundant objects; vernacular labels (in English, Gurmukhi, Hindi, and Urdu); the introduction of new educational subjects in lectures; and the sale of guidebooks, catalogs, duplicates of coins in the collection, and postcards (Bhatti 2012:72). The museum's first Indian curator, Dr. K. N. Sitaram (1889–1940), was hired in 1928, a calculated move by the colonial government to make Indian nationals more visible in the museum service. Sitaram instituted further reforms, including the elimination of some galleries and the addition of guided tours in both English and local languages. Nevertheless, the transition to an Indian director was not smooth:

> In the early twentieth century, museums were becoming complex spaces that now included three types of participants—the colonials, elite Indians, and subalterns—and for the colonial museum project *some* success of the "civilizing mission" that had been associated so deeply with public museums in Europe . . . was at least gained in the construction of employable modern Indian subjects. (Bhatti 2012:75)

The first comprehensive inventory of the Lahore Museum was not undertaken until 1942, corresponding to a shift during the 1940s in the museum's mission from the colonial emphasis on raw materials, crafts, and trade to a new mission of education about the history and culture of Punjab.

(continued)

BOX 8.2.
(continued)

The partition that separated India and Pakistan had many impacts on the Lahore Museum, as on the society at large, occurring at a time when the Lahore Museum was undergoing a process of modernization that took decades to play out. In 1947 (before partition), the museum had seven galleries; by 2003, it had expanded to twenty-two galleries through a "gradual process guided in part by shifting political ideals" (Bhatti 2012:111).

As Bhatti eloquently articulates in her study, the transformation of museums in postcolonial societies is a complex process involving the "ambiguities entailed in transforming colonial museums into national icons" (Bhatti 2012:84). The process of decolonialization itself is a process of "conversion and reinscription through remits of national rhetoric and identity, with those not complying being popularly imagined as barren, dusty storehouses of the past that are of little interest to the public, curators, or researchers, who are attracted to the new museological splendours of the modern nation" (Bhatti 2012:84). Bhatti also makes the point that the remaining old colonial museums should not be "sidelined" because "they occupy a tantalizing position that disrupts the presumed chronological progression from colonial to national museum representation, while deposing the lifeless image associated with colonial museums through local visitor's curiosity and attractions for them" (Bhatti 2012:85).

Ultimately, "[o]bjects in the museum are subject to ideological narratives—colonial or postcolonial; however, they are also the mainstay of the habitual discourse on museum practice" (Bhatti 2012:117).

(1896–1990) and dedicated to the memory of his son, Raja. Kelkar started the collection about 1920. It now contains more than 20,000 objects, of which about 12 percent (2,500) are exhibited to the public. The collection includes sculptures dating back to the fourteenth century, ornaments, musical instruments, weapons, and vessels, with a strong emphasis on the "arts of everyday life—pots, lamps, containers, nutcrackers, pen stands, and the like—objects one would find in the homes of the village landlord, the farmer, the merchant and shopkeeper" (Punja 1991:226).

Several prominent museums in India were established by the new government after independence. These include the National Gallery of Modern Art at Jaipur House in New Delhi, which was founded in 1954 and now has branches in Mumbai and Bangalore. The National Handicrafts and Handlooms Museum (also in New Delhi) was established in the 1950s and now houses more than 35,000 craft objects and has a handcrafts demonstration area (Punja 1991). Memorial museums have been established for both Mahatma Gandhi and Jawaharlal Nehru.

MUSEUMS IN WESTERN EUROPE AND THE AMERICAS

For much of the twentieth century, European museums were largely in recovery mode after two world wars and a prolonged economic depression. As a result, changes in European museums were relatively minor but included subdivision of very spacious exhibit halls and installation of plain backgrounds in exhibits, a general thinning-out of objects on display, and a preference for chronological or geographic arrangements in the galleries. The architecture of new museums was on a more human scale than the temple-inspired or palace-inspired museums of the past, with museums more people-oriented and less object-oriented and both centralization and decentralization taking place in different areas (Wittlin 1970). The situation was different in the Americas, which had not suffered the physical destruction of the first half of the century as did Europe.

In the early part of the twentieth century, collecting in American museums was often opportunistic rather than planned. Many objects from the Near East, particularly from Egypt, were acquired by American museums, not necessarily because the museums wished to acquire them to fulfill their missions, but because the objects were available, were popular with the public, were donated, or simply were found to be too tempting to resist (Redman 2005). In part, this was due to the fact that people liked museums because they were "repositories of the 'real thing'" (Lewis 1985:482). But as museums grew and their collections expanded, it became necessary to develop professional standards for managing the collections. When Henry Watson Kent (1866–1948) became the assistant secretary of the Metropolitan Museum of Art in 1905, he was "appalled by the lack of system that he found" (Alexander 1997:52). The previous director had made all decisions, the museum office had only one typewriter and one telephone, there was no information desk, communication was poor, and relationships among the staff were not good. The Metropolitan Museum of Art had been founded by a group of prominent, wealthy Americans who met in Paris on the Fourth of July in 1866 and decided that the United States needed a "National Institution and Gallery of Art" (Danziger 2007:xi). The museum was incorporated in 1866 and has been adding to its collections ever since. Kent instituted regular business procedures in the office; standardized systems for the accession, registration, and cataloging of the collections; improved communication; and worked to make the museum more of an educational institution than it had been previously by improving publications and programs. Kent was also responsible for installing the museum's first information desk (Alexander 1997). Today, the Metropolitan Museum of Art is the second-largest museum in the world (after the Louvre), occupying four city blocks, with two million square feet of space in twenty contiguous buildings and a security staff of more than six hundred employees (Danziger 2007).

While European museums were busy restoring churches, castles, and vernacular architecture in outdoor museums, Americans developed their own distinctive version of historic preservation based on the historic-house museum. Local and regional historical societies began appearing in the United States shortly after the country gained independence, with the goal of collecting documents and objects as aids to the interpretation and dissemination of history (Alexander 1997). The earliest historical societies include the Massachusetts Historical Society (founded in 1791), the New-York Historical Society (established in 1804), and the American Antiquarian Society (begun in 1812). By the time of the Centennial Exposition of 1876 in Philadelphia, there were more than seventy independent historical societies around the country, many supporting museums or historic houses or sites (Alexander 1997). The first historic-house museum in the United States was Hasbrouck House, which had been George Washington's headquarters in Newburgh, New York (Alexander and Alexander 2008). The Mount Vernon Ladies' Association, chartered in 1856, raised sufficient funds to purchase Washington's Mount Vernon plantation in 1860 and restore it as a historic site. Numerous local historical societies and historic preservation groups formed in communities across the country, frequently based on the preservation of a historic house or other significant site (Alexander and Alexander 2008). Other outdoor museums of the era and later include the restored medieval walled cities of Suzdal and Vladimir in Russia; the restored former slave-trading station of Gorée Island, Senegal; and the preservation of the Museum of Qin Shi Huang (the terra-cotta warriors) and mausoleum at Xi'an, China (Lewis 1992).

During the twentieth century, especially between World War I and World War II, the importance and scope of the educational function came to dominate most museums in the United States, although not without some controversy, as this diverted limited museum resources from other functions. Some critics "who doubted the power of instruction as an all-purpose nostrum raised strong objection to the didactic bias in art museums which was blamed on the 'atrophy of perception in Anglo-Saxons'—on their absorption in effort and their aversion to pleasure" (Wittlin 1970:151). John Dewey (1859–1952), who had a particular interest in museums as educational institutions, published an influential book, *The School and Society*, based on three public lectures and later printed in book form in 1899 and in a second edition in 1915 (Dewey 1915). Dewey's conception of an ideal school includes studios and laboratories for making discoveries about science, art, and music, all clustered around a central museum, in which the discoveries could be integrated and presented. The emphasis on using museums to disseminate knowledge to the public resulted in the development of many new exhibition concepts (and the importation of some techniques from Europe), including the use of period rooms, dioramas, and habitat groups and sometimes long-running, complex controversies (box 8.3).

There were disagreements among those who thought that museum objects, particularly works of art, were social documents and that their history and other musealized attributes should receive as much attention as their aesthetic qualities. In some museums, curators analyzed "forgotten works," comparing them to textual sources, including such often-neglected decorative art objects as medals and wax sculptures. In *Die Kunst und Wunderkammern der Spätrenaissance* (*The Art and Wonder Chambers of the Late Renaissance*), Julius von Schlosser (1866–1938) raises the possibility that "[i]ndeed, the work of art was already no longer the embodiment of an ideal of beauty related to taste, but rather a reflection on the period that witnessed its birth; it thus became one document among the others, serving an authentic intellectual investigation" (Davenne and Fleurent 2012:29). By the end of the twentieth century, art museums were far more open to an astoundingly diverse variety of art, now "legitimized by the museum setting," and referencing the early cabinets of curiosities by asking if postmodern art had become a "movement without movement, producing art without art—in short a compilation before classification, as the cabinet of curiosities sometimes was" (Davenne and Fleurent 2012:32).

Other museum controversies during this period include debate over which objects were worthy of exhibition. The Museum of Modern Art in New York was founded in 1929 to exhibit the sort of art that other museums refused to show or were criticized for displaying. Reactions to art that people did not like were often extreme. In 1921, when the Metropolitan Museum of Art exhibited a group of postimpressionist paintings, the "anonymous sponsors of a circular were quick in perceiving a link between degenerate art and a Bolshevist attempt to destroy social order in the United States" (Wittlin 1970:155). The situation was similar with abstract art, which had great difficulty finding acceptance in American museums. In the 1930s,

[a]bstract art in America was a voice crying out in the wilderness. With no hope of winning a mass audience away from the realistic styles, abstract art was spurned by the museum as hopelessly out of date—the modern style of the twenties. Although the Whitney [Museum] had lent impetus to the movement by holding an exhibition of abstract painting in America in 1935, when the Abstract Artists wished to hold its annual showing there in the late thirties, it was refused. In 1940, members of the Abstract Artists picketed the Museum of Modern Art, demanding that the museum show American Art. (Rose 1975:124)

BOX 8.3.
The Long, Strange Saga of the Barnes: What Is (and Is Not) a Museum?

One of the most controversial museum issues of the last half-century (at least in the United States) involves the Barnes Foundation. Albert Coombs Barnes (1872–1951) was born into a poor family in Philadelphia, but through grit and determination, he managed to earn both an MD and a PhD in chemistry, supporting himself at various times by tutoring his fellow students, playing semiprofessional baseball, and boxing.

Barnes made a fortune selling a silver-nitrate-based antiseptic called Argyrol, which enabled him to begin collecting art. In 1912, Barnes commissioned American artist William Glackens (1870–1938) to purchase $20,000 worth of paintings for him in Europe. Pleased with the pictures that Glackens brought back, Barnes took over the task of collecting himself and built up an astounding collection of works by Cézanne (69 paintings), Matisse (60 paintings), Modigliani (14 paintings), Picasso (44 works), Renoir (180 paintings), Rousseau (18 paintings), and others at a time when modern art was not widely appreciated or valued. Barnes had a lifelong interest in learning and self-improvement and began teaching art appreciation classes to his factory staff in Philadelphia.

In 1922, Barnes established the nonprofit Barnes Foundation, chartered as an educational institution and botanical garden in 1925 in Merion, Pennsylvania (in suburban Philadelphia). Although the Barnes Foundation included galleries full of art, the works were presented in a very particular way for the teaching of Barnes's personal philosophy of art appreciation. Barnes did not intend for his institution to be a museum. In fact, Barnes had a contemptuous attitude toward museums in general, particularly after the negative reaction of curators and critics to the foundation's first major public exhibition in 1923 at the Pennsylvania Academy of the Fine Arts. Despite the negative reception, Barnes remained convinced that "works of art could be employed as tools in an educational experiment" (quoted in Anderson 2003:34) and went on to write several books on art appreciation (one coauthored with John Dewey). During Barnes's lifetime, he consistently ran his foundation as a school, limiting public access primarily to students in the foundation's classes.

In an attempt to set a course for the foundation that would ensure it continued as a school for art appreciation and did not become a public museum, Barnes made several changes to the foundation's trust documents just before his death in a car accident in 1951. Unfortunately, Barnes's gruff personality and strong opinions made him many enemies during his lifetime. A short seven months after Barnes's death, a long series of legal maneuvers and lawsuits began that resulted at first in a gradual weakening and later in major changes to the terms of Barnes's trust, forcing the Barnes Foundation to admit members of the public to view the collection as if it were a museum. After years of legal battles, in 2001, the foundation was essentially broke, and talk began of moving the art collection to a place where it would be more easily accessible to paying visitors. Ultimately, the very thing Barnes feared most occurred—the collection was moved to a specially designed building on museum row in Philadelphia and opened to the public in 2012 as a museum.

One of the most fascinating aspects among all of the intrigue and backroom dealing that consumed the Barnes Foundation is how a school for teaching art appreciation became a museum, contrary to the explicit and well-documented intentions of its founder. Among other things, the forced metamorphosis occurred slowly over the course of several decades, beginning with a crusading newspaper owner's personal dislike for Barnes. The story serves as an instructive case and a cautionary tale for collectors, collections, and museums in general, as it involves a perceived (though contested) need for conservation of the paintings and renovation of the foundation's buildings; limitations on endowment investments due to restrictions imposed by the original trust; an attempt by the foundation's board (as its composition changed) to use the collection to produce income by subverting the purpose of the organization to become a museum; and the erosion of the foundation's endowment to pay for a series of complex legal issues, many of which involved the simple act of building a larger parking lot.

At the heart of the issue is what it means to be a museum. As discussed in chapter 1, there are many ways to define a museum, and as the history of collections shows, many collectors have explicit desires for the fate of their objects, usually thwarted after their deaths. While it is widely accepted that donors' wishes cannot always be carried out exactly as they might wish, it is fascinating that the concept of the museum is so compelling and powerful that a donor's wishes can be reversed and a school for art appreciation can be turned into the opposite of the founder's wishes.

Sources: Anderson 2003; Argott 2009; Dewey 1934; Higonnet 1994; Meisler 1993; numerous press reports.

The new museum idea of the previous century—the separation of collections into those for exhibition and those for study—continued to affect museum development, including museum architecture, as museums were now designed with large collection storage areas to hold more objects than could ever be placed before the public, laboratories and study rooms, and both permanent and temporary exhibition galleries. Benjamin Ives Gilman (1852–1933), the secretary of the Boston Museum of Fine Arts, "insisted that art museums differ from science and history museums in that their collections exist to allow their viewers to experience beauty rather than to convey information. This aesthetic emphasis in a sense meant 'art for art's sake,' not education"; however, John Cotton Dana (1856–1929) of the Newark Museum had a "very different idea—to emphasize art in the everyday activities of the community, to make immigrant and minority groups as well as factory workers proud of their culture and their products, to show how even everyday household wares could be well designed; in short, to define the museum as an instrument for community betterment" (Alexander and Alexander 2008:42).

The children's museum was a distinctive American invention, beginning with the Brooklyn Children's Museum in 1899, which had its roots in the children's galleries of the Victoria and Albert Museum, the Metropolitan Museum of Art, and the Smithsonian Institution. John Dewey was especially influential in the children's museum movement (Alexander and Alexander 2008). Dewey believed that

> [n]ot merely individuals, but communities and nations, put their cultural good taste in evidence by building opera houses, galleries, and museums. These show that a community is not wholly absorbed in material wealth, because it is willing to spend its gains in patronage of art. It erects these buildings and collects their contents as it now builds a cathedral. These things reflect and establish superior cultural status, while their segregation from the common life reflects the fact that they are not part of a native and spontaneous culture. They are a kind of counterpart of a holier-than-thou attitude, exhibited not toward persons as such but toward the interests and occupations that absorb most of the community's time and energy. (Dewey 1934:7)

In Dewey's opinion, the "growth of capitalism has been a powerful influence in the development of the museum as the proper home for works of art, and in the promotion of the idea that they are apart from the common life" (Dewey 1934:7).

The Museum of Science and Industry in Chicago, which opened in 1933 in the old Palace of Fine Arts building that was a leftover from the Columbian Exposition of 1893, is based on the Deutsches Museum in Munich (Alexander and Alexander 2008). The museum was envisioned as a "museum of progress" that would "crystallize the discoveries of science" and "explain the implications of new technology," and therefore, it was never intended to be finished (Pridmore 1997:16). The idea for the museum came from a businessman named Julius Rosenwald (then the president of Sears, Roebuck and Company), who saw the Deutsches Museum while on a trip to Munich with his family in 1916. The Museum of Science and Industry includes such diverse objects as a coal mine, dozens of hands-on interactive exhibits, a train, a German submarine, and a series of preserved slices through two human bodies (Pridmore 1997).

What is generally considered to be the first science center was the Palais de la Découverte, which opened in Paris in 1937 (it was built for the International Exposition of 1937 and was affiliated with the University of Paris). There was a surge in growth of science centers in the United States in the post-Sputnik climate of the space race. The Exploratorium in San Francisco, which like the Museum of Science and Industry in Chicago was inspired by the Deutsches Museum in Munich, was created by physicist Frank Friedman Oppenheimer (1912–1985). The Exploratorium opened in 1968, as did the Ontario Science Center (Alexander and Alexander 2008). Oppenheimer conceived the idea for his new kind of science and technology museum in 1950 when, as a professor of physics, he created a "Library of Experiments" in a large open space in the attic of a building at the University of Colorado in Boulder that eventually featured eighty experiment stations (Alexander 1997). In 1965, Oppenheimer visited Europe to study European science museums firsthand and was particularly impressed by the Palais de la Découverte in Paris and the Deutsches Museum in Munich, then widely considered to be the two best museums of science and industry in the world. Oppenheimer established his hands-on museum in 1969 in 86,000 square feet of space inside San Francisco's Palace of Fine Arts, with 300 experiment stations. By this time, Oppenheimer had decided that he disliked the word *museum*, as he thought it had a passive connotation for many people, so he coined the word *Exploratorium* for his new institution (Alexander 1997). Indeed, the Exploratorium did not fit the traditional conceptual model of a museum, as its main purpose was not collecting and preserving objects but rather teaching scientific and technological principles using interactive experiments. Oppenheimer started what he called the School in the Exploratorium (SITE) for elementary and junior high science teachers, also modeled on the Deutsches Museum's schools for teachers, and "aimed to acquaint them with scientific phenomena and to stimulate their perceptual awareness" (Alexander 1997:121).

The rapid expansion of highway systems in the United States after World War I inspired the creation of museums outside of urban centers, particularly historic-house museums and such total-environment museums as Colonial Williamsburg in Virginia and Greenfield Village in Dearborn, Michigan, with facilities designed to encourage visitors to extend their time on-site, including hotels and restaurants (Wittlin 1970). Greenfield Village was founded by automobile pioneer Henry Ford (1863–1947), who began accumulating objects early in the century for an outdoor museum to be based on the Scandinavian folk museums. Ford's museum opened in 1929 as the Greenfield Village and Edison Institute to showcase the development of industry in America—it is now known as The Henry Ford (Alexander and Alexander 2008).

The proliferation of folk museums had started in Sweden when a teacher and folklorist named Artur Hazelius (1833–1901), traveling about the country for his folklore research, became concerned about the erosion of Swedish culture and the disappearance of traditional folkways in the country. Hazelius founded the Nordiska Museet in Stockholm in 1873 and the first open-air museum, Skansen, in 1891 (Lewis 1992).

As the number of visitors to museums grew, museum educators and psychologists became interested in why people visited museums and what they got out of their visits (see also box 8.1). Some of the earliest research in this area was conducted by Edward S. Robinson (1893–1937) of Yale University in the 1920s. In 1928, the American Association of Museums published Robinson's summation of two years of observations of visitors in art museums, *The Behavior of the Museum Visitor*. Robinson remarked, "The museum may be an intellectual and aesthetic delight to its financial supporters, to its curators, or to some other select group of the sophisticates" but asked what about "that casual, self-conscious crowd which, on Saturday and Sunday afternoons, moves like some inanimate current from picture to picture and from glass case to glass case. . . . What does the 'average' man do in a museum?" (Robinson 1928:7). Robinson investigated the recently named phenomenon of museum fatigue and offered suggestions based on his study for the placement of art in museums to reduce fatigue and increase visitor satisfaction, concluding, "The behavior of the museum visitor offers an inexhaustible stock of problems" (Robinson 1928:66). This pioneering study and others that followed (particularly the work of Alma S. Wittlin) refocused attention in museum design from the objects as ends in themselves to the humans who came to see the objects and how information is transmitted in a museum. In Wittlin's early work, she determined that "museums offered to people experiences they did not find elsewhere: the direct confrontation with authentic objects and even with copies or models of authentic specimens, resulted in a speedy and forceful communication. Value was found in the variety of museum materials" (Wittlin 1970:162).

The main trends in museums in the United States between 1900 and 1970 included the diversification of collections in art museums, increasing emphasis on ecology and ecological principles in natural history museums, greater awareness of minority groups in museums, emphasis on research and working with schools on educational endeavors, and museums as multifaceted institutions (Wittlin 1970).

A significant change occurred in museums of science and natural history during the latter three-quarters of the twentieth century—research activity overall decreased (although it remained strong in museums associated with colleges and universities), while educational activities overall increased (Rader and Cain 2008). In large part, this change was driven by economic factors, including the increasing cost of research, the need to attract more paying visitors to museums, and the increase in funding available for research through institutions of higher education. In part, the shift was driven by changes in science itself, as biology (and particularly natural history) became more theoretical and less descriptive. In addition, science museum budgets (like the budgets of most museums) eroded badly during the period of the Great Depression in the 1930s (Rader and Cain 2008). This is not to say that research ceased in natural history museums—such large institutions as the American Museum of Natural History, the Field Museum, and the British Museum (Natural History), as well as many university museums, continued to be leaders in scientific research throughout the century.

The nature of natural history museum exhibits also changed significantly during this period, with an overall de-emphasis on habitat dioramas and systematic displays and an overall increase in exhibits that explained scientific phenomena, often in a very mechanistic style (Rader and Cain 2008).

In Canada, the number of museums increased from 385 just after World War II to more than 650 in 1970 (Wittlin 1970) and to more than 1,400 by 1980, clustered in its major population centers (Segger 1987).

Attempts to establish a museum in Cuba began in 1910, just eight years after independence, when members of the Academia Nacional de Artes y Letras met to discuss the formation of a formal collecting institution. After several years of acquisition of objects and fund-raising, the Museo Nacional de Bellas Artes opened in Havana in 1919 (Singleton 2008). A private museum was founded by the family of the rum magnate Emilio Bacardí in Havana in 1928 to exhibit their large collection of art and antiquities (Singleton 2008). In Latin America (as in Asia and Africa) during the second half of the twentieth century, there have been movements to integrate museums more fully into their communities. Latin American museum curators from several countries met in Santiago, Chile, in 1972 to promote museums as institutions for lifelong education and the development of social, economic, and political awareness of scientific, technological, and environmental development (Lewis 1992).

The use of museums to promote cultural identity has occurred in many parts of the world at one time or another. For example, the Council of Europe "encouraged its member states to develop 'European Rooms' in museums to present a public view of the European heritage" (Lewis 1992:16). The movement has been particularly strong in Latin America and the Caribbean. During most of the twentieth century, museums in the Caribbean countries reflected the relationships between planters and slaves that had been established in the seventeenth century, based on a culture that was a "derivative of European values (for generations the most dominant force) and bound to African sensibilities," even though slavery had been abolished in the West Indies in 1834 (Cummins 1994:192). On the island of Bermuda, a public library was established in 1843, along with a public museum that was to contain a "collection of natural history and works of art [that] would be beneficial to the community" (quoted in Cummins 1994:194), with similar institutions established in St. Lucia, the Bahamas,

Barbados, and Grenada between 1847 and 1848. However, limited transportation and restrictive social standards made these institutions largely inaccessible to the general population that was of African descent. As with colonial Indian museums of the same period, the collections of these institutions were focused on natural history and ethnography in order to demonstrate the wealth of natural resources of the region that was available for exploitation.

Typically, early Caribbean museums were founded as private organizations to meet the needs of commercial and agricultural interests and operated with only token assistance from the government. The museums were usually started with lofty missions and ideals but in reality served the self-interests of the founders, were designed to bring investment and business opportunities to the attention of their visitors, and had little or no presentation of island folk cultures (Cummins 1994). This began to change in the 1950s, when there was an increase in tourism to the West Indies due to improved airline services throughout the Caribbean and as Cuba was closed to most visitors. An analysis of regional museums by the Caribbean Conservation Association in 1967 concluded that most of the institutions were small, underfunded, poorly organized, understaffed, and generalized in their exhibits.

As most of the Caribbean nations gained independence during the 1970s, museums began to pay more attention to the complete histories of their communities. An analysis of the Barbados Museum in 1977 concluded that the institution was "not fully representative of national history and culture" and its exhibitions only told the story of the merchants and planters' lives, with "little or nothing about slaves, plantation labourers, or peasant farmers" in the galleries (Cummins 1994:213). Most Caribbean museums became more inclusive in their representations after the formation of the Museums Association of the Caribbean in 1989.

In Mexico, museums played a role in defining the Mexican nationalist character after independence (Morales-Moreno 1994), as

[e]l museo, como institución, ha sido uno de los espacios privilegiados de construcción y legitimación de la "cultura nacional" Mexicana. . . . Es también el lugar donde atisbar los significados diversos que las clases y grupos hegemónicos generan sobre su pasado, y donde esos significados se vuelven naturales, o al menos predominantes para buena parte de la sociedad.

the museum, as an institution, has been one of the privileged spaces of construction and legitimation of the Mexican "national culture." . . . It is also where the various meanings that classes and hegemonic groups generated about their past are observed and where those meanings become naturalized or at least predominant for a good part of society. (Schmilchuk 1995:21)

Much of the preconquest history of Mexico was destroyed by the Spanish conquistadors, including religious objects, fine gold and silver work, art, and written records. By the middle of the eighteenth century, however, interest in the region's indigenous past was increasing among Creoles and mestizos—the people of Spanish and Indian descent who had been born in Mexico, particularly as "Creole intellectuals tried to establish enlightened ideas of what was actually 'Mexican'" (Morales-Moreno 1994:173). During the war for independence (1810–1821), there was an emphasis on the continuity of Mexican history from Aztec times forward, which later became a "process of appropriation and expropriation of history, taken from the Indians and their culture to represent the Mexicans. Patriotism-motivated collecting provided the principle cornerstone of the modern National Museum at the end of the 19th century" (Morales-Moreno 1994:175).

A presidential decree calling for the formation of a Mexican national museum was issued in 1825, marking the

> beginning of the Mexican government's control over and husbandry of cultural heritage. The museum would legitimize the practice of successive Mexican government's gathering together all objects considered of "use and national glory." Finally, and most importantly, the decree of 1825 initiated the museological process of converting idolatrous objects into museum pieces. (Morales-Moreno 1994:177)

The result was that a symbiotic relationship formed among archaeology, the state, and the museum to forge a new definition of Mexican national identity. This was strengthened in 1910, when the Mexican president, Porfirio Díaz (1830–1915), became the first official visitor to the new Museo Nacional de Arqueología, Historia, y Etnología (now the Museo de Antropología), demonstrating that the "relationships among the museum, archaeology, and power were part of a strategic plan by the state to control the past through the image exhibited in the National Museum" (Morales-Moreno 1994:181–82).

MUSEUMS IN AFRICA AND ASIA

As one African museologist notes,

> The museum is by far the most positive cultural phenomenon borrowed by contemporary Africa from the West as a result of European colonization; not that Africans wished to make the museum an instrument reserved for a social élite, as was the case in Europe until recent times, but rather because they saw

in it far-reaching qualities and possibilities which were readily exploitable provided that the approach to the institution was pragmatic. (Diop 1973:250)

Several newly independent African countries have used museums to help define nationality. The government of Nigeria created a museum network with the aim of simultaneously preserving heritage and fostering national unity. The National Museum (Musée National du Niger) in Niamey, Niger, includes craft workshops for professional craftsmen and to train people who are seeing impaired or have other disabilities (Lewis 1992). In African museums, the "museological decolonization has brought new motivations to the museums. Their historical, ethnological, and art collections are imbued with a dynamism which breathes life into them and brings out to the maximum their inherent value" (Diop 1973:252). However, museum growth in Africa has not been rapid. As of 1980, the ratio of museums to inhabitants in Europe was 1:43,000, while in Africa it was 1:1,300,000 (Lewis 1992).

The Nakhon Si Thammarat National Museum was established by the regional office of Archaeology and National Museums of the Royal Thai Government in 1971 to interpret archaeological excavations that had begun in 1964 in the region surrounding the city of Nakhon Si Thammarat, the largest city in southern Thailand (Chandavij and Traikasem 2000:7). The museum's collections include prehistoric objects, ancient art objects, ancient artifacts of everyday life, trade ceramics from other countries found in archaeological sites, and objects related to a Buddhist patriarch named Phra Rattanathatcharmunee. Thailand, which has a thriving tourist trade, is relatively rich in museums, particularly in the capital city of Bangkok, where the first public museum in the country was founded in 1874 to commemorate the birthday of King Rama V (Pulsap 2004). Museum growth is often related to tourism—in 1949, it was estimated that there were only about 50 museums in China; by 1985, there were more than 800; and by the end of the century (with an enormous increase in tourists visiting China), there were more than 3,500 museums (Jisheng 1987).

THE PROFESSIONALIZATION OF MUSEUMS

When David Murray's *Museums, Their History and Their Use* was published in 1904, the study of museums (now called *museology* or *museum studies*) hardly existed as an academic discipline. In fact, the museum profession was not even recognized as such, and instead

scholar-curators undertook almost all of the museum's specialized work: acquiring collections, specimens, and works of art, researching, cataloguing, and documenting their collections, and interpreting and communicating their significance through the museum's permanent display galleries, temporary exhibitions, publications, and educational programs such as lectures and guided visits. The "generalist" scholar-curators . . . were in turn supported by a single category of non-professional support staff, lowly regarded manual workers mainly undertaking security, cleaning, and building maintenance duties. (Boylan 2006:418)

The first museological works published were chiefly concerned with practice, not theory, and formal museum training courses were preceded by in-house training courses at various museums in Europe and in the United States (Lorente 2012). Although the discussion of how to best train professionals for museum work had begun in the 1890s, as the twentieth century got under way, museum training was still limited to on-the-job training, training offered through professional museum associations, or the limited training opportunities available at a few universities or museums (Simmons 2015). Most museum workers had, in fact, been invisible for centuries (Latham and Simmons 2015).

In an insightful study of the history of museum studies, Jesús Lorente identifies three pillars of modern museology as (1) specialized publications addressing museological issues, (2) professional associations, and (3) formal training courses (Lorente 2012). As Lorente notes, during the last century, training for museum professionals has evolved from practical courses and apprenticeships to university courses and eventually formal university programs, as museological theory was developed and applied to museum practice (Lorente 2012). During the early period of this development, key museology publications included

- *Bibliography of Museums and Museology* by William Clifford, published by the Metropolitan Museum of Art in New York in 1923;
- *Museumskunde* by Otto Homburger, published by Hirt in 1924;
- *A Bibliography of Museums and Museum Work* by Ralph Clifton Smith, published by the American Association of Museums in 1928;
- *Mouseion* magazine, established in Madrid in 1934;
- *Concepto Actual del Museo Artístico* by Andrés Ovejero Bustamente, published in 1934; and
- *Le Temple des Muses* by Jean Capart, published in 1936.

Professional museum associations were first formed in Europe, among the oldest being the Museums Association organized in the United Kingdom in 1889 (Lorente 2012) and the American Association of Museums (now the American Alliance of Museums) founded in 1906 (Schwarzer 2006). Professional organizations were subsequently formed in several other countries, such as the Art Galleries and Museums Association of Australia and New Zealand, established in 1977 (McCarthy and Cobley 2009).

An indication of the nature of the field early in the twentieth century can be found in a statement made by Benjamin Ives Gilman (1852–1933), then a board member of the American Association of Museums, who stated,

> Two years ago at our meeting in Chicago I gave a simple definition of museums, which seemed to arouse some amusement. I said it often seemed to me that a museum of art or history is a place where things out of date were gathered in order to become more so. If this is true it makes evident the clear and direct connection between the teaching of history and museums. The teaching of history tells us about the very things that are in museums, and it seems singular that we have not taken advantage of the opportunity museums afford for illustrating history. (Gilman 1916:53)

Clearly, change was needed in the form of trained museum professionals who would have the practical knowledge necessary for daily museum operations and the theoretical understanding of their institutions that would enable them to critique and improve them. Although inexorable, it was a change that was slow in coming.

The Louvre Museum in Paris established the Ecole du Louvre in 1882, primarily to teach archaeology; a chair of museology was added in 1927 and began offering museological classes in about 1929 (Lorente 2012). Germain Bazin (1901–1990) was later appointed to the Ecole du Louvre and published his influential *Le Temps des Musées* in 1967 (published in English as *The Museum Age*). Other early courses in museology include

- a course at the University of Moscow offered by Georgy Leonidovich Malitsky (1886–1953) between 1919 and 1924;
- a course taught beginning in 1927 by Jaroslav Helfert (1883–1972), director of the Moravian Museum and founder of the Museology Faculty at the University of Masaryk in Brno;
- courses at the University of Halle, beginning in 1930, by Alois J. Schardt (1889–1955);
- instruction offered by E. Lionel Judah (1880–1967), the head curator of the McGill University museums, beginning about 1930 in Montreal;
- a course provided through the Museu Histórico Nacional in Rio de Janeiro in Brazil in 1932; and
- courses in curation offered by the Courtauld Institute of Art in London beginning in 1932.

Museum associations have played an important role in training people for museum work in several countries, beginning with the first standard diploma course established in Great Britain through the Museums Association in 1930. In the United States, museum training courses were organized primarily through colleges and universities, beginning in 1908, when Sarah Yorke Stevenson (1847–1921), the assistant curator of the Pennsylvania Museum, began teaching a two-year course for students (who were required to have at least a high school diploma) to prepare for work in art museums (Cushman 1984). At about the same time, Homer Ray Dill (1877–1964), the director of the Museum of Natural History at the State University of Iowa in Iowa City, began teaching a single class in museum studies that later grew into a four-year degree program in natural sciences, with a minor in museum work. Students in Dill's program studied taxidermy, exhibition techniques, drawing, and modeling (Cushman 1984). In 1910, Myrtilla Avery (1869–1959) of the Farnsworth Museum at Wellesley College began training women students to work as art museum assistants (Alexander 1997; Cushman 1984; Glaser 1987). As with earlier programs, the intention was to train museum workers, not museum administrators or museum directors. Paul Joseph Sachs (1878–1965) taught a course at Harvard through the Fogg Museum for graduate students who wished to become curators or directors of art museums, beginning about 1921 (Alexander 1997). At the Newark Museum, John Cotton Dana (1856–1929) initiated a one-year training course in 1925 that was supervised by Katherine Coffey (1900–1972) for students with a college degree (Alexander 1997; Cushman 1984). The biggest obstacle all these programs faced was the failure of the American Association of Museums—the largest museum organization in the United States—to endorse formal museum training, despite establishing a committee to survey museum studies training opportunities in 1917 (Glaser 1987; Simmons 2006).

Elsewhere, university training for museum professionals was initiated in Argentina (during the 1920s), Czechoslovakia (1921), India (1952), England (1966), Australia (1975), Italy (1984), and New Zealand (1989; Bedekar 1987; Fedi 1987; Hodge 1987; Lewis 1985; Lewis 1987; McCarthy and Cobley 2009). Postgraduate studies in museology were established at the University of Zagreb in 1966, later headed by Ivo Maroević (Lorente 2012).

In most regions of the world, professionalization of museum staff was haphazard at best. An independent regional training center for museum assistants was established in Jos, Nigeria, in 1963 (Arinze 1987). It was not until 1974 that the Lahore Museum got its first professional "museologist" when director Dr. Saifur Rhaman Dar was hired. Dar sought to train and inspire the museum staff—of the seventeen officers then at the museum, not one had ever visited another museum in Pakistan, much less elsewhere in the world, so Dar sent staff members the United Kingdom, Germany, and the United States for training and to see museums firsthand. The first formal museum training course was held at the Lahore Museum in 1979 (Bhatti 2012).

In her 1970 publication, museum research pioneer Alma Wittlin (1899–1990) expresses the view that the "diversified tasks in museums call for knowledge in many disciplines or skills of increasing specialization. No single individual can be an expert in 'museology.' If he aspires to work at a professional level, he has to limit himself to a well-defined sector of museum work." She also notes, "The demand for specialists in many fields leads to the need for an adequate provision of training facilities for a variety of museum personnel" (Wittlin 1970:187).

At midcentury, two texts that would prove crucial to the development of museology as an academic discipline were published in France (Lorente 2012). In *Le Museé Imaginaire* (*The Imaginary Museum*), published in 1947, André Malraux (1901–1976) argues that the nature of works of art is changed when they are removed from their original surroundings and added to a museum collection (presaging the later theory of musealization) and proposes the creation of a museum without walls (which presaged the virtual museum, discussed in chapter 9). In 1966, Pierre Bourdieu (1930–2002) published *L'Amour de l'art* (*Love of Art*), a detailed analysis of European art museums and visitors intended to help museums better understand their audiences.

During the 1970s, in most of Europe and the United States, museum studies training was dominated by university postgraduate programs. In 1978, ICOM formed the International Committee for Museology (ICOFOM). The largest growth in museum studies programs in the United States began in the late 1970s (Simmons 2006).

RESTORATION AND CONSERVATION

Museums have long confronted the dilemma of preservation of collections versus the use of objects. All objects deteriorate—some rapidly, some slowly, depending on the materials they are composed of and the environment they are kept in—but the use of objects for study, research, exhibition, and education puts objects at much greater risk of damage and deterioration. Although some of the factors that contribute to object deterioration have long been known (such as the risks posed by exposure to pests or sunlight), significant improvements in preservation technology have only occurred over the last one hundred years as our understanding of how materials deteriorate has advanced (Muñoz Viñas 2005).

The practice of *restoration* (making old or damaged collection objects look new again) has a long history, with its origins in late medieval and early Renaissance collecting practices. Restoration techniques and materials have traditionally been cloaked in secrecy, with few restorers willing to share their methods with others. Although restorers may make objects look good again, restoration rarely preserves the historical integrity of the object, and most of the techniques and materials used are not reversible or documented. There are many examples of the restoration of museum objects creating more damage to the object than they repaired.

Beginning in the mid-nineteenth century, concern for the integrity of museum objects led to the creation of a new profession called *conservation*, which has gradually replaced the practice of restoration in museums. Unlike restoration, the focus of conservation is to ameliorate damage while preserving the historic and artistic integrity of the object and to prevent further deterioration from occurring (Zubiaur Carreño 2004). The early development of conservation was greatly influenced by such authors as John Ruskin (1819–1900) in his books *The Seven Lamps of Architecture* (1849) and *The Stones of Venice* (published in three volumes between 1851 and 1853) and Eugène Viollet-le-Duc (1814–1879) in his ten-volume 1856 work *Dictionnaire raisonné de l'architecture française du XIe au XVIe siècle* (*Dictionary of French Architecture from the 11th to 16th Centuries*). The theories advanced by Ruskin and Viollet-le-Duc eventually led to the abandonment of secret and often damaging restoration methods in favor of techniques of conservation that were grounded in science, reversible, and well documented (Muñoz Viñas 2005). Rather than the restorer's concern with the external appearance of an object, a conservator is concerned with the object's materials, history, and overall integrity (Appelbaum 2010).

Beginning in the 1960s, the theory of preventive conservation has gained dominance in museums, as reliable and efficient technologies for controlling collection storage environments have become available (see box 9.4). The principle of preventive conservation is to prolong the useful life of objects in collections by controlling the agents of deterioration (Canadian Conservation Institute 2015) in a stable storage environment. Preventive conservation employs a combination of preventive care (the avoidance of deterioration), reversible treatment methods, documentation of conservation materials and procedures, and research on object deterioration.

ZOOLOGICAL PARKS AND BOTANICAL GARDENS

During the early years of the twentieth century, zoological parks and botanical gardens, like museums, began to change their admissions policies to admit all members of the public, which resulted in a surge of zoo visitors during the first half of the twentieth century. Many zoos doubled their visitor numbers during this period (Baratay and Hardouin-Fugier 2002). Like museums, zoos and botanical gardens were recast as educational institutions rather than purely entertainment venues, as the welfare, housing, and presentation of living organisms became more sophisticated.

Many of the newer zoos put an emphasis on scientific animal care and exhibition and established direct links to both museums and universities where zoological research was conducted. For example, the New York Zoological Society (popularly known as the Bronx Zoo), founded in 1895, was created with the idea that it would be an institution on par with the American Museum of Natural History and play an active role in conservation. Henry Fairfield Osborn (1857–1935), who already held joint appointments as professor of biology at Columbia University and curator at the American Museum of Natural History (which enabled the two organizations to work more closely together on research), became president of the board of trustees of the American Museum of Natural History in 1908 and was instrumental in the founding and development of the New York Zoological Society (Alexander 1997; Bridges 1974). To achieve the lofty goal of a scientifically based zoological park, the first director hired was William Temple Hornaday (1854–1937), a well-known and widely respected naturalist, scientific animal collector, and taxidermist at the US National Museum (Bridges 1974). Hornaday brought many of the exhibit concepts he had developed at the museum to the zoo's presentation of animals in natural settings. Hornaday worked tirelessly to save the American bison from extinction and encouraged his curators to publish scientific papers. In 1907, the society took the then-unusual step of organizing research expeditions (Bridges 1974), and in 1922, the society established a Department of Tropical Research with a full-time, dedicated staff (Gould 2004).

Beginning in 1907, the concept of the zoo without bars was pioneered by Carl Hagenbeck (1844–1913) in Stellingen, Germany, using hidden walls, moats, and other unobtrusive barriers to allow visitors to see zoo animals in a more natural setting (Baratay and Hardouin-Fugier 2002). The concept quickly came to dominate zoos across Europe and North America.

The intensely anthropomorphic "individualization of animals" became very popular between the 1930s and 1950s, in which zoo animals were given pet names, their birthdays were celebrated with parties, and they were humanized in other ways (Baratay and Hardouin-Fugier 2002). Although this brought much attention (and more visitors) to zoos, it did little or nothing to further the public's understanding of animals in nature. On the positive side, particularly after World War II, most zoos began to seriously tackle issues of wildlife conservation with a combination of educational programming, research, and carefully managed captive breeding programs (Rabb 2004).

LITERATURE

After 1900, books became much less expensive to produce, literacy rates rose dramatically, the means of distribution of books continued to improve, and literature became more international in scope, as more books were available in languages other than those of their authors. As a result, more people not only read more books but also purchased more books to own. Books with paper covers had been sold commercially since the mid-nineteenth century, but these were either very inexpensive editions or were designed for the purchaser to bind in hard covers. In the 1930s, the first mainstream, mass-market paperback books were released—Penguin Books in England brought out *Ariel* by André Maurois (1885–1967) in 1935, and in the United States, Pocket Books released *The Good Earth* by Pearl Buck (1892–1973) in 1938. The publications of these well-respected books in paperback marked a major milestone in the publishing industry, as now quality literature was accepted in a lower-priced soft-cover format, making books even more widely available to readers. Following World War II, publishers began releasing paperbacks with high-quality cover art and, after 1950, began to release paperback originals of literary fiction.

Modernist literature dominated the period from 1900 to 1950, first with the disillusionment of the fin de siècle tales of lost faith and broken dreams, often dwelling on the inner workings of the mind, sometimes with wildly experimental styles of writing. *The Autobiography of Alice B. Toklas* (1933) by Gertrude Stein (1874–1946) captured the creation of the sensational new art being made in Paris that was causing controversies in major staid art museums. Joseph Conrad (1857–1924) embodied the new internationalization of writing. Born Józef Teodor Konrad Korzeniowski to a Polish family in the Ukraine, Conrad spent the first half of his life as a mariner, before embarking on a writing career in 1894 to become one of the greatest novelists writing in the English language. Austrian-born Gustav Meyrink (1868–1932) used the Jewish ghetto in Prague (where he lived for twenty years) as the setting for his best-known work, *The Golem* (1915), a dark and shadowy story of an art restorer, based on an old Jewish folktale. Marcel Proust (1871–1922), born in France, published one of the most influential novels of the twentieth century, *Á la recherche du temps perdu* (*Remembrance of Things Past*), between 1914 and 1927, using multiple perspectives, hundreds of characters, and exploring a theme closely related to musealization—the relationship between memory and writing—which greatly influenced the writers of the beat generation thirty years later.

Reacting to the horrors and massive casualties of World War I, the Lost Generation of writers, including Ernest Hemingway (1899–1961) and Sherwood Anderson (1876–1941), produced introspective, subjective, and self-revealing fiction based closely on personal experiences and a sense of place. William Faulkner (1897–1962) created the mythical Yoknapatawpha County based on his southern childhood. A combination of Faulkner's creation of a place, the freedom of surrealism, and the non-traditional chronological order and stream-of-consciousness narration of Virginia Woolf (1882–1941) inspired the magical realism of a group of Latin American writers in the second half of the twentieth century, including the Colombian-born Gabriel García Márquez (1927–2014) and the Peruvian author and literary scholar Mario Vargas Llosa (b. 1936). Much like the changes that were occurring in museum exhibitions, magical realism extrapolated complex meanings from concrete objects and events. In his 1941 story *La Biblioteca de Babel* (*The Library of Babel*), the Argentine author Jorge Luis Borges (1899–1986; Borges 1962) describes an enormous universal library of adjoining hexagonal rooms, each randomly filled with books composed using every possible order of twenty-two letters, the period, the comma, and the space, rendering some volumes incomprehensible while others contain all the useful information in the universe.

The postmodern writers, finding the world utterly gone awry after World War II, confronted a confining and unreliable culture with the use of highly experimental language, imagery, and storylines, particularly the beat generation writers of the 1950s and 1960s, such as William Burroughs (1914–1997), Jack Kerouac (1922–1969), and Alan Ginsberg (1926–1997).

SUMMARY

In the short span of time between 1900 and 1970, the number and variety of museums in the world grew exponentially, as did their complexity and activities. Over seventy years of abrupt and often unexpected changes, museums came full circle from the collections of objects used by humans to navigate their way through a complex and often hostile world to educational institutions that helped humans better understand their place in the world.

9

—◦◊◦—

Learning to Read Objects (Again)

The Post-Postmodern Museum

Recent history seems more complex than the distant past due to our distorted narrative perspective—we are awash in the details of what has just occurred and find it difficult to discern the significant trends that are enmeshed in contemporary events. This problem is made worse as the pace of change in the world has accelerated tremendously along with the speed of communication. As a result, it is "not just as a succession of events that history has speeded up. The rapidity of the changes it has brought has often had wider and deeper implications, and more influence than in the past, just because of the speed with which the changes came about" (Roberts and Westad 2013:991–92). This makes identifying important trends in the recent history of museums somewhat problematic—it can be difficult to understand the tides while one is still dodging the waves. Nevertheless, in this chapter, I parse out some of the major trends in museums since the 1970s.

The digitization of information and the ease with which it can be accessed are having a profound effect on museums and on people's attitudes toward museums. Although recent surveys show that museums still rank high as credible information sources, museum visitors have more options for access to knowledge than they did in the past. Internet use has increased astronomically from its origin in 1969. What we now know as the Internet began as ARPANET, developed by the Advanced Research Projects Agency for the US Department of Defense. Access to ARPANET was expanded in 1981 with funds from the National Science Foundation and morphed into the universal Internet during the mid-1990s. By 2000, the Internet had 738 million users worldwide, but just a decade later, in 2010, there were more than 2 billion users. As 2015 drew to a close, the number of Internet users was estimated to be 3.2 billion, which is 43 percent of the world's population (Davidson 2015; Roberts and Westad 2013).

Despite the astounding number of Internet users, the digital divide—the gap between those who have ready access to electronic communication and those who do not—remains significant, even as it is shrinking. The increased availability of the Internet has affected museums in a number of ways, from largely replacing written texts as the primary source of information to enabling even small, remote museums to communicate with a worldwide audience (Keene 2005). The digitization of paper-based materials has proven to be a double-edged sword, as it has resulted in another form of digital divide—while there is an astonishing amount of books, journals, handwritten museum catalogs, and other paper-based documents available electronically, printed materials that have not been digitized (and may never be digitized) are largely overlooked and ignored.

Paradoxically, the digital information age has brought about an unanticipated anti-intellectual movement, particularly within the United States. Beginning in the 1970s, "it became clear that a new skepticism about science itself was abroad, even though only among a minority and only in rich countries," which has made the task of communicating complex ideas and concepts (not just about science but about the arts and humanities as well) more difficult for museums (Roberts and Westad 2013:1019). The Internet does not speed up the communication of only verified information but marginal and extreme ideas, as well.

During the present decade, the impact of technology on museums has been the subject of extensive speculation and wild prediction. Lost in most of this rhetoric is the reality that the vast majority of new technology—including computers, cellular telephones, barcodes and QR (quick response) codes, and most especially social media—does not empower museums to do things they did not do before but instead enables museums to do faster and more efficiently what they were already doing. The history of museums is the story of striving to reach new audiences, better understanding the needs of visitors, making innovations in collections management and exhibition practices, creating and disseminating knowledge, and finding better ways to preserve and restore objects of value to society. Most museums are doing all of these things better now, often aided by new technology, but very rarely are they doing them because of new technology. A good example is the history of computers in museums, which have made many museum functions—from registration to member services to communication of collection-related information—faster and easier but have not fundamentally changed museums' missions (box 9.1). There is always a tendency for the introduction of new technology to dis-

BOX 9.1.
From Binary to Primary: Computers in the Museum

Museums are restricted in how much information they can manage by the physical limitations of information storage and retrieval. Prior to the introduction of electronic data processing, accessing collection information was labor intensive, slow, and often inadequate—the old card catalog for the collection at the Metropolitan Museum of Art in New York grew to occupy a series of cabinets that were a full city block in length, but the information they contained was organized only by accession number (Vance 1986, cited in Jones 2008). The introduction of computers brought about a significant improvement in the ability of museums to function as repositories of information as well as repositories of objects. Improved access to collection information means that museums can now better fulfill their missions and serve the public.

A computer is a device that stores, manipulates, and retrieves information, one of a series of devices in a long progression from the clay tablets of the Babylonians to the more efficient papyrus scrolls of the Egyptians and the knotted, colored strings of the quipu of the Inca empire and on to punch cards and microchips. A database is a set of software programs that controls how data is organized, stored, and retrieved in computers. Computers and databases in museums now do much of the work that used to be done by hand (once upon a time) by inscribing information in bound ledger books in longhand and later retyping information on cards to sort in file drawers. The advantage that computers and electronic databases bring to museums is that they can manage large amounts of information rapidly, efficiently, and with few mistakes (although it should be noted that computers and databases are also excellent means to perpetuate human errors).

The work that a computer does is based on mathematics and sorting systems, whose history begins with the abacus, the oldest known mechanical device for making mathematical computations, in use since at least 2700 BCE in Babylonia (and probably invented much earlier). The original abacus used pebbles rather than the familiar beads-on-wires design of the Chinese version, which dates back to the fourteenth century (the word *calculus* comes from the Latin word *calculi*, meaning "pebble"). The oldest programmable analog computer was an astronomical clock built in 1206 by Abū al-'Iz Ibn Ismā'īl ibn al-Razāz al-Jazarī (1136–1206), an Islamic scholar from Mesopotamia. The clock displayed the zodiac and the orbits of the sun and moon, had doors that opened every hour, and was equipped with five robot musicians that played music. The clock mechanism was operated by a camshaft attached to a water wheel.

In 1617, a Scotsman named John Napier (1540–1617) invented logarithms, which allow complex mathematical operations to be performed very quickly. Napier originally produced his logarithm tables as series of numbers printed

(continued)

BOX 9.1.
(continued)

on paper but later engraved them on ivory sticks (called Napier's bones) that could be used to do calculations faster than the paper tables. Napier's bones are the basis of a calculating device called the slide rule, first made in England in 1632. Slide rules were so efficient for calculating that they were used until well after the invention of the modern computers (the calculations necessary for the first space flights and the moon landing were made using slide rules, not computers).

The first gear-driven calculating machine was invented by Wilhelm Schickard (1592–1635) in 1623 to calculate astronomical tables. Schickard's marvel could add and subtract six-digit numbers. In 1642, Blaise Pascal (1623–1662) designed a more efficient calculating machine called the Pascaline, a one-function, gear-driven calculator that could add by incrementing a wheel after each full revolution of the prior wheel. Unfortunately, due to the lack of precision in gear production at the time, the manufactured machines were not very accurate and did not sell well. Between 1672 and 1694, a German named Gottfried Wilhelm Leibniz (1646–1716) built a four-function calculating machine that could add, subtract, multiply, and divide, but rather than using gears, it employed metal drums with ten flutes (for the decimal number system) arranged around the circumference in a stair-step fashion. Leibniz called his device a *Staffelwalze*, or stepped reckoner system.

In 1801, Joseph Marie Jacquard (1752–1834) invented a power loom for weaving that used holes punched through flat wooden blocks to make patterns in the woven products. English mathematician Charles Babbage (1791–1871) invented an analytic engine that used Jacquard's punched wooden blocks to make problem statements, later changing the wooden blocks for stiff paper cards. A contest was held prior to the 1890 census in the United States for a system that could automate the process of data analysis. The contest was won by Herman Hollerith (1860–1929), who adopted Jacquard's punched cards into a mechanical tabulator that did the mathematical computations using a gear-driven mechanism with electric connections made through the holes in the cards. The results were displayed on dial indicators. Hollerith later started his own company, the Tabulating Machine Company, which eventually became International Business Machines (IBM), and parlayed the punched cards into a multimillion-dollar industry, using them for everything from highway tolls to library cards.

The next impetus for more powerful computers came from the US military and the need to make complex calculations of rocket and missile trajectories, which led to the invention of the Harvard Mark I computer, built in partnership with IBM in 1944—the first programmable digital computer. The computational mechanism consisted of switches, relays, rotating shafts, and clutches. The Mark I was huge—it weighed more than five tons, was eight feet tall and fifty-one feet long, had a fifty-foot-long rotating shaft that was turned by a five-horsepower electric motor, and used five hundred miles of wire. A Mark I programmer named Grace Hopper (1906–1992), called to fix an error in the machine, found that a dead moth had fallen into the computer's mechanism and was blocking the holes in the paper tape, preventing the electrical transmission from taking place, which is why we now call eliminating computer errors "debugging." Hopper invented the first true high-level computer language, Flow-matic, in 1953, which was more understandable by humans than the standard binary language. By today's standards, the Mark I was slow, limited by the speed of its rotating shaft.

The next big computer breakthrough was the ENIAC (Electronic Numerical Integrator and Calculator), built at the University of Pennsylvania between 1943 and 1945. The ENIAC weighed 30 tons, read data from punch cards, and required 18,000 vacuum tubes for its electric brain. A calculation that took 6 seconds on the Mark I took only 2.8 thousandths of a second on the ENIAC, but the vacuum tubes produced so much heat that the computer had to have its own air conditioning system, and the vacuum tubes had short life spans. An entire team of people was required to manually reset patch cords and switches in order to reprogram the machine.

Transistors, invented in 1947, replaced vacuum tubes, and microchips that contained millions of transistors on fingernail-sized pieces of silicon then replaced simple transistors. However, it wasn't until the 1960s that computers became sufficiently cost-effective for private businesses to begin using them to store and process large quantities of information, and even then, data had to be coded for input, manipulation, and retrieval—the memory of these computers was very limited and expensive to increase. Libraries began using computers toward the end of the 1960s, which attracted the interest of museums.

In 1965, the first attempt to develop a universal computer program for all museum collections was initiated at the University of Oklahoma using a records management software program called GIPSY (Generalized Information Processing System). The program was not widely used, but the attempt attracted the attention of the museum community, and so the Museum Computer Network (MCN) was founded in 1967 as the first professional organization to promote the use of computers in museums. A number of MCN member organizations began using the GRIPHOS program (an acronym for General Retrieval and Information Processor for Humanities-Oriented Studies), but it also failed to achieve widespread use. Nevertheless, by 1970, the Metropolitan Museum of Art and the Museum of Modern Art had computer-based catalogs, and in the early 1970s, the Smithsonian Institution launched a program called SELGEM (the name is derived from *Self-Generating Master*). Another program that went into operation in 1975 was REGIS (the official name was Arizona State Museum's Interactive REGIStration System). Due to limited computer memory, the information put into REGIS and SELGEM was limited, had to be coded, and was loaded in batches, all of which was very time consuming.

(continued)

BOX 9.1.
(continued)

After sinking a lot of time and money into GRIPHOS, REGIS, and SELGEM, without many tangible results, many museums abandoned attempts to find a universal system to catalog their collections in the late 1970s and began to develop highly idiosyncratic individual database systems. As a result, by the end of the 1970s, there were hundreds of different programs in use, none compatible with any of the others. This situation began to change when the relational model for databases was proposed by Edgar Frank "Ted" Codd (1923–2003), a British scientist who worked for IBM. The relational database model fundamentally changed the way databases were developed and how data were stored and retrieved by organizing data into sets and storing it in tables.

Once museums began digitizing their collection information, the importance of adopting standard nomenclatures (taxonomies) became glaringly apparent. With a computerized system, it was possible for a museum to process much more information about the objects in its collection, but sharing and combining that information with other institutions was difficult without standardized systems. Sharing and combining information was not too complicated a problem for natural history museums, which had long used standardized systems of nomenclature (see box 7.2), but it was a more serious issue in other disciplines where competing and conflicting taxonomies were common (there are at least twenty accepted variant spellings for the name of the composer Peter Ilyich Tchaikowsky, but to a computer, those would be twenty unique names). Many museums began to use the taxonomic system developed by Robert Chenhall (1978), later amplified by Blackaby and Greeno (1988), then by Bourcier and Rogers (2010), and finally Bourcier and Dunn (2015), now known as *Nomenclature 4.0 for Museum Cataloging*. The system provides names for human-made objects in a controlled hierarchical structure. The 2015 version includes more than 14,600 preferred object names—the purpose is not to provide a specific name for every object that might be in a collection but rather to provide a framework for cataloging in a hierarchical structure.

By the mid-1980s, computers were at last reliable enough and sufficiently inexpensive for museum use, and relational databases were available on the commercial market. In most museums, the recording of documentation had historically taken a backseat to collecting and preserving the collections, but now in many museums (particularly in natural history museums), collections care is secondary to electronic data management. As the management of information in the museum has become as much in demand as the management of the collections, it has resulted in an increase in value of both the information and the objects, leading to some interesting sociotechnical interactions as human beings, technology, and information all intersect (Marty 2008a). Collections management has now become a delicate balance of caring for the objects, making them available for use, and managing collection information (Simmons 2015).

Prior to electronic data management, how files were organized and which data were recorded were pretty much at the whim of the registrar or curator, with the result that the kind of information kept and the way it was kept were usually highly eccentric and specialized. It is still rare to find two systems in museums that are exactly alike. With the advent of computerization, these eccentric and personalized systems were converted to eccentric and personalized computer databases, and often the prejudices or nonrational ideas of registrars or curators continued to drive system design. The standard of evaluation was usually low—if a database system worked at least as well as the old paper-based system, then it was considered good. There has been little questioning of how well systems work or what they are supposed to do, and the design of collection management systems has been largely driven by users of collections data rather than by those in charge of collections care (Simmons 2013). The next generation of collection management systems must be designed to provide the tools needed to better manage all aspects of the collections, not just the documentation.

Current computer technology now allows museums to share data on distributed databases, even though their individual database structures are different.

Sources: Arnone 2010; Baron 1991; Jones 2008; Jones-Garmil 1997; Quigley 2010; Sarasan 1981; Simmons 2013; Vance 1986; Williams 1987.

tract museum staff from the core mission of the musealization of objects. Electronic data management has led some people to argue that, once collection information has been captured electronically and the object digitized, the information assumes a greater value than the objects it came from (this is particularly a problem in natural history museums, which now dispense more collection-based information than loans of specimens to researchers). However, this ignores not only the multiple contexts and stories of each object or specimen but also one of the great values of museums—the new uses that are continually discovered for the collections and the new knowledge that is subsequently extracted from them. As discussed in chapter 1, musealization is continual throughout the lifespan of the object. Collections management systems can be very good at creating surrogates (extracting subunits of information) and aggregates (new groupings of information from more than one source) as the information is manipulated electronically (Marty 2008b), but this enhances rather than diminishes the importance of the original objects.

Since the end of World War II, the number of nation-states (geographically recognized entities with legislative and political sovereignty) has increased from fewer than fifty to more than two hundred, due primarily to realignments of former spheres of power and influence, the decline of colonialism, and the diffusion of the forms of state machinery through the exportation of European cultural systems (Roberts and Westad 2013). The economic disintegration of the Soviet Union culminated in its dissolution in 1991, and China emerged as a world economic and political power after thousands of years of relative isolation. The growth of urban populations has reached the point that "[a]s the twentieth century ended nearly half of us lived in cities. The city is becoming the typical habitat of *Homo sapiens*," a significant change from how people lived throughout most of human history (Roberts and Westad 2013:998).

Along with the increase in the number of nations and the growth of urban populations has come an increase in museums—by one estimate, there are now more than 55,000 museums worldwide, twice as many as there were in 1990 (Beanland 2014). The website of the International Council of Museums (ICOM) also uses the estimate of 55,000 museums in 202 countries, based on the listings in the 2014 edition of the *Museums of the World* directory, which ICOM acknowledges is an undercount of world museums (ICOM 2015).

According to one estimate, 95 percent of museums in the world today were founded after World War II (Lowenthal 1998). As a result of changes in communication, "[t]oday, some museums and galleries are brands. They've begun colonising in the way that countries did while the institutions themselves were being formed, back in Victorian days" (Beanland 2014:n.p.). It is possible that, in the near future, the continued digitization of information and communication may mean that patrons demand nothing less than personalized museums with visitor experiences designed expressly for them.

UNIVERSAL MUSEUMS

The descriptor *universal museums* (also *encyclopedic museums*) refers primarily to older, larger institutions with extensive collections, usually founded during the Enlightenment. Universal museums have been criticized as "instruments of the state" because they present cultural heritage to the public as an "essentialized, state-derived cultural identity," but their defenders respond that universal museums "respect the individual agency" of the visitors, who have the option to look at, or not look at, whatever they wish in the exhibitions, and argue that nonprofit museums are public institutions, open to all, that provide something the public cannot find elsewhere—carefully developed collections of objects assembled by curators with extensive expertise (Cuno 2011:3). In effect, because of the breadth and depth of their collections, universal museums offer an experience that is as close as many visitors can get to the sort of knowledge that can otherwise only be gained by world travel. In large part, the criticism of encyclopedic museums stems from their imperial origins, but as their defenders respond, although many of these museums were, indeed, once instruments of imperialism, they are now the legacy of imperialism, no longer a means of gaining and retaining power. Other criticisms of universal museums have been directed at the objects in the collections that have suspect histories, were obtained by conquest or outright theft, or simply were never returned to their rightful owners. Some critics have questioned why certain museums should be deemed universal when all museums ultimately share a common purpose (Abungu 2004).

In 2002, the directors of several large, comprehensive museums issued a joint *Declaration on the Importance and Values of Universal Museums*, arguing that the objects in their collections that were "acquired in earlier times must be viewed in the light of different sensitivities and values, reflective of that earlier time" (Lewis 2004:4). The directors made the point that, because their collections were universal in nature and their institutional roots were so deep in the European Enlightenment, their institutions should have more protection from repatriation claims because the objects had long been cared for in their museums and, by extension, had become part of the heritage of the nation that now housed the objects, regardless of the original source of the objects. The directors of the twenty-two self-declared universal museums stressed that the admiration we have today for ancient civilizations is due to their museums safeguarding the objects in their collections and promoting respect for them (Schuster 2004). Although this idea resonated well in some quarters, in others it was roundly condemned because the "presumption that a museum with universally defined objectives may be considered exempt from such demands is specious" (Lewis 2014:3).

A key justification for the universal museum declaration is that the demand for repatriation of objects that have a long history in collections is not always straightforward, and object provenance can be very complicated. Consider, for example, a "Greek Attic vase of the 5th century BC . . . which was exported 2,500 years ago from Athens to Etruria, was legally excavated by a Delegation from the Vatican, sold to a Prussian monarch, and lastly transferred from the royal collection to the nascent public museum some 170 years ago" (Schuster 2004:4). Furthermore, some of the objects now involved in repatriation demands were saved from destruction by their long residence in universal museums—had these objects remained at their original source, they would likely have been destroyed or would have ended up in private hands (see also box 7.1).

The universal museum directors consortium recognized four categories of repatriation cases and how each could be resolved using existing laws and agreements: (1) historic objects that were purchased legally by the museums (and hence present no legal issues); (2) war booty that was seized as reparations or trophies (the resolution of which is addressed in the Geneva Convention); (3) cultural possessions that were acquired as a consequence of persecution (which is covered by several existing international laws); and (4) stolen, plundered, or illegally excavated objects (which are covered by the UNESCO and UNIDROIT conventions).

History cannot be rewritten nor past errors corrected simply by the redistribution of the collections of encyclopedic museums to their points of origin, but a better understanding of how the world got to be the way it is may be obtained by studying the collections of these museums and how they were acquired (MacGregor 2011). In terms of correcting the errors of the past, as discussed here, many imperial museums have been converted into national museums, decolonized in the name of defining independent nationhood.

MUSEUMS IN THE UNITED STATES POST-1970

The trend in professionalization of museums and museum staff and diversification of types of museums that was established in the twentieth century continued into the twenty-first century, and museum collections continued to grow. The popular Newseum, which opened in its present Washington, DC, location in 2008, contains fifteen exhibit galleries but also fifteen theaters (figure 9.1). The Interior Museum Program of the US

Figure 9.1.   The Newseum, Washington, DC.

Figure 9.2. Visitor center, White Sands National Monument, New Mexico.

Department of the Interior (which includes the National Park Service, the Bureau of Land Management, and many other agencies) is responsible for managing an estimated 194 million objects and documents housed in archives, museums, and visitor centers (figure 9.2).

A report by the American Association of Museums (AAM) published in 1994 provides a detailed analysis of museums in the United States based on an extensive survey that was launched in 1987 (AAM 1994). The report provides a fascinating snapshot of the 8,200 museums and 15,600 historic sites that responded. The data revealed that 38 percent of museums had budgets of $50,000 or less, 57 percent had budgets of $100,000 or less, and just 8 percent of museums had budgets of more than $1,000,000. Only 4 percent of museums in the United States were founded before 1900, 75 percent were founded after 1950, and 40 percent were founded after 1970. More than half of all museums (59 percent) were private, nonprofit institutions, with 41 percent belonging to a city, county, state, or federal government agency. Ninety-three percent of museums in the United States were described as traditional collecting institutions. In 2014, the Institute for Museum and Library Services (IMLS) conducted a much more thorough accounting of museums in the United States, combining data from the US Department of the Treasury, the Internal Revenue Ser-

Table 9.1. Museums in the United States

Type of Museum	Percent
Museums in the United States in the Early 1990s	
Aquariums	0.2
Arboretums and botanical gardens	3.9
Art museums	14.8
Children's museums	0.8
General museums	8.6
Historic sites	25.5
History museums	29.4
Natural history and anthropology museums	3.1
Nature centers	3.6
Planetariums	0.5
Science and technology centers	2.2
Specialized museums	5.7
Zoological parks	1.6
Museums in the United States in 2014	
Arboretums, botanical gardens, and nature centers	2.4
Art museums	4.5
Children's museums	1.0
Historic societies, historical preservation, and historic houses and sites	48.0
History museums	7.5
Natural history and natural science museums	0.9
Science and technology museums and planetariums	1.1
Unclassified and general museums	33.1
Zoos, aquariums, and wildlife conservation	1.4

Sources: AAM 1994; IMLS 2014b.

vice, and IMLS files to compile a database of approximately 35,000 active museums, doubling the previous estimate for the number of museums (IMLS 2014b). The IMLS report counted 169 million library users over the age of fourteen and 148 million museum users over the age of eighteen. Because the two reports used different sources to count museums and categorized them differently, the data are not directly comparable. The information from both reports is presented in table 9.1.

Although the IMLS count of museums is widely assumed to be more accurate than previous estimates (based on the data sources used), it is probably an undercount of the number of active museums, and it does not include for-profit museums. No estimates on the number of for-profit museums in the United States are available, although they have been described as a "small but highly visible group" (Arroyo 2008:64). Many for-profit museums report very high numbers of paying visitors (the Ripley's Believe It or Not! franchise operates thirty-two for-profit museums in eleven countries and fourteen states of the United States). The distinction between nonprofit and for-profit museums is fairly recent in museum history (it did not occur until the late nineteenth century), but it is a significant one. Many well-known early museums in the United States were for-profit enterprises (such as the Peale Museum), but neither AAM, ICOM, nor IMLS recognize for-profit institutions as museums. For-profit museums account for some truly oddball institutions, including the Museum of Menstruation, Leila's Hair Museum, the Museum of Death, the Cockroach Hall of Fame, and the National Mustard Museum (Rubin 1997), as well as many corporate museums, the St. Augustine Pirate and Treasure Museum, the Voodoo Museum of New Orleans, and a number of more mainstream institutions.

For-profit museums are run like any other business, which means that all proceeds they earn are paid to the owners, who are under no ethical or legal obligation to serve the public. In for-profit museums, collections are treated as financial assets that can be bought and sold at will, and the collections are not held in the public trust. By contrast, in nonprofit museums, proceeds must be used to fulfill the institutional mission, the collections are held in the public trust, and there are certain ethical and legal restrictions on the sale of collection objects (Latham and Simmons 2014). There are some well-run and respected for-profit museums, and the visiting public is usually unaware whether the museum they are visiting is a nonprofit or for-profit institution.

In 1970, the American Alliance of Museums initiated a program of accreditation for museums in the United States, with the first sixteen institutions receiving accreditation the following year. AAM accreditation is a peer-review process run by an appointed AAM accreditation commission that is composed of working museum professionals who are assisted by AAM staff. The process of accreditation requires a museum to demonstrate that it meets established standards for all phases of its operation, collections care, exhibitions, and public programming—in short, accreditation means that the museum is operating at the highest professional standards. Despite extensive promotion by the AAM, few American museums have sought accreditation. Although the accreditation program was revised and the accreditation process streamlined in 2005, of the estimated 35,000 museums in the United States, fewer than 800 were accredited as of 2014. By contrast, of the estimated 2,500 museums in Great Britain, some 1,500 are accredited.

Of the museums accredited by the AAM, nearly half (41 percent) are art museums; 22 percent are history museums; and 10 percent are considered general, multidisciplinary museums. The majority of accredited museums (63 percent) are private, nonprofit institutions, with a staff size of six to fifteen employees.

In 2012, the American Association of Museums was renamed the American Alliance of Museums. According to data provided on the

AAM website, museums in the United States remain very popular, with approximately 850 million visitors each year (almost twice the annual attendance of all major league sporting events and theme parks combined). In addition to about 400,000 paid staff, museum volunteers combine to contribute more than one million hours of service to museums each week. The collections of American museums contain more than one billion objects, and museums spend more than $2 billion on educational programming each year and contribute $21 billion to the economy each year. About 74 percent of museums in the United States are located in urban areas and about 24 percent in rural areas.

MUSEUMS WORLDWIDE POST-1970

Museums are widely recognized as instrumental in the presentation and interpretation of history and culture, but this may sometimes make a museum the object of criticism. During the Great Proletarian Cultural Revolution of 1965–1977, the Chinese government cracked down on museums and their traditional interpretations and presentations of Chinese history and culture. Museums have been used as instruments to help forge national identity but have also been used to promote particular political viewpoints, sometimes despite evidence of the fallacies in the viewpoints. The Museo del Hombre Dominicano (Museum of Dominican Man) once presented Dominican racial identity in line with what had been the official government position since the long dictatorship of Rafael Leónidas Trujillo Molina (1891–1961), despite the fact that it neglected the culture of the majority African Dominican population (Ginetta and Candelario 2007). Members of the US Congress have, on more than one occasion, threatened to cut federal funding to museums when representatives have disagreed with the content of an exhibit, the best-known instance being the 1994 firestorm of protest and threatened loss of the National Air and Space Museum's budget over a planned exhibit of the *Enola Gay* and the dropping of the atomic bomb in 1945 on Hiroshima—congressional pressure only relented when the plans for the exhibit were scrapped (Dubin 1999).

Museums in many Eastern European countries that had proliferated or expanded initially under the new post-Communist governments later struggled to survive the vagaries of faltering free-market economies and changing political winds. For example, during the 1980s and 1990s, as a result of the spread of democracy in Slovenia, there was a sharp increase in the number of museums and consequently in the number of museum visitors. In large part, this change of fortunes for museums was due to the cooperative work of the Slovene Museum Society, the Association of

Museums, and the Slovene ICOM Committee, which provided professional meetings and museum conferences and assisted museums with international projects (Cepic 2002).

Museums have always suffered during the ravages of war, the most recent examples being museums in the former Yugoslavia and the Middle East. Museums in Afghanistan, Iraq, Syria, and Tunisia (along with monuments and archaeological sites) have suffered collateral damage from warfare and direct purposeful assault by radical fundamentalist forces who claim museums are examples of Western decadence.

The period from 1970 to the present has been one of gradual decline in the dominance of US museums worldwide, particularly between 1970 and 1999,

> [w]here once the educational, architectural, and curatorial innovations of American museums had created a clear standard of world performance, now in all of Europe, Canada, and in parts of Asia, boldly assertive museums, often armed with generous public support and significant private collections as well, [have] opened to the public with elaborate programs of education and publicity. (Harris 1999:48)

In a provocative tract titled *Museum, Inc.: Inside the Global Art World*, Paul Werner (a former gallery lecturer at the Guggenheim Museum in New York City) offers a biting and often hilarious critique of the international art market in general and art museums in particular, a thesis that can in part be extended to other kinds of museums as well. Werner postulates that art museums define and authenticate which art is worthy, establish and control the value of art, and thus manipulate the market for the art, so that it's not about art and it's not about money, but rather it's about the art and the money combined. Werner explains,

> Here's how it works: a museum (any museum) has accumulated a collection that it leverages the way a bank leverages capital. The museum puts its own capital ("the collection") or the capital of others ("loans") into circulation ("shows"). As the capital circulates it accumulates more capital, which in turn is put back in circulation or leveraged for more capital. (Werner 2005:4)

This works, Werner says, because of the control exerted by museums over what is in collections and what is deaccessioned for sale. For example, "[i]f one-tenth of the Picassos in the world came on the market in one day the market would collapse. If ninety-nine percent of the Rembrandts in the world were kept off the market (and they are) then the demand for the one percent left would be tremendous—and it is" (Werner 2005:16). Werner chronicles how, under the controversial leadership of Thomas Krens (b. 1946), the Guggenheim Museum expanded on-site and opened several new museums in other countries (some of which are now closed), including the Guggenheim Museum Bilbao (1997) and Deutsche Guggenheim in Berlin (1997). While Krens was director, the Guggenheim's endowment grew from $20 million to $118 million, but Krens was criticized for a management style that many considered too businesslike, changing the museum into a populist and commercial enterprise, a Guggenheim brand.

Latin America has many museums of history and art and a good number devoted to anthropology and archaeology, but the region is deficient in science and technology museums due to lack of economic resources, industrial underdevelopment, bureaucracy, and lack of interest on the part of governments (Teruggi 1973). Buenos Aires, Argentina—which is the most densely populated Spanish-speaking city in Latin America—did not get its first planetarium (El Planetario Galileo Galilei) until 1966. As of 1992, there were approximately 1,176 natural history museums in the United States but only 326 in all of Latin America.

The adoption of the museum concept in Asia has produced both institutions based directly on the traditional Western model and some that are unique to a particular culture or region. Japan was first exposed to the museum concept when Japanese observers began to visit Western countries in the 1860s. The observers found that "they needed new words with which to describe the museums, exhibitions, and other institutions of visual culture that were so numerous in Europe and America" (Lockyer 2008:100) because the European exhibitions were very different from displays of culture in Japan. The word invented by the Japanese was *hakubutsukan*, which literally means "hall of diverse objects." The Tokyo Kokuritsu Hakubutsukan (Tokyo National Museum), founded in 1872, is now the largest art and archaeology museum in Japan, but in Osaka, one can find the Momofuku Ando Instant Ramen Museum.

Among the one hundred museums selected for inclusion in a guidebook to museums of Bangkok are the expected government-run national museums, famous temples and shrines, royal palace museums, and science centers but also the Congdon Anatomical Museum and Songkram Niyomsane Forensic Medical Museum (both associated with the Siriraj Hospital, a teaching institution), the Tilleke and Gibbins Museum of Counterfeit Goods, the House of Bicycles Museum, Ban Lan Laem Museum of Thai Farmer Lifestyle, and the Siamese Cats Museum (Pulsap 2004).

Museology in China was introduced from Western sources in the first half of the twentieth century, influenced by the Soviet Union beginning in the 1950s, and finally began to take shape as Chinese museology beginning in the 1980s (Su 2000). Once Chinese museums began to open to the outside world after 1978, the number of museums in China began to increase, with an average of one new museum opening every ten days between 1980 and 1985. By the end of the 1980s, there were more than one thousand museums in China. Cultural heritage preservation legislation passed into law in 1982 provides a legal framework for heritage protection across China.

In many Asian countries, science museums are seen as important for promoting an understanding of industrialization and the development of technological expertise. Pakistan, Korea, Thailand, Singapore, and India have all established science and technology museums that are expected to shoulder more of the responsibility to stimulate and educate the public about science and technology than do similar museums in Europe or North America (Danilov 1984). India was the first Asian country to develop a contemporary science and technology museum when it opened the Birla Industrial and Technological Museum in Calcutta (now Kolkata) in 1959 (Danilov 1984). The museum's interactive exhibits and mobile exhibitions proved popular with the public and eventually developed into a network of science centers around the country. In Bangkok, the first planetarium opened in 1964 and the National Science Centre for Education in 1979. South Korea has two science and technology museums, both in Seoul—the National Science Museum was founded in 1926, primarily as a natural history museum, but was destroyed during World War II. It reopened in 1972 as a comprehensive science and technology center and was expanded in 1979. Other science museums in Asia include the Nagoya City Science Museum (1962) in Japan; the Singapore Science Centre (1977), which focuses on interactive exhibits; the National Museum of Natural Science in Taichung, Taiwan (1986); the China Science and Technology Museum in Beijing (1988), the Hong Kong Science Museum (1991); and the National Science Centre that opened in Kuala Lumpur in 1996 (Yip 2001).

After apartheid ended in South Africa in the 1990s, public museums came to be perceived as places where a new, more inclusive society could be represented, built around narratives of repression, resistance, and reconciliation (Witz 2006). Among the new national museums founded in this era were the Nelson Mandela National Museum in Mthatha and the Robben Island Museum in Cape Town. This new South African initiative for museums included altering some existing museums to make them more fully inclusive of South African society and history and in several instances led to the renovation, closing, or complete removal of inaccurate exhibits. Some museums were established to interpret neglected aspects of South African society, such as the Lwandle Migrant Labour Museum, which opened in 2000 in a township about forty kilometers north of Cape Town to commemorate the system that under apartheid had employed hundreds of thousands of migrant laborers at very low wages, forcing them to live and work in isolation from their families and native villages.

The first museum in Morocco was the Dar Batha Museum in Fez, founded in 1915 under the French colonial administration. Morocco now has more than thirty museums, of which sixteen are under the government's Ministry of Culture and three are public institutions—the remainder are private. Despite the presence of these museums (most of which are located in major population centers), according to a recent survey, 75 percent of the citizens of Morocco have never visited a museum (El Azhar 2013). One of the reasons seems to be that most museums in Morocco offer little to attract national visitors, and even the Moroccan museum professionals agree that "Moroccan museums are unwelcoming institutions, often housed in gloomy, lifeless, crumbling buildings that are simply seen as depositories for miscellaneous objects from the past" (El Azhar 2013:26). Most of the visitors to Moroccan museums are foreign tourists. To change this situation, the Ben M'sik Community Museum was founded in a poor neighborhood in 2006 as a cooperative project with the Museum of History and Holocaust Education in Kennesaw, Georgia, with a mission to document the life of the people of the neighborhood (El Azhar 2013).

EDUCATION AND LEARNING IN MUSEUMS

A publication issued by UNESCO (UN Educational, Scientific, and Cultural Organization) in 1956 provides an interesting look at museum education in the mid-nineteenth century. The document reports that it was "widely assumed that education ends when the child leaves school and, in the same way, museum educational work is often thought of as being concerned only with children," so the work of museum educators included making the case that museum education is for all ages and that it involves the museum building design, exhibitions, and activities inside and outside of the museum and all of the museum staff (Harrison 1956:5). The lack of data concerning adult learning in museums was problematic because "[m]useum work with adults has not been considerably documented, perhaps because it shades into very general practice," but the author notes, "Lectures, meetings, discussion groups, recitals, film shows, and special exhibitions are a normal provision, since World War II, in many museums in many different countries" (Harrison 1956:6). The UNESCO document cautions that object labels should be neither too short nor too long, content specialists (usually curators) are necessary to provide correct and authoritative information, and only museum educators can judge what the right amount of label text is and recommends that museums develop school loan programs to serve areas where children have little opportunity to visit a museum themselves, adding, "There are few of these in continental Europe . . . , but they are very general in the United States of America and the British Commonwealth" (Harrison 1956:7).

Professional museum education is an American innovation, stemming from the egalitarian ideal behind museums and the importance of self-education in the newly established museums of postrevolutionary America that eventually fully opened their doors to the general public (Roberts 1997). The history of museum education is closely linked with the study of learning (see box 9.2).

Museum education is intimately connected to the interpretation of the objects in the collection, which is determined by the epistemological position of the staff. Any museum presentation (be it an exhibit, lecture, children's program, or website) has a particular taxonomy and epistemology, thus the "way a museum is organized carries implicit assumptions about the manner in which visitors learn" and what they will learn (Russell 1994:19). All of a museum's activities are interpretation—the museum chooses which objects to collect, which objects to exhibit, and how to exhibit them. A museum's interpretation may be intended or inadvertent, but it is interpretation just the same: "Whether we like it or not, every acquisition (and indeed disposal), every juxtaposition or arrangement of an object or work of art, together with other objects or works of art, within the context of a temporary exhibition or museum display means placing a certain construction upon history" (Vergo 1989:2).

Most visitors come to museums as part of a social group—what the visitors see, do, and remember is mediated by that group. The visitor's experience within the museum includes the docents, guards, concessionaires, and other visitors. A poorly trained docent, a rude guard, or an unfriendly gift shop clerk may have a very negative impact on the quality of a museum visitor's experience. Visitors are strongly influenced by the physical aspects of museums, including their architecture, ambience, smells, sounds, and overall feel.

Despite all the research that has been done on learning in museums, moments of learning are hard to pinpoint—there are many signs of learning and many learning outcomes. The traditional assumption was that learning occurred when knowledge was transmitted by experts and absorbed by learners, so learning was measured by testing to see how much of the transmitted information the learners retained. By shifting the concept of learning away from the idea of accumulating information and toward an emphasis on active engagement, there are many more possible places to look for evidence of learning (Falk and Dierking 2013).

Millions of visitors every year learn from their experiences in museums, but little of this learning is documented. In part, this is because it is not easy to provide clear evidence of museum learning, but there have been some interesting studies with intriguing results. Face-to-face interviews were conducted with visitors to *Points in Time*, a multimedia exhibit at the John Heinz Pittsburgh Regional History Center in Pennsylvania. The visi-

BOX 9.2.
Learning How We Learn

What does it mean to learn something? A general definition of *learning* is the "process of developing knowledge, skills, or dispositions through study, instruction, or expertise" (Tishman, McKinney, and Straughn 2007:5). An evolutionary definition of *learning* is the "product of hundreds of millions of years of survival-oriented evolution, a continually refining capacity for humans and other animals to intelligently navigate an ever changing social, cultural, and physical world. . . . [O]ne of the aspects of learning that makes it so challenging to understand is that it is always a process and a product, a verb and a noun" (Falk and Dierking 2000:xii).

After decades of research, we now know that learning is a nonlinear process in which a personally motivated learner has considerable choice of what to learn, where to learn, and when to participate. Learning in a traditional classroom setting is termed *formal learning*; learning outside the classroom (and hence in the museum) is termed *informal learning*, although it has been proposed that the name *free-choice learning* is a more descriptive term than *informal learning*. Most of what we know we construct over the course of our lives through free-choice learning. In short, the learning process brings together cognitive, emotional, and environmental influences and experiences to acquire, enhance, or make changes in one's knowledge, skills, values, or worldviews.

The learning theories that have most affected the development of museum education can be grouped into three broad categories: (1) behaviorism, (2) cognitivism, and (3) constructivism. Understanding the similarities and differences among these three theories is crucial for understanding the history of museum education.

The theory of behaviorism was developed primarily by Burrhus Frederic "B. F." Skinner (1904–1990). Behaviorism assumes that learning is demonstrated by changes in behavior, that environment shapes behavior, and that how close in time events happen and how they are reinforced explains the learning process. In short, the theory of behaviorism holds that learning is the acquisition of new behavior through conditioning (a response to a stimulus or behavior reinforced by reward or punishment), which means that the locus of control over learning is in the environment. The shift away from behaviorist views of learning began as research revealed that learning was complex, involved a range of influences, and was not easy to understand.

The theory of cognitivism was advocated as a challenge to behaviorism by a gestalt psychologist named Boyd Henry Bode (1873–1953), who thought that behaviorists were too dependent on overt behavior to explain learning. Cognitivism assumes that the memory system is an active, organized processor of information and that prior knowledge plays an important role in learning. For cognitivists, the locus of control over learning is within the individual learner.

The behaviorist and cognitivist paradigms of learning ignore motivation, both intrinsic and extrinsic. Extrinsic motivation refers to anticipated benefits that are external to the activity (such as getting good grades or a high salary), while intrinsic motivation refers to actions that are taken for their own sake (such as exercising or visiting a museum). This brings us closer to what happens in museum learning because, although we are constantly inundated with information from our external environment, the "human brain is designed to sift through this abundance of information to selectively determine what to attend to and what to ignore. One filter for this selection process is interest" (Falk and Dierking 2002:40).

The theory of constructivism assumes that learning is part of a process in which an individual actively constructs new ideas or concepts based on current and past knowledge or experience, so that learning is very personal. Constructivism was formulated by Jean Piaget (1896–1980), who conducted research on the intellectual development of children and created the field of genetic epistemology. Piaget theorized that children develop knowledge through assimilation (the process of integrating reality or the perception of reality with an internal structure of knowledge) and accommodation (the modification of internal structural conflicts to reflect experience). The development of constructivism owes much to Lev Vygotsky (1896–1934), a psychologist from Belarus who suggested that all learning is contextually and socially mediated, therefore intellectual development is the result of interaction with the environment, and social interactions with other people influence the level of performance exhibited by the individual. Vygotsky believed that play is an effective tool for learning because it enables children to advance from one stage of knowledge to another. Play is often incorporated into informal learning environments now that constructivism has become widely accepted in museum education (Spock 2012).

Applying constructivist principles in a museum means assuming that learning is an active process in which a learner gains information by using sensory input and then constructs meaning out of the information. Physical actions are part of learning but are not sufficient in themselves for the constructing of meaning, thus interactive exhibits that "offer visitors a way to provide input and, in return, perceive a response tailored to their specific action" must be meaningful, not merely involve some physical manipulation, which means that "[s]uccessful interactives are usually hard to develop, difficult to design, and challenging to build" (Russick 2010:220–22).

The bottom line is that there must be a connection between actions and learning because constructivism emphasizes the active and imaginative dimensions of learning and discovery. Museum visitors bring in their own vernacular theories about why things happen the way they do, which means the museum must engage the visitors' ideas in order to develop their understanding and awareness. To some degree, the museum must be sensitive to

(continued)

tors related what was in the exhibit to their own stories or those of their families to give them a richer understanding of Pittsburgh's history (Falk 1999). A study at the National Zoo in Washington, DC, evaluated the impact of an exhibit called *Think Tank*, in which live animals were used for demonstrations and to provide interactive experiences. The study used previsit and postvisit surveys of visitors, with follow-up telephone surveys thirteen months later. The researchers found that what the visitors had learned while at the exhibit remained unchanged more than a year later (Falk 1999). In another study, local schoolchildren were brought to the National Gallery of Art in Washington, DC, for a program called *Art around the Corner* and then evaluated annually for several years beginning in 1993. Most of the participants expressed positive attitudes toward art and art museums, even years after their experience in the program, compared to students who had not been in the program (Falk 1999).

INDIGENOUS MUSEUMS

In 2006, there were about two hundred Native American tribal and community museums in Canada, Mexico, and the United States (Cooper 2006). A community museum is one formed by a community initiative that responds to local needs and demands, directed by a community organization, created and developed with direct involvement of the local population, and owned by the community. In the context of globalization, the

community museum is not a luxury, and its value is not simply decorative: it is a necessity that allows communities to repossess their heritage, both physically and symbolically. It is a tool for rethinking the future, for facing rapid transformations within the strength born of a core identity rooted in the past. It is a concrete image of the values that bind a people together, and a vehicle to project and legitimize these values. It is an opportunity to remember the vital experiences that should not be forgotten, but should be preserved to educate the generations who will inherit them. (Camarena and Morales 2006:78)

Community museums are usually centers for cultural organization and cultural action that help mobilize the community and develop new community initiatives. Because of this, "[c]ommunity-based museums and cultural centers strengthen the bonds that connect generations. We remember ourselves in these places and dream about who we want to be. At their best, these places are homes for cultural expression, dialogue, learning, and understanding" (Sandoval 2006:7).

In North America, indigenous museums often take the form of tribal museums, which began to appear in the middle of the twentieth century—only three tribal museums were established before 1940, but the number steadily increased after that, with nearly seventy more founded by the end of the 1970s, and more than seventy-five in the 1980s and 1990s (Cooper 2006).

Indigenous museums can be found in many countries. There are indigenous museums in Australia, where "[i]nterest in Aboriginal art in Australian art museums can be traced back at least to the 1950s. However, the efflorescence of Aboriginal art in our museum exhibitions, collecting, and public programming, and its presence in art activity internationally, has occurred only since the early 1980s" (Murphy 2005:54). The Museum of World Culture, which opened in Gothenburg, Sweden, in 2004, is considered to be "working on the same agenda as the National Museum of the American Indian, namely, transcending colonialist and imperialist legacies, of going behind or beyond evolutionary positions and interpretations, and of developing paradigmatic and epistemological shifts that can explore and facilitate a range of other perspectives and world views" (Sandahl 2005:35).

The significance of indigenous museums is that "Native communities are no longer entrusting non-Native institutions to define who they are" (Cooper 2006:9). Because they are community oriented, most tribal museums have advisory boards to help make decisions on access, use, and storage of objects and to help establish policy, but it is "critical for established institutions to create museum study programs for Natives" (Scalplock 2006:68).

In the United States, as more Native American tribes have formed connections with museums (often related to NAGPRA [Native American Graves Protection and Repatriation Act of 1990] reporting) or established their own indigenous museums, there have been changes not just in presentation of indigenous cultures but in collections care as well. A good example of the latter can be found in the Makah Cultural and Research Center (MCRC), founded in 1979 by the Makah Tribe in Neah Bay, Washington, to interpret a site where artifacts were excavated from a Makah village that had been buried in a mudslide around 1750.

Initially, the newly excavated artifacts were arranged and stored, and the collection was managed as in a standard archaeological research collection, which made the objects available but "failed to reflect Makah values and cultural concerns centering around tribal traditional property rights and sanctions concerning the handling of certain items" (Mauger and Bowechop 2006:58). When a new collections facility was built in 1993, it "provided the opportunity for developing a system that allows for the care of and access to the collection, in addition to reflecting the values and concerns of the Makah people" (Mauger and Bowechop 2006:58).

In the new facility, the objects were sorted according to both artifact categories and the households from which they were recovered (information that was identified on shelf labels, as space did not permit grouping all of the artifacts from each household together). Objects that could be identified as belonging to particular individuals were labeled appropriately. In the new facility, traditional Makah gender restrictions were applied to collection storage. For example, because "[w]haling gear . . . could not be touched or handled by women below a certain age," the "shelves containing these artifacts are flagged with symbols indicating a gender restriction. These restrictions apply to staff, researchers, and visitors alike. The imposition of gender restrictions in MCRC collections management defined the need for both male and female curators in the MCRC" (Mauger and Bowechop 2006:61).

A goal of the MCRC is to support the preservation and use of the Makah language, so artifacts are labeled in both Makah and English, using physical groupings of artifacts based on the Makah words, which "encouraged analysis of the cultural meanings and affinities between artifacts in the collection and provides insight into both Makah language and thought" (Mauger and Bowechop 2006:62), an example of unexpected new information arising from the musealization and juxtaposition of objects, in this case a very special indigenous form of musealization. The Makah artifacts are now housed in modern, environmentally controlled storage. There is a computer database for the collection, but the system is based on both standard collection management concerns and Makah tradition. This example reinforces the observation that the "ways in which tribal collections are stored, managed, and accessed may have profound significance to their host communities as agents of preservation and support or as agents of change" (Mauger and Bowechop 2006:63).

An example from Alberta, Canada, concerning Blackfoot tribal objects demonstrates that an

> object the museum professional may classify as a cultural artifact may also, to the Native, hold sacred beliefs and require care within Native tradition. To the Blackfoot, sacred items require spiritual cleansing. Sacred objects are likened to children, and need to be treated with respect and reverence. Given greater accessibility to collections, the Blackfoot were able to go into collections and

traditionally smudge their ceremonial material. "Smudging" is the burning of sweetgrass in a blessing. In designated smudging areas in the museum, smoke alarms are disabled and elders may offer the blessing. (Scalplock 2006:67)

Similar accommodations have been made for the spiritual care of Native American collections in many nonindigenous museums in the United States and elsewhere in the world (see box 9.3). As in Canada, "[b]ecause

---

BOX 9.3.
The Case of the Māori

Beginning in the 1980s, a number of scholars in New Zealand began to reexamine museums as postcolonial institutions, with particular attention paid to their collections and how material culture was managed and presented by museums.

The first museums in New Zealand had been established during the colonial era (from the 1850s to the 1890s), following contemporary western museological practices. As with most colonial museums, there was friction involving the objects collected, how they were exhibited, and how they were interpreted.

At the beginning of the 1980s, most New Zealand museums categorized and exhibited Māori objects according to standard ethnological and archaeological frameworks, with little or no input from the Māori themselves (the first Māori museum workers were not hired until the early 1980s). An exhibit of Māori art called *Te Māori* marked a turning point in indigenous influence in New Zealand museums that ultimately returned control of Māori representation back to the Māori. These changes involved the recognition of a Māori perspective of objects; input from Māori leaders concerning collection care and interpretation; collaborative planning for exhibitions with Māori communities; the use of Māori cultural protocols for exhibit openings and closings; and Māori representation in museum governance, management, and operations. The process was not always easy, as "moments of awkwardness, tension and confusion, but also instances of learning, exchange and genuine personal growth" occurred between the Māori and non-Māori museum staff members (McCarthy 2011:83).

In 1992, the Museum of New Zealand Te Papa Tongarewa Act blended the National Museum and the National Art Gallery into a single institution with integrated collections, the Museum of New Zealand Te Papa Tongarewa, a "bicultural museum with its own distinctive museological practice" that incorporates Māori spiritual practices in object handling and collections care (McCarthy 2011:96). The accommodations made in collections care include that certain sacred objects are treated as living ancestors, not as artifacts; collections managers are guardians of the collections, not gatekeepers; objects are classified and documented using the Māori language and corresponding philosophical frameworks; objects are handled, stored, packed, and transported by means that reflect a Māori worldview; and appropriate Māori ritual practices are observed in collections management activities.

Source: McCarthy 2011.

of the powerful nature of the ceremonial bundles, museum professionals are encouraged to participate in ceremonies to ensure their safety and to help them understand the significance of holy bundles" (Scalplock 2006:68).

MUSEUMS OF MEMORY

Museums of memory or commemoration, sometimes called museums of remembrance or museums of conflict (Keene 2005), help people cope with conflict and loss, such as Yad Vashem, the Holocaust remembrance museum founded in 1953 in Jerusalem or the National September 11 Memorial and Museum in New York City. The Nanjing Massacre Memorial Hall in Nanjing, China, was established in 1985 to commemorate the Chinese citizens who were killed by the Imperial Japanese Army in 1937, and the Museo Memorial de la Resistencia Dominicana (the Memorial Museum of the Dominican Resistance) in Santo Domingo commemorates citizens of the Dominican Republic who were imprisoned, tortured, and killed during the 1930–1961 dictatorship of Rafael Trujillo (1891–1961). Museums of memory typically contain artifacts related to those being commemorated and are often built at the site of a particular tragic event.

There are museums of memory that commemorate events that were widespread and took place over long spans of years, such war memorials or the slavery museums in the Americas and Africa. Wilberforce House in Hull, England, commemorates the abolition of slavery in Great Britain and its colonies in 1833 (Duffy 2001). In Colombia, several museums have presented programming and exhibits to reflect on the country's ongoing sixty years of internal armed struggle, which has had profound social and cultural consequences for the country (López Rosas 2013), because:

> [e]sta situación se ha traducido en una separación casi absoluta entre las instituciones de la memoria y los actores democráticos comprometidos con las luchas por los derechos humanos, la verdad y la reparación, representados por un abigarrado panorama de instituciones y movimientos sociales, agrandada por la ausencia de una separación temporal entre el pasado violent y los procesos de rememoración.

this situation has resulted in an almost complete separation between memory institutions and the democratic actors engaged in struggles for human rights, truth, and reparation, represented by a varied panorama of institutions and social movements, and enlarged by the lack a provisional separation of the violent past and the processes of remembrance. (López Rosas 2013:17–18)

ECOMUSEUMS

The ecomuseum concept originated in the 1960s with French museologists Georges-Henri Rivière (1897–1985) and Hugues Michet de Varine-

Bohan (b. 1935). The idea was based on the adaptation of the open-air museum concept of Scandinavia to the French Regional Nature Parks, which would allow the communities within the parks to remain where they were rather than be relocated and would enable the community members to participate in the planning and running of the museum.

The name *ecomuseum* was coined in 1971 based on the concept of a "reappropriation of a heritage by the people" (Hubert 1985:187). An ecomuseum is "designed around and within the community in order to combine the natural and social environments. . . . The collections consist of the whole environment of buildings, artefacts, and people" (Simpson 2001:71). The ecomuseum concept has been embraced by many indigenous communities as the best way for them to both preserve and present their history and culture while creating a future based on it, emphasizing the management of heritage in a sustainable environment.

Ecomuseums are not intended to replace traditional museums but rather to broaden the concept of what a museum is. Whereas a traditional museum is a building containing collections, an ecomuseum is heritage that is preserved in situ so that the territory of the community and the space of the museum are the same, applying a definition of *heritage* that includes "landscape, buildings, moveable objects, and traditions." The concept of the ecomuseum is intentionally vague. Ecomuseums are not supposed to be easily defined but are to serve as long-term working models, part of a continuous cultural process, with the goal of strengthening the cultural identity of a group (Davis 2011).

Georges-Henri Rivière described an ecomuseum as an "instrument conceived, fashioned and operated jointly by a public authority and a local population," with the public authority providing expertise, facilities, and resources, while the local population contributed aspirations, knowledge, and an individual approach (Rivière 1985:182). According to Rivière, the ecomuseum is variously a mirror for the community, an interpretation of space, a laboratory, a center of conservation, and a school. The cocreator of the concept, Hugues de Varine, saw it as a "renewal of the museum as a necessary instrument of service to society. To serve a global heritage for global development. To serve man in his totality, embedded in nature in its totality, yesterday and today, seeking above all his future in the intellectual and material means to master it" (de Varine 1985:185). Ecomuseums include collections because "objects are signs to which the collective memory clings. However, it is more concerned with the 'safeguarding of skills' than with the 'museification' of artefacts. The objects that it does assemble are bound up with everyday life" (Querrien 1985:199).

Several ecomuseums have been established in Quebec, where there were few public museums prior to 1970 and little strong museological tradition. In 1974, the ecomuseum concept was adopted by Parks Canada for the preservation of a group of historic buildings in Forillon National Park, and several French ecomuseum experts subsequently visited Quebec to help plan museums (Rivard 1985). The first true ecomuseums established in Quebec were the Musée et Centre Régional d'Interprétation de la Haute-Beauce (1979), which "enabled the neglected region to recover a measure of pride through a clearer idea of its own identity in the form of a museum supported by its own people and with its own financial resources" (Rivard 1985:202), and the Écomusée de la Haute-Beauce, comprised of thirteen villages.

The theoretical and practical principles of the ecomuseum movement were well received in Portugal, where the idea for establishing an ecomuseum was first discussed in 1979 for the Natural Park of Serra de Estrela. Georges-Henri Rivière was invited to visit the site as a consultant. Although the Serra de Estrela project did not materialize, an ecomuseum was established by the municipal museum of Seixal and Santiago do Cacém in 1984 in a traditionally constructed shipyard (Nabais 1985). Although as of 1985 Sweden had a number of open-air museums that closely resembled ecomuseums (Engström 1985), none quite fit the concept until the Ekomuseum Bergslagen was founded in 1986 (Davis 2011).

The ecomuseum concept began to attract attention in China in the 1980s, as industrialization and economic development accelerated, producing substantial environmental damage and pollution (Su 2005). At this time, there were approximately one thousand museums in China. By 2005, seven ecomuseums had been established that preserved the living cultural traditions of various ethnic groups, working on the principle that the people of a village are the true owners of their culture and have the right to interpret it, that the meaning of culture and its values can only be defined by perceptions and interpretations that are based on cultural competence, that public participation is essential to an ecomuseum, that preservation takes precedence over tourism, and that long-term holistic planning is crucial to an ecomuseum's success.

Some urban ecomuseums have been dubbed "combat ecomuseums" for their proactive engagement with social issues, particularly in addressing issues of migration and multiculturalism (Montanari 2015:379). One of these is the Écomusée du Val de Bièvre in Fresnes, on the southern outskirts of Paris. Unlike most other French ecomuseums, which are located in rural settings, the Écomusée du Val de Bièvre interprets a suburban community and has a collection of objects connected to the community through documents and audiovisual recordings. Museum programming often addresses such issues as unemployment, drug use, and gender roles in the community.

The concept of the ecomuseum continues to evolve. In rural Iran, ecomuseums have been proposed as a means of safeguarding traditional desert water systems called *qanats* (Mahmoodi and Nezhad 2015). A *qanat* consists of a series of vertical shafts on a slope that connect to a gently sloping horizontal underground shaft that uses gravity to collect water at an outlet at the base of the slope. Because ecomuseums are publicly accountable and could sustain tourism, they are seen as a way to protect these environmentally friendly traditional water-collecting systems with the participation and management of local communities.

ISSUES

In this section I consider a number of issues that have significantly affected the development of museums since 1970. Some of these are new issues; others are problems that have always confronted museums but have taken on more urgency over the last few decades.

Deaccessioning

Since 1970, deaccessioning has become a controversial topic in many museums, particularly in the United States but in several other countries as well. Deaccessioning is the process of legally removing an accessioned object from a collection. Deaccessioned objects may be destroyed or given to or traded with another museum, but more commonly they are sold. The 1990s was a period of rapid expansion of museums and rising visitor numbers across the United States, accompanied at some museums by a wave of deaccessioning of objects from the collections to finance the expansions.

Deaccessioning is an old practice in collections (few museums can afford to keep every object in their collections permanently), but the word *deaccessioning* did not appear in the museum literature until the early 1970s. Attitudes toward deaccessioning have changed greatly over the history of museums. In the United States in 1927, the executive secretary of the American Association of Museums, Lawrence Vail Coleman (1893–1982), wrote, "On occasion, worthless material may be accepted and later thrown away rather than give offence by refusing it" (Coleman 1972:122), but few museums would operate in such a cavalier manner today. Often more controversial than the deaccessioning is what the museum chooses to do with the deaccessioned objects. The 1991 AAM Code of Ethics for Museums limits the "use of proceeds from the sale of collections materials . . . to the acquisition of collections" (Simmons 2015:241), but many museum professionals felt that this was too restrictive. The code was revised in 1994 by the AAM Ethics Commission to state that the proceeds from the sale of deaccessioned objects could not be used for "anything other than the acquisition or direct care of collections" (AAM 2014:n.p.). However, the Ethics Commission did not define what was meant by direct care of collections, which has been fiercely debated ever since. In any case, the AAM Code of Ethics is a voluntary standard. Under US law, there are very few legal restrictions against a museum deaccessioning objects or how the proceeds from a deaccession are used, provided it is in compliance with laws regulating nonprofit status (Cirigliana 2011; Courtney 2015; Malaro and DeAngelis 2012). Laws in other countries vary greatly.

There are cultural differences regarding deaccessioning. In general, European and Latin American museums are more reluctant to deaccession than are museums in the United States, in large part because most European and Latin American museums follow the International Council of Museums Code of Ethics, which states that "there must always be a strong presumption against the disposal of objects to which a museum has assumed formal title" (Lewis 2003:3). By contrast, the American Alliance of Museums Code of Ethics states, "Museums must remain free to improve their collections through selective disposal . . . and intentionally to sacrifice objects for well-considered . . . purposes" (AAM 2014:n.p.).

Interpretation

More than one hundred years ago, William Henry Flower, director of the British Museum (Natural History), stated, "It is not the objects placed in a museum that constitute its value, so much as the method in which they are displayed and the use made of them for the purpose of instruction" (Flower 1898:55). How objects in museums are presented and interpreted, long-contentious issues, have become a point of unending debate in many museums since 1970 (Keene 2005).

Museum professionals have long acknowledged that objects may not be understood by the visitor the way the collector or curator intended them to be, but the degree of difference in some instances may be startling (Siegel 2008). For example, the Hope Diamond has long been a popular exhibit at the National Museum of Natural History of the Smithsonian Institution in Washington, DC, but a good part of the public comes to see the stone not because of its qualities as a gemstone or jewel but because of the legend that it has brought misfortune and tragedy to most of its previous owners (Dickinson 1965; Kurin 1997).

Controversies may arise over the content and presentation of the museum itself. The Creation Museum, founded by a religious organization called Answers in Genesis, opened in Petersburg, Kentucky (near Cincinnati, Ohio), in 2007. The museum promotes the long-discredited ideas that the Earth is just six thousand years old and that all species of plants and animals arose by divine creation, not as the result of millions of years of organic evolution. Despite the fact that a young Earth and divine creation are fringe ideas without scientific merit, the 60,000-square-foot complex (with a planetarium) was built with $27 million in private donations. Since its opening, the museum has consistently drawn large numbers of visitors and expanded its facilities to include a petting zoo and a zip-line feature (Arroyo 2007; Jennings 2008). In a more whimsical vein, the artist David Wilson explores the intentional use of the "museum voice" to communicate inaccurate information in an installation known as the Museum of Jurassic Technology in Culver City, California (Weschler 1995).

Some postmodernists posit that museums are entirely artificial constructs because

> [w]ith the recent exception of modern art, the museum can never be understood to be the natural home of any of the material it contains. Objects tend to enter the museum when their world has been destroyed, and so they are relics and witnesses of loss. The collapse of older political and cultural arrangements was an important factor in the emergence of the modern museum. (Siegel 2008:4–5)

Because the acquisition of an object by a museum means that the object was lost elsewhere, "disruption and profound disassociation . . . underlies every museum" (Siegel 2008:5).

Although in the past many scholars believed that it was possible for an expert to apply scientific principles to collecting and exhibition decisions and thus be neutral in the process, this idea has long been debunked. A more common position is one similar to that stated by George R. Goldner (b. 1943), a curator at the Metropolitan Museum of Art, who explains, "A curator should collect what the museum needs, but anyone who claims he isn't affected by his own biases and preferences is lying. Therefore, who's head of the department is tremendously important" (quoted in Danziger 2007:75). Goldner goes on to say that he also believes it is the responsibility of the museum to try to expand the public's perceptions of what they can see in a museum. Rather than simply filling the galleries of the Met with popular works by Van Gogh, the museum should design its exhibits to stimulate the curiosity of visitors who come because they are interested in Van Gogh: "If you go back to the nineteenth century, when museums were first founded, they were founded with an explicit obligation to instruct and elevate people. They weren't founded in order to get more people in the building just because you had given them what they wanted. . . . It's not the entertainment industry, it's an educational establishment" (Danziger 2007:76).

A large part of stimulating the curiosity of visitors has to do with how objects are presented and how information is conveyed to them. Another Met employee, Jessie McNab, observes, "It's nice to have a label, and every exhibit now has a label, but very often the labels distract you from truly seeing something. To draw an analogy, you could sit at home and read a book about Beethoven's life, or you could go to a concert and actually be moved by the music itself" (quoted in Danziger 2007:144).

The historian Steven Conn coined the term *object-based epistemology* to describe the orientation toward objects in many US museums during the late nineteenth and early twentieth centuries (Conn 1998, 2010; see also Evans, Mull, and Poling 2002). Conn postulates,

> The intellectual architecture used to build the museums of the late nineteenth century was predicated on the assumption that objects could tell stories "to the untrained observer," an assumption that I will call "object-based epistemology." . . . In this epistemology, objects are not precisely transparent, but neither are they hopelessly opaque. The meanings held within objects would yield themselves up to anyone who studied and observed objects carefully enough. (Conn 1998:4)

Conn goes on to say, "The object-based epistemology around which museums were organized had two parts: the objects themselves, and the systematics into which those objects were placed. . . . Objects had inherent meaning, but that meaning could only be revealed by the way they were presented in the museum exhibits" (Conn 1998:23). Another way to put it is, "Objects are not simply objects. . . . The meaning of each object relies on its place in a semiotic system" (Rowe 2002:30). As Conn points out, museums are no longer using objects as if they were self-interpretive, but "[o]bjects can evoke novel questions and stories that unfold among participants" visiting the museum (van Kraayenoord and Paris 2002:227). In fact, "Just as texts can be problematized, so can objects be positioned as problems or questions" (van Kraayenoord and Paris 2002:227). In other words, objects cannot speak entirely for themselves, but they do speak to us, and we still need museums because, "[w]hen objects are read in isolation, like sentences that are not integrated in their meaning, the result is piecemeal or superficial comprehension of insular bits of information" (van Kraayenoord and Paris 2002:226).

A theoretical construct receiving a lot of consideration at present is the idea that the objects in museums are documents, meaning they can provide accurate representation and transmission of information. In this sense, objects serve as "thinking devices" or "cultural tools for generating meaning" because all objects support multiple interpretations and multiple activities (Rowe 2002:30). The idea of objects as documents is not a new idea:

> It is not novel for us to consider objects as texts. Anthropologists, psychologists, curators, and museum educators have noted how collected objects are like and unlike libraries of collected texts. . . . The object is like a text because

it may be a representation of a class of similar objects, available for viewing, discussion, and analysis. Or it may be a unique object that might be sacred, frightening, valuable, or bizarre. (van Kraayenoord and Paris 2002:223)

Nevertheless, as a theoretical construct, the object-as-text has proven to be a powerful tool for understanding the role of objects and object-based learning in museums. Wood and Latham make the point that "[o]nce objects enter a museum, they become 'documents.' . . . Not merely a text or artifact, a document is so named because it has a level of intentionality, which stems from its place as evidence of something" (Wood and Latham 2009:n.p.). Wood and Latham identify four parameters of objects as documents:

1. Materiality (objects are physical things). "Materiality . . . recognizes that all physical things, whether they are human-made or natural, are imbued with meaning by human beings and that humans exist in a physical world in which all thoughts and actions occur both *within* their own material bodies and *with* external material things" (Wood and Latham 2011:54).
2. Intentionality (museum objects are intended to be treated as evidence).
3. Process (objects are made into documents).
4. Phenomenological position (objects are perceived as documents).

Similarly, Peter Gathercole argues, "Curators are the catalysts who determine the way relationships are established between publicly seen artefacts and consumers" and

museum artefacts are analogous to commodities in that they have properties bestowed upon them by virtue of their museum existence. They do not possess these properties intrinsic to themselves. . . . They are often regarded as evidence *per se* of cultural behaviour, but until this evidence is recognized, they remain, literally speaking, mere objects. Thus, in museum terms, the cultural status of artefacts, that is, the attribute which transforms objects into artefacts, depends upon the extent to which this attribute is perceived by curators, and is used by them in both research and display. (Gathercole 1989:74)

Dioramas

Dioramas (three-dimensional scenes, either life-sized or scaled) have been a staple of museums, particularly history and natural history museums, since the 1800s (see chapter 7). Paradoxically, dioramas have both fallen out of favor and received hearty support since the 1970s (Poliquin 2012).

Considered by some people to be static and old-fashioned, dioramas were removed from many museums without due consideration of their artistic and historic values and enormous educational potential. Museum professionals who would never dream of tossing out an old painting or sculpture may think nothing of destroying a diorama in the name of fashion, ignoring the fact that dioramas are complex entities, cultural artifacts, and works of art that bring together a subject (typically history or natural science) and several art forms, including sculpture and painting (Wonders 1993). Dioramas can be powerful icons that, as many studies have shown, evoke memories and emotions in viewers and stimulate learners to observe and ask questions. As with any complex work of art, dioramas need to be properly cared for and maintained and are more effective if supplemented with appropriate interpretation and hands-on activities (Rader and Cain 2008, 2014; Schwarzer and Sutton 2009).

The habitat diorama—a three-dimensional scene that depicts nature using some real animals and plants—was developed in natural history museums beginning about 1860 (Hornaday 1905). According to Stephen Quinn, the classic habitat diorama has three basic components acting together: (1) the taxidermy preparations, (2) the foreground, and (3) the painted background (which may be flat but is usually curved; Quinn 2006). In harmony, these three components create the illusion of space and show the diversity of nature. Most dioramas represent a specific place, time of year, and time of day. The plants and animals in habitat dioramas may be species that are rare or extinct in the wild, and they may have scientific value as specimens, in addition to their cultural and artistic value as part of the diorama.

Some critics have characterized dioramas as often inaccurate, too theatrical, imperialist, and sexist (particularly Haraway 1984), but as with any historic work, dioramas are representative of the way people understood the world at the time of their creation. Dioramas are complex historic and cultural documents that capture the imagination, tell stories, provide instruction, and continue to be popular with museum visitors. The faults or shortcomings of dioramas can usually be rectified with proper interpretation that explains them in terms of chronology and worldview.

NAGPRA

The Native American Graves Protection and Repatriation Act of 1990 (NAGPRA) gave Native Americans and native Hawaiians the legal right to make a claim for custody of human remains, funerary objects, sacred objects, and objects of cultural patrimony that are in the control of agencies and museums of the US federal government and institutions receiving federal funding. The legislation came about in response to a troubled history of abuses in the collection, study, and display of Native American human remains and cultural objects in museums across the United States and because of a lack of understanding of (or disagreement with) the missions of museums. The problems were compounded by the fact that complaints about the desecration of graves, looting of cultural property, and inappropriate exhibition of Native American remains and material culture had long been ignored (Kawasaki 2000; Mihesuah 2000; Thomas 2000).

Attitudes toward human remains can be grouped into four basic categories: (1) human remains are sources of cultural, biological, and historical information, for which the imperative for research is most important; (2) the human rights of the deceased are more important than the research imperative; (3) gravesites are places of sacred memory but not necessarily sacred sites; and (4) human remains and gravesites (whether they still contain physical remains of the deceased or not) are sacred and are always the home of the spirits of the deceased (Grimes 1990). These differences in beliefs and attitudes concerning human remains lie at the heart of NAGPRA.

The legislation was signed into law on November 16, 1990, requiring federal agencies and museums that receive federal funds (including grants) to compile an inventory of Native American and native Hawaiian collections and human remains in their control and work with appropriate tribes to repatriate human remains and certain objects. NAGPRA stipulated that requests for repatriation must come from the lineal descendants of the identified Native American or native Hawaiian group, which led to issues with remains that cannot be linked directly to an extant cultural group. Since 1990, the enactment of NAGPRA has resulted in the reburial of thousands of human remains and the return of hundreds of thousands of artifacts to Native American tribes and native Hawaiian groups. NAGPRA has affected more than 5,000 institutions (the Field Museum repatriated about 2,000 skeletons from its collections, and the American Museum of Natural History repatriated about 14,000). Because repatriated remains and objects can no longer be studied, NAGPRA has been described as a case of human rights versus scientific rights. Because repatriation under NAGPRA has ended many practices that Native Americans found abhorrent, it has been called a long-overdue step toward correcting past wrongs against native peoples.

In 2000, the AAM magazine *Museum News* published a roundtable discussion called "NAGPRA at 10: Examining a Decade of the Native American Graves Protection and Repatriation Act" (AAM 2000), with reflections by five representatives from museums, Native American communities, and government agencies. The participants agreed that, although the process had not always proceeded smoothly, NAGPRA had changed the museum field and in many instances created new links between museums and Native American tribes.

NAGPRA has attracted international attention as a model law. Similar legislation is under consideration in several other countries (including several in Latin America), with concerns about the museum interpretation of indigenous history and repatriation of human remains and material culture (Gonzáles de Oleaga, di Liscia, and Bohoslavsky 2011). Although many Latin American museums have become more engaged with indigenous communities, a significant change has still not "permeated the discourse of the history museum" in Latin America (Gonzáles de Oleaga, di Liscia, and Bohoslavsky 2011:51).

Virtual Museums

A virtual museum may be defined as a "logically related collection of digital objects composed in a variety of media" (Andrews and Schweibenz 1998, quoted in Schweibenz 2004:3). Although the term *virtual museum* is most commonly used for museums that exist only in cyberspace, without physical collections or traditional physical locations, some museum professionals prefer to use a wider definition that includes digital interfaces of physical museums (Correia Lima and de Barros Mendes 2009).

The first virtual museums appeared during the mid-1990s as rates of Internet usage were rapidly increasing (Schweibenz 2004). Although some museum professionals do not consider them to be museums, others maintain that virtual museums are "inevitable because of the increasing digitisation of cultural heritage and the demand to make collections more accessible," predicting that "[e]ventually, these trends will blur the differences between cultural heritage institutions and in the long run these institutions will merge into one memory institution [that] combines digital surrogates of the collections of archives, libraries and museums in rich interactive environments" (Schweibenz 2004:3), with an emphasis on collections of knowledge rather than collections of objects (Keene 2004). Supporters argue that, although virtual museums cannot offer real objects to visitors, they can extend ideas and concepts in ways that traditional museums cannot.

Controversies

More than thirty years ago, Wilcomb E. Washburn (1925–1997) cautioned that, in a museum, the "object can become a fetish that, if we merely worship it, impedes our understanding of the object itself and its place in our society" (Washburn 1984:15). Treating objects as religious fetishes may lead to controversy as well, particularly when a collection contains objects that are considered culturally sensitive or sacred. While all objects in a museum collection should be treated with respect, just how far collections care staff should go to accommodate cultural traditions in caring for objects must be carefully evaluated (Flynn and Hull-Walski 2001; Simpson 2001; see also the section "Indigenous Museums"). Moving statues of the Buddha from a lower shelf to a higher shelf or reorienting objects to face a certain direction is a fairly easy accommodation. Limiting staff members who can enter the room where certain objects are stored to only those of one gender or not housing objects from two particular cultures or religious traditions in the same space may be more difficult to comply with. Some requests (such as smudging Native American objects with sage smoke and feeding with corn pollen) may conflict with other institutional policies (e.g., concerning conservation or pest management). In addition to storage concerns, there may be restrictions on conservation work that can be done on some sacred objects (Greene 1992). The British social critic Tiffany Jenkins (b. 1973) has argued that such actions are contrary to the purposes of museums because the "very point of these institutions is to open up other worlds to people, not to lock the ones inside or shut the others out" (Jenkins 2005:n.p.). Jenkins believes that such actions as the Hancock Museum in Newcastle preventing female staff members from looking at Australian male churinga totems from the Arrente people or the British Museum wrapping up eleven Ethiopian wooden tablets that are believed to represent the Ark of the Covenant and not allowing any staff members to see them will mean that the "pursuit of truth is sacrificed on the altar of veneration" (Jenkins 2005:n.p.).

Controversies over museum exhibits tend to flare up suddenly and die away quickly, but some have longer-lasting consequences than others. One of the most far-reaching controversies in American museums in the last fifty years was the reaction to an exhibition titled *Harlem on My Mind: Cultural Capital of Black America, 1900–1968*, which opened at the staid Metropolitan Museum of Art in New York in early 1969. The exhibit was the brainchild of the museum's new director, Thomas Hoving (1931–2009), and a guest curator, Allon Schoener (b. 1926). The exhibit has been referred to as "possibly the most controversial American exhibition ever mounted" because "this exhibit or its catalogue infuriated blacks, horrified Jews, purportedly smeared the Irish, slighted Puerto Ricans, teed off artists and art critics, and propelled the Jewish Defense League, the Black Emergency Cultural Coalition, and members of the right-wing John Birch Society all into upper Fifth Avenue to man picket lines in front of the Met" (Dubin 1999:19).

The show presented sixty years of history using seven hundred photographs, hours of voice and music recordings, and five hundred rapidly changing projected images. The combination of racial tension in American society, provocative language in the catalog (which was withdrawn from sale), lack of inclusion of traditional paintings and sculptures by African American artists in the exhibit, feelings of exclusion on the part of individuals and groups who felt they should have had a voice in the exhibition, and charges of paternalism and prejudice all contributed to make the exhibition "political dynamite" (Dubin 1999:51). Although intended to inspire dialogue and conversation, the exhibit instead generated enormous opposition and criticism. Reflecting on the exhibit many years later, Holland Cotter wrote that he had "never seen an art show so much like a science-museum display. I didn't know what to do with any of this. So I left thinking: What was that about?" (Cotter 2015:C1). As Cotter notes, it was the response to the exhibit, not the exhibit itself, that most made it significant, and ultimately it was "through protest, not cooperation, that African-American artists finally started getting in the door. 'Harlem on My Mind' did what Mr. Hoving claimed he wanted it to do, but in an unexpected way" (Cotter 2015:C1).

MUSEUM STUDIES AND THE TRAINING OF MUSEUM PROFESSIONALS

In the 1960s, several French museologists, notably Georges-Henri Rivière and Hugues de Varine, began talking about *nouvelle muséologie*, or new museology, the impact of which was felt in museum studies programs throughout the next two decades. The new museology advocated the introduction of theoretical perspectives into museum studies and a reconsideration of change, as museums transformed from being exclusive and socially divisive institutions into more inclusive and accessible institutions (Ross 2004). The new museology included new concepts of what museums could be (particularly in the form of the ecomuseum, discussed previously) and how museums communicated with society at large (Lorente 2012). In fact, exactly what new museology included (or did not include) has been controversial from its inception. In his 1989 book, Peter Vergo "diagnosed a widespread dissatisfaction with the 'old museologies.' He argued in favour of a theoretical and humanistic approach to museums, which examined their purposes, politics, values, and histories. His call resonated and the following decade saw a flood of literature on these topics" (Candlin 2012:10). For some museum studies programs, the new museology meant a significant shift away from practice to a focus almost entirely on theory and criticism, but in most American universities, the new museology became critical museology, in reference to the critical analysis of museums and their functions and how that criticism impacts museum practice, the representation of minority and peripheral cultures, and challenges to colonial discourse (Lorente 2012).

In the 1980s and early 1990s, most North American museum studies programs still emphasized practice, in part because of a dire need for better-trained collections care personnel in museums. This need became apparent during the 1980s, when the Institute for Museum Services conducted a survey that revealed that 38 percent of the collections in American museums needed conservation work and the condition of another 40 percent was unknown. The American Association of Museums issued a report called *Caring for Collections: Strategies for Conservation, Maintenance and Documentation* in 1984 that points to the need for better training of museum staff in techniques of preventive care and maintenance. In response, the Bay Foundation funded a series of extensive Collections Care Pilot Training Programs (for archaeology and ethnography, fine arts, history, and natural history) administered by the National Institute of Conservation (NIC) that brought together working collections care personnel from the Americas and conservators, material scientists, and other professionals for intensive training. A series of publications were issued under the general title *Training for Collections Care and Maintenance: A Suggested Curriculum*:

- *Volume I: Archaeology and Ethnography* (1990, based on a training program at the Arizona State Museum, University of Arizona, Tucson)
- *Volume II: History* (1991, based on a training program at the Panhandle-Plains Historical Museum, Canyon, Texas)
- *Volume III: Natural Sciences* (1991, based on a training program at the Los Angeles County Museum of Natural History, Los Angeles, California)
- *Volume IV: Fine Arts* (1991, based on a training program at the Art Institute of Chicago, Chicago, Illinois)

Although the training programs were of great benefit to the participants and although parts of each of the programs have been incorporated into various training programs, none of the curricula were used in full by an educational institution to establish a postgraduate course in collections care as was initially anticipated. Nevertheless, the impact of the program on museums has been extensive, particularly in raising the awareness of conservation issues, achieving the integration of preventive conservation measures as a standard part of collections management (Rose and Hawks 1995; Simmons 2013, 2015), and promoting improvements in collection storage environments (see box 9.4).

BOX 9.4.
Changing Environmental Standards

Environmental standards for museums have undergone several revisions as knowledge has accumulated about the effects of the storage environment on museum objects, our ability to measure environmental parameters has improved, and we have developed better means of controlling museum environments.

The first museum in the United States to attempt year-round control of relative humidity was the Boston Museum of Fine Arts, which installed a system in 1908 designed to maintain a relative humidity of 55 to 60 percent. In 1915, the Cleveland Museum of Art followed, with the installation of a humidification and heating system intended to maintain a range of 50 to 55 percent. The first International Conference for the Study of Scientific Methods for the Examination and Preservation of Works of Art was held in Rome in October 1930. From this meeting came the *Manual on the Conservation of Paintings* in 1940, which concludes, "We have no adequate information at present to enable us to fix an absolute standard. The reason for choosing 60 to 65% as the figure for relative humidity for practical purposes is that in many climates it is the nearest approach to the conditions in which a degree of stability may be easily obtained" (quoted in Boersma, Dardes, and Druzik 2014:5).

Following the Second World War, many advances were made in understanding the deterioration mechanisms that affect museum objects and how they might be regulated or ameliorated, leading George Stout to advocate for the concept of long-term conservation at the 1949 meeting of the American Association of Museums in Chicago. The International Council of Museums (ICOM) conducted a survey in 1955 to determine the effects of climate on museum objects. The results of the ICOM survey were published in 1960 by Harold Plenderleith and Paul Philippot as *Climatology and Conservation in Museums*. Plenderleith and Philippot recommended a range of relative humidity of 50 to 65 percent, with no abrupt changes.

The first conference on museum climatology was held at the International Institute for Conservation (IIC) meeting in London in 1967. By this time, central heating and cooling systems that allowed for better climate control were becoming common in museums. Beginning in the 1970s, new museum construction typically featured far more sophisticated climate systems than it had been possible to build before, although the set points were still often unachievable and idealistic. Garry Thomson wrote an extraordinarily influential book, *The Museum Environment* (first edition 1978, second edition 1986), in which he argues for choosing appropriate ranges of temperature and humidity based on the museum's climate zone, heating and cooling systems, and the composition of objects in the collection.

In the following decades, further accumulation of scientific evidence and technological advances in climate control systems (particularly the work of the Canadian Conservation Institute and the Smithsonian Institution's Museum

Conservation Institute) led to reconsiderations of museum climate standards, including moving beyond the idea that strict targets should be set for an ideal building environment. Maintaining stable, nonfluctuating year-round temperature and humidity indoors is simply not practicable given museum budgetary constraints and how museums are used, and we now better understand the reactions of museum objects to environmental fluctuations. New environmental standards based on a better understanding of science and the limitations of environmental controls that are realistically attainable in museums now generally allow a more flexible range of variation than previous standards.

Sources: Boersma, Dardes, and Druzik 2014; Erhardt, Tumosa, and Mecklenburg 2007; IPI 2012.

An assessment of the state of museum studies programs in the United States in 1996 concludes, "From the beginning, the academic training of museum workers has taken place amid a diversity of conflicting circumstances. Museums, as educational institutions, operate quite differently from academic ones, yet the collegiate training of museum workers has always been organized around the principles of the classroom" (Spiess 1996:32). This seems a curious criticism, given that the same is true for all professions for which people are trained in university programs. There is no reason that the museum profession should be any different, aside from the fact that, at the point in time the article was published, most museum workers were not graduates of museum studies programs and many viewed university training in museum studies with suspicion. However, the situation was changing even as this criticism appeared due to the expansion in the number of museum studies programs and the corresponding number of graduates entering the profession. Another of Spiess's observations—that museum programs were searching for the right balance between theory and practice—was still true ten years later, when another review of museums studies programs in North America was published (Simmons 2006), and to some extent remains true today (Simmons 2015; Welsh 2013).

There are some museum studies programs that teach little or no theory, some that teach little or no practice, and others that have found the correct balance. There remains an unsubstantiated belief among some museum professionals in the United States that there are too many museum studies programs producing too many graduates for the size of the job market, a criticism mentioned in the 1996 review and one that still arises on discussion lists from time to time. This is another criticism that can be leveled at almost any academic program, particularly most liberal arts programs, even though we don't expect everyone who gets a graduate degree in architecture to become an architect or everyone who gets a graduate degree in history to become a historian. A graduate program should equip students with a detailed knowledge of an academic field but should also instill the skills necessary to do scholarly research, criticism, and writing—skills that are transferable to many other occupations outside the specific academic discipline.

A 2005 review of the museum studies program at Leicester University in the United Kingdom (in its fortieth year) examines the changes that had occurred in the museum field and in museum studies over four decades and points out that "[m]useum studies is no longer about established practice, it must set the agenda and build an adaptive and creative museum workforce capable of responding to change, opportunity and cultural context. In the process, museum studies has become research-active" and "[t]his type of creative museum studies is now widespread" worldwide (Knell 2005:3).

LAM: THE CONVERGENCE OF LIBRARIES, ARCHIVES, AND MUSEUMS

From our exploration of the history of museums, we know that, once upon a time, museums, libraries, and archives were one and the same, before diverging as each became more specialized in the nineteenth century. An interesting ongoing trend is the convergence (or reconvergence) of these institutions around their commonalities to provide better access to information through shared digitization processes; collection management systems; collection storage; exhibitions; and, in some cases, shared physical spaces (Given and McTavish 2010; Waibal and Erway 2009). Although there are certainly differences in how collections are cataloged, stored, and used among libraries, archives, and museums, all three types of institutions are concerned with objects and information derived from objects. The convergence of libraries, archives, and museums (LAM) has the potential to create new information environments. By capitalizing on their commonalities, the institutions involved could provide more cost-effective services and new synergies.

LEARNING TO READ OBJECTS (AGAIN)

The objects in the collection should be the "starting point, not the ending, of a visitor's experience because objects stimulate thought and reflection" (Paris 2002:44). Museums remain relevant and significant institutions because we keep finding new ways to derive information from objects.

An exhibit at Harvard University in 2011 challenged the "nineteenth-century categories that still divide art museums from science museums and historical collections from anthropological displays and assume that history is made only from written documents" by reconsidering objects, how they are classified, and what new information can be learned by their juxtaposition across informational boundaries (Ulrich et al. 2015:ix). The curators of the exhibition were able to explore the "instability of categories, the permeability of boundaries, and the tenet that there were no unvarnished facts" (Ulrich et al. 2015:xiv), something that could only be done in a museum.

The examination of objects and the study of their musealization has brought fresh understanding to such diverse subjects as former Chilean dictator Augusto José Ramón Pinochet Ugarte (1915–2006) and his book-collecting habits (Peña 2012) and the intimate lives of the Brontë family (Lutz 2015).

Museums began with objects, and despite occasional museological deviations to emphasize aesthetics, interpretation, technology, or visitor experiences, museums are still, at their core, object-based institutions. The clear theme running through museum history is that, the better we have learned to read objects, the better we have been able to use them to navigate our way through the world. The process of musealization means that object meanings are dynamic, not static, and thus the "museum remains integral to the idea of Western culture through the exchanges it encourages and the changes that it initiates" (Davenne and Fleurent 2012:32).

ZOOS AND BOTANICAL GARDENS

Since the start of the twentieth century, the four main functions of zoos have been recognized as recreation, education, research, and conservation (Baratay and Hardouin-Fugier 2002), missions that zoos share with botanical gardens. The American Zoo and Aquarium Association estimates that there are about 10,000 zoos worldwide. Botanic Gardens Conservation International estimates that there are 1,775 botanical gardens and arboreta in nearly 150 countries.

The number of zoos in Europe grew from just 50 in 1912 to 180 in 1965 to more than 300 by 1995. Beginning in the late 1960s, drive-through observation parks became popular for visitors willing to spend more time to see fewer animals but to be able to observe them not confined in traditional enclosures (Baratay and Hardouin-Fugier 2002). During the 1970s, there was an increase in the number of such specialized institutions as aquariums, marine parks, safari parks, petting zoos, aviaries, and zoos that specialize in local wildlife or farm animals.

Although there is a long history of deceased zoo animals being given to natural history museums for study, recently there has been increased "interest in the 'cultural biography' of their collection items" because "[e]very specimen has its own history of acquisition, preparation and exhibition . . . objects are documents of biodiversity as well as documents of the history of the study of biodiversity" (van Mensch 2011:6). This led to controversy when Knut, a popular polar bear that had been born and raised at the Zoologische Garten in Berlin, died unexpectedly in 2011 at four years of age. The zoo announced that the bear's body would be sent to the Museum für Naturkunde in Berlin to be prepared as a taxidermy mount for an exhibit on climate change. Public reaction was swift and negative. Polls showed that 73 percent of the German public was against having the bear stuffed, despite the good intentions for its use in an important exhibit, which raised questions concerning the cultural value versus the scientific value of the specimen—in other words, Knut had become musealized (van Mensch 2011).

LITERATURE

Reading habits have been changing for the last two decades due to the increased availability of digitized materials and portable electronic readers, although the long decline in sales of traditional books and magazines seems to have leveled out (Salkowitz 2014). These changes have come despite the fact that research has shown that reading on a screen is significantly slower (as much as 20 to 30 percent slower) than reading from paper, and reading accuracy may also be significantly reduced (Dillon 1992). Changes in reading habits have been reflected in museum practice, with more digital information in museum exhibits and available in museums on hand-held devices, as well as a general reduction in the number of traditional text labels.

Despite the changes in the way information is now accessed (or perhaps because of them), the diversity of literature has increased. Rather than attempting to parse out trends in this rapidly changing landscape, a few examples of literature published since about 1970 related to museums are considered instead.

Three notable children's books touch on a fantasy that many adults also share—spending the night inside a museum. In 1968, the book *From the Mixed-up Files of Mrs. Basil E. Frankweiler* by Elaine Lobl "E. L." Konigsburg (1930–2013) won a Newbery Medal for excellence in children's literature. The book tells the story of twelve-year-old Claudia Kincaid and her nine-year-old brother Jamie, who run away from home and hide out in the Metropolitan Museum of Art for a week. While in the museum, the children manage to solve a mystery involving a purported Michelangelo sculpture through careful observation and research in the museum's library. The book was made into a major film (1973), a television movie (1995), and an opera. In 1993, Milan Trenc (b. 1962) published a picture book called *The Night at the Museum,* in which Hector, a night watchman at the Museum of Natural History in New York, discovers that the dinosaur skeletons come alive every night. The book was made into three feature films of the same name (2006, 2009, and 2014) but with the watchman's name changed to Larry and, instead of just the dinosaurs, all of the museum exhibits came to life at night (the idea that museum exhibits come to life at night was also used in a 1939 German film, *Salonwagen E 417* or *Luxury Train Car E 417*). Brian Selznick's (b. 1966) 2011 book *Wonderstruck: A Novel in Words and Pictures* tells two stories simultaneously, set fifty years apart. The stories are initially told in parallel, one only in graphic form, the other in text, and both involve children running away to hide in museums who, while hiding, unravel important secrets. As the book advances, the two plots intermingle and then converge (although no exhibits come to life at night).

Graphic novels, which first appeared in the 1920s, have surged greatly in popularity since the 1970s. The 2009 graphic novel *Stuffed!* is the story of two brothers who inherit their late father's museum of curiosities only to discover that the contents include a taxidermy preparation of an African man (Eichler and Bertozzi 2009). Although a comic novel, the book addresses many of the serious issues involved in the repatriation of human remains.

A 2008 novel by the Turkish Nobel-laureate Orhan Pamuk (b. 1952), *The Museum of Innocence* (*Masumiyet Müzesi*), is set in the time period 1975–1984 in Istanbul. The novel concerns a complicated love affair between a wealthy businessman and a poor distant relative. Pamuk cites the influence of the Bagatti Valsecchi Museum (a historic-house museum featuring decorative arts from the Italian Renaissance located in Milan, Italy) as the inspiration behind the creation by the protagonist of a museum devoted to his obsessive though frustrated romance. In 2012, Pamuk opened an actual Museum of Innocence in Istanbul containing many of the objects mentioned in his novel, thus simultaneously preserving both fictional and real memories (Yackley 2012). A free admission ticket that is honored at the real museum is included in the final pages of the published novel. Pamuk has told interviewers that he thought of establishing the actual museum at the same time he thought of writing the novel, in which a fictional character establishes a museum. Objects in Pamuk's collection came from junk shops and other sources in Istanbul.

Another example of fiction becoming musealized reality can be found in the sleepy little agricultural town of Aracataca on the Caribbean coastal plain of Colombia. Aracataca is the hometown of Nobel-laureate Gabriel García Márquez (1927–2014), who used it as the model for the town of Macondo in his 1967 novel *One Hundred Years of Solitude* (*Cien Años de Soledad*). Until recently, Aracataca received few visitors due to security issues related to guerrilla and paramilitary activity in the area. Now that the area is safe to visit, the number of literary tourists from both Colombia and abroad is gradually increasing. Following a pattern first established in Victorian England, when it became fashionable to visit the homes of beloved writers and the real settings of fictional events, Aracataca is becoming musealized—in effect, it is being turned into an outdoor museum (figure 9.3). When I visited Aracataca in 2007, a collection of objects from the author's family was on exhibit, two local tour guides were employed by the municipality to show visitors the locations mentioned in the novel, and the house the author grew up in was being reconstructed. García Márquez is one of the best-known writers of the literary form called magical realism, in which real events are blended with magical elements (see chapter 8), thus it is somewhat ironic that the physical locations in Aracataca that are mentioned in the novel are presented by the local guides as if the events of the novel actually took place there, in Macondo.

Figure 9.3. Former telegraph office in Aracataca, Colombia; now a municipal museum.

SUMMARY

What we can learn from the history of museums is how these institutions have evolved to serve different needs at different periods of history by interpreting nature and culture. Museums were once perceived as the "institutions charged with furthering knowledge and creating order" (Conn 1998:15), and in an era of massive globalization, museums continue to serve as "centers of education and enlightenment and purveyors of cultural values" (Dickey, Azhar, and Lewis 2013:12).

Although early museums were, in essence, reliquaries or storehouses with limited intellectual justification for their existence, beginning in the mid-1700s, museums began to reflect the intellectual ferment of the Enlightenment, and "Enlightened men made a fetish of reason, and they demanded proof to substantiate claims. This need for evidence gave the museum, for the first time, a strong raison d'être" (Orosz 1990:13). As a result, museums became "indispensable for the preservation of the artifacts of history, the taxonomy of the natural world, the apparatus of science, and the legacy of great art from the past" (Orosz 1990:13).

However, museums are far more than just holders of evidence—they are also places of learning, stimulation, consolation, and entertainment. A museum can both affirm and provoke, inspire and amuse, help us understand the world or serve as a refuge from it. In an interview, Sabine Rewald of the Metropolitan Museum of Art spoke about an exhibit that she curated with Gary Tinterow called *Moonwatchers*, explaining,

> The show opened on September 11, 2001, strangely enough. The public didn't come, because we closed the galleries half an hour after the Museum opened on that extraordinary day. But this exhibition, with these very moving, meditative pictures, became a favorite with the public, because the public was in need of consolation, and people streamed to it and felt solace. (quoted in Danziger 2007:198–99)

Museums will continue to be important as long as humans remain curious about the world around them.

References

AAM. 1984. *Caring for Collections: Strategies for Conservation, Maintenance and Documentation.* American Association of Museums, Washington, DC, 44 pp.

———. 1994. *Museums Count: A Report by the American Association of Museums.* American Association of Museums, Washington, DC, 104 pp.

———. 2000. NAGPRA at 10: Examining a Decade of the Native American Graves Protection and Repatriation Act. *Museum News*: 42–49, 67–75.

AAM. 2014. *Code of Ethics for Museums.* http://www.aam-us.org/resources/ethics-standards-and-best-practices/code-of-ethics.

———. 2015. Museum Facts. *American Alliance of Museums.* http://www.aam-us.org/about-museums/museum-facts.

Abungu, G. 2004. The Declaration: A Contested Issue. *ICOM News* 57(1):5.

Ackley, J. S. 2014. Re-approaching the Western Medieval Church Treasury Inventory, c. 800–1250. *Journal of Art Historiography* 11:1–37.

Aimi, A., V. de Michele, and A. Merandotti. 1985. Towards a History of Collecting in Milan in the Late Renaissance and Baroque Periods. Pp. 24–28 in O. Impey and A. MacGregor (eds.), *The Origins of Museums: The Cabinet of Curiosities in Sixteenth- and Seventeenth-Century Europe.* Clarendon Press, Oxford, x + 431 pp.

Alberti, S. J. M. M. 2005. Objects and the Museum. *Isis* 96(4):559–71.

Alderson, W. T. (ed.). 1992. *Mermaids, Mummies, and Mastodons: The Emergence of the American Museum.* American Association of Museums, Washington, DC, 104 pp.

Alexander, E. P. 1979. *Museums in Motion: An Introduction to the History and Functions of Museums.* American Association for State and Local History, Nashville, xii + 308 pp.

———. 1992. Mermaids, Mummies, and Mastodons: An Exhibition on the Evolution of Early American Museums. Pp. 17–21 in W. T. Alderson (ed.), *Mermaids,*

Mummies, and Mastodons: The Emergence of the American Museum. American Association of Museums, Washington, DC, 104 pp.

———. 1996. *Museum Masters: Their Museums and Their Influence.* AltaMira Press, Walnut Creek, 448 pp.

———. 1997. *The Museum in America: Innovators and Pioneers.* AltaMira Press, Walnut Creek, 224 pp.

Alexander, E. P., and M. Alexander. 2008. *Museums in Motion: An Introduction to the History and Functions of Museums.* AltaMira Press, Lanham, xiii + 352 pp.

Allen, D. E. 1994. *The Naturalist in Britain: A Social History.* 2nd ed. Princeton University Press, Princeton, xix + 270 pp.

Anderson, J. 2003. *Art Held Hostage: The Battle over the Barnes Collection.* W. W. Norton, New York, xiv + 237 pp.

Anderson, L. I., and M. Lowe. 2010. Charles W. Peach and Darwin's Barnacles. *Journal of the History of Collections* 22(2):257–70.

Andrews, C. 1998. *Egyptian Mummies.* British Museum Press, London, 96 pp.

Andrews, J. E., and W. Schweibenz. 1998. A New Medium for Old Masters: The Kress Study Collection Virtual Museum Project. *Art Documentation* 17(1):19–27.

Appelbaum, B. 2010. *Conservation Treatment Methodology.* CreateSpace, New York, xxix + 437 pp.

Argott, D. (dir.). 2009. *The Art of the Steal.* Produced by Lenny Feinberg.

Arinze, E. N. 1987. Training in African Museums: The Role of the Centre for Museum Studies, Jos. *Museum* 156:278–80.

Arnone, O. 2010. Digital Asset Management. Pp. 184–92 in R. A. Buck and J. A. Gilmore (eds.), *Museum Registration Methods.* 5th ed. American Association of Museums Press, Washington, DC, xi + 516 pp.

Arriaza, B. T. 1995. *Beyond Death: The Chinchorro Mummies of Ancient Chile.* Smithsonian Institution Press, Washington, DC, xv + 176 pp.

Arroyo, L. 2007. Science on Faith at the Creation Museum. *Museum News* 86(6): 42–49.

———. 2008. Sex, Drugs and Pirates: The Rise of For-Profit Museums. *Museum News* 87(6):62–68, 75–77.

Ayers, J. 1985. The Early China Trade. Pp. 259–66 in O. Impey and A. MacGregor (eds.), *The Origins of Museums: The Cabinet of Curiosities in Sixteenth- and Seventeenth-Century Europe.* Clarendon Press, Oxford, x + 431 pp.

Bacon, F. 1688. *Gesta Grayorum: or, the History of the High and Mighty Prince Henry.* W. Canning, London, 82 pp.

Bailey, N. (ed.). 1730. *Dictionarium Britannicum: Or a More Compleat Universal Etymological English Dictionary.* T. Cox, London.

Baratay, E., and E. Hardouin-Fugier. 2002. *Zoo: A History of Zoological Gardens in the West.* Reaktion Books, London, 400 pp.

Barber, L. 1980. *The Heyday of Natural History 1820–1870.* Doubleday, Garden City, 320 pp.

Baron, R. A. 1991. The Computerized Accession Ledger: A View from a Computer Consultant. *Registrar* 8(2):41ff.

Barwise, J. M., and N. J. White. 2002. *A Traveler's History of South East Asia.* Windrush Press, Morton-in-Marsh, Gloucestershire, x + 342 pp.

Battles, M. 2015. *Library: An Unquiet History.* W. W. Norton, New York, x + 253 pp.

Baucon, A. 2008. Italy, The Cradle of Ichnology: The Legacy of Aldrovandi and Leonardo. *Studi Trentini di Scienze Naturali: Acta Geologica* 83:15–29.

Bauer, A. M., A. Ceregato, and M. Delfino. 2013. The Oldest Herpetological Collection in the World: The Surviving Amphibian and Reptile Specimens of the Museum of Ulisee Aldrovandi. *Amphibia-Reptilia* 34:305–21.

Bazin, G. 1967. *The Museum Age*. Universe Books, New York, 302 pp.

Beanland, C. 2014. Is There a Future for the Traditional Museum? *Independent*, 30 November. http://www.independent.co.uk/arts-entertainment/is-there-a -future-for-the-traditional-museum-9855822.html.

Bedekar, V. H. 1987. The Museum Training Situation in India. *Museum* 39(4):284–90.

Bennett, T. 1995. *The Birth of the Museum: History, Theory, Politics*. Routledge, London, x + 278 pp.

Bergreen, L. 2011. *Columbus: The Four Voyages*. Viking Penguin, New York, xvii + 423 pp.

Berti, M., and V. Costa. 2009. The Ancient Library of Alexandria: A Model for Classical Scholarship in the Age of Million Book Libraries. Preprint from *CLIR Proceedings of the International Symposium of the Scaife Digital Library*.

Berry, A. (ed.). 2002. *Infinite Tropics: An Alfred Russel Wallace Anthology*. Verso, London, xvii + 430 pp.

Betts, J. R. 1959. P. T. Barnum and the Popularization of Natural History. *Journal of the History of Ideas* 29(3):353–68.

Bhatti, S. 2012. *Translating Museums: A Counterhistory of South Asian Museology*. Left Coast Press, Walnut Creek, 300 pp.

Biddle, W. 1995. *A Field Guide to Germs*. Henry Holt, New York, xix + 196 pp.

Bjurström, P. 1993. Physiocratic Ideals and National Galleries. Pp. 28–60 in P. Bjurström (ed.), *The Genesis of the Art Museum in the 18th Century*. Nationalmuseum, Stockholm, 130 pp.

Blackaby, R. J., and P. Greeno. 1988. *The Revised Nomenclature for Museum Cataloging: A Revised and Expanded Version of Robert G. Chenhall's System for Classifying Manmade Objects*. Nomenclature Committee of the American Association for State and Local History, Nashville, 520 pp.

Blom, P. 2002. *To Have and to Hold: An Intimate History of Collectors and Collecting*. Overlook Press, Woodstock, xiv + 273 pp.

Blunt, W. 2001. *Linnaeus: The Compleat Naturalist*. Princeton University Press, Princeton, 264 pp.

Boersma, F., K. Dardes, and J. Druzik. 2014. Precaution, Proof, and Pragmatism: Evolving Perspectives on the Museum Environment. *Conservation Perspectives* 29(2):4–9.

Borges, J. L. 1962. The Library of Babel. Pp. 79–88 in *Ficciones*. Grove Press, New York, 174 pp.

Born, P. 2002. The Cannon Is Cast: Plaster Casts in American Museums and University Collections. *Art Documentation* 21(2):8–13.

Bounia, A. 2004. *The Nature of Classical Collecting: Collectors and Collections, 100 BCE–100 CE*. Ashgate, Aldershot, xvi + 354 pp.

Bourcier, P., and R. Rogers. 2010. *Nomenclature 3.0 for Museum Cataloging: Robert G. Chenhall's System for Classifying Man-Made Objects*. 3rd ed. AltaMira Press, Lanham, 750 pp.

Bourcier, P., and H. Dunn. 2015. *Nomenclature 4.0 for Museum Cataloging: Robert G. Chenhall's System for Classifying Cultural Objects*. 4th ed. AltaMira Press, Lanham, 752 pp.

Boylan, P. J. 1999. Universities and Museums: Past, Present and Future. *Museum Management and Curatorship* 18(1):43–56.

———. 2006. The Museum Profession. Pp. 415–30 in S. Macdonald (ed.), *A Companion to Museum Studies*. Blackwell, London, 592 pp.

Bray, W. (ed.). 1901. *The Diary of John Evelyn*. Vol. 1. M. Walter Dunne, New York, xv + 380 pp.

Bredekamp, H. 1995. *The Lure of Antiquity and the Cult of the Machine: The Kunstkammer and the Evolution of Nature, Art and Technology*. Markus Wiener, Princeton, xiii + 140 pp.

Brennan, N. 1992. Foreword. Pp 7–11 in W. T. Alderson (ed.), *Mermaids, Mummies, and Mastodons: The Emergence of the American Museum*. American Association of Museums, Washington, DC, 104 pp.

Bridges, W. 1974. *A Gathering of Animals: An Unconventional History of the New York Zoological Society*. Harper and Row, New York, viii + 518 pp.

Brier, B. 1994. *Egyptian Mummies: Unraveling the Secrets of an Ancient Art*. Brockhampton Press, London, 352 pp.

Brinkman, P. D. 2009. Frederic Ward Putnam, Chicago's Cultural Philanthropists, and the Founding of the Field Museum. *Museum History Journal* 2(1):73–100.

Browne, J. 2002. *Charles Darwin: The Power of Place*. Princeton University Press, Princeton, 591 pp.

Bruhns, K. O., and N. L. Kelker. 2010. *Faking the Ancient Andes*. Left Coast Press, Walnut Creek, 220 pp.

Buchanan, H. C. 1901. To What Extent Should a State Library Enter the Field of a State Museum? *Public Libraries* 6(1):41–43.

Burton, R. F. 1878. *The Gold-Mines of Midian*. C. Kegan Paul, London, xvi + 395 pp. [1995 reprint by Dover, Mineola].

Butler, B. 2007. *Return to Alexandria: An Ethnography of Cultural Heritage Revivalism and Museum Memory*. Left Coast Press, Walnut Creek, 299 pp.

Camarena, C., and T. Morales. 2006. The Power of Self-Interpretation: Ideas on Starting a Community Museum. Pp. 77–85 in K. C. Cooper and N. I. Sandoval (eds.), *Living Homes for Cultural Expression: North American Native Perspectives on Creating Community Museums*. National Museum of the American Indian, Washington, DC, 119 pp.

Camin, G. 2007. *Los Grandes Museos del Mundo*. Numen, Mexico City, 304 pp.

Canadian Conservation Institute. 2015. Ten Agents of Deterioration. http://www.cci-icc.gc.ca/caringfor-prendresoindes/articles/10agents/index-eng.aspx.

Candlin, F. 2012. Independent Museums, Heritage, and the Shape of Museum Studies. *Museum and Society* 10(1):28–41.

Capart, J. 1926. *Thebes: The Glory of a Great Past*. Dial Press, New York, 362 pp.

Carrier, D. 2006. *Museum Skepticism: A History of the Display of Art in Public Galleries*. Duke University Press, Durham, xiii + 313 pp.

Carrighar, S. 1965. *Wild Heritage*. Houghton, Mifflin, Boston, ix + 276 pp.

Casson, L. 2001. *Libraries in the Ancient World*. Yale University Press, New Haven, xii + 177 pp.

Cepic, T. V. 2002. The City Museum of Ljubljana. *ICOM News* 55(2):7.

Chandavij, N., and S. Traikasem (eds.). 2000. *Visitors Guide to the Nakhon Si Thammarat National Museum.* Office of Archaeological and National Museums, Fine Arts Department, Ministry of Education, Bangkok, 160 pp.

Chappell, W. 1970. *A Short History of the Printed Word.* Alfred A. Knopf, New York, xviii + 244 + xv pp.

Chatwin, B. 1988. *Utz.* Jonathan Cape, London, 154 pp.

Chenhall, R. G. 1978. *Nomenclature for Museum Cataloging.* American Association for State and Local History, Nashville, viii + 512 pp.

Chickering, H. D. (trans.). 2005. Beowulf: The Treasure and the Dragon. Pp. 119–20 in S. Keene, *Fragments of the World: Uses of Museum Collections.* Elsevier Butterworth-Heineman, Oxford, x + 198 pp.

Chongkol, C. 1999. *Guide to the National Museum Bangkok.* 4th ed. Office of Archaeology and National Museum, Bangkok, 159 pp.

Cirigliana, J. A. 2011. Let Them Sell Art: Why a Broader Deaccession Policy Today Could Save Museums Tomorrow. *Southern California Interdisciplinary Law Journal* 20(2):365–93.

Clark, L. R. 2013. Collecting, Exchange, and Sociability in the Renaissance *Studiolo. Journal of the History of Collections* 25(2):171–84.

Cohn, S. K. 2002. The Black Death: End of a Paradigm. *American Historical Review* 107(3):703–38.

Cole, F. J. 1921. The History of Anatomical Injections. Pp. 285–343 in C. J. Singer (ed.), *Studies in the History and Method of Science.* Vol. 2. Oxford at the Clarendon Press, Oxford, xxii + 559 pp.

———. 1944. *A History of Comparative Anatomy from Aristotle to the Eighteenth Century.* Macmillan, London, viii + 524 pp.

Coleman, L. V. 1927. *Manual for Small Museums.* G. P. Putnam's Sons, New York, 395 pp.

Coleridge, T. S. 1821. Selection from Mr. Coleridge's Literary Correspondence with Friends, and Men of Letters. *Blackwood's Edinburgh Magazine* 10(56): 243–64.

Collin de Plancy, J. A. Sn. 1821. *Dictionnaire Critique des Reliques et des Images Miraculeuses.* 3 vols. Guien et Compagnie, Libraires, Paris, 478 pp.

Conn, S. 1998. *Museums and American Intellectual Life, 1876–1926.* University of Chicago Press, Chicago, viii + 305 pp.

———. 2010. *Do Museums Still Need Objects?* University of Pennsylvania Press, Philadelphia, 262 pp.

Cooper, K. C. 2006. Preface. Pp. 8–9 in K. C. Cooper and N. I. Sandoval (eds.), *Living Homes for Cultural Expression: North American Native Perspectives on Creating Community Museums.* National Museum of the American Indian, Washington, DC, 119 pp.

Correia Lima, D. F., and P. de Barros Mendes. 2009. Virtual Museum: Identifying Models through a Conceptual Study and Museology Practices: Museology: Back to Basics, *ICOFOM Study Series* 38:237–49.

Cotter, H. 2015. What I Learned from a Disgraced Art Show on Harlem. *New York Times,* 19 August, http://www.nytimes.com/2015/08/20/arts/design/what-i-learned-from-a-disgraced-art-show-on-harlem.html?_r=0.

Courtney, J. (ed.). 2015. *The Legal Guide for Museum Professionals*. Rowman and Littlefield, Lanham, xiii + 301 pp.

Crook, J. M. 1972. *The British Museum: A Case-Study of Architectural Politics*. Penguin Books, London, 252 pp.

Cruz, J. C. 1977. *The Incorruptibles. A Study of the Incorruption of the Bodies of Various Catholic Saints and Beati*. Tan Books, Rockford, 310 pp.

———. 1984. *Relics*. Our Sunday Visitor, Huntington, 308 pp.

Cruz-Ramirez, A. 1985. The Heimatmuseum: A Perverted Forerunner. *Museum International* 37(4):242–44.

Csikszentmihalyi, M. 1975. *Beyond Boredom and Anxiety*. Jossey-Bass, San Francisco, 231 pp.

Cummins, A. 1994. The "Caribbeanization" of the West Indies: The Museum's Role in the Development of National Identity. Pp. 192–220 in F. E. S. Kaplan (ed.), *Museums and the Making of "Ourselves": The Role of Objects in National Identity*. Leicester University Press, London, xi + 430 pp.

Cunliffe, B. (ed.). 1987. *Origins: The Roots of European Civilization*. Dorsey Press, Chicago, xi + 195 pp.

Cuno, J. 2011. *Museums Matter: In Praise of the Encyclopedic Museum*. University of Chicago Press, Chicago, xii + 148 pp.

Cushman, K. 1984. Museum Studies: The Beginnings, 1900–1926. *Museum Studies Journal* 1(3):8–18.

Dahlström, Å., and L. Brost. 1996. *The Amber Book*. Geoscience Press, Tucson, 134 pp.

Dahlbom, T. 2009. Biographies of Zoological Specimens. *Museum History Journal* 2(1):51–72.

Dampier, W. 1927. *A New Voyage round the World*. Argonaut Press, London, 448 pp. [2007 reprint by Dover, Mineola, under the title *Memoirs of a Buccaneer: Dampier's New Voyage round the World, 1697*].

Damrosch, D. 2008. Toward a History of World Literature. *New Literary History* 39(3):481–95.

Danilov, V. J. 1984. Science Centers in the Far East. *Museum Studies Journal* 1(4):24–30.

Danziger, D. 2007. *Museum: Behind the Scenes at the Metropolitan Museum of Art*. Viking, New York, xxii + 277 pp.

Daston, L., and K. Park. 2001. *Wonders and the Order of Nature, 1150–1750*. Zone Books, New York, 511 pp.

Davenne, C., and C. Fleurent. 2012. *Cabinets of Wonder*. Abrams, New York, 232 pp.

Davidson, J. 2015. Mobile Is Fueling Global Connectivity. *Money*, 26 May, http://time.com/money/3896219/internet-users-worldwide.

Davis, P. 2011. *Ecomuseums: A Sense of Place*. 2nd ed. Continuum International, London, 320 pp.

Dechen, L. 2004. Buddhism. Pp. 158–88 in S. T. Hitchcock and J. L. Esposito (eds), *Geography of Religion: Where God Lives, Where Pilgrims Walk*. National Geographic Society, Washington, DC, 416 pp.

Deetz, J. 1977. *In Small Things Forgotten: The Archaeology of Early American Life*. Anchor Books/Doubleday, Garden City, 184 pp.

Dembeck, H. 1965. *Animals and Men*. Natural History Press, Doubleday, New York, x + 390 pp.

d'Errico, F., H. Salomon, C. Vignaud, and C. Stringer. 2010. Pigments from the Middle Palaeolithic Levels of Es-Skhul (Mount Carmel, Israel). *Journal of Archaeological Science* 37(12): 3099–3110.

Derry, T. K., and T. I. Williams. 1961. *A Short History of Technology from the Earliest Times to A.D. 1900*. Oxford University Press, Oxford, xviii + 782 pp. [1993 reprint by Dover, Mineola].

Dewey, J. 1915. *The School and Society*. 2nd ed. University of Chicago Press, Chicago, 101 pp. [2001 reprint by Dover, Mineola].

———. 1916. *Democracy and Education: An Introduction to the Philosophy of Education*. Macmillan, New York, 375 pp.

———. 1934. *Art as Experience*. Penguin Books, London, viii + 371 pp.

Desvallées, A., and F. Mairesse (eds.). 2010. *Key Concepts of Museology*. Armand Colin and ICOM, Paris, 83 pp.

de Varine, H. 1985. The Word and Beyond. *Museum* 37(148):185.

Dickey, J. W., S. El Azhar, and C. M. Lewis (eds.). 2013. *Museums in a Global Context: National Identity, International Understanding*. AAM Press, Washington, DC, 224 pp.

Dickinson, J. Y. 1965. *The Book of Diamonds*. Crown, New York, xiv + 240 pp. [2001 reprint by Dover, Mineola].

Dillon, A. 1992. Reading from Paper versus Screens: A Critical Review of the Empirical Literature. *Ergonomics* 35(10):1297–1326.

Diop, A. S. G. 1973. Museological Activity in African Countries: Its Role and Purpose. *Museum* 25(4):250–56.

di Pasquale, G. 2005. The Museum of Alexandria: Myth and Model. Pp. 1–11 in M. Baretta (ed.), *From Private to Public: Natural Collections and Museums*. Science History, Sagamore Beach, 272 pp.

Dirda, M. 2013. Introduction. Pp. vii–xvi in S. Butler (trans.), *The Iliad and the Odyssey*. Barnes and Noble, New York, xvi + 731 pp.

Diringer, D. 1953. *The Hand-Produced Book*. Hutchinson's Scientific and Technical Publications, London, xii + 603 pp. [1982 reprint by Dover, Mineola, under the title *The Book before Printing: Ancient, Medieval and Oriental*].

Dubin, S. C. 1999. *Displays of Power: Controversy in the American Museum from the Enola Gay to Sensation*. New York University Press, New York, xiii + 325 pp.

Duellman, W. E. 2015. *Herpetology at Kansas: A Centennial History*. Society for the Study of Amphibians and Reptiles Contributions to Herpetology, Number 31, Ithaca, xiv + 346 pp.

Duffy, T. M. 2001. Museums of "Human Suffering" and the Struggle for Human Rights. *Museum International* 53(1):10–16.

Dugatkin, L. A. 2009. *Mr. Jefferson and the Giant Moose: Natural History in Early America*. University of Chicago Press, Chicago, xii +166 pp.

Eichler, G., and N. Bertozzi. 2009. *Stuffed!* First Second, New York, 124 pp.

El-Abbadi, M. 1990. *The Life and Fate of the Library of Alexandria*. UNESCO Press, Paris, 250 pp.

El Azhar, S. 2013. The Ben M'sik Community Museum: Beyond Cultural Values. Pp. 24–43 in J. W. Dickey, S. El Azhar, and C. M. Lewis (eds.), *Museums in a Global Context: National Identity, International Understanding*. AAM Press, Washington, DC, 224 pp.

Empereur, J. Y. 2002. *Alexandria: Jewel of Egypt.* Harry N. Abrams, New York, 159 pp.

Engel, F. A. 1976. *An Ancient World Preserved: Relics and Records of Prehistory in the Andes.* Crown, New York, 114 pp.

Engström, K. 1985. The Ecomuseum Concept Is Taking Root in Sweden. *Museum* 37(148):206–10.

Erhardt, D., C. S. Tumosa, and M. F. Mecklenburg. 2007. Applying Science to the Question of Museum Climate. Pp. 11–18 in T. Padfield and K. Borchersen (eds.), *Proceedings from Museum Microclimates.* National Museum of Denmark, Copenhagen, 283 pp.

Evans, E. M., M. S. Mull, and D. A. Poling. 2002. The Authentic Object? A Child's-Eye View. Pp. 55–77 in S. G. Paris (ed.), *Perspectives on Object-Centered Learning in Museums.* Lawrence Erlbaum Associates, Mahwah, xxii + 383 pp.

Falk, J. H. 1999. Museums as Institutions of Personal Learning. *Daedalus* 128(3):259–75.

Falk, J. H., and L. D. Dierking. 2000. *Learning from Museums: Visitor Experiences and the Making of Meaning.* American Association for State and Local History/ AltaMira Press, Walnut Creek, xv + 288 pp.

———. 2002. *Lessons without Limit: How Free-Choice Learning Is Transforming Education.* AltaMira Press, Walnut Creek, x + 208 pp.

———. 2013. The Museum Experience Revisited. Left Coast Press, Walnut Creek, 416 pp.

Fedi, F. 1987. Postgraduate Course in Museography and Museology in the Faculty of Architecture in Milan. *Museum* 39(4):261–64.

Feliciano, H. 1997. *The Lost Museum: The Nazi Conspiracy to Steal the World's Greatest Works of Art.* Basic Books, New York, vii +280 pp.

Fenner, F. J., B. R. McAuslan, and C. A. Mims. 1974. *The Biology of Animal Viruses.* 2nd ed. Academic Press, 834 pp.

Findlen, P. 1989. The Museum: Its Classical Etymology and Renaissance Genealogy. *Journal of the History of Collections* 1(1):59–78.

———. 1994. *Possessing Nature: Museums, Collecting, and Scientific Culture in Early Modern Italy.* University of California Press, Berkeley, xvii + 449 pp.

———. 1998. Possessing the Past: The Material World of the Italian Renaissance. *American Historical Review* 103(1):83–114.

———. 2000. Introduction: Mr. Murray's Cabinet of Wonder. Pp. i–xvii in D. Murray. 1904. *Museums, Their History, and Their Uses: With a Bibliography and List of Museums in the United Kingdom.* Vol. 1. James L. MacLehose and Sons, Glasgow. [2000 reprint by Pober, Staten Island, xiv + 339 pp.].

———. 2004. The Museum: Its Classical Etymology and Renaissance Genealogy. Pp. 23–50 in B. M. Carbonell (ed.), *Museum Studies: An Anthology of Contexts.* Blackwell, Malden, xxxiii + 640 pp.

Fischer, S. R. 2001. *A History of Writing.* Reaktion Books, London, 352 pp.

Flower, W. H. 1898. *Essays on Museums and Other Subjects Connected with Natural History.* Macmillan, London. [1972 reprint by Books for Libraries Press, Freeport, 394 pp.].

Flynn, G., and D. Hull-Walski. 2001. Merging Traditional Indigenous Curation Methods with Modern Museum Standards of Care. *Museum Anthropology* 25(1):31–40.

Frazer, M. E. 1986. Medieval Church Treasuries. *Metropolitan Museum of Art Bulletin* 43(3):1–56.

French, R. 1994. *Ancient Natural History*. Routledge, London, xxii +357 pp.

Funk, I. K. 1913. *Standard Dictionary of the English Language*. Funk and Wagnalls, New York, xxxvii + 2916 pp.

García Márquez, G. 1970. *One Hundred Years of Solitude*. HarperCollins, New York, 458 pp. [English reprint of the original, published in Spanish in 1967].

Gathercole, P. 1989. The Fetishism of Artefacts. Pp. 73–81 in S. M. Pearce (ed.), *Museum Studies in Material Culture*. Leicester University Press, Leicester, 174 pp.

George, W. 1985. Alive or Dead: Zoological Collections in the Seventeenth Century. Pp. 179–87 in O. Impey and A. MacGregor (eds.), *The Origins of Museums: The Cabinet of Curiosities in Sixteenth- and Seventeenth-Century Europe*. Clarendon Press, Oxford, x + 431 pp.

Gilman, B. I. 1916. [Discussion]. *Proceedings of the American Association of Museums* 10:53.

Ginetta, E., and B. Candelario. 2007. *Black behind the Ears: Dominican Racial Identity from Museums to Beauty Shops*. Duke University Press, Durham, xiii + 360 pp.

Given, L. M., and L. McTavish. 2010. What's Old Is New Again: The Reconvergence of Libraries, Archives, and Museums in the Digital Age. *Library Quarterly* 80(1):7–32.

Glaser, J. R. 1987. Museum Studies Training in the United States: Coming a Long Way for a Long Time. *Museum* 39(4):268–74.

Goldhill, S. 2011. *Freud's Couch, Scott's Buttocks, Brontë's Grave*. University of Chicago Press, Chicago, vii + 129 pp.

Gonzáles de Oleaga, M., M. S. di Liscia, and E. Bohoslavsky. 2011. Looking from Above: Saying and Doing in the History Museums of Latin America. *Museum and Society* 9(1):49–76.

Goode, G. B. 1889. Museum-History and Museums of History. *Papers of the American Historical Association* 3(2):253–75.

Goodwin, M. 1990. Objects, Belief and Power in Mid-Victorian England: The Origins of the Victoria and Albert Museum. Pp. 9–49 in S. M. Pearce (ed.), *Objects of Knowledge*. Athlone Press, London, x + 235 pp.

Gould, C. G. 2004. *The Remarkable Life of William Beebe, Explorer and Naturalist*. Island Press, Washington, DC, xv + 447 pp.

Grant, M. A. 1966. *The History of the Wilcox Collection and the Department of Classics and Classical Archaeology at the University of Kansas, 1866–1966*. Privately printed.

Greene, V. 1992. "Accessories of Holiness": Defining Jewish Sacred Objects. *Journal of the American Institute for Conservation* 31(1):31–39.

Grene, D. (trans.). 1987. *Herodotus: The History*. University of Chicago Press, Chicago, x + 699 pp.

Grethlein, J. 2008. Memory and Material Objects in the *Iliad* and the *Odyssey*. *Journal of Hellenic Studies* 128:27–51.

Grew, N. 1681. *Musaeum Regalis Societatis; Or, A Catalog and Description of the Natural and Artificial Rarities Belonging to the Royal Society and Preserved at Gresham College. Whereunto Is Subjoyned the Comparative Anatomy of Stomachs and Guts*. London: W. Rawlins, 386 + 43 pp.

Grimes, R. 1990. Breaking the Glass Barrier: The Power of Display. *Journal of Ritual Studies* 4(2):239–62.

Gudeman, A. 1894. The Alexandrian Library and Museum. *Columbia Literary Monthly* 3(3):97–107.

Gundestrup, B. 1985. From the Royal *Kunstkammer* to the Modern Museums of Copenhagen. Pp. 128–35 in O. Impey and A. MacGregor (eds.), *The Origins of Museums: The Cabinet of Curiosities in Sixteenth- and Seventeenth-Century Europe*. Clarendon Press, Oxford, x + 431 pp.

Haberly, L. 1959. The American Museum from Baker to Barnum. *New-York Historical Society Quarterly* 43(3):273–87.

Hafstein, V. T. 2003. Bodies of Knowledge: Ole Worm and Collecting in Late Renaissance Scandinavia. *Ethnologia Europaea* 33(1):5–20.

Hagen, H. A. 1876. The History of the Origin and Development of Museums. *American Naturalist* 19(2):80–89.

Hamilton, H. C., and W. Falconer. 1903. *The Geography of Strabo: Literally Translated, with Notes*. 3 vols. George Bell and Sons, London, 515 pp. (vol. 1), 466 pp. (vol. 2), 422 pp. (vol. 3).

Haraway, D. 1984. Teddy Bear Patrimony: Taxidermy in the Garden of Eden, New York City, 1908–1936. *Social Text* 11:19–64.

Harkness, D. E. 2007. *The Jewel House: Elizabethan London and the Scientific Revolution*. Yale University Press, New Haven, xviii + 349 pp.

Harmand, S., J. E. Lewis, C. S. Feibel, C. J. Lepre, S. Prat, A. Lenoble, X. Boës, R. L. Quinn, M. Brenet, A. Arroyo, N. Taylor, S. Clément, G. Daver, J. P. Brugal, L. Leakey, R. A. Mortlock, J. D. Wright, S. Lokorodi, C. Kirwa, D. V. Kent, and H. Roche. 2015. 3.3-Million-Year-Old Stone Tools from Lomekwi 3, West Turkana, Kenya. *Nature* 521:310–15.

Harris, M. H. 1995. *Histories of Libraries in the Western World*. 4th ed. Scarecrow Press, Lanham, 311 pp.

Harris, N. 1999. The Divided House of the American Art Museum. *Daedalus* 128(3):33–56.

Harrison, M. 1956. Museums in Education. *UNESCO Education Abstracts* 8(2):3–10.

Hawass, Z., Y. Z. Gad, S. Ismail, R. Khairat, D. Fathalla, N. Hasan, A. Ahmed, H. Elleithy, M. Ball, F. Gaballah, S. Wasef, M. Fateen, H. Amer, P. Gostner, A. Selim, A. Zink, and C. M. Pusch. 2010. Ancestry and Pathology in King Tutankhamun's Family. *Journal of the American Medical Association* 303(7):638–47.

Hein, G. E. 2006. Progressive Education and Museum Education: Anna Billings Gallup and Louise Connolly. *Journal of Museum Education* 31(3):161–74.

———. 2012. *Progressive Museum Practice: John Dewey and Democracy*. Left Coast Press, Walnut Creek, 254 pp.

Henderson, C. 2013. *The Book of Barely Imagined Beings. A 21st Century Bestiary*. University of Chicago Press, Chicago, xix + 427 pp.

Heritage Preservation. 2005. *A Public Trust at Risk: The Heritage Health Index Report on the State of America's Collections*. Heritage Preservation, Washington, DC., 79 pp.

Higham, T., L. Basell, R. Jacobi, R. Wood, C. B. Ramsey, and N. J. Conard. 2012. Testing Models for the Beginnings of the Aurignacian and the Advent of Figurative Art and Music: The Radiocarbon Chronology of Geißenklösterle. *Journal of Human Evolution* 62(6):664–76.

Higham, T. K., Douka, R. Wood, C. B. Ramsey, F. Brock, L. Basell, M. Camps, A. Arrizabalaga, J. Baena, C. Barroso-Ruíz, C. Bergman, C. Boitard, P. Boscato, M. Caparrós, N. J. Conard, C. Draily, A. Froment, B. Galván, P. Gambassini, A. Garcia-Moreno, S. Grimaldi, P. Haesaerts, B. Holt, M. J. Iriarte-Chiapusso, A. Jelinek, J. F. Jordá Pardo, J. M. Maíllo-Fernández, A. Marom, J. Maroto, M. Menéndez, L. Metz, E. Morin, A. Moroni, F. Negrino, E. Panagopoulou, M. Peresani, S. Pirson, M. de la Rasilla, J. Riel-Salvatore, A. Ronchitelli, D. Santamaria, P. Semal, L. Slimak, J. Soler, N. Soler, A. Villaluenga, R. Pinhasi, and R. Jacobi. 2014. The Timing and Spatiotemporal Patterning of Neanderthal Disappearance. *Nature* 512 (7514):306–9.

Higonnet, A. 1994. Whither the Barnes? *Art in America* 82(3):62–ff.

Hitchcock, S. T., and J. L. Esposito (eds.). 2004. *Geography of Religion: Where God Lives, Where Pilgrims Walk*. National Geographic Society, Washington, DC, 416 pp.

Hodge, J. C. 1987. Museum Studies Training in Australia. *Museum* 39(4):249–51.

Holdengräber, P. 1987. "A Visible History of Art": The Forms and Preoccupations of the Early Museum. Pp. 107–17 in J. Yolton and L. E. Brown (eds.), *Studies in Eighteenth-Century Culture*. Colleagues Press, East Lansing, xi + 371 pp.

Hooper-Greenhill, E. 1989. The Museum in the Disciplinary Society. Pp. 61–72 in S. Pearce (ed.), *Museum Studies in Material Culture*. Leicester University Press, Leicester, 174 pp.

———. 1992. *Museums and the Shaping of Knowledge*. Routledge, London, ix + 232 pp.

Hornaday, W. T. 1905. *Taxidermy and Zoological Collecting: A Complete Handbook for the Amateur Taxidermist, Collector, Osteologist, Museum-Builder, Sportsman, and Traveller*. 8th ed. Charles Scribner's Sons, New York, xxi + 364 pp.

Hubert, F. 1985. Ecomuseums in France: Contradictions and Distortions. *Museum* 37(148):186–90.

Huisman, T. 2009. *The Finger of God: Anatomical Practice in 17th-Century Leiden*. Primavera Pers, Leiden, 215 pp.

Hunter, M. 1985. The Cabinet Institutionalized: The Royal Society's "Repository" and Its Background. Pp. 159–68 in O. Impey and A. MacGregor (eds.), *The Origins of Museums: The Cabinet of Curiosities in Sixteenth- and Seventeenth-Century Europe*. Clarendon Press, Oxford, x + 431 pp.

Hunter, R., and C. Morris. 1897. *Universal Dictionary of the English Language*. Vol. 3. Peter Fenelon Collier, New York, 1330 pp.

ICOM. 2015. Frequently Asked Questions. *International Council of Museums*. http://icom.museum/resources/frequently-asked-questions.

———. 2016. Development of the Museum Definition According to ICOM Statutes (2007–1946). *International Council of Museums*. http://archives.icom.museum/hist_def_eng.html.

Iliad. 2016. http://classics.mit.edu/Homer/iliad.html.

IMLS. 2014a. Distribution of Museums by Discipline, FY 2014. https://www.imls.gov/assets/1/AssetManager/MUDF_TypeDist_2014q3.pdf.

———. 2014b. Institute of Museum and Library Services Performance and Accountability Report for Fiscal Year 2014. https://www.imls.gov/assets/1/AssetManager/2014_PAR.pdf.

International Commission on Zoological Nomenclature. 1999. *International Code of Zoological Nomenclature*. 4th ed. International Trust for Zoological Nomenclature, London, xxiv + 306 pp.

IPI. 2012. *IPI's Guide to Sustainable Preservation Practices for Managing Storage Environments*. Image Permanence Institute, Rochester, 113 pp.

Jackson, D. J. 1992. How Lord Elgin First Won—and Lost—His Marbles. *Smithsonian Magazine* 23(9):135–46.

James, E. O. 1962. *Prehistoric Religion: A Study in Prehistoric Archaeology*. Barnes and Noble, New York, 300 pp.

Jenkins, T. 2005. The Censoring of Our Museums. *New Statesman*, 11 July, http://www.newstatesman.com/node/162442.

Jennings, G. 2008. Inbox: But Is It a Museum? *Museum* 87(3):87–89.

Jisheng, L. 1987. Museum Training in China. *Museum* 156:291–95.

Jones, K. B. 2008. The Transformation of the Digital Museum. Pp. 9–25 in P. F. Marty and K. B. Jones (eds.), *Museum Informatics: People, Information, and Technology in Museums*. Routledge, New York, xiii + 340 pp.

Jones, R. 1708. The Resurrection Rescued from the Soldier's Calumnies: In Two Sermons Preach'd at St. Mary's in Oxford, about the Year 1619. Pp. 476–98 in J. Dunton (ed.), *The Phenix: or, A Revival of Scarce and Valuable Pieces No Where to Be Found but in the Closets of the Curious*. Vol. 2. J. Morphew, London, xvi + 552 pp.

Jones, R. F. 1961. *Ancients and Moderns: A Study of the Rise of the Scientific Movement in Seventeenth-Century England*. Rev. ed. Washington University Press, St. Louis, xii + 354 pp. [1982 reprint by Dover, Mineola].

Jones-Garmil, K. (ed.). 1997. *The Wired Museum: Emerging Technology and Changing Paradigms*. American Association of Museums, Washington, DC, 250 pp.

Juvenal. 1974. *The Sixteen Satires: Translated with an Introduction and Notes by Peter Green*. Penguin Books, Middlesex, 320 pp.

Kawasaki, A. 2000. *The Changing Presentation of the American Indian*. National Museum of the American Indian in association with University of Washington Press, Seattle, 118 pp.

Keating, J., and L. Markey. 2011. Introduction: Captured Objects: Inventories of Early Modern Collections. *Journal of the History of Collections* 23(2):209–13.

Keegan, J. 1976. *The Face of Battle*. Military Heritage Press, New York, 355 pp.

Keene, S. 2004. The future of the museum in the digital age. *ICOM News* 57(3):4.

———. 2005. *Fragments of the World: Uses of Museum Collections*. Elsevier Butterworth-Heineman, Oxford, x + 198 pp.

Kendall, A. 1973. *Everyday Life of the Incas*. Dorset Press, New York, 216 pp.

Kenseth, J. 1991. The Age of the Marvelous: An Introduction. Pp. 25–59 in J. Kenseth (ed.), *The Age of the Marvelous*. Hood Museum of Art, Hanover, 485 pp.

Kiernan, M. (ed.). 1995. *The Essayes or Counsels, Civill and Morall*. Clarendon Press, Oxford, cxviii + 351 pp.

Kluge, A. 2005. Taxonomy in Theory and Practice, with Arguments for a New Phylogenetic System of Taxonomy. Pp. 7–14 in M. A. Donnelly, B. I. Crother, C. Guyer, M. H. Wake, and M. E. White (eds.), *Ecology and Evolution in the Tropics: A Herpetological Perspective*. University of Chicago Press, Chicago, xv + 675 pp.

Knell, S. 2005. Museum Studies: Past, Present, Future. *ICOM News* 58(4):3.

Kohler, R. E. 2006. *All Creatures: Naturalists, Collectors, and Biodiversity, 1850–1950.* Princeton University Press, Princeton, xxiii + 363 pp.

Kohlstedt, S. G. 1992. Entrepreneurs and Intellectuals: Natural History in Early American Museums. Pp. 23–29 in W. T. Alderson (ed.), *Mermaids, Mummies, and Mastodons: The Emergence of the American Museum.* American Association of Museums, Washington, DC, 104 pp.

Konigsburg, E. L. 1995. *From the Mixed-Up Files of Mrs. Basil E. Frankweiler.* Aladdin Paperbacks, New York, 162 pp. [Reprint of the original, published in 1967].

Krajewski, M. 2011. *Paper Machines: About Cards and Catalogs, 1548–1929.* MIT Press, Cambridge, 215 pp.

Kramer, S. N. 1944. *Sumerian Mythology: A Study of Spiritual and Literary Achievement in the Third Millennium B.C.* American Philosophical Society, Philadelphia, xiv + 125 pp.

Kurin, R. 1997. The Hope Diamond: Gem, Jewel, and Icon. Pp. 47–60 in A. Henderson and A. L. Kaeppler (eds.), *Exhibiting Dilemmas: Issues of Representation at the Smithsonian.* Smithsonian Institution Press, Washington, DC, vi + 285 pp.

Lai, Y. 2013. Images, Knowledge and Empire: Depicting Cassowaries in the Qing Court. *Transcultural Studies* (1):7–100. http://heiup.uni-heidelberg.de/journals/index.php/transcultural/article/view/10769.

Langbehn, J. 1890. *Rembrandt als Erzieher.* C. L. Hirshfield, Leipzig, 329 pp.

Langer, W. L. 1964. The Black Death. *Scientific American* 210(2):114–21.

Langone, J., B. Stutz, and A. Gianopoulos. 2006. *Theories for Everything: An Illustrated History of Science.* National Geographic Society, Washington, DC, 407 pp.

Larson, F. 2009. *An Infinity of Things: How Sir Henry Wellcome Collected the World.* Oxford University Press, Oxford, xi + 343 pp.

Latham, K., and J. E. Simmons. 2014. *Foundations of Museum Studies: Evolving Systems of Knowledge.* Libraries Unlimited, Santa Barbara, xvii + 155 pp.

Laurencich-Minelli, L. 1985. Museography and Ethnological Collections in Bologna during the Sixteenth and Seventeenth Centuries. Pp. 17–22 in O. Impey and A. MacGregor (eds.), *The Origins of Museums: The Cabinet of Curiosities in Sixteenth- and Seventeenth-Century Europe.* Clarendon Press, Oxford, x + 431 pp.

Lawell, S., and M. Mack. 2001. *The Norton Anthology of World Literature,* vol. A: *Beginnings to A.D. 100.* 2nd ed. W. W. Norton, New York, xxiii + 1199 + A17 pp.

Lee, P. Y. 1997. The Musaeum of Alexandria and the Formation of the Muséum in Eighteenth-Century France. *Art Bulletin* 79(3):385–412.

Levey, M. 1951. The First American Museum of Natural History. *Isis* 42(1):10–12.

Lewis, G. 1987. Museum, Profession and University: Museum Studies at Leicester. *Museum* 39(4):225–58.

———. 1992. Museums and Their Precursors: A Brief World Survey. Pp. 5–21 in J. M. A. Thompson (ed.), *Manual of Curatorship: A Guide to Museum Practice.* 2nd ed. Butterworth-Heinemann, Oxford, 756 pp.

———. 2003. Deaccessioning and the *ICOM Code of Ethics for Museums. ICOM News* 56(1):3.

———. 2014. The Universal Museum: A Special Case? *ICOM News* 57(1):3.

Lewis, G. D. 1985. Museums. *Encyclopedia Britannica,* 24:480–92.

References

Lindauer, M. A. 2010. Cabinets of Curiosities. Pp. 721–24 in M. J. Bates and M. N. Maack (eds.), *Encyclopedia of Library and Information Sciences*. 3rd ed. CRC Press, Boca Raton, 946 pp.

Lockyer, A. 2008. National Museums and Other Cultures in Modern Japan. Pp. 97–123 in D. J. Sherman (ed.), *Museums and Difference*. Indiana University Press, Bloomington, x + 386 pp.

López Rosas, W. A. 2013. *Museo en Tiempos de Conflicto: Memoria y Ciudadanía en Colombia*. Cuadernos de Museologia, Universidad Nacional de Colombia, Bogotá, 54 pp.

Lorente, J. P. 2012. *Manual de la Historia de la Museología*. Ediciones Trea, España, Gijón, 111 pp.

Lowenthal, D. 1998. *The Heritage Crusade and the Spoils of History*. Cambridge University Press, Cambridge, 338 pp.

Lutz, D. 2015. *The Brontë Cabinet: Three Lives in Nine Objects*. W. W. Norton, New York, xvii + 310 pp.

MacDonald, D. W. 2006. *The Encyclopedia of Mammals*. Facts on File, New York, xli + 936 pp.

Macdonald, S. J. 2003. Museums: National, Postnational and Transcultural Identities. *Museum and Society* 1(1):1–16.

MacGregor, A. (ed.). 1983. *Tradescant's Rarities: Essays on the Foundation of the Ashmolean Museum 1683 with a Catalogue of the Surviving Early Collections*. Clarendon Press, Oxford, xiii + 382 pp.

MacGregor, N. 2011. *A History of the World in 100 Objects*. Viking (Penguin Group), New York, xxvi + 707 pp.

MacLeod, R. (ed.). 2000. *The Library of Alexandria: Centre of Learning in the Ancient World*. I. B. Tauris, London, xii + 196 pp.

Mahmoodi, M. R., and S. F. Nezhad. 2015. Feasibility Study on the Establishment of Ecomuseums in Areas under the Influence of Qanats in Iran. *Journal of Applied Environmental Science* 5(11):72–80.

Malaro, M. C., and I. DeAngelis. 2012. *A Legal Primer on Managing Museum Collections*. 3rd ed. Smithsonian Books, Washington, DC, xx + 540 pp.

Maranda, L. 2009. Museology, Back to the Basics: Musealization. ICOM International Committee for Museology. *ICOFOM Study Series* 38:251–58.

Marean, C. W., M. Bar-Matthews, J. Bernatchez, E. Fisher, P. Goldberg, A. I. R. Herries, Z. Jacobs, A. Jerardino, P. Karkanas, T. Minichillo, P. J. Milssen, E. Thompson, I. Watts, and H. M. Williams. 2007. Early Human Use of Marine Resources and Pigment in South Africa during the Middle Pleistocene. *Nature* 449: 905–8.

Marinetti, F. T. 1909. The Foundation and Manifesto of Futurism. *Gazzetta dell'Emilia* (Bologna), 5 February; and *Le Figaro* (Paris), 20 February.

Marketos, S. G., and G. J. Androustos. 2009. The Healing Art in the *Iliad*. Pp. 275–81 in S. A. Paipetis (ed.), *Science and Technology in Homeric Epics*. Springer, New York, 536 pp.

Maroević, I. 1998. *Introduction to Museology: The European Approach*. C. Müller-Straten, Munich, 358 pp.

Marty, P. F. 2008a. An Introduction to Museum Informatics. Pp. 1–8 in P. F. Marty and K. B. Jones (eds.), *Museum Informatics: People, Information, and Technology in Museums*. Routledge, New York, xiii + 340 pp.

———. 2008b. Informational Representation. Pp. 29–34 in P. F. Marty and K. B. Jones (eds.), *Museum Informatics: People, Information, and Technology in Museums*. Routledge, New York, xiii + 340 pp.

Marvin, U. B. 1992. The Meteorite of Ensisheim: 1492–1992. *Meteoritics* 27:28–72.

Mauger, J. E., and J. Bowechop. 2006. Tribal Collections Management at the Makah Cultural and Research Center. Pp. 57–62 in K. C. Cooper and N. I. Sandoval (eds.), *Living Homes for Cultural Expression: North American Native Perspectives on Creating Community Museums*. National Museum of the American Indian, Washington, DC, 119 pp.

Mauriès, P. 2002. *Cabinets of Curiosities*. Thames and Hudson, London, 256 pp.

Mayor, A. 2011. *The First Fossil Hunters: Dinosaurs, Mammoths, and Myth in Greek and Roman Times*. Princeton University Press, Princeton, 400 pp.

Mayr, E. 1969. *Principles of Systematic Zoology*. McGraw-Hill, New York, 428 pp.

———. 1982. *The Growth of Biological Thought: Diversity, Evolution, and Inheritance*. Belknap Press, Cambridge, 974 pp.

McCarthy, C. 2011. *Museums and the M ori: Heritage Professionals, Indigenous Collections, Current Practices*. Left Coast Press, Walnut Creek, xvii + 315 pp.

McCarthy, C., and J. Cobley. 2009. Museums and Museum Studies in New Zealand: A Survey of Historical Developments. *History Compass* 7:2–19.

McClellan, A. 1993. The Museum and Its Public in Eighteenth-Century France. Pp. 61–80 in P. Bjurström (ed.), *The Genesis of the Art Museum in the 18th Century*. Nationalmuseum, Stockholm, 130 pp.

McMillan, B. C. (ed.). 2002. *Captive Passage: The Transatlantic Slave Trade and the Making of the Americas*. Smithsonian Institution Press, Washington, DC, 208 pp.

McNamara, K. J. 2010. *The Star-Crossed Stone: The Secret Life, Myths, and History of a Fascinating Fossil*. University of Chicago Press, Chicago, 280 pp.

Meadow, M. A. 2013. Introduction. Pp. 1–41 in M. A. Meadow and B. Robertson, *The First Treatise on Museums: Samuel Quiccheberg's Inscriptiones 1565*. Getty Research Institute, Los Angeles, xiii + 145 pp.

Meadow, M. A., and B. Robertson (trans.). 2013. *The First Treatise on Museums: Samuel Quiccheberg's Inscriptiones 1565*. Getty Research Institute, Los Angeles, xiii + 145 pp.

Medals. 1900. *Journal of the Society of Arts* 48:589.

Meisler, S. 1993. Say What They May, the Feisty Doctor Had an Artful Eye. *Smithsonian Magazine* 24(2):96–109.

Melton, J. V. H. 2001. *The Rise of the Public in Enlightenment Europe*. Cambridge University Press, Cambridge, xiv + 284 pp.

Melville, R. 1995. *Towards Stability in the Names of Animals: A History of the International Commission on Zoological Nomenclature 1895–1995*. International Commission on Zoological Nomenclature, London, xi + 92 pp.

Merrill, L. L. 1989. *The Romance of Victorian Natural History*. Oxford University Press, New York, x + 288 pp.

Mihesuah, D. A. (ed.). 2000. *Repatriation Reader: Who Owns American Indian Remains?* University of Nebraska Press, Lincoln, viii + 335pp.

Miller, L. B. 1979. The Peale Family: A Lively Mixture of Art and Science. *Smithsonian* 10(1):66–77.

Milner, G. R. 2004. *The Moundbuilders: Ancient Peoples of Eastern North America.* Thames and Hudson, London, 224 pp.

Montanari, E. 2015. Ecomuseums and Contemporary Multi-Cultural Communities: Assessing Problems and Potentialities through the Experience of the Écomusée du Val de Bièvre, Fresnes. *Museum and Society* 13(3):375–90.

Morales-Moreno, L. G. 1994. History and Patriotism in the National Museum of Mexico. Pp. 171–91 in F. E. S. Kaplan (ed.), *Museums and the Making of "Ourselves": The Role of Objects in National Identity.* Leicester University Press, London, xi + 430 pp.

Moser, S. 2006. *Wondrous Curiosities: Ancient Egypt at the British Museum.* University of Chicago Press, Chicago, xxi + 328 pp.

Muensterberger, W. 1994. *Collecting: An Unruly Passion: Psychological Perspectives.* Harcourt Brace, San Diego, xiii + 295 pp.

Muñoz Viñas, S. 2005. *Contemporary Theory of Conservation.* Elsevier, Amsterdam, xiii + 239 pp.

Murphy, B. L. 2005. Establishing Connections, Releasing Capacities: A Reflection on the Resurgence of Indigenous Arts in Australia. Pp 53–67 in M. Hirsch and A. Pickworth (eds.), *The Native Universe and Museums in the Twenty-First Century: The Significance of the National Museum of the American Indian.* National Museum of the American Indian, Washington, DC, 144 pp.

Murray, D. 1904. *Museums, Their History and Their Use: With a Bibliography and List of Museums in the United Kingdom.* 2 vols. James MacLehose and Sons, Glasgow. [2000 reprint of the 1904 edition by Pober, Staten Island].

Murray, S. A. P. 2009. *The Library: An Illustrated History.* Skyhorse, New York, x + 310 pp.

Müsch, I. 2001. Albertus Seba's Collection of Natural Specimens and Its Pictorial Inventory. Pp. 6–24 in A. Seba (ed.), *Cabinet of Natural Curiosities: The Complete Plates in Colour 1734–1765.* Taschen, Köln, 587 pp.

Nabais, A. 1985. The Development of Ecomuseums in Portugal. *Museum* 37(148):211–16.

Nagel, S. 2005. *Mistress of the Elgin Marbles: A Biography of Mary Nisbet, Countess of Elgin.* William Morrow Paperbacks, New York, 336 pp.

Nasrallah, N. 2011. *Dates: A Global History.* Reaktion Books, London, 136 pp.

Neverov, O. 1985. "His Majesty's Cabinet" and Peter I's Kunstkammer. Pp. 54–61 in O. Impey and A. MacGregor (eds.), *The Origins of Museums: The Cabinet of Curiosities in Sixteenth- and Seventeenth-Century Europe.* Clarendon Press, Oxford, x + 431 pp.

NIC. 1990–91. *Training for Collections Care and Maintenance: A Suggested Curriculum.* Vol. 1: *Archaeology and Ethnology*, v + 103 pp.; vol. 2: *History*, v + 92 pp.; vol. 3: *Natural Sciences*, v + 94 pp.; vol. 4: *Fine Arts*, v + 70 pp. National Institute for the Conservation of Cultural Property, Washington, DC.

Nicolson, D. H. 1991. A History of Botanical Nomenclature. *Annals of the Missouri Botanical Garden* 78(1):33–56.

Nieto Olarte, M. 2013. *Las Máquinas del Imperio y el Reino de Dios: Reflexiones Sobre Ciencia, Tecnología y Religión en el Mundo Atlántico del Siglo XVI*. Ediciones Uniandes, Bogotá, xviii + 306 pp.

Nigosian, S. A. 2004. *Islam: Its History, Teaching and Practices*. Indiana University Press, Bloomington, 200 pp.

Olmi, G. 1985. Science-Honor-Metaphor: Italian Cabinets of the Sixteenth and Seventeenth Centuries. Pp. 5–16 in O. Impey and A. MacGregor (eds.), *The Origins of Museums: The Cabinet of Curiosities in Sixteenth- and Seventeenth-Century Europe*. Clarendon Press, Oxford, x + 431 pp.

Orosz, J. J. 1985. Pierre Eugène du Simitière: Museum Pioneer in America. *Museum Studies Journal* 1(5):8–18.

———. 1990. *Curators and Culture: The Museum Movement in America, 1740–1870*. University of Alabama Press, Tuscaloosa, xii + 304 pp.

Pamuk, O. 2008. *The Museum of Innocence*. Alfred A. Knopf, New York, xiii + 530 pp.

Paris, S. G. 2002. Children Learning with Objects in Informal Learning Environments. Pp. 37–54 in S. G. Paris (ed.), *Perspectives on Object-Centered Learning in Museums*. Lawrence Erlbaum Associates, Mahwah, xxii + 383 pp.

Parrinder, G. 1971. *World Religions: From Ancient History to the Present*. Facts on File, New York, 528 pp.

Partington, J. R. 1957. *A Short History of Chemistry*. Macmillan, London, xiii + 428 pp. [1989 reprint by Dover, Mineola].

Pavord, A. 2005. *The Naming of Names: The Search for Order in the World of Plants*. Bloomsbury, New York, 471 pp.

Payne, A. 1990. *Medieval Beasts*. New Amsterdam Books, New York, 96 pp.

Pearce, S. 2010. The Collecting Process and the Founding of Museums in the Sixteenth, Seventeenth, and Eighteenth Centuries. Pp. 12–32 in S. Pettersson, M. Hagedorn-Saupe, T. Jyrkkiö, and A. Weij (eds.), *Encouraging Collections Mobility: A Way Forward for Museums in Europe*. Finnish National Gallery, Helsinki, 299 pp.

Pearce, S. M. 1992. *Museums, Objects, and Collections: A Cultural Study*. Smithsonian Institution Press, Washington, DC, xii + 300 pp.

———. 1994. The Urge to Collect. Pp. 157–59 in S. M. Pearce (ed.), *Interpreting Objects and Collections*. Routledge, London, 360 pp.

———. 1995. *On Collecting: An investigation into Collecting in the European Tradition*. Routledge, London, 440 pp.

Peña, C. 2012. Viaje al Fondo de la Biblioteca de Pinochet. Pp. 334–45 in D. Jaramillo Agudelo (ed.), *Antología de Crónica Latinoamericana Actual*. Alfaguara, Bogotá, 650 pp.

Petiver, J. 1695–1703. *Musei Petiveriani*. Sam. Smith and Chr. Bateman, London, 93 pp.

Petrie, W. F. 1900. A National Repository for Science and Art. *Royal Society of Arts Journal* 48:525–36.

Petrovka-Campbell, G. 2010. Museum Representations in the Process of "Culturing" the Public in Bulgaria. *Museum History Journal* 3(2):171–88.

Pitman, B. 1999. Uses, Museums, and Memories. *Daedalus* 128(3):1–31.

Plenderleith, H., and P. Philippot. 1960. Climatology and Conservation in Museums. *Museum* 13(4):242–89.

Plotz, J. 2008. *Portable Property: Victorian Culture on the Move*. Princeton University Press, Princeton, xvii + 268 pp.

Podgorny, I. 2012. *Un Repositorio Nacional para la Ciencia y el Arte: Traducción, Notas y Palabras Preliniares*. Cuadernos de Museología, Universidad Nacional de Colombia, Bogotá, 53 pp.

Poliquin, R. 2012. *The Breathless Zoo: Taxidermy and the Cultures of Longing*. Pennsylvania State University Press, University Park, ix + 259 pp.

Pomian, K. 1990. *Collectors and Curiosities: Paris and Venice, 1500–1800*. Polity Press, Oxford, 348 pp.

Potter, J. 2006. *Strange Blooms: The Curious Lives and Adventures of the John Tradescants*. Atlantic Books, London, xxix + 404 pp.

Pridmore, J. 1997. *Museum of Science and Industry, Chicago*. Harry Abrams, New York, 160 pp.

Prioreschi, P. 1991. Possible Reasons for Neolithic Skull Trephining. *Perspectives in Biology and Medicine* 34(2):296–303.

Puchner, M., S. C. Akbari, W. Denecke, V. Dharwadker, B. Fuchs, C. Levine, P. Lewis, and E. Wilson (eds). 2012. *The Norton Anthology of World Literature*. 3rd ed. Vols. A–F. W. W. Norton, New York.

Pulsap, S. (ed.). 2004. *100 Museums in Bangkok and Its Vicinity*. Plan Readers, Bangkok, 160 pp.

Punja, S. 1991. *Museums of India*. Odyssey Guides, Hong Kong, 307 pp.

Purcell, R. W., and S. J. Gould. 1986. *Illuminations: A Bestiary*. W. W. Norton, New York, 120 pp.

Pyenson, L., and S. Sheets-Pyenson. 1999. *Servants of Nature: A History of Scientific Institutions, Enterprises, and Sensibilities*. W. W. Norton, New York, xiv + 496 pp.

Querrien, M. 1985. Taking the Measure of the Phenomenon. *Museum* 37(148): 198–99.

Quigley, S. 2010. Computerized Systems. Pp. 161–83 in R. A. Buck and J. A. Gilmore (eds.), *Museum Registration Methods*. 5th ed. American Association of Museums Press, Washington, DC, xi + 516 pp.

Quinn, S. C. 2006. *Windows on Nature: The Great Habitat Dioramas of the American Museum of Natural History*. Abrams, New York, 179 pp.

Rabb, G. B. 2004. The Evolution of Zoos from Menageries to Centers of Conservation and Caring. *Curator* 47(3):237–46.

Raby, J. 1985. Exotica from Islam. Pp. 251–58 in O. Impey and A. MacGregor (eds.), *The Origins of Museums: The Cabinet of Curiosities in Sixteenth- and Seventeenth-Century Europe*. Clarendon Press, Oxford, x + 431 pp.

Rader, K. A., and V. E. M. Cain. 2008. From Natural History to Science: Display and the Transformation of American Museums of Science and Nature. *Museum and Society* 6(2):152–71.

———. 2014. *Life on Display: Revolutionizing U.S. Museums of Science and Natural History in the Twentieth Century*. University of Chicago Press, Chicago, xiv + 467 pp.

Radovčić, D., A. O. Sršen, J. Radovčić, and D. W. Frayer. 2015. Evidence for Neandertal Jewelry: Modified White-Tailed Eagle Claws at Krapina. *PLoS ONE* 19(3):e0119802.

Ransome, H. M. 1937. *The Sacred Bee in Ancient Times and Folklore.* George Allen and Unwin, London, 320 pp.

Ray, J. 1693. *Travels through the Low-Countries, Germany, Italy and France, with Curious Observations, Natural, Topographical, Moral, Physiological, &c. Also, A Catalogue of Plants, Found Spontaneously Growing in Those Parts, and Their Virtues: To Which Is Added, An Account of the Travels of Francis Willughby, Esq.; Through Great Part of Spain.* 2nd ed. vol. 1. Printed for J. Walthoe, London, iv + 428 pp.

Redman, S. J. 2005. "What Self-Respecting Museum Is without One?" The Story of Collecting the Old World at the Science Museum of Minnesota 1914–1988. *Collections: A Journal of Museum and Archives Professionals* 1(4):309–28.

Riding, A. 2001. Stranger Than Chatwin's Fiction. *New York Times,* 17 October. http://www.nytimes.com/2001/10/17/arts/arts-abroad-stranger-than-chatwin-s-fiction.html.

Ridley, G. 2004. *Clara's Grand Tour: Travels with a Rhinoceros in Eighteenth-Century Europe.* Atlantic Monthly Press, New York, xvii + 222 pp.

Rigby, D., and E. Rigby. 1944. *Lock, Stock and Barrel: The Story of Collecting.* J. B. Lippincott, Philadelphia, xix + 570 pp.

Rivard, R. 1985. Ecomuseums in Quebec. *Museum* 37(148):202–5.

Rivière, G. H. 1985. The Ecomuseum: An Evolutive Definition. *Museum* 37(148):182–83.

Roberts, J. M., and O. A. Westad. 2013. *The Penguin History of the World.* 6th ed. Penguin Books, London, xiv + 1260 pp.

Roberts, L. C. 1997. *From Knowledge to Narrative: Educators and the Changing Museum.* Smithsonian Institution Press, Washington, DC, ix + 205 pp.

Robertson, B. 2013. Preface: Wonderful Museums and Quiccheberg's *Inscriptiones.* Pp. vi–xi in M. A. Meadow and B. Robertson (trans.), *The First Treatise on Museums: Samuel Quiccheberg's Inscriptiones 1565.* Getty Research Institute, Los Angeles, xiii + 145 pp.

Robinson, E. S. 1928. *The Behavior of the Museum Visitor.* Publications of the American Association of Museums, no. 5, 71 pp.

Roebroeks, W., M. J. Sier, T. K. Nielsen, D. De Loecker, J. M. Parés, C. E. S. Arps, and H. J. Mücher. 2012. Use of Red Ochre by Early Neanderthals. *Proceedings of the National Academy of Sciences USA* 109(6):1889–94.

Rogers, S. 1932. *Crusoes and Castaways: True Stories of Survival and Solitude.* George G. Harrap, London, 255 pp. [2011 reprint by Dover, Mineola].

Rose, B. 1975. *American Art since 1900.* Rev. ed. Praeger, New York, 320 pp.

Rose, C. L., and C. A. Hawks. 1995. A Preventive Conservation Approach to the Storage of Collections. Pp. 1–20 in C. L. Rose, C. A. Hawks, and H. H. Genoways (eds.), *Storage of Natural History Collections: A Preventive Conservation Approach.* Society for the Preservation of Natural History Collections, x + 448 pp.

Roser, M. 2015. Literacy. *OurWorldInData.org.* http://ourworldindata.org/data/education-knowledge/literacy.

Ross, M. 2004. Interpreting the New Museology. *Museum and Society* 2(2):84–103.

Rowe, S. 2002. The Role of Objects in Active, Distributed Meaning-Making. Pp. 19–35 in S. G. Paris (ed.), *Perspectives on Object-Centered Learning in Museums*. Lawrence Erlbaum Associates, Mahwah, xxii + 383 pp.

Rubin, S. 1997. *Offbeat Museums: A Guided Tour of America's Weirdest and Wackiest Museums*. Black Dog and Leventhal, New York, 237 pp.

Ruskin, J. 1849. *The Seven Lamps of Architecture*. John Wiley, New York, viii + 186 pp.

———. 1851–1853. *The Stones of Venice*. 3 vols. Vol. 1: *The Foundations*, 1851, 431 pp.; vol. 2: *The Sea-Stories*, 1853, 396 pp.; vol. 3: *The Fall*, 1853, 393 pp. Smith, Elder, London.

Russell, T. 1994. The Enquiring Visitor: Usable Learning Theory for Museum Contexts. *Journal of Education in Museums* 15:19–21.

Russick, J. 2010. Making History Interactive. Pp. 219–39 in D. L. McRainey and J. Russick (eds.), 2010. *Connecting Kids to History with Museum Exhibitions*. Left Coast Press, Walnut Creek, 333 pp.

Salkowitz, R. 2014. The Future of Reading: 10 Trends for 2014 and Beyond. *Publisher's Weekly*, 20 January, http://www.publishersweekly.com/pw/by-topic/industry-news/publisher-news/article/60700-the-future-of-reading-10-trends-for-2014-and-beyond.html.

Sandahl, J. 2005. Living Entities. Pp. 27–39 in M. Hirsch and A. Pickworth (eds.), *The Native Universe and Museums in the Twenty-First Century: The Significance of the National Museum of the American Indian*. National Museum of the American Indian, Washington, DC, 144 pp.

Sandars, N. K. 1972. *The Epic of Gilgamesh: An English Version with an Introduction*. Rev. ed., with new material. Penguin Books, Harmondsworth, 128 pp.

Sandoval, N. 2006. Foreword. Pp. 6–7 in K. C. Cooper and N. I. Sandoval (eds.), *Living Homes for Cultural Expression: North American Native Perspectives on Creating Community Museums*. National Museum of the American Indian, Washington, DC, 119 pp.

Sandys, G. 1621. *A Relation of a Journey begun An. Dom. 1610: Foure Bookes: Containing a Description of the Turkish Empire, of Aegypt, of the Holy Land, of the Remote Parts of Italy, and Ilands Adjoying*. W. Barrett, London, 240 pp.

Sarasan, L. 1981. Why Museum Computer Projects Fail. *Museum News* 59(4):41–49.

Sarton, G. 1970a. *Ancient Science through the Golden Age of Greece*. W. W. Norton, New York, xxvi + 646 pp. [1993 reprint by Dover, Mineola].

———. 1970b. *Hellenistic Science and Culture in the Last Three Centuries B.C.* W. W. Norton, xxvi + 554 pp. [1993 reprint by Dover, Mineola].

Scalplock, I. J. 2006. Tribal Museums and the Sikiska Experience. Pp. 65–69 in K. C. Cooper and N. I. Sandoval (eds.), *Living Homes for Cultural Expression: North American Native Perspectives on Creating Community Museums*. National Museum of the American Indian, Washington, DC, 119 pp.

Scheiches, E. 1985. The Collection of Archduke Ferdinand II at Schloss Ambras: Its Purpose, Composition and Evolution. Pp. 29–38 in O. Impey and A. MacGregor (eds.), *The Origins of Museums: The Cabinet of Curiosities in Sixteenth- and Seventeenth-Century Europe*. Clarendon Press, Oxford, x + 431 pp.

Schmilchuk, G. 1995. Historia, Antropología y Arte: Notas Sobre la Formación de los Museos Nacionales en México. *RUNA: Archivo para las Ciencias del Hombre* 22:21–38.

Schmitz, H., N. Uddenberg, and P. Östensson. 2007. *A Passion for Systems: Linnaeus and the Dream of Order in Nature*. Natur och Kultur, Stockholm, 256 pp.

Schulz, E. 1994. Notes on the History of Collecting and of Museums. Pp. 175–87 in S. M. Pearce (ed.), *Interpreting Objects and Collections*. Routledge, London, 360 pp.

Schumacher, G. H. 2007. *Theatrum anatomicum* in History and Today. *International Journal of Morphology* 25(1):15–32.

Schuster, P. K. 2004. The Treasures of World Culture in Public Museums. *ICOM News* 57(1):4–5.

Schuyl, F. 1723. *A Catalogue of All the Cheifest Rarities in the Theater and Publick Anatomie-Hall of the University of Leyden*. Diewertje vander Boxe, Leyden, 16 pp.

Schwarzer, M. 2006. *Riches, Rivals, and Radicals: 100 Years of Museums in America*. American Association of Museums, Washington, DC, x + 263 pp.

Schwarzer, M., and M. J. Sutton. 2009. The Diorama Dilemma: A Literature Review and Analysis. http://museumca.org/files/gallery-documentation/Diorama-Lit-Review_Schwarzer_Sutton.pdf.

Schweibenz, W. 2004. The Development of Virtual Museums. *ICOM News* 57(3):3.

Segger, M. 1987. Canada: Great Distances Require Distance Learning. *Museum* 156:244–48.

Selznick, B. 2011. *Wonderstruck: A Novel in Words and Pictures*. Scholastic Press, New York, 608 pp.

Senter, P., L. C. Hill, and B. J. Moton. 2013. Solution to a 330-Year-Old Zoological Mystery: The Case of Aldrovandi's Dragon. *Annals of Science* 70(4):531–37.

Shannon, J. 1974. The Icing Is Good but the Cake Is Rotten. *Museum News* 52(5):29–34.

Sheets-Pyenson, S. 1988. *Cathedrals of Science: The Development of Colonial Natural History Museums during the Late Nineteenth Century*. McGill-Queens University Press, Kingston, xii + 144 pp.

Siegel, J. (ed.). 2008. *The Emergence of the Modern Museum: An Anthology of Nineteenth-Century Sources*. Oxford University Press, New York, xix + 381 pp.

Simmons, J. E. 2006. Museum Studies Programs in North America. Pp. 113–28 in S. L. Williams and C. A. Hawks (eds.), *Museum Studies: Perspectives and Innovations*. Society for the Preservation of Natural History Collections, Washington, DC, 281 pp.

———. 2013. Application of Preventive Conservation to Solve the Coming Crisis in Collections Management. *Collection Forum* 20(1–2):89–101.

———. 2014. *Fluid Preservation: A Comprehensive Reference*. Rowman and Littlefield, Lanham, 347 pp.

———. 2015. Collections Management: History, Theory, and Practice. Pp. 221–47 in C. McCarthy (ed.), *The International Handbook of Museum Studies*. Vol. 4. John Wiley and Sons, London, lii + 652 pp.

Simmons, J. E., and Y. Muñoz-Saba. 2003. The Theoretical Bases of Collections Management. *Collection Forum* 18(1–2):38–49.

Simmons, J. E., and J. Snider. 2012. Observation and Distillation: Preservation, Depiction, and the Perception of Nature. *Bibliotheca Herpetologica* 9(1–2):115–34.

Simons, J. 2008. *Rossetti's Wombat: Pre-Raphaelites and Australian Animals in Victorian London*. Middlesex University Press, London, 142 pp.

Simpson, M. G. 2001. *Making Representations: Museums in the Post-Colonial Era.* Rev. ed. Routledge, London, xi + 336 pp.

Singleton, L. R. 2008. For Revolutionaries and Rum: A Preliminary Study on Museum History and Structure in Cuba. *Museum History Journal* 1(2):235–52.

Smith, P. H. 2008. Collecting Nature and Art: Artisans and Knowledge in the *Kunstkammer.* Pp. 115–32 in B. Hannawalt and L. Kiser (eds.), *Engaging with Nature: Essays on the Natural World and Early Modern Europe.* University of Notre Dame Press, Notre Dame, 248 pp.

Smith, W., W. Wayte, and G. E. Marindin (eds). 1890. *A Dictionary of Greek and Roman Antiquities.* John Murray, London, 1090 pp.

Spiess, P. D. 1996. Museum Studies: Are They Doing Their Job? *Museum News* 75(6):32–40.

Spock, D. 2012. Imagination: A Child's Gateway to Engagement with the Past. Pp. 117–35 in D. L. McRainey and J. Russick (eds.), 2010. *Connecting Kids to History with Museum Exhibitions.* Left Coast Press, Walnut Creek, 333 pp.

Sprague de Camp, L., and W. Ley. 1952. *Lands Beyond.* Rinehart New York, 329 pp.

Stearns, R. P. 1953. James Petiver: Promoter of Natural Science, c. 1663–1718. *Proceedings of the American Antiquarian Society* 62:243–365.

Stenhouse, W. 2014. Roman Antiquities and the Emergence of Renaissance Civic Collections. *Journal of the History of Collections* 26(2):131–44.

Stimpson, D. 1948. *Scientists and Amateurs: A History of the Royal Society.* Henry Schuman, New York, xiii + 270 pp.

Stone, B. (trans.). 1964. *Sir Gawain and the Green Knight.* Penguin Books, Baltimore, 144 pp.

Stránsky, Z. Z. 1970. Pojam Muzeologije. *Muzeologija* 8:2–9.

Su, D. 2000. Museology and Cultural Heritage in China. Museology. *ICOM Study Series* 8:13–14.

———. 2005. Ecomuseums in China. *ICOM News* 58(3):7.

Summerhorn, J. 1984. *A New Description of Sir John Soane's Museum.* 6th ed. Trustees of Sir John Soane's Museum, London, 83 pp.

Swallow, D. A. 1991. Preface. Pp.12–13 in S. Punja, *Museums of India.* Odyssey Guides, Hong Kong, 307 pp.

Swann, M. 2001. *Curiosities and Texts: The Culture of Collecting in Early Modern England.* University of Pennsylvania Press, Philadelphia, 280 pp.

Teruggi, M. E. 1973. Museums and Scientific and Technological Development. *UNESCO Museum* 25(3):150–56.

Thomas, D. H. 2000. *Skull Wars: Kennewick Man, Archaeology, and the Battle for Native American Identity.* Basic Books, New York City, 368 pp.

Thomson, G. 1986. *The Museum Environment.* 2nd ed. Butterworths, London, 293 pp.

Thwaite, A. 2002. *Glimpses of the Wonderful: The Life of Philip Henry Gosse 1810–1888.* Faber and Faber, London, xx + 387 pp.

Tishman, S., A. McKinney, and C. Straughn. 2007. *Study Center Learning: An Investigation of the Educational Power and Potential of the Harvard University Art Museums Study Centers.* Harvard University Art Museums, Cambridge, 104 pp.

Tradescant, J. 1656. *Musaeum Tradescantianum; Or, A Collection of Rarities: Preserved at South-Lambeth neer London by John Tradescant.* John Grismond, London, 177 pp.

Trenc, M. 1993. *The Night at the Museum*. Barron's Educational Series, Hauppauge, 32 pp.

Tribby, J. 1992. Body/Building: Living the Museum Life in Early Modern Europe. *Rhetorica: A Journal of the History of Rhetoric* 10(2):139–63.

True, W. P. 1934. *The Smithsonian Institution*. Smithsonian Institution Series, Washington, DC, 330 pp.

Twain, M. 1869. *The Innocents Abroad; or, The New Pilgrim's Progress*. American Publishing Company, Hartford, 651 pp. [2003 reprint by Dover, Mineola].

Tyerman, C. 2007. *The Crusades*. Sterling, New York, ix + 212 pp.

Ullberg, A, P. Ullberg, A. H. Grogg, and R. Lind. 2002. A Short History of the Museum. Pp. 425–31 in R. C. Lind, R. M. Jarvis, and M. E. Phelan (eds.), *Art and Museum Law: Cases and Materials*. Carolina Academic Press, Durham, xxiv + 718 pp.

Ulrich, L. T., I. Gaskell, S. J. Schechner, and S. A. Carter. 2015. *Tangible Things: Making History through Objects*. Oxford University Press, Oxford, xvii + 259 pp.

Vance, D. 1986. The Museum Computer Network in Context. Pp. 37–47 in R. B. Light, D. A. Roberts, and J. D. Stewart (eds.), *Museum Documentation Systems: Developments and Applications*. Butterworths, London, 346 pp.

van der Veen, S. 2001. *Hortus botanicus Leiden*. Universiteit Leiden, Leiden, 105 pp.

Vanhaereny, M., F. d'Errico, C. Stringer, S. L. James, J. A. Todd, and H. K. Mienis. 2006. Middle Paleolithic Shell Beads in Israel and Algeria. *Science* 312(5781):1785–88.

van Kraayenoord, C. E., and S. G. Paris. 2002. Reading Objects. Pp. 215–34 in S. G. Paris (ed.), *Perspectives on Object-Centered Learning in Museums*. Lawrence Erlbaum Associates, Mahwah, xxii + 383 pp.

van Lawick-Goodall, J. 1971. Tool-Using in Primates and Other Vertebrates. *Advances in the Study of Behavior* 3:195–249.

van Mensch, P. 2000. Museology as a Profession. *ICOM International Committee for Museology Study Series* 8: 20–21.

———. 2011. The Musealisation of Knut: Dilemmas in the Relationship between Zoos and Museums. *COMCOL Newsletter* 13:4–7.

Vergo, P. (ed.). 1989. *The New Museology*. Reaktion Books, London, viii + 238 pp.

Viollet-le-Duc, E. E. 1856. *Dictionnaire raisonné de l'architecture française du XIe au XVIe siècle*. 10 vols. B. Bance, Paris.

Voth, G. L. 2007. *The History of World Literature*. Pt. 1: *Teaching Company*. http://www.alysion.org/HistoryWorldLiterature.pdf.

Waibal, G., and R. Erway. 2009. Think Global, Act Local: Libraries, Archive and Museum Collaborations. *Museum Management and Curatorship* 24(4):323–36.

Walker, C. 2015. The First Artists. *National Geographic* 227(1):32–57.

Wallace, I. 1959. *The Fabulous Showman: The Life and Times of P. T. Barnum*. Alfred A. Knopf, New York, viii + 279 pp.

Washburn, W. E. 1984. Collecting Information, Not Objects. *Museum News* 62:15.

Watson, B. 2002. Rising Sun. *Smithsonian* 33(1):78–88.

Webster, N. 1841. *An American Dictionary of the English Language: Exhibiting the Origin, Orthography, Pronunciation, and Definitions of Words*. Rev. ed. White and Sheffield, New York, xxiii + 1079 pp.

Webster, N., W. G. Webster, and W. A. Wheeler. 1872. *A Dictionary of the English Language, Explanatory, Pronouncing, Etymological, and Synonymous*. Rev. ed. Ivison, Blakeman, Taylor, New York, xxxi + 1079 pp.

Welsh, P. H. 2013. Preparing a New Generation: Thoughts on Contemporary Museum Studies Training. *Museum Management and Curatorship* 28(5):436–54.

Welty, J. C. 1979. *The Life of Birds*. 2nd ed. Saunders College, Philadelphia, xv + 623 pp.

Werner, P. 2005. *Museum, Inc.: Inside the Global Art World*. Prickly Paradigm Press, Chicago, 76 pp.

Wershler-Henry, D. 2005. *The Iron Whim: A Fragmented History of Typewriting*. McClelland and Stewart, Toronto, 331 pp.

Weschler, L. 1995. *Mr. Wilson's Cabinet of Wonder*. Pantheon Books, New York, 164 pp.

Whitehead, P. J. P. 1970. Museums in the History of Zoology. *Museums Journal* 70(2):50–57.

———. 1971. Museums in the History of Zoology. *Museums Journal* 70(4):155–60.

Whittaker, J. C. 1994. *Flintknapping: Making and Understanding Stone Tools*. University of Texas Press, Austin, 341 pp.

Wicke, J. 1992. Vampiric Typewriting: *Dracula* and Its Media. *ELH: English Literary History* 59(2):467–93.

Williams, D. W. 1987. A Brief History of Museum Computerization. *Museum Studies Journal* 3(1):58–65.

Willmann, R., and J. Rust. 2001. The Zoology and Botany in Albertus Seba's Thesaurus. Pp. 27–39 in A. Seba (ed.), *Cabinet of Natural Curiosities: The Complete Plates in Colour 1734–1765*. Taschen, Köln, 587 pp.

Wittlin, A. S. 1970. *Museums: In Search of a Usable Future*. MIT Press, Cambridge, Massachusetts, xiii + 300 pp.

Witz, L. 2006. Transforming Museums on Postapartheid Tourist Routes. Pp. 107–34 in I. Karp, C. A. Kratz, L. Szwaja, and T. Ybarra-Frausto (eds.), *Museum Frictions: Public Cultures/Global Transformations*. Duke University Press, Durham, xxii + 602 pp.

Wonders, K. 1993. Habitat Dioramas: Illusions of Wilderness in Museums of Natural History. *Acta Universitatis Upsaliensis Figura Nova Series* 15:1–262.

Wood, E., and K. F. Latham. 2009. Object Knowledge: Researching Objects in the Museum Experience. *Reconstruction* 9(1). http://reconstruction.eserver.org/Issues/091/wood&latham.shtml.

———. 2011. The Thickness of Things: Exploring the Curriculum of Museums through Phenomenological Touch. *Journal of Curriculum Theorizing* 27(2):51–65.

———. 2014. *The Objects of Experience: Transforming Visitor-Object Encounters in Museums*. Left Coast Press, Walnut Creek, 175 pp.

Wood, M. 2000. *Conquistadors*. University of California Press, Berkeley, 288 pp.

Woolley, C. L. 1935. *Ur of the Chaldees: A Record of Seven Years of Excavation*. Faber and Faber, London, 272 pp.

Wrag Sykes, R. M. 2015. To See a World in a Hafted Tool: Birch Pitch Composite Technology, Cognition and Memory in Neanderthals. Pp. 117–37 in F. Coward, R. Hosfield, M. Pope, and F. Wenban-Smith (eds.), *Settlement, Society and Cogni-*

tion in Human Evolution: Landscapes in the Mind. Cambridge University Press, Cambridge, 440 pp.

Yackley, A. J. 2012. Nobel Winner Pamuk Opens Novel Museum in Istanbul. Reuters, 27 April.

Yaya, I. 2008. Wonders of America: The Curiosity Cabinet as a Site of Representation and Knowledge. *Journal of the History of Collections* 29(2):173–88.

Ying-Hsing, S. 1966. *Chinese Technology in the Seventeenth Century.* Translated by E. Z. Sun and S. C. Sun. Pennsylvania State University Press, University Park, xii + 372 pp. [1997 reprint by Dover, Mineola].

Yip, C. K. 2001. Science and Technology Museums in Asia. *ICOM News* 55(2):7.

Yoon, C. K. 2009. *Naming Nature: The Clash between Instinct and Science.* W. W. Norton, New York, viii + 341 pp.

Zbarsky, I., and S. Hutchinson. 1997. *Lenin's Embalmers.* Harvill Press, London, 215 pp.

Zubiaur Carreño, F. J. 2004. *Curso de Museología.* Ediciones Trea, S. L., Gijón, 111 pp.

Index

Italicized page numbers indicate figures, tables, or boxes.

AAM. *See* American Alliance of Museums

AAM Code of Ethics for Museums, 241–242

Academia Nacional de Artes y Letras (Havana), 201

Academy of Sciences (Bologna), 119

Academy of Sciences (Russian), 134

accreditation, 5, 225

acquisition of collections, 241

acquisition of objects, 2, 58, 63, 115, 128, 140, 231, 243, 256

Acropolis Museum (Athens), 30, *146*

Adolphus, Gustavus, 112

Aeschylus, 37

Agassiz, Louis, 152

Agassiz Museum of Comparative Zoology (Cambridge), *142*

Age of Enlightenment, 10, 93, 172

Age of the Marvelous, 64

Agricola, Georgius, 61, 66, *90*

Á la recherche du temps perdu, 211

Albrecht V, 66, 86, *141*

Alcuin of York, 46

Aldrovandi, Ulisse, 68, 79, *81–83*, *107–109*, 119

Alexander (the Great), 31, *32*, 33, *35*, 36, *74*

Alexandria, 31, *32*, 33, *35*, 36

Alexandria National Museum (Alexandria), *175*

Alezeyevich, Peter. *See* Peter the Great

Alighieri, Dante, 56, 118

All Souls' Church (Wittenberg), 49

Alte Pinakothek (Munich), *142*, 161

Altes Museum (Berlin), *142*, 161, *168*, 185

Amerbach, Basilius, 120

Amerbach Cabinet (Basel), *141*

Amenhotep, 24

American Alliance of Museums (AAM), 5, 205, 225–226, 242. *See also* American Association of Museums

American Antiquarian Society, 194

American Association of Museums, 4, 5, 179, *181–182*, 200, 205, 206, 207, 223, 225, 241, 251, *252*

American Museum (New York),
169–170
American Museum of Natural History
(New York), 96, *142*, 201, 210, 247
American Philosophical Society, 136,
137
American Zoo and Aquarium
Association, 255
Amsterdamse Courant, 99
Analects of Confucius, 42
Ancanthe Museum (Hobart), *142*
Anderson, Sherwood, 212
Angeloni, Francesco, 120
anthropology museum, *224*
Antigone, 37
antiquitas, 66, 67
antiquities, 24, 30, 38, 39, 54, 66, *68*,
72, *77*, *100*, 113, *114*, 134, 140, 159,
162, 185, *191*, 201; African, 135;
Egyptian, 39, 76, 112, 114, 120,
140, 151; Greek, *147–148*, 150, 162;
Indian, 41, 135, 187; Mediaeval, 162;
Roman, 78, 120, 151, 162
aquarium, 4, 5, 152, 163, *224*, 255
Arabian Nights. See *One Thousand and
One Nights*
Aracataca (Colombia), 257–258
arboretum, *224*
Ashmolean Museum (Oxford), *68*, 106,
108–111, *141*
Ashmole, Elias, 103, 106
Ashutosh Museum of Indian Art
(Kolcata), *144*, 189
Araujo Sánchez, Ceferino, 172
Aristotle, *35*, 37, 52, 56, 57, *62*, 63, *74*,
79, *157*
Aristyllus, 36
Art Around the Corner, 234
Art Galleries and Museums
Association of Australia and New
Zealand, 206
artifact, xiii–xvi, 13, *70*, 167, 169,
183, 204, 235–236, 238, 245, 247;
archaeological, 78, 98, 134, *169*, 186,
191, 236; cultural, 246; Egyptian,
112, 114, 115, 140, 173, 185;
ethnographic, 100, 112, 116, 134,

186; historical, 96, 259; Roman, 78,
114
artificialia, 64–66, *67–68*, *82*, 116
Art Institute of Chicago, *143*, 251
art museum, 96, 97, 125, 148, 152, 167,
170, *180*, 194, 195, 197, 200, 207, 208,
224, 225, 227, 234, 255
Asiatic Museum (St. Petersburg), 134
Asiatic Society of Bengal (Kolcata),
141, 167
Association of Museums (Slovenia),
226–227
Assyria, 21, 38
Auckland Institute and Museum
(Auckland), *141*
Augustus, 39–40
Aurelianus, 38
Australian Museum (Sydney), *142*
Australopithecus afarensis, 131
The Autobiography of Alice B. Toklas, 211
Avery, Myrtilla, 207

Babur, Zahir ud din Muhammad, 87
Babylon, 19, 24, 25, 28, 33, 38, 69, *215*
Bacon, Francis, *62*, 73, 95, 99, *100*
Bagatti Valsecchi Museum (Milan),
145, 257
Baghdad, 52
Baltimore City Life Museum
(Baltimore), 165
Baltimore Museum and Gallery of
Paintings (Baltimore), 167
Banks, Joseph, 164
Ban Lan Laem Museum of Thai
Farmer Lifestyle (Bangkok), 228
Barbados Museum and Historical
Society (Bridgetown), *144*, 202
Barbo, Pietro, 77
Barnes Foundation (Philadelphia), *144*,
196–197
Barnum, Phineas Taylor (P. T.),
169–170
Bauer, Georg. *See* Agricola, Georgius
Bazin, Germaine, 175, 206
beat generation, 211–212
The Behavior of the Museum Visitor, 200
Bel-Shalti-Nanna, 39

Belvedere Palace (Vienna), 126, *141*
Benavides, Andrea Mantova, 120
Ben M'sik Community Museum
(Casablanca), *146*, 230
Beowulf, 57
Besler, Basilius, 85, 124
Bhagavad Gita, 41
Biavati, Sebastiano, 118
Bible, *32*, 52, *89–90*, 94, *108–109*
Bibliography of Museums and Museology,
205
*A Bibliography of Museums and Museum
Work*, 205
Biringuicco, Vannoccio, 61
Birla Industrial and Technological
Museum (Kolcata), *144*, 229
Black Death, 46
Blackmail, xi
Bode Museum (Berlin), *143*, 185
Bonapart, Napoleon, 125
Bordes, François, *13*
Borel, Pierre, 121
Borges, Jorge Luis, 34, 212
Boston Museum of Fine Arts. *See*
Museum of Fine Arts
Botanic Gardens Conservation
International, 255
botanical garden, xvii, 4, 5, 37, 40, 56,
78, *81*, 85, 94, 139, 163, *196*, 209–210,
224, 255–256
Bourdieu, Pierre, 208
Bourgeois, Francis, 8
British East India Company, 87
British Museum (London), 113–115,
128, 131, 132, 140, *141*, 146, *148*, 150,
153–156, 161–162, 163, 249
British Museum (Natural History)
(London), *143*, 152, *158–159*, 162,
201, 242
Brontë, Anne, 173
Brontë, Charlotte, *51*, 173
Brontë, Emily, 173
Bronx Zoo. *See* New York Zoological
Society
Brooking, Albert M., 8
Brooklyn Children's Museum (New
York), *143*, *180*, 198

Bruce, Thomas, *147*
Buck, Pearl, 211
Buddhism, 25, 41, 45–46, 54–55
Buffon, Georges-Louis Leclerc, 126,
128, 136–137
Burroughs, William, 212
Burton, Richard Francis, 38
Bustamente, Andrés Ovejero, 205
Byzantine Empire, 48, 53

cabinet de curieux, 72
Cabinet d'Histoire Naturelle (Paris),
125
Cabinet du Roi (Paris), 125
cabinets of curiosities, xvi, 10, 25, *35*,
58, 59, *62*, *67*, 71–73, *74*, 77–79, 84,
91, 96, 99, *100*, 101, 106, *107–111*,
112, 115, 121, 122, 123, 134, 139, 153,
162, 195
Calico Museum of Textiles
(Ahmedabad), *144*, 189
Callimachus, 37
Calzolari, Francesco, 79, 83, 124
Canterbury Tales, 42, 57
Capart, Jean, 205
card file. *See* documentation
Caribbean Conservation Association,
202
*Caring for Collections: Strategies for
Conservation, Maintenance and
Documentation*, 251
Carré d'art (Nîmes), *145*
Cartier, Jacques, 99
catalog. *See* documentation
*Catalogue of all the cheifest Rarities in
the Publick Anatomie-Hall of the
University of Leyden*, *90*, 112
cathedral, 198; in Brunswick, 49; of
Hakberstadt, 51; of Merseburg, 49;
of Milan, 47
Catherine the Great, 135
Centennial Exposition (Philadelphia),
194
Central Lenin Museum (Moscow), *144*,
187
Central Museum of Indonesian
Culture (Jakarta), *141*

Centre Georges Pompidou (Paris), *145*

Century of History, 179

Čermák, Klimet, 172

Cervantes, Miguel, 88

Charlemagne, 46

Charles V, 52

Charleston Library Society
(Charleston), 135

Charleston Library Society Cabinet
(Charleston), *141*

Charleston Museum (Charleston), 135

Chatwin, Bruce, 7

Chhatrapatī Shivaji Mahārāj Vastu
Saṅgrahālay (Mumbai), *143*, 189

Children's Civilization and Creativity
Museum (Cairo), *146*

children's museum, 198, *224*

China, 18, 25, 41, 42, 45, 54–55, 60, 76,
87, *89*, 93, *143*, *145*, 150, 194, 204,
220, 228–229, 238, 240

China Science and Technology
Museum (Beijing), *145*, 229

Chou, Chuang, 42

Christianity, 46, 178

Chulalongkorn, Phra Bat Somdet Phra
Poraminthra Maha. *See* Rama V

church treasury, 47, 49, 150

Cicero, 39

*Cien Años de Soledad. See One Hundred
Years of Solitude*

Ciudad de las Artes y las Ciencias
(Valencia), *145*

clay tablet, 9, 19, *20*, 21, 23, 38, *215*

Clemens, Samuel Langhorne. *See*
Twain, Mark

Cleopatra, 33

Cleveland, Grover, 177–178

Clifford, George, 123

Clifford, William, 205

Clusius, Carolus, 78

Cockroach Hall of Fame (Plano), 225

Codd, Edgar Frank, *218*

coffeehouses, 94

Cole, Henry, 149

Coleman, Lawrence Vail, 241

collecting: as a human trait, xii, 1–2,
58; by animals, *3*; by individuals,

xv, 39, 59, 68; by institutions, xvii,
49, 201, 223; the process of, 9;
rationale for, 41, *62*, 69, 71, 83, 94,
139, *158*, 203

collection categories, *70–71*, 72, 95

collection classification schemes, *67–68*

collection of Archduke Ferdinand
(Schloss Ambras), 86, 120, *141*

collections: acquisition, 241; archives,
23; art, 6, 36, 39, *75*; conservation,
196–197, 208–209, 249, 251, *252–253*;
digital, 248; historic, 6, 49, 255;
natural history, 6, 36, 38, 65, 76, 78,
79; relics, 47, 49, *75*; research, xx,
68, 83, *95*, 96, 97, 98, 120, 152, 201,
208, 236, 245; storage, 69, *71*, 106,
156, *159*, 183, 197, 209, 236, *252–253*,
254; teaching, 150, 159, 167; tribal,
236–237, 247

Collections Care Pilot Training
Programs, 251

collectors, xii, xiii

College of Charleston, 135

Collin de Plancy, Jaques Albin Simon,
47

colonialism, 165–167, 220

colonial museums, 165, 167, *190–192*,
237

Colonial Williamsburg (Williamsburg),
144, 161, 199

Columbian Exposition (Chicago), 150,
198

Columbus, Christopher, 59–60

community museum, *146*, 179, 230,
234–235

Concepto Actual del Museo Artístico, 205

Confucius, 42

Congdon Anatomical Museum
(Bangkok), 228

Congreve, William, 137

Conn, Steven, 244

Conrad, Joseph, 211

conservation, *197*, 208–209, 210, *224*,
239, 249, 251, *252–253*, 255

Constantinople, *32*, 48, 53, *147–148*

Coptic Museum (Cairo), *144*

Córdoba, 52

Cortés, Hernán, 56, 87
Cospi, Ferdinando, *83*, 118–119, 120
Cotton, Robert, 78, 113
Council of Europe, 201
Courtauld Institute of Art (London), 206
Creation Museum (Petersburg), *146*, 242
Crook, Joseph Mordaunt, 4
crusader, 47–48, 53
Crusades, 46–48, 57
Crystal Palace Exhibition (London), 146
cuneiform, 19, *20*
Cuvier, Frédéric, 139
Czartoryski Museum (Krakow), *141*

Dampier, William, 125
Dana, John Cotton, *180*, 197, 207
Dandolo, Benedetto, 71
Danmarks Nationalmuseum (Copenhagen), *143*
Dar Batha Museum (Fez), *144*, 229
Darius, 33, *35*
Dar, Saifur Rhaman, 207
Darwin, Charles, 139, 146, 156, *157–159*, 163, 174
Das Kapital, 146
deaccessioning, 241–242
Decameron, 42
Decimus Iunius Iuvenalis. *See* Juvenal
Declaration on the Importance and Values of Universal Museums, 221
Defoe, Daniel, 137
De la Pirotechnia, 61
De re Metallica, 61, 66, *90*
Descartes, René, 73, 95
Desenfans, Noel, 8
Deutsche Guggenheim (Berlin), *145*, 228
Deutsches Museum (Munich), *143*, 198, 199
Deutsches Museum für Kunst in Hnadel und Gewerbe. *See* German Museum of Applied and Commercial Arts
Dewey decimal classification, 133, 156

Dewey decimal system. *See* Dewey decimal classification
Dewey, John, *180*, 194, *196*, 198
Dewey, Melvil, 156
Díaz, Porfirio, 203
Dickens, Charles, 173
Dictionnaire raisonné de l'architecture française du XIe au XVe siècle, 209
Diderot, Denis, 125
Die Kunst und Wunderkammern der Spätrenaissance, 195
Dill, Homer Ray, 207
diorama, xi, 164, 195, 201, 245–246
Divina Commedia, 56
docents, *180–181*, 231
doctrine of magnificence, 63
documentation, 63, *95*, *148*, 179, 209, 214, *218–219*, 254; card catalog, 86, 183, *215*; collection catalog, 10, 23, 24, 54, 63–66, 71, 79, *81–82*, 84, 86, *89–90*, 99, 101, 103–106, *107–111*, 112, 115–116, 117–118, 121–124, 127, 128, *129–131*, 135, 138, *217*; cataloging, 38, 95, 106, 124, 131, 133, 153, 183, 193, 204, *218*; databases, *215*, *217–219*, 236; illustrations, *81–82*, *90*; inventories, 24, 63, 86; photographs, 183. *See also* clay tablet
documents, *20*, 23, 26, 38, 39, 96, 122, 194–195, 223, 240, 244–246, 255–256
Dom João VI, 137
Dracula, 173
Dr. Alvaro de Castro Museum (Maputo), *144*
Dulwich Picture Gallery (London), 8
Dürer, Albrecht, *89*, 138
Du Simitière, Pierre Eugène, 135
Du Simitière's Curio Cabinet (Philadelphia), *141*
Düsseldorf Gallery (Düsseldorf), 126
Dutch East India Company, 86

East India Museum (London), *141*, 150
Ebla, 23
Ecole du Louvre, 206

Écomusée de la Haute-Beauce (Canada), 240

Écomusée du Val de Bièvre (Fresnes), *145*, 240

Ecomuseum, 185, 238–241, 250

Ecomuseu Municipal do Seixal (Seixal), *145*

Egkl, Wilhelm, 86

Egypt, 18, *20*, 22, 24, 31, 33, *35*, 36, 48, 58, 114–115, 193

Egyptian Museum (Cairo), *142*

Ekomuseum Bergslagen (Bergslagen), *145*, 240

element, xiv–xv

Elgin marbles, 140, *147–148*

Eliot, George, 173

El Museo de los Niños Abasto (Buenos Aires), *145*

encyclopedic museums. *See* universal museums

Encyclopédie ou Dictionnaire raisonné des sciences, des arts et des métiers, par une Société de Gens de letters, 125

Enlightenment, 10, 91, 93–94, 96, 98, 99–102, 113, 116, 132, 133, 134, 136, 137, 172, 173, 220, 221, 259

Ennigaldi-Nanna. *See* Bel-Shalti-Nanna

Epic of Gilgamesh, xvii, 21

Epigrams, 41

Erasistratus, 36

An Essay Towards a Real Character, And a Philosophical Language, 127

Ethics (of Aristotle), 63

Euclid, 36, 52

Euripides, 37

Evelyn, John, 78, *80*, 121

The Exhumation of the Mastodon, 165

The Exploratorium (San Francisco), *145*, 198, 199

The Face of Battle, 184

Farnsworth Museum (Wellesley College), 207

Fasciculus rariorum et aspectiv dig norum varii generis, 85

Faulkner, William, 212

Faust , 172

Ferdinand of Tirol, 78

Ferdinando II (Grand Duke), 118

Field, Marshall, 150

Field Museum (Chicago), *143*, 149, 150, 201, 247

Five Classics, 42

flint knapping, 12, *14*

Flower, William Henry, 152, 175, 242

Fogg Museum (Cambridge), *143*, 207

Folger, Emily Jordan, 8

Folger, Henry Clay, 8

Forbes, Edward, 156

Ford, Henry, 199

Forillon National Park (Canada), 239

for-profit museums, 224–225

Fortuÿn, J., 122

fossils, 24, 28, 30, 39, 40, 41, *67*, 73, *74–75*, *114*, 136, 137, 163

Frederic II, 116

French Regional Nature Parks, 239

From the Mixed-up Files of Mrs. Basil E. Frankweiler, 256

Gaius Plinius Secundus. *See* Pliny the Elder

Galleria Borghese (Rome), *143*

Galleria degli Uffizi (Florence), 77, *141*

Galleria dell'Accademia (Florence), *141*

gallery, 72

García Márquez, Gabriel, 9, 212, 258

gazophylacia, 72

general museum, *179*, 224

Geographical and Geological Museum (São Paulo), *143*

German Museum of Applied and Commercial Arts (Hagen), 155

Gessner, Konrad, 66, *76*, 79, 86

Getty Center (Los Angeles), *145*

Ghini, Luca, 78

Gilman, Benjamin Ives, 4, *181*, 197, 206

Ginsberg, Alan, 212

Giornale dei letterati, 73

Giovio, Paolo, 78

glassmaking, 61

globalization, 60, 177, 234, 259

Goethe, Johann Wolfgang von, 172

Golden Age of Museums, 98

Goldner, George R., 243
The Golem, 211
The Good Earth, 211
Goode, George Brown, 4, 152, 172, 175, 180
Grammaticus Aristonicus, 36
Grand Palace Collections. *See* National Museum, Bangkok
graphic symbols, 16, *21*
grave goods, 43, *50*, 139
Great North Museum (Newcastle upon Tyne), *143*
Greece, 24, 27, 29, 34, 49, 56, 77, *90*
Greenfield Village and Edison Institute. *See* The Henry Ford
Greenwood, Thomas, 172
Grew, Nehemiah, *90*, 127–128
Grimani family, 78
Grimani Gallery (Venice), *143*
Grollier de Servière, Nicolas, 117
Guggenheim Museum (New York), *144*, 227
Guggenheim Museum Bilbao (Bilbao), *145*, 228
Gutenberg, Johannes, 88, *89–90*

Hagenbeck, Carl, 210
Hainhofer, Philipp, 112
hakubutsukan, 228
Hamilton, Mary, 135
Hancock Museum (Newcastle upon Tyne), *143*, 249
Hardy, Thomas, 173
Harlem on My Mind: Cultural Capital of Black America, 1900–1968, 249, 250
Hasbrouck House (Newburgh), *142*, 194
Hastings Museum (Hastings), 8
Hazelius, Arthur, 161, 199
Hecuba, 37
Heeresmuseum, 185
Heimatmuseum, 185
Helfert, Jaroslav, 206
Hemingway, Ernest, 212
Henry Ford Greenfield Village, *144*, 161, 199
herbarium, 24, *81*, 113

Hermitage, xii, 133, *141*, 186, 187
Herodotus, 30
Herophilos, 36
Hesiod, 37
Hezekiah, 25, 69
hieroglyph, 22, 24, 114, 140
The High-Brow Ladies, 137
Hinduism, 25, 41, 55
Hippolytus, 37
Historia animalium, 35, 79
historic site, *95*, 96, 179, 194, 223, *224*
Historie Naturelle Générale et Particulière, 136
history museum, xv, 97, 156, 161, 167, 174, 179, 197, *224*, 225, 248
The History of the World in 100 Objects, xvi
Hitler, 185
Homburger, Otto, 205
homeland museum. See *Heimatmuseum*
Homer, 26, 27, *32*
Homo erectus, 12
Homo neanderthalensis, 12, 15
Homo sapiens, 12, 15, 220
Hong Kong Science Museum (Hong Kong), *145*, 229
Hooke, Robert, 126
Hornaday, William Temple, 210
Horniman, Frederick John, 182
Horniman Museum and Gardens (London), 139, *140*, *143*, 182
hortus academicus, 78
Hortus Botanicus (Leiden), 78, *79*
hortus medicus, 78
hortus siccus, 78
House of Bicycles Museum (Bangkok), 228
House of Slaves (Gorée Island), *144*
Hoving, Thomas, 249, 250
Hultman, David, 131
Hundred Years War, 48
Hungarian National Museum (Budapest), *141*
Huxley, Thomas Henry, 175

ICOM. *See* Internal Council of Museums

Iliad, xvii, 26–28, 37
The Imaginary Invalid, 137
IMLS. *See* Institute for Museum and Library Services
Imperato, Ferrante, 84, 115
Independence Hall, 136
Indian Museum (Kolcata), *141, 143,* 167, 188, *190*
indigenous museums, 234–237
Industrial Revolution, 98, 172
Inhotim (Brumadinho), *146*
The Innocents Abroad, or The New Pilgrim's Progress, 174
interpretation, 2, 63, 96–98, 165, 187, 194, 226, 231, 235, *237,* 239, 240, 242–245, 246, 248, 256
Inscriptiones; vel, tituli theatric amplissimi, 66
Inscriptions, or, Titles of the Most Ample Theater. See Inscriptiones; vel, tituli theatric amplissimi
Institut d'Égypte, 125
Institute for Museum and Library Services (IMLS), 5, 223, 224, 225
Instituto Ricardo Brennand (Recife), *145*
Instructio Musei Rerum Naturalium, 131
Interior Museum Program (United States Department of the Interior), 222
International Council of Museums (ICOM), 4, 5, 179, 208, 220, 225, 227, *242, 252*
International Exhibition (1937), 198
International Marionette Museum (Palermo), *145*
Islam, 9, 46, 52–54, 86
Istituto delle Scienze (Bologna), *83,* 120
item, xvi
Iziko South African Museum (Cape Town), *142*

Japan, 55, 76, *90,* 99, 150, 184, 228
Jardin des Plantes (Paris), 139, *141,* 156
J taka, 41
Jean de Berry, 52

Jefferson, Thomas, 137, *168*
Jenequel, Kaspar Friedrich, 131
Jenkins, Tiffany, 249
Jerusalem, 25, 48, *50,* 90, 170, 238
Jevons, W. Stanley, 160
The Jewel of Seven Stars, 173
Jewish Museum (Berlin), *145*
Jigsaw, xi
John Heinz Pittsburgh Regional History Center (Pittsburgh), *145,* 231
Johnson, Samuel, 1–2
Journal des savants, 73
Judah, E. Lionel, 206
Jüdisches Museum. *See* Jewish Museum
Julius Caesar, 38
Juvenal, 40, 41

Kaiser Friedrich Museum of Western Art. *See* Bode Museum
Keegan, John, 184
Kelkar, Dinkar G., 189, 192
Kent, Henry Watson, 193
Kentman, Johannes, 66, *90*
Kerouac, Jack, 212
Kiasma Museum of Contemporary Art (Helsinki), *145*
Kircher, Athanasius, 101–102
Kircher Museum, *101*
Klemm, Gustav, 171
Korzeniowski, Józef Teodor Konrad. *See* Conrad, Joseph
Krahe, (Wilhelm) Lambert, 121, 126
Krens, Thomas, 227–228
Kunsthistorisches Museum (Vienna), *143*
Kunstkammer, *67, 72,* 86, 120
Kunstkammer (St. Petersburg), 134, *141*

L'Amour de l'art, 208
L.C. Bates Museum (Hinckley), *143*
l'Ecluse, Charles. *See* Carolus Clusius
La biblioteca de Babel, 212
Lahore Museum (Lahore), *142, 190–192,* 207

LAM. *See* Libraries, Archives, and Museums
Lamark, Jean-Baptiste Pierre Antoine de Monet Chevalier de, 128
Langbehn, Julius, 2
learning, 2, 31, 34, 43, 52, 59, 63, 93, 128, 149, 160, *180–182, 196,* 230–231, *232–234,* 259; informal, xix, *232–233;* formal, *232;* free-choice, *232;* object-based, 134, 244, 245
Legati, Lorenzo, 118
Leila's Hair Museum (Independence), 225
Le Musée Imaginaire, 208
Le Temple des Muses, 205
Le Temps des Musées, 206
Les Musées d'Europe: Guide et Memento de l'artiste et du voyageur, 172
The Library of Babel. See La biblioteca de Babel
libraries, archives, and museums (LAM), 254
library, 2, 21, 31, *32,* 34, 36, 37, 38, 40, 46, *71, 76,* 86, 113, 120, 133, 156, 160, 163, 175, 212, 224, 257
lighting, 61, 123, 132, 156, 164, 179, 183
Linnaeus, Carl (Carl von Linné), *111,* 122, 123, 126, 128, 133, 136, 156, *157*
literacy, 56, 57, 61, 94, 137, 151, 155, 173, 177, 211
Locupletissimi rerum naturalium thesauri accurata description, 121
Lorente, Jesús, 205
Lorenzo the Magnificent. *See* Medici, Lorenzo
Los Museos de España, 172
The Lost Symbol, xi
Louvre (Paris), 7, 125, *141,* 153, 193, 206
Lucius Licinius Lucullus, 40
Luxembourg Gallery (Luxembourg), 126, *141*
Lwandle Migrant Labour Museum (Lwandle), *145,* 229

magical realism, 212, 258
Mahabharata, 41

Maison des Esclaves. *See* House of Slaves
Makah Cultural and Research Center (MCRC) (Neah Bay), *145,* 235, 236
Malitsky, Georgy Leonidovich, 206
Malpighi, Marcello, 132
Malraux, André, 238
Mantegna, Andrea, 78
Māori, *237*
Marcus Aemilius Scaurus, 40
Marcus Terentius Varro, 40
Marcus Valerius Martialis. *See* Martial
Marinetti, Filippo, 4
Mark Antony, 33
Maroević, Ivo, xi, xvi, xxi, 6, 7, 207
Marsigli, Luigi Ferndinando, 120
martial, 40
Marx, Karl, 146
Massachusetts Historical Society (Boston), *147,* 161, 194
Masumiyet Müzesi. See The Museum of Innocence
material culture, 12, 13, *16,* 17, 22, 162, *237,* 247, 248
Matthias Corvinus. *See* Matthias I
Matthias I (Matthias Corvinus), 78
Maurois, André, 211
Mazzarino, Giulio Raimondo, 7
McGill University Museum (Montreal), 206
MCRC. *See* Makah Cultural and Research Center
McNab, Jessie, 243
Mechel, Christian von, 126
Medea, 37
Medici collection (Florence), 72, 76, 77, *141*
Medici, Cosimo, 76, 77
Medici (family), 40, 72, 76, 77
Medici, Lorenzo, 76, *77,* 78
memory theater, 72
Mendeleev, Dimitri, 144
Mercedes-Benz Museum (Stuttgart), *146*
Mercer, Henry Chapman, 161
Mercer Museum (Doylestown), *144,* 161

Mercure de France, 73
Mesopotamia, 18, 19, *21*, 22, 25, 38, 42, 58, *108, 215*
metallurgy, 17
Metropolitan Museum of Art (New York), *142, 168*, 193, 195, 198, 205, *215, 217*, 243, 249, 256, 259
Meyrink, Gustav, 211
microcosm, xii, 61, 63, 72, 95, 121
military museum (*Heeresuseum*), 185
Mint (Münzhof), 86, *141*
mirabilia, 66, 67
miracula, 65, 66, 67
The Misanthrope, 137
The Miser, 137
Modern Art Gallery (Venice), 150
Mohammed, *50, 52*
Molière, 137
Momofuku Ando Instant Ramen Museum, 228
Mons, Willem, 135
Montaigne, Michel Eyquem, 88
Moonwatchers, 259
Moravian Museum (Brno), 206
Moravian Pottery and Tile Works (Doylestown), 161
Moravské Múzeum (Brno), *142*
More, Thomas, 88
Morris, Margaret, 8
Mound Builders, 43
Mount Vernon, *142*, 194
Mount Vernon Ladies' Association, 194
mouseion, 1, 31, 34, 37, 125
Mouseion (magazine), 205
Mummius, 39
Münzhof. *See* Mint
Murray, David, 174, 204
musaeum, 2, 31, *32*, 34, 36, 37, 38, 59, 63, 79, *81, 83*, 130
Musaeum Calceolarium, 79, *83*
Musaeum Regalis Societatis: or, a Catalogue and Description of the Natural and Artificial Rarities belonging to the Royal Society and preserved at Gresham College, 90
Musaeum Tradescantianum: or, A Collection of Rarities. Preserved at

South-Lambert neer London By John Tradescant, 103, *107*
musealia, 6
museality, 6
musealization, xvi, 6, 7, 9, 15, 18, 22, 25, 27, 28, 38, 38, 43, 45, 47, 55, 58, 195, 208, 211, 219, 236, 255, 256, 257, 258
Musée Alaoui (Tunis), *143*
Musée des Beaux-Arts et d'archéologie (Besançon), *141*
Musée d'Orsay (Paris), *145*
Musée du Quai Branly (Paris), *146*
Musée et Centre Régional d'Interprétation de la Haute-Beauce (Saint-Évariste-de-Forsyth), *145*, 240
Musée les Abattoirs (Toulouse), *145*
Musée Napoléon. *See* Louvre
Musée National des Arts Asiatiques Guimet (Paris), *143*
Museé National des Arts et Traditions Populaires (Paris), *144*
Musée Océanographique (Monaco-Ville), *144*
Musei Capitolini (Rome), *141*
Musei Vaticani (Rome), *141*
museo, 72
Museo Archeologico Nazionale di Napoli (Naples), 40
Museo d'Arte Moderna e Contemporanea di Trento e Rovereto (Rovereto), *145*
Museo de Antropología (Mexico City), *144*, 203
Museo de Arte Latinoamericano de Buenos Aires (Buenos Aires), *145*
Museo de Geologia (Lima), *143*
Museo de Historia Natural (Mexico City), *141*
Museo de Historia Natural de la Plata (Buenos Aires), *142*
Museo de Historia Natural de la Universidad de San Marcos (Lima), *144*
Museo del Hombre Dominicano (Santo Domingo), *145*, 246
Museo del País (Buenos Aires), *142*

Museo del Prado (Madrid), *141*
Museografica Oder Anleitung Zum rechten Begriff und nützlicher Anlegung der Museorum oder Raritäten-Kammern, 131
museological, xvi, 7, 26, 66, 131, 163, 171, 185, 187, *192*, 203, 204, 205, 206, *237*, 239, 255
museology, xiii, 7, 131, 174, 187, 204, 205, 206, 207, 208, 228, 250
Museo Memorial de la Resistencia Dominicana (Santo Domingo), *146*, 238
Museo Nacional (Montevideo), *142*
Museo Nacional (San José), *143*
Museo Nacional (Santiago), *142*
Museo Nacional de Arqueología, Historia, y Etnología. *See* Museo de Antropología
Museo Nacional de Bellas Artes (Havana), *144*, 201
Museo Nacional de Ciencias Naturales (Madrid), *141*
Museo Nacional de Colombia. *See* National Museum of Colombia
Museo Nacional de Guayaquil (Guayaquil), *142*
Museo Nacional Reina Sofía (Madrid), *145*
Museo Pio-Clementino (Rome), 133
Museorum Museum, 99
Museo Sacro (Rome), 133, *141*
Muses, xii, 1, 29, *31*, 33, 34, *35*, 36, 37, 59
Museu de Historia Natural de São Paulo (São Paulo), *143*
Museu Histórico Nacional (Rio de Janiero), 206
The Museum Age. See Le Temps des Musées
museum, definition of, xi, xii, xvi, 1, 2, 4, 5, 10, 166, *197*, 198, 206, 239, 248
Museum de Nordiske Oldsager (Copenhagen), *141*
museum fatigue, 200
Museum für Naturkunde (Berlin), 256

Museum, Inc: Inside the Global Art World, 227
Museum Island (Berlin), 185, 186
Museu Nacional. *See* National Museum of Brazil
Museu Nacional de Belas Artes (Rio de Janeiro), *141*
Museum News, 247
Museum of Comparative Zoology (Cambridge), *142*, 152
Museum of Death (Los Angeles), 225
Museum of Fine Arts (Boston), 27, *142*, *168*, *169*, *181*, 197, 252
Museum of History and Holocaust Education (Kennesaw), 230
The Museum of Innocence, 257
Museum of Islamic Art (Cairo), 153
Museum of Jurassic Technology (Culver City), *145*, 243
Museum of Manufactures (London), 148
Museum of Marrakech (Marrakech), *145*
Museum of Menstruation (New Carrollton), 225
Museum of Modern Art (New York), *144*, 195, *217*
Museum of Natural History (Iowa City), *142*, 207
Museum of New Zealand Te Papa Tongarewa (Wellington), *142*, *237*
Museum of Ornamental Art (London), 148
Museum of Qin Shi Huang (Lintong), 97, 194
Museum of Science and Industry (Chicago), *144*, 198
Museum of the History of Riga and Navigation (Riga), *141*
Museum of World Culture (Gothenburg), *146*, 235
Museums and Art Galleries, 172
Museums Association (UK), 205
Museums Association of the Caribbean, 202
museums of memory, 238

Museums of the World, 220
museum staff, 207, 219222, 230, 251
Museums, Their History and their Use, with a Bibliography and List of Museums in the United Kingdom, 175, 204
Museumskunde, 205
museum studies, xx, 204, 205, 207, 208, 250, 251, 253, 254
Museum Wormianum (Copenhagen), 115, 116, *141*
Museu Paraense Emilio Goeldi (Belém), *142*

Nabonidus, 38, 39
Nagoya City Science Museum (Nagoya), *144*, 229
NAGPRA. *See* Native American Graves Protection and Repatriation Act
Nakhon Si Thammarat National Museum (Nakhon Si Thammarat), *145*, 204
Nanjing Massacre Memorial Hall (Nanjing), *145*, 238
Nant'ung Museum (Kaingsu), *143*
National Archeological Museum (Athens), *144*
National Archeological Museum (Naples). *See* Museo Archeologico Nazionale di Napoli
National Archeological Museum (Sofia), *143*, 187
National Art Gallery (Sofia), *144*, 187
National Ethnological Museum (Sofia), 187
Nationalgalerie (Berlin), 143, 185
National Gallery (London), *144*, 154, 155
National Gallery of Art (Washington, D.C.), *144*, 234
National Gallery of Canada (Ottawa), *143*
National Gallery of Modern Art (New Delhi), *144*
National Gallery of Victoria (Melbourne), *142*

National Gallery of Zimbabwe (Harare), *144*
National Gandhi Museum (New Delhi), 192
National Handicrafts and Handlooms Museum (New Delhi), *144*, 192
National Institute of Design (Ahmedabad), 189
National Museum (Bangkok), *143*, 167
National Museum (Bulawayo), *143*
National Museum (Musée National du Niger) (Niamey), 204
National Museum (Tokyo), *142*
National Museum of Brazil, 167
National Museum of Budapest (Budapest), *141*, 155
National Museum of Canada (Ottawa), *142*
National Museum of Colombia (Bogota), 167
National Museum of Ethnology (Leiden), *142*
National Museum of Health and Medicine (Silver Springs), *51*
National Museum of India (New Delhi), *144*, 188
National Museum of Kenya (Nairobi), *144*
National Museum of Natural History (Sofia), *143*
National Museum of Natural History (United States), 242
National Museum of Natural Science (Tachung), *145*, 229
National Museum of Nature and Science (Tokyo), *142*
National Museum of Prague (Prague), 155
National Museum of Victoria (Melbourne), *142*
National Museum of the American Indian (Washington, D.C.), 235
National Mustard Museum (Middleton), 225
National Science Centre (Kuala Lumpur), *145*, 229

National Science Centre for Education (Bangkok) , *145,* 229

National Science Museum (Seoul), *144,* 229

National September 11 Memorial and Museum (New York), *146,* 238

National Zoological Park (Washington, D.C.), *146,* 238

Native American Graves Protection and Repatriation Act (NAGPRA), 235, 246, 247, 248

Natural History Institutes (Bulgaria), 187

natural history museum, 85, 123, *157–159,* 163, 164, 200, 201, *218,* 219, *224,* 228, 229, 245, 246, 256

The Natural History Museum (London), *143,* 152, *158–159,* 162

naturalia, 65, 66, *67–68, 82,* 96, 112, 116, 120, 123, 134

Naturalis Historia, 40, 58, 116

naturalism, 173

nature center, *224*

Naturhistorisches Museum (Basle), 79

Neanderthal, 7, 15, *16*

Nebuchadnezzar, 33, 38

Nehru Memorial Museum and Library (New Delhi), *144,* 192

Neikelius, Caspar. *See* Jenequel, Kaspar Friedrich

Nelson Mandela National Museum (Mthatha), *145,* 229

Nelson Provincial Museum (Stoke), *142*

Neues Museum (Berlin), *142*

Newark Museum (Newark), *144, 180, 181,* 197, 207

A New Description of Sir John Soane's Museum, 151

new museology, 250

Newseum (Washington, D.C.), *222*

New-York Historical Society (Manhattan), 194

New York Zoological Society (New York), *153,* 210

Niépce, Joseph Nicéphore, 146

Night at the Museum, xi, 257

Nineveh, 38

Nippur, *19,* 22, 23

non-profit museums, 5, *196,* 220, 223, 224, 225, 242

Nordiska Museet (Stockholm), *142,* 199

The Norton Anthology of World Literature, xvi

Notes on the State of Virginia, 137

nouvelle muséologie. See new museology

object, xiii

object-based epistemology, 244

objects: acquisition of, 2, 58, 63, 115, 128, 134, 231, 243; power of, xii, 45–46, 77

Octavian, 33

Odyssey, xvii, 26, 28, 37

off-site storage, 183

Olmec, 42, 55

One Hundred Years of Solitude, 9, 258

One Thousand and One Nights, 58

Ontario Science Center (Toronto), *145,* 199

On the Expression of the Emotions in Man and Animals, 146

On the Nature of Metals. See De re Metallica

On the Origin of Species, 156, *157,* 163

Openluchtmuseum (Arnhem), *144*

Oppenheimer, Frank Friedman, 199

oral tradition, xii, xvii, 17, 18, *19,* 21, 26, 28, 41, 55, 57

order, systems of, xi, xii, xvi, 6, 9, 17, *20, 23,* 58, 61, 64, 73, 77, *82,* 86, 88, *108–111,* 117, 128, 139, 153, 156, *157–159,* 187, 188, *190,* 212, 259

Oresteia trilogy, 37

Osborn, Henry Fairfield, 210

Owen, Richard, 152

Oxford University, *32, 68,* 106, 107, *111, 141, 143,* 163

Palace of the Louvre. *See* Louvre

Palais de la Découverte (Paris), *144,* 198, 199

Palazzo dei Conservatori (Rome), *141*

Palazzo Pubblico (Bologna), *83,* 118

Palazzo San Marco (Palazzo Venezia), 78
Palazzo Venezia. *See* Palazzo San Marco
Paludanus, Bernard, 115, 134
Pañcatantra, 41
paper making, *89–90*, 151, 173
Parker, John Henry, 128
Patel, Surendra, 188
Pausanias, 31, 40
Peale, Charles Willson, 135, 136, 137, 165, 167
Peale Museum (Philadelphia), *141*, 164, 165, 167, 170, 225
Peale, Rembrandt, 137
Pearce, Susan, 6
The Penguin History of the World, xvi
Pennsylvania Museum (Philadelphia), *143*, 207
Pergamon Museum (Berlin), *144*, 185
Pergamonmuseum. *See* Pergamon Museum
Peshāwar Museum (Peshāwar), *143*
Peter I, 135
Peter the Great (Peter Alexeyevich), 121, 122, 134, 135
Petiver, James, 113, 124
Petöfi, Sándor, 155
Petrie, William Matthew Flinders, 24, 183, 184
petroglyph, *17*
Phigalian marbles, 140
Philadelphia Zoological Park (Philadelphia), *143*
Philosophical Transactions, 127
photo documentation, 183
Physiologus, 58, 85
pictogram, 19, *21*
Pictou Academy (Pictou), *142*
Pinochet Ugarte, Augusto José Ramón, 225
Pintard, John, 167
Pirotechnia. See *De la Pirotechnia*
Pitt Rivers, Augustus Henry Lane-Fox, 162, 163
Pitt Rivers Museum (Oxford), *143*
Pizarro, Francisco, 87

Planetario Galileo Galilei, 228
planetarium, 5, *224*, 228, 229, 243
Plato, 34, *35*, 37, 52, *157*
Pliny (the Elder), 40, 58, 65, 116
Points in Time, 231
Pope Paul II. *See* Barbo, Pietro
Poquelin, Jean Baptiste. *See* Molière
postcolonial museums, 187–189
Potter, Felix, 79
pottery, 18, 55, 187
Prado. *See* Museo del Prado
preservation. *See* conservation; restoration
Prince of Wales Museum. *See* Chhatrapatī Shivaji Mahārāj Vastu Saṅgrahālay
The Principles of Museum Administration, 152
printing, 42, 56, 61, 65, 87, 88, *89–90*, 94, *106*, 131, 138, 162, 173, 179, 214
Proust, Marcel, 211
Ptolemy II (Philadelphus), *35*, 37
Ptolemy Soter, 33, 34
public art and monuments, 18, 22, 30, 31, 34, 39, 78, 87
Pushkin Museum (Moscow), *144*
Putnam, Henry Ward, 150

Qin Shi Huang, 97, 194
Queensland Museum (Brisbane), *142*
Querci, Giuseppe, 133
Quicchebert, Samuel, *67*
Quinn, Stephen, 264
Quran, 52, *109*

Raffles Museum and Library (Singapore), *142*
Raja Dinkar Kelkar Museum (Pune), *144*, 189
Rama V, 167, 204
Ramayana, 44
Rattanathatcharmunee, Phra, 204
Ray, John, 112
Red Castle Archaeological Museum (Tripoli), *144*
relic, 24, 30, 46, 47, 48, 49, *50–51*, 52, *68*, 72, 73, *75–76*, 78, 112, 174, *190*, 243

The Relic, xi
Remembrance of Things Past. See *Á la recherche du temps perdu*
repatriation, 221, 235, 246, 247, 248, 257
restoration, 161, 186, 208, 209
Rewald, Sabine, 259
Ricci, Matteo, 87
Rigveda, 25
Rijksmuseum (The Hague), *144*
Rivière, Georges-Henri, 238, 239, 240, 250
Robben Island Museum (Robben Island), 229
Robinson Crusoe, 137
Robinson, Edward S., 200
Rock and Roll Hall of Fame (Cleveland), 96, *145*
romanticism, 173
Rome, *32,* 39, 40, 41, 71, *75, 77, 81,* 100, 101, 114, 133, 140, *141, 142,* 168, 184, 252
Roosevelt, Theodore, 178
Rosenwald, Julius, 198
Rossetti, Dante Gabriel, 8
Rova of Antananarivo (Antananarivo), *143*
Royal Academy, 132, 188
Royal Ontario Museum (Toronto), *142*
Royal Society of Arts, 184
Royal Society of London for Improving Natural Knowledge, 126, 138, *141*
Rudolph II, 76
Ruhmeshalle (Munich), 96
Rumyantzev Museum of Russian Art (Moscow), *142,* 186
Ruskin, John, 209
Russian Ark, xi
Rustkammer, 72
Ruysch, Frederick, 121, 122, 134
Ruzzini, Carlo, 78, *80*

Sachs, Paul Joseph, 207
Saint-Hilaire, Étienne Geoffroy, 139
Saint Kilian's Church, 49
saints, 49, *51,* 120
Salonwagen E 417, 257

Sandys, George, 31, *32*
Sarabhai, Gautam, 189
Sarabhai, Gira, 189
Sarawak State Museum (Kuching), *143*
scala naturae, 35, 57–58, 79, *157*
Schardt, Alois J., 206
Schatzkammer, 72
Schiaparelli, Ernesto, 24
Schloss Ambras (Innsbruck), 86, 120, *141*
Schloss Bensberg (Bensberg), 121
Schlosser, Julius von, 195
Schlosskirche. *See* All Soul's Church
Schoener, Allon, 249
The School and Society, 194
School in the Exploratorium (SITE), 199
Schumacher, Johann, 134
Schynvoet, Simon, 134
science center, 198, 228, 229
science and technology center, *95, 96, 224,* 229
Scott, Walter, 173
Scudder, John, 169
Scudder's American Museum (New York), 169
Seba, Albertus, 121–122, 123, 134
Select Committee on National Monuments and Works of Art, 153
Settala, Lodovico, *67,* 117
Settala, Manfredo, *67,* 117, 119, 120
The Seven Lamps of Architecture, 209
Shakespeare, William, 88
Shōsō-in, 55
Siamese Cats Museum (Bangkok), 228
Siddal, Elizabeth, 8
Silk Road, 54
Singapore Science Centre (Singapore), *145,* 229
Sir Gawain and the Green Knight, 57
Sir John Soane Museum (London), *142,* 151, 154
SITE. *See* School in the Exploratorium
Skansen Museum (Stockholm), *143,* 161, 199
Sloane, Hans, 113, *114,* 164, 183
Slovene Museum Society, 226

Smith, Ralph Clifton, 205
Smithsonian Institution (Washington, D.C.), 4, *142*, 151, 152, 155, 170, *171*, 175, *180*, 198, *217*, 242, *252*
Smithson, James, 170
snake stone, 73, *74–75*
Soane, John 150
Solomon, 25, 48, *51*, 69
Songkram Niyomsane Forensic Medical Museum, 228
Sophocles, 37
South African Museum (Cape Town), 167
South Kensington Museum (London), *142*, 148, 150, 155, *190*
specialized museum, 133, *224*
Species Plantarum, *111*, 123
specimen, xiv, 160, 162, 200
Squarcione, Francesco, 77, 78
Sri Lanka National Museum (Colombo), *143*
Stallburg Museum (Vienna), 126
State Hermitage Museum (St. Petersburg), *141*
St. Augustine Pirate and Treasure Museum (St. Augustine), 225
Stein, Gertrude, 211
Stevenson, Sarah Yorke, 207
Stoker, Abraham (Bram), 173
The Stones of Venice, 209
Strabo, 36
Studiolo, 72, 77
study, 2, 72
Stuffed!, 257
stupa, *50*
Sumer, 18
Swainson, William, 132
Swammerdam, Jacob, 117
Swammerdam, Jan, *68*, 117
symbolic expression, 12, 13, 15, 16, 18
A Synopsis of the Contents of the British Museum, 154
Systema Naturae, 123, 133

Tanakh, xvii, 25
Taoism, 42
Tartuffe, 137

Tata, Dorab, 189
Tata, Ratan, 189
Tate Modern (London), *145*
taxonomy, 9, 35, 133, 136, 158, 218, 231, 259
teatro, 72
technology, xv, 16, 54, 60, 61, *89*, 93, 98, 123, 133, 183, 184, 187, 198, 199, 208, 214, *219*, 255
technology center. *See* science and technology center
The Tempest, 88
temple of the muses, 1
Temple of the Muses (Alexandria), 1, 31–37, 59
Ten Brocke, Berend. *See* Paludanus, Bernard
terrarium, 152, 163
Thackeray, William, 173
Theater, 68, 72, 222
Theatrum Anatomicum (Leiden), 112, *141*
The Henry Ford (Dearborn), *144*, 161, 199
thesaurus, 30, 49, 63
Thesaurus. See Locupletissimi rerum naturalium thesauri accurata description
thing, xiv, 9, 131
Think Tank, 234
Tilleke and Gibbins Museum of Counterfeit Goods (Bangkok), 228
Timocharis, 36
Tinterow, Gary, 259
Tocqueville, Alexis de, 169
Tokyo Kokuritsu Hakubutsukan (Tokyo), 228
tool making, 12, 13
tool use, 12
Torah, *25*
Tradescant Catalog, *107–111*, 138
Tradescant, Hester Pookes, 106
Tradescant, John the Elder, 101, 103
Tradescant, John the Younger, *67*, 101, 103, 106
Tradescant's Ark (London), 102–103, 113, *141*

Training for Collections Care and Maintenance: A Suggested Curriculum, 251
treasury, 29, 30, 47, 48, 49, 63, 69, 150
trepanation, 17
tribal museums, 235
Trujillo Molina, Rafael Leónidas, 226
Tutankhamen, 24
Tuthmosis, 24
Twain, Mark, 174

Upanishads, 25
Uffizi Gallery. *See* Uffizi Palace
Uffizi Palace (Florence), 77, *141*
Uganda Museum (Kampala), *144*
UNESCO, 222, 230
United Nations Educational, Scientific, and Cultural Organization. *See* UNESCO
universal museums, 220–221
University of Leiden, 78, 112
University of Pennsylvania Museum of Archaeology and Anthropology (Philadelphia), *143*
University of Santo Tomas Museum of Arts and Sciences (Manila), *144*
The Use and Abuse of Museums, 160
Utopia, 88

Valentini, Michael Bernhard, *68*, 99
Vallisnieri, Antonio, 121
Vargas Llosa, Mario, 212
Varine-Bohan, Hugues Michet de, 238, 239, 250
Vasamuseet. See Vasa Museum
Vasa Museum (Stockholm), *145*
Vechaar Utensils Museum (Ahmedabad), *145*, 188
Venice, *32*, 48, 77, 78, 99, 150
Vergo, Peter, 250
Verres, 39
Viardot, Luis, 172
Victoria and Albert Museum (London), *142*, 149, 198
Vincent, Levinus, 119
Viollet-le-Duc, Eugène, 209
virtual museums, 208, 248

visitor studies, *181, 182*
Vitra Design Museum (Weil am Rhein), *145*
Vivant Denon, Dominique, 125
Von Mechel, Christian. *See* Mechel, Christian von
von Quicchebert, Samuel. *See* Quicchebert, Samuel von
Voodoo Museum (New Orleans), 225
Vorontsova-Dashkova, Yekaterina Romanovna, 135
The Voyage of the Beagle, 174
Vychova v Museologii, 172

Wadsworth Atheneum (Cambridge), *142*, 170
Wallace, Alfred Russel, *159*, 163
Wang Fu, 53
waqf, 53
Washburn, Wilcomb E., 248
Wat Phra Mahathat (Nakhon Si Thammarat), *50*
The Way of the World, 137
Wellcome, Henry Solomon, 182, 183
Wellcome Library (London), 183
Wellcome Trust Centre for the History of Medicine (London), 183
Wendeborn, Gebhard Friedrich August, 132
White Sands National Monument (New Mexico), *223*
Whitney Museum (New York), 195
Wilberforce House (Hull), *143*, 238
Wilhelm II, Johann, 121
Wilhelm IV and Albrecht V collection (Munich), 86, *141*
Wilkins, John, 127
Wittlin, Alma S., 5, 11, *181*, 200, 208
wonder cabinet, 72
Wonderstruck: A Novel in Words and Pictures, 257
Wondertooneel der Nature, 119
Woolf, Virginia, 212
Woolley, Leonard, 38–39
World's Columbian Exposition (1893), 150
World War I, 156, 184, 194, 199, 212

World War II, 184, 185, 186, 187, 194, 201, 210, 211, 212, 219, 220, 229, 230
Worm, Ole (Olaus), *67*, 115–117
writing, xiii, xvi, 16, 18–19, *20–21*, 21–22, 23, *31*, 38, 42, 55–56, 211
wunderkammer, *67*, 69, 72, 73, 117, *119*
Wuthering Heights, 173

Yad Vashem (Jerusalem), *144*, 238

Zenedotus, 37
Zenobia, 38
zoo. *See* zoological park
zoological park, xvii, 5, 56, 139, 163, 209–210, 224
Zoologische Garten (Germany), 256
Zur Geschichte der Sammlungen für Wissenschaft und Kunst in Deutschland, 171